The French Legal System
An Introduction

Fourmat Publishing

The French Legal System
An Introduction

Andrew West, *Solicitor, Diplômé de l'Université d'Aix-Marseille III, Lecturer Cardiff Law School University of Wales, Maître de Conférences invité à l'Université de Nantes*

Yvon Desdevises, *Docteur en Droit, Professeur à l'Université de Nantes, Visiting Fellow, Institute of Advanced Legal Studies*

Alain Fenet, *Docteur en Droit, Professeur à l'Université de Picardie*

Dominique Gaurier, *Docteur en Droit, Maître de Conférences à l'Université de Nantes*

Marie-Clet Heussaff, *Docteur en Droit, Maître de Conférences à l'Université de Nantes, Visiting Academic, London School of Economics*

London
Fourmat Publishing
1992

ISBN 1 85190 156 6

First published 1992

A catalogue record for this book is available from the British Library

© 1992 Andrew West, Yvon Desdevises, Alain Fenet, Dominique Gaurier, Marie-Clet Heussaff.

Published by Fourmat Publishing
133 Upper Street, London NI 1QP
Printed by Antony Rowe Ltd, Chippenham, Wiltshire

Preface

The French legal system has in recent years become a subject of increasing interest to lawyers from Britain and other countries of the common law tradition. Certain institutions of the French system have held a particular fascination: the separate administrative courts headed by the *Conseil d'Etat;* the existence of a constitutional court, the *Conseil Constitutionnel;* the role and function in criminal procedure of the examining magistrate, the *juge d'instruction;* indeed, the inquisitorial nature of criminal procedure in general. However, this interest has tended to be surrounded by a lack of knowledge as to how the French legal system operates. Are the Napoleonic codes really the sole source of law in France? What place is left for caselaw? Is it really true, as some journalists would have us believe, that in France you are presumed guilty until proved innocent? In this book we endeavour to present the French legal system to the lawyer or student of the common law tradition clearly and in terms that are readily understandable.

We have sought to explain the French legal system in sufficient breadth and depth to give the reader a full understanding of how the system operates, although we have not attempted to go into all of the detail that is contained in French textbooks (to which the reader's attention is drawn in a bibliography). We have therefore included not only such topics as the court structure, legal professions, and sources of law, but also matters of proof and procedure before the criminal, civil and administrative courts. We have also included a chapter on the historical development of the system, as many of the aspects of the present system can only be understood in an historical context; the Napoleonic codifications will thus be seen not to have represented as much of a break with the past as may have been thought. Furthermore, we have sought to convey something of the way in which the French themselves perceive their system; thus when examining the constitutional framework, we look at the important role in French constitutional and political thinking played by the notions of *la République* and *la Nation.*

The book assumes no knowledge of the French language or indeed of French law or politics on the part of the reader; the French terms which are used are explained when first mentioned. However, for the reader who is able to read French, we have included a wide range of primary and source texts and materials in French to enable the reader to carry out further study if he or she wishes to do so. We thus include (in the chapter on the constitutional framework) the text of many of the provisions of the 1958 Constitution, and several important judgments of the *Conseil Constitutionnel*. Similarly, in the chapter on criminal procedure we cite many of the provisions of the Criminal Procedure Code and several decisions of the supreme court (the *Cour de Cassation*). We have also drafted pleadings and a judgment of an imaginary civil case in the lower civil court (the *Tribunal d'Instance*).

This book results from long-standing co-operation between Cardiff Law School of the University of Wales and the law faculty of the *Université de Nantes*. The writers from each institution have experience in teaching comparative law in the other institution. Although each chapter is the product of *trans-manche* collaboration, primary responsibility for the writing of the chapters was taken as follows: Chapter 1, Dominique Gaurier; Chapter 2, Dominique Gaurier and Andrew West; Chapter 3, Yvon Desdevises and Andrew West; Chapter 4, Alain Fenet; Chapter 5, Marie-Clet Heussaff and Andrew West; Chapter 6, Yvon Desdevises and Andrew West.

We wish to express our sincere gratitude to colleagues in Cardiff and Nantes who kindly agreed to read part of the manuscript: Gérard Brovelli (parts of Chapters 3 and 6), Jacques Fialaire (parts of Chapter 2), Stewart Field (Chapter 5), Raphaël Romi (Chapter 4), and to Rachel Trost of the University of Southampton who read the entire manuscript. Their helpful comments and criticisms have been much appreciated. Any errors remain, of course, those of the writers alone. We are also grateful to our respective deans/*doyens* for the encouragement and support given to the exchanges between our law schools and for specific support for this joint project, and to the Journal of the Society of Public Teachers of Law for permission to use material for Chapter 3 based on an article (*Reforming the French legal profession; towards increased competitiveness in the single market)* which appeared in (1991) 11 LS 189–204.

A. W.
Y. D.
A. F.
D. G.
M-C. H.

June 1992.

Contents

Chapter 1

Historical development of the French legal system

To be properly understood, the modern French legal system must be viewed in the context of its historical development; it is the product of a long evolution which began effectively during the twelfth century with the move towards the reduction into writing of substantive customary law, a process which was largely completed by the end of the sixteenth century. Reforms to both substantive law and procedure were increasingly introduced by royal ordinance during the seventeenth and eighteenth centuries. It is wrong to consider the 1789 Revolution and the promulgation of the Civil Code in 1804 as representing a completely fresh start, as the Code draws heavily on the substantive law of pre-revolutionary times. The Revolution does, however, represent a fundamental break with the past in respect of constitutional law, with the introduction of a written constitution separating legislative, executive and judicial powers. In this chapter, we will examine the development of the legal system from the period of Roman Gaul to modern times.

A. Roman Gaul to feudal France

1. Roman Gaul

Little is known about the legal system before the Roman conquest of Gaul in 52 BC, as writing was not used by the Celts; the sole record of Celtic customs in Gaul is to be found in the *Commentarii de Bello Gallico* of Caesar. Following the conquest, Roman Gaul became a Roman province, into which was implanted the Roman legal system; by the Edict of Caracalla (212 AD) its inhabitants were accorded the status of Roman citizens. The third and fourth centuries AD witnessed the progressive settlement in the north-eastern part of Roman Gaul of groups of people of Germanic origin, and by the time that the western Roman empire fell to the Ostrogoths (476 AD) large parts of Roman Gaul had come under the control of such tribes as the Salic Franks (north-western region), the Burgundians (south-eastern), and the Visigoths (south-western).

2. From ethnic to local customary law

Gaul was thus divided into independent ethnic kingdoms, the most important of which was the Salic Frank kingdom (as it was called by the end of the fifth century), controlled by the Merovingian dynasty (482–751) and later the Carolingian dynasty (751–987). Each ethnic group continued to apply its own customary laws, the Salic Frank kingdom being subject to Salic customs, the Burgundian kingdom to Burgundian customs, etc. However, these ethnic customs were not imposed on the Gallo-Roman inhabitants of the various kingdoms; their right to continue to be subject to Roman law was recognised, at least in respect of private law matters.

In 438 AD the Emperor Theodosius issued a collection of imperial constitutions passed since Constantine (*Codex Theodosianus*). The rulers of the ethnic kingdoms themselves adopted the practice of reduction to writing in an attempt to ensure the survival of their own customs; the Salic laws (*lex Salica*) were thus codified during the reign of Clovis (482–511) (and subsequently amended under the Carolingian dynasty), the Visigoth customs by Euric in 480, and the Burgundian customs (*lex barbara Burgundionum*) by Gundobad (474–516). There were also codifications of the Roman law applying to Gallo-Roman subjects of the Burgundians (*lex Romana Burgundionum*) and the Visigoths (*lex Romana Visigothorum* (also known as Breviary of Alaric), drawn up by Alaric II in 506); the latter was in time recognised as applying to all Gallo-Romans, and indeed was to prove to be the major source of Roman law until the late eleventh century.

This "personal" principle of law, whereby a person was subject to the customary law of his ethnic group of origin, was progressively abandoned as the various ethnic groups (and hence their customs) became intermingled through marriage and migration. In due course, there grew up a number of sets of customs of local or regional effect, each set reflecting the customs of the differing local ethnic groupings; a general development that can be observed was the waning of influence of Roman law in the northern part of Gaul, although influence was retained in the south-east.

3. The evolution of royal authority

The term *lex* (law) has been used to refer to written customary law; this was not, however, legislation in the modern sense, Germanic custom not recognising the power of the king to legislate without the approval of

2

assemblies of the freemen of the group; thus the *lex Salica* was not promulgated by royal ordinance of King Clovis but rather approved at assemblies of the Salic Frank freemen.

(a) Attempts to recognise royal authority

The rise to power of the Carolingian dynasty in 751 with the accession of King Pippin (the Short) was to lead to the re-establishment of the Western Roman Empire in 800 with the coronation by Pope Leo III of Charlemagne (the son and successor of Pippin) as Emperor of the Western Empire. Charlemagne sought to establish his imperial authority by promulgating edicts (*capitulaires*) which purported to apply to all subjects of the Empire, regardless of their ethnic origin. This attempt to re-establish imperial power after the Roman model did not last long; the unity of the Empire could not be maintained after the death of Louis the Pious, the son of Charlemagne, and was formally brought to an end in 843 when the Treaty of Verdun divided the Empire into three parts, ruled by separate kings (the grandsons of Charlemagne), Francia Occidentalis (roughly equivalent to the western part of modern France, excluding Brittany, but including part of Belgium, Pamplona and Catalonia), Germania (modern Germany), and Lotharingia (Benelux, Provence and Lombardy); the latter proved to be unviable as a separate kingdom, most of its territory in time being absorbed into Germania.

(b) Towards feudalism

The mid-ninth century saw incursions into Francia Occidentalis particularly by Norse Vikings in the north and west and to a lesser extent by Hungarians and Arabs in the east and south; the Carolingian kings (replaced by the Capetian dynasty (named after Hugues Capet) in 987) found themselves unable to exercise effective authority over their kingdom, and increasingly had to leave the *comtes, ducs* and other noblemen to defend their own territories. The monarchy had little power to resist the demands of the noblemen to exercise powers of administration and control within their territories; indeed, as early as 877 at the meeting of Quierzy-sur-Oise, the Carolingian king Charles the Bald was forced to accept a system of government in which power was shared with a council (*conseil*) of *comtes* and bishops. The authority of the Capetian monarchy in time became effectively limited territorially to the region of Paris and parts of the Loire valley, the other regions being autonomous counties or duchies (among the most important of which were the *comtés* of Flandres, Maine, Champagne, and Toulouse, and the *duchés* of Normandie, Bourgogne, Aquitaine, Bretagne and Gascogne).

(c) Feudal France

From the ninth to the thirteenth century, France was a feudal society, at the heart of which was the feudal bond between the lord (*seigneur*)

3

and his vassals, whereby the latter swore personal loyalty (homage) and service (fealty) to the former, and agreed to serve as advisers in his courts; the lord for his part guaranteed the protection of his vassals. During the ninth century the practice grew of a lord granting to a vassal whose services he valued a gift or *bénéfice* of land; in time, this developed into tenure, the vassal's right to remain on the land (his *fief*, which was heritable) being conditional on the fulfilment of a tenurial service, usually military in nature.

The lord ruled over his own domain (*seigneurie*; which was regarded as comprising not only the land but also the serfs), and exercised administrative and judicial powers over his subjects. The land constituting the domain was regarded as belonging to him, in contrast with the English feudal system in which all land was held of the king as tenant-in-chief; this is because, as we have seen, the Capetian king exercised effective control only over his own domain. He was, however, regarded as being sovereign amongst the feudal lords, as he was the successor to the Carolingian kings, his authority thus being sacred, deriving from God alone; indeed, the other feudal lords swore loyalty to him as his vassals. This notional sovereignty (suzerainty) was not to become true sovereignty until royal authority was effectively established within the kingdom.

(d) Reassertion of royal authority

The king, like all other members of society, was bound by custom. Indeed, it was his duty to uphold custom; thus, he would confirm the customs of a town or district by means of charters, and make rulings on the content of disputed customs. From the twelfth century, the practice evolved of granting privileges to certain towns or churches by way of exception to the general custom.

Where situations arose to which custom provided no answer, the king was recognised as having the authority to promulgate legislation of general effect (known as *nouveaux établissements* or *ordonnances*). However, this power was subject to the consent of the *Conseil* (of nobles and bishops), as the king ruled the kingdom only by consent, and a royal *ordonnance* would only be effective throughout the land with the consent of the various nobles and lords. The first *ordonnance* to have general effect in this way was that of Louis VII in 1155, in which the nobles, sitting in *Conseil*, agreed to keep the peace in the land for a period of ten years. This important provision emphasised the growing authority of the monarchy, recognising as it did that it was for the king to guarantee peace within the realm, this not being simply a local issue for the feudal lords.

There was a gradual assertion of royal legislative authority, and by the middle of the thirteenth century the king had sufficient authority to be able to promulgate *ordonnances* of general effect to which only a majority of the members of the *Conseil* had assented; the legislation was no longer issued in the name of all of the consenting lords, just that of the king. By 1285, Philippe IV found it sufficient to obtain the consent of merely some of the members of his *Conseil* (whose members were in any event appointed at his sovereign choice).

This growing royal authority was buttressed by the recognition by doctrinal writers (especially Philippe de Beaumanoir) of the sovereign power of the king to legislate. A primary source of this theory was Roman law (the study of the Code of Justinian (525 AD) having been revived), which recognised the inherent sovereign legislative power of the ruler (*quod principi placuit habet legis vigorem*). Thus in his work on customary law (*Les Coutumes de Beauvaisis*) Beaumanoir accepted the right of the king to legislate by royal ordinance in certain circumstances (ie times of war or necessity, or in times of peace where the ordinance was "reasonable" and for the common good, and promulgated with the consent of the *Conseil*). Philippe IV promulgated much royal legislation, a practice which was to be adopted by subsequent monarchs.

4. Evolution of the judicial system and legal procedure

(a) Merovingian and Carolingian dynasties

Germanic peoples had traditionally had a system of "popular justice" whereby disputes were brought before an assembly, known as a *mallus* (or Hundred Court), presided over by an elected judge (*thunginus*), who sat with the tribal elders (to confirm the customs) and freemen. This assembly, acting jointly, identified the appropriate customary rule and applied it to the case in question. The custom would prescribe tariffs of compensation payable to the victim in any given circumstance. No appeal was possible from such a decision, a "popular" judgment being regarded as sovereign.

A modified form of this system of popular justice was introduced into Gaul by the conquering Germanic groups. A local assembly, dealing with criminal and civil matters, was presided over by a royal appointee, the *comte*, who sat with at least seven nobles (the *rachimbourgs* (later known as *scabini*) appointed by the *comte*; they had the role of law-finders) and with the freemen of the *hundred*. The *comte* would go on circuit around his county. In time, the role of the freemen diminished, and most cases were dealt with by the *scabini* (sitting with the *comte* or his deputy), the freemen meeting in assembly only three times a year to deal with major cases and to discuss the general affairs of the county (*comté*). Some authors consider that this marks the origin of the distinction between later seigneurial high and low justice. A Carolingian reform was the introduction of an itinerant superior jurisdiction (the *missi dominici*, whose authority came directly from the king) which acted as a supervisory and appellate court from the proceedings of the courts of the *comtes* and also heard cases involving the king's interests.

As in England during the Anglo-Saxon period, procedure was essentially accusatorial and oral in nature; it was for the plaintiff or accuser to prove his case against the defendant. As there was no public authority who could issue a writ, an action was commenced by the plaintiff physically bringing the defendant to the *mallus* (the procedure of *mannitio; lex Salica, Tit. 1*). There was public prosecution (by the *mallus*) only in respect of certain serious criminal offences (which could lead to the imposition of the death penalty). In respect of other criminal offences it was for the victim to prosecute the alleged offender before the *mallus*. Means of proof were not rational; a defendant could successfully counter the allegations against him by swearing an oath corroborated by the production in court of a given number of character witnesses (*co-jureurs*; the number, which varied with the seriousness of the case, being fixed by custom). If he were unable to do this satisfactorily, he could have recourse to the judgment of God and claim trial by battle (between the two parties or their champions) in civil cases, or ordeal (hot iron or boiling water) in criminal cases. If the case was proved against the defendant, the penalty took the form of the payment of compensation in accordance with tariffs fixed by custom. The procedure of the *missi dominici* contrasted with that of the *mallus*, as it favoured written evidence, and was inquisitorial in nature; it also relied on more rational means of proof, such as the interrogation of witnesses of fact.

(b) Feudal courts

During the feudal period, the local courts gradually came under the control of the lord of the domain. The lord's vassals were obliged to act as his advisers in his court, which dealt with feudal issues such as the failure of a vassal to meet his feudal obligations. Vassals were entitled to be judged by their equals, a right which did not extend to those of lower social standing, the serfs, who were judged by an appointee of the lord. The feudal court system was subject to a great deal of local variation, but for the majority of the population it can be said to have represented a reduction of justice compared with that of the Frankish Hundred Courts. Criminal and civil procedure was very similar to that of the latter, with continued recourse to ordeals and other irrational means of proof; this was to be a cause of the withering of the feudal courts to the profit of the royal courts, particularly following the prohibition in 1215 (by the Fourth Lateran Council) of the participation of the clergy in trials by ordeal.

(c) Royal courts

(i) Parlements

During the tenth and eleventh centuries there was a royal feudal court which, due to the monarch's limited authority, was of little importance outside the king's domain. However, from the mid-twelfth century Louis

VII began to have sufficient military strength to be able to impose the judgments of the royal court on his vassals. The influence of the royal court was to increase markedly during the mid-thirteenth century, when the judicial functions of the *Conseil du Roi* were assumed by a newly created royal court of justice consisting of professional judges appointed by the king. The court, which was based in Paris, was known as the *Cour en Parlement* (later simply *Parlement*), and used more rational means of proof than had the feudal courts, trial by battle being abolished by an *ordonnance* of 1258, which also introduced an inquisitorial written procedure based on the Roman-canonical *cognitio* system, whereby trial procedure was from beginning to end under the control of a state official; there was no lay participation. The early requirement that all French trainee lawyers and judges read Roman and Canon law at university made the use of such procedures possible. It should be noted that in addition to its judicial function the *Parlement* played its part in the legislative process, being involved both in the drafting of royal *ordonnances* and their registration (*enregistrement*), which was necessary before they took effect. It also exercised supervision over local administrators.

During the fourteenth century, the *Parlement de Paris* was itself divided into four divisions, each having a particular function; a claim would first be vetted by the *chambre des requêtes* (pleas division) and, if a triable issue was found, it was passed on to the *grande chambre*, where oral pleadings would take place; thereafter an investigation (*enquête*) would be carried out by the *chambre des enquêtes* in the absence of the parties and their representatives. Its report was transmitted with the dossier to the *grande chambre* (to the *tournelle* in criminal cases) for judgment. Inquisitorial procedures remain an important feature of French court procedure to the present day, particularly in criminal and administrative law (see Chapters 5 and 6).

The jurisdiction of the *Parlement de Paris* was sovereign, in that no appeal lay from its decisions, the court in effect having delegated to it the king's inherent power of exercising justice. It had competence for cases throughout the kingdom until the expansion of royal political power permitted the creation of regional *Parlements*, firstly at Toulouse (1443), then Grenoble (1453), Bordeaux (1462), Dijon (1477) and Aix-en-Provence (1501); by the time of the 1789 Revolution there was a total of 17 *Parlements* (or the equivalent *Conseils Souverains*; TEXTS NO. 1).

(ii) Cours de Bailliage

The *Parlements* had first instance jurisdiction in respect of certain cases involving high nobles, but their primary role was to act as an appeal court from the local royal jurisdictions, the *Cours de Bailliage*. These had been created during the thirteenth century, based on the Norman institution of the *bailli*. The *bailli* was the local royal representative in respect of financial, administrative, military and judicial matters. As the political influence of the king spread throughout France during the fourteenth and fifteenth centuries, so did the system of *Cours de Bailliage*. The *bailli* himself was replaced during the fifteenth century by two *lieutenants de bailliage*, one *civil*, and one *criminel* who, sitting with assessors (*prud'hommes*) but without jury, acted as the first instance court in civil and criminal matters involving nobles, royal officers, and *cas royaux*. Less important cases were dealt with by a lesser royal officer known as a *prévôt*, and feudal matters continued to be dealt with by the feudal courts (which dispensed justice to the majority of the population which was agrarian). The function of the *Cours de Bailliage* was carried out by *Sénéchaussées* (presided over by a *sénéchal*) in western and southern parts of the kingdom, and by the *Tribunal du Châtelet* in Paris. Appeal lay from the *Cours de Bailliage, Sénéchaussées* or *Châtelet* to the regional *Parlement*.

Because of the increasing number of appeals being made to the *Parlements*, it was decided in 1552 to create a new appellate jurisdiction between the *Parlements* and the *Cours de Bailliages* and *Sénéchaussées*. These *Sièges Présidiaux* were the final appeal court for cases involving less than a certain monetary figure; this reduced the work-load of the *Parlements*, to whom a right of appeal lay only in respect of more important cases; the *Parlements* regarded this reform as being an unwelcome curtailment of their jurisdiction.

(iii) Increasing jurisdiction of the royal courts

Although the feudal courts were not finally to disappear until the Revolution, they were to be eclipsed by the royal courts from the thirteenth century onwards. Three factors contributed towards this decline. Firstly there was the notion of appeal; if a subject failed to obtain justice at the hand of his lord, it was recognised (from the mid-thirteenth century) that he could appeal to the sovereign lord, the king; appeal thus lay in civil and criminal matters from the feudal courts to the royal courts. Secondly, a litigant in the feudal courts could elect to have his case transferred to the royal courts (usually the *Cours de Bailliage*) if the feudal court delayed unreasonably in the hearing of his case; this right of preferment (*la prévention*) was often made use of by litigants, who preferred the superior means of proof of the royal courts. Thirdly, during the thirteenth century it was accepted that cases involving the king's interests (*cas royaux*; cases affecting the person, property or authority of the king or his agents) could be withdrawn from the feudal courts as coming within the sole jurisdiction of the royal courts.

Moreover, the king's authority over judicial matters was underlined by his position as head of the hierarchical system of royal courts; the notion thus came to be accepted that the king was entitled to quash (*casser*) a judgment of a royal court in which in his opinion there had been an incorrect application of the law, and to send the case back to the court for the law to be correctly applied. This power of cassation (formalised in a 1667 *ordonnance* and the 1738 *règlement du conseil*) was not

8

exercised personally by the king, but rather by a particular division of the *Conseil du Roi* called the *Conseil des Parties*, also known as the *Conseil d'Etat*. As will be seen below, in the modern French legal system appeal by way of *cassation* lies in the ordinary court system to the *Cours de Cassation* from the decision of courts of last instance (such as the *Cours d'Assises* and *Cours d'Appel*) and similarly to the *Conseil d'Etat* in the administrative court system.

B. Sources of pre-revolutionary law (Ancien Droit)

The period from the sixteenth century to the Revolution (known as the *Ancien Régime*; hence *Ancien Droit*) was characterised by an absolute monarchy. Six sources of law can be identified, customary law and royal ordinances having the greatest authority, but in different domains; secondary sources included the caselaw of the *Parlements* (which, however, never acquired the binding authority of the decisions of English courts) and Roman law (to which recourse was had as written reason (*ratio scripta*) when no other authority could be found). Other sources that should be noted are Canon law and academic writings (*la doctrine*).

1. Customary law

(a) Oral tradition

Customary law may be defined as being the recognised legal practices within any given society or locality; it is to be contrasted with legal rules which are imposed by some legislative or judicial authority. Custom represents practices that have become accepted over a period of time, and is thus essentially static and lacking in dynamism. The traditional drawback of oral customary law as a source of law is the identification of its precise contents. A party to an action would have to prove to the court the existence and content of any customary rule on which he intended to rely; some customs were so well established (notorious) as to need no proof; from the late thirteenth century onwards, non-notorious customs could be established only by the unanimous decision of a group inquest or *turba* (*enquête par turbes*), usually of ten local inhabitants.

During the twelfth and thirteenth centuries legal practitioners reduced to writing some of the local customs in order to facilitate the task of the courts; examples of these unofficial compilations are the *Coutumes de Beauvaisis* of Beaumanoir, the *Vieux coustumier de Poictou* and the *Très ancienne coustume de Bretagne*. The customs of the Midi (the southern part of France) drew heavily on Roman law usages, and it is from this period that the distinction can be drawn between the romanised south (known as the *pays de droit écrit*) and the customary north (*pays de coutumes*; TEXTS, NO. 2).

(b) Reduction to writing of customary law

At the conclusion of the Hundred Years War between France and England, Charles VII, as part of a reorganisation of the kingdom, sought to reduce the complexity of court procedure and ordered (by the 1454 *ordonnance de Montil-lès-Tours*; TEXTS, NO. 3) the reduction into writing of all customs and rules of procedure. However, the process was slow, and by the end of the fifteenth century there were only a few written texts (eg the *Coutumes de Touraine* (1462), *Berry* (1483), and *Boulogne* (1495)).

A revised procedure for the reduction to writing of the customs was introduced in 1497 by Charles VIII in an attempt to accelerate the process; the procedure is of importance because the participation of both the *Parlements* and the king's representatives in the recognition and confirmation of the different regional customs substantially buttressed their authority, and made a unified national system of law impossible until the *Ancien Régime* was itself swept away by the Revolution. The revised procedure most frequently used consisted of several stages; firstly a draft of the customs was prepared by the local *Cour de Bailliage* (if a local custom) or the *Parlement* (if regional) with the participation of other judges, lawyers and notables. Secondly, two royal commissioners were appointed to visit the district and, having examined the draft, chair a discussion of its provisions in an assembly of representatives of the three social classes: clergy, nobles and commons (*tiers état*). Once the provisions were agreed (if agreement was not forthcoming, the provisions were referred to the *Parlement* for determination) the written custom was promulgated in the name of the king by the royal commissioners, and the regional *Parlement* took judicial notice of the customary law. Having thus been reduced to writing under the supervision of the king's commissioners with the collaboration of the courts and an assembly of representatives of the people, customary law from this time can no longer truly be regarded as a law of purely popular origin.

Paradoxically, the fact of having customary rules written down only emphasised their limitations; they were quite restricted in their subject matter, dealing primarily with land law, the law of succession, and some areas of family law, such as marriage contracts; the important area of the law of obligations was not covered – judges dealing with such issues therefore made use of Roman law concepts. Other areas, such as criminal procedure and commercial law, were regulated by royal legislation.

In 1579 (by the *ordonnance de Blois*) the king agreed to repeat the whole process of reduction to writing with a view to the up-dating and reform of the customs. The role of the royal commissioners in this second process was pronounced, particularly in the implementation of reforms to the rules of civil procedure; they also sought to reduce the divergence of the different customs where possible. At the end of this second round of reduction to writing (the last custom to be put in writing was that of Artois in 1741) France was still a long way from having a unified body of legal rules in force throughout the kingdom. There were some 60 customs of regional application (TEXTS, NO. 2) and over 300 local customs (ie customs which diverged to some degree from the regional custom; thus within the region of application of the *Coutume de Bretagne*, the towns of Rennes, Nantes, Vannes and Goello had their own particular rules of *aménagement* (town planning)).

In the north and east of France customs tended to be of limited territorial application, because during the procedure of reduction to writing, individual towns had been unable to agree on the existence of a common provincial custom, holding out instead for the preservation of their own local practices (thus no regional custom could be agreed for the province of Champagne, and separate local customs were reduced into writing for Reims, Chalons, Vitry, Troyes and Chaumont).

(c) Pays de droit écrit and pays de coutumes

As we have seen, during the thirteenth century the southern region of France became known as the *pays de droit écrit*, as its customs relied to a large extent on principles of Roman law; Roman law was initially recognised as being a secondary source of custom to which recourse could be had in the absence of any other customary rule. Several southern towns had their own municipal customs, some of which were in written form (Avignon, Arles, Cahors, Marseille, Montpellier, and Toulouse). However, with the reappearance of classical Justinian Roman law during the thirteenth century, Roman law came to be recognised as having general application as the primary source of customary law in the south, thus restricting the domain of the pre-existing municipal customs, which were regarded as exceptional.

The Roman law which was applied comprised principles of Roman law as interpreted and applied by the *Parlements* of the Midi (Aix-en-Provence, Bordeaux, Grenoble and Toulouse). This customary Roman law was never reduced to writing under the *ordonnance de Montil-lès-Tours* (although the latter did result in the writing down of some of the pre-existing municipal customs, such as those of Bordeaux, Dax, St. Sever and Bayonne). The classical distinction between the *pays de coutumes* and the *pays de droit écrit* is therefore not strictly accurate, the northern region of the kingdom in effect becoming the *pays de droit écrit* in the fifteenth century with the reduction to writing of customary law.

(d) The impact of written custom

The most important impact on the courts of the writing down of customary law was that the judges, like the litigants, could no longer claim the existence of any other, unwritten, customary rule; in effect, the sole admissible proof of the existence of any given custom was that it had been reduced to writing. It should be noted that customary law, even though now in writing, was not considered to be an appropriate subject for study in university law faculties, which taught exclusively Roman law and Canon law. Scant attention was paid to the need for the lawyers to know the customary rules they would actually be applying in practice; these they had to learn through experience. The study of customary law was introduced in 1679, but even then only as a secondary subject.

2. Caselaw of the Parlements

(a) Introduction

As we have seen, following the division of the king's *Conseil*, the *Parlements* became autonomous royal courts of appeal. The jurisdiction of most of the *Parlements* extended over a province, but that of the *Parlement de Paris* covered nearly one-third of the entire kingdom; it thus had competence over a number of different customary areas (Ile de France, Nivernais, Bourbonnais, Maine, Poitou, Touraine, Champagne, Anjou, Auvergne). It tended to interpret and apply the differing rules of custom in the light of the *Coutume de Paris*, which it regarded as the model customary law. This process gradually whittled away at the distinctiveness of the various customs. The *Parlements* also adapted the various customary rules to the needs of contemporary society and supplemented them where they were lacking, usually by reference to Roman law concepts. This process would help prepare the ground for the introduction of a unitary body of legal rules, although customary diversity was to remain until the Revolution, each *Parlement* seeking to retain its influence by upholding its own provincial customs within its area of jurisdiction.

(b) A doctrine of precedent?

The *Parlements* had for many years exercised quasi-legislative power to make regulations in respect of court procedure; they purported to extend this power, arguing that they were entitled to exercise delegated royal authority, by passing regulations on matters which were not covered by custom or royal ordinance. These regulations (known as *arrêts de règlement*; TEXTS, NO. 4) were regarded as binding on courts within the jurisdiction (not, however, on the other *Parlements*, although they were of persuasive value). Theoretically, these *arrêts de règlement* were meant to be of temporary effect, pending the passing of royal legislation on the matter, but in practice such legislation was rarely forthcoming.

Arrêts de règlement apart, the decisions of *Parlements* were not binding, although there was a tendency for them to be of persuasive value for the courts within the jurisdiction of the *Parlement*, to whom any appeal would lie. One of the reasons militating against the development of a system of binding precedent was the absence of an official system of recording and publishing court decisions. Although from as early as 1254 the *Parlement de Paris* kept a register of its deliberations in summary form (some examples of which dating from 1254 to 1328 were published during the nineteenth century under the title of the *Olim*), the practice of systematically recording judgments was lost after the mid-fourteenth century, and there was no official publication of court decisions during the Ancien Régime.

However, some of the most important decisions were reported by private lawyers in the form of commentaries or dictionaries of principles of law; these lawyers became known as the *arrêtistes* (the court's decision being called an *arrêt*). These commentaries reveal that although custom remained the fundamental source of law, the way it was interpreted and applied was influenced and moulded by the caselaw of the courts.

3. Royal ordinances

(a) Introduction

An ordinance (*ordonnance*) was a legislative command of general effect issued in the name of the king. In the preceding pages we traced the gradual recognition of the inherent power of the king as sovereign to legislate for the whole kingdom. The royal legislative power was limited only by the requirement that legislation should conform with reason and justice; he thus had to respect traditional social privileges and the various customary rules (unless shown to be bad). The king could not alter the fundamental constitutional principles of the kingdom (known as the *lois fondamentales*). Early royal ordinances dealt essentially with public law matters, particularly taxation and public finances, the armed forces, judicial and administrative organisation, the regulation of religious observance, and the maintenance of public order. Private law matters were largely regulated by customary law which, as has been examined, had been reduced to writing by the sixteenth century.

Three forms of royal ordinance can be distinguished during the seventeenth century; the *ordonnance* itself, dealing with a variety of different matters, the edict (*édit*) which legislated on a particular matter, or applied to part only of the kingdom, and the *déclaration* which clarified or modified an *ordonnance* or *édit*. The first two forms of royal legislation were implemented by means of formal letters patent (*grandes lettres patentes*) issued by the Chancellor; *déclarations*, as well as executive instructions to the king's administrative officers and executive decisions of the king affecting individuals (such as the conferment of an office or the granting of a pardon) were implemented by the less formal *petites lettres patentes*.

(b) Consultation in the legislative process

Although *ordonnances* were the expression of royal intention alone, the king's legislative power not being shared, in practice the king always took the advice of his *Conseil* in the drafting of *édits* and *ordonnances*. During the fourteenth century, with the cost of the Hundred Years War and the creation of national institutions (such as a nationally funded army and navy, royal courts and other public services) income from the royal domain was insufficient to meet all the demands placed upon it, and it became necessary to raise income from additional taxation. The practice became established of the king soliciting the consent of the people to the raising of finance by means of occasional formal meetings (known as the *Etats Généraux*) of locally elected representatives of the three social orders − the nobility, the clergy and the commons (which comprised the urban bourgeoisie and representatives of rural communities).

Recourse was first had to the *Etats Généraux* by Louis XI in 1483. Such meetings, which could be summoned only at the request of the king, were also called in times of political or religious crisis to consult the people on how best to resolve the situation. Once convened, the *Etats Généraux* could propose reforms of the institutions of the realm. This they did by submitting formal petitions (*doléances*) to the king. The latter was free to accept or reject the petitions. Those he accepted were implemented by the promulgation of an *ordonnance*. This happened, for example, at the end of the sixteenth century, at a time when there was great strife between the Catholic and Protestant communities of France; the *Etats* were summoned three times − in 1560 at Orléans and in 1576 and 1588 at Blois. The resulting *ordonnances d'Orléans* (1566) and *Blois* (1579) dealt with the general policing of the realm (the latter also provided, as we have seen, for the re-drafting of written customary law).

Attempts by the deputies to the *Etats Généraux* during the fifteenth and sixteenth centuries to develop the *Etats* into a true legislative assembly were unsuccessful, the king keeping firm control of the convocation of meetings, and strictly limiting their role to one of an advisory nature. During the seventeenth century the importance of the *Etats Généraux* faded, their involvement in the process of government as a representative body proving to be incompatible with the absolute nature of the monarchy of the *Ancien Régime*; a 1614 meeting, summoned in an attempt to resolve the crisis occasioned by the assassination of Henri IV, broke up without any agreement being reached by the three orders as to the measures which should be proposed to Louis XIII. A meeting of the *Etats* was not to be called again until 1789, when it would lead to the formation of the National Assembly.

(c) Role of the Parlements in implementing royal legislation

The *Parlements* had a role to play both in the formation and implementation of royal legislation. They were recognised as having an advisory function; the king consulted them not only in times of crisis and war (when they were particularly involved in the conclusion of treaties), but also at other times in respect of administrative and judicial reforms (thus they were involved in the elaboration of the important *ordonnance de Montil-lès-Tours* of 1454 (see page 10)). Additionally, since the fourteenth century, as part of this advisory function, all important letters patent (and hence royal ordinances and edicts) were sent to them for registration (*enregistrement*) and publication, failing which they would be ineffective. If a *Parlement* took the view that the legislation was contrary to reason, or against the king's interests, it would point this out to him by the use of formal documents known as *remontrances*, thus giving him an opportunity to reconsider the legislation. However, as legislative authority rested with the king alone, he had the power to constrain *Parlements* to register royal legislation; he would do this by issuing letters of command (*lettres de jussion*). If his will were still resisted, he would attend in person at the court (sitting on his throne (*lit de justice*)), as he was entitled to do as the "fount of justice". His physical presence had the effect of suspending the delegation of royal judicial powers to the *Parlement*, and he would command the court clerk to register the legislation.

During the sixteenth century some *Parlements* used their power of referral to oppose the legislative reforms of the monarchy, particularly in religious matters; thus the *Parlement de Paris* took nearly a year to register the important *édit de Nantes* of 1598 (see page 18), and then did so only after forcing the king into accepting certain amendments. During the eighteenth century, the *Parlements* also fought against attempts to introduce a more egalitarian tax system, which would have reduced the privileges of the nobility. They thus consistently refused to register tax legislation, arguing that the right of the *Etats Généraux* to consent to the levying of taxes was now vested in the *Parlements*, as the *Etats* had effectively ceased to be convened. In 1766, Louis XV was constrained to attend the *Parlement de Paris* in person and point out in forceful terms that their judicial role was a delegated one only, and that legislative initiative belonged solely to the king (see TEXTS, NO. 5(a)(b)). Such direct warnings went unheeded, and both Louis XV and XVI had to have recourse to the *lit de justice* procedure to push through reforms of the legal system and the introduction of a liberal commercial policy.

The frequent opposition to royal authority displayed by the *Parlements* had the effect (according to Voltaire writing in 1764) of sowing the seeds of an inevitable revolution. Louis XV's Chancellor Maupeou had an edict passed in 1771 which effected major reforms of the court system and judicial offices; had the reforms been fully implemented, a modern system of justice could have ensued, and the obstructive power of the *Parlements* broken. However, Louis XV died soon afterwards, and the reforms were abandoned by Louis XVI in 1774. The last chance of the monarchy to prevent revolution by reforming from within had gone; when in 1788 Lamoignon, the Minister of Justice of Louis XVI, tried to push through major reforms of the legal system, the *Parlements* revolted against this renewed attempt to reduce their influence, and the ensuing civil disturbances led the king to agree to convene the fateful meeting of the *Etats Généraux* during May 1789.

(d) Royal ordinances of the seventeenth and eighteenth centuries

(i) Seventeenth century

During the seventeenth and eighteenth centuries, royal legislation was to become the pre-eminent source of law. In the second half of the seventeenth century the method of drafting *ordonnances* became more methodical, signalling the use of royal legislation as a means of unifying the legal system. The systematic programme of reform of procedure and commercial law carried out between 1667 and 1681 by Jean Baptiste Colbert, the Finance Secretary to Louis XIV, can be regarded as a forerunner of the codification of French law that was to occur under Napoleon Bonaparte.

The series of ordinances that Colbert had promulgated were prepared by a group of specialist draftsmen from within the king's secretariat, and vetted by a committee of lawyers. Five fundamental ordinances were issued in this way: the 1667 *ordonnance civile* (TEXTS, NO. 6) which set out a detailed and precise civil procedure code, and was greatly to inspire the 1806 *Code de Procédure Civile*; the 1670 *ordonnance criminelle*, which reinforced the secretive nature of inquisitorial criminal procedure; the 1673 *ordonnance du commerce* and the 1681 *ordonnance maritime* which in effect codified the customary law merchant and maritime law – their provisions were to form the basis of the 1807 *Code Commercial*; lastly the 1679 *ordonnance des eaux et forêts*, which reorganised the legal rules relating to both seigneurial and royal forests, and which served as the model for the 1827 *Code Forestier*. There was in fact a sixth ordinance promulgated in 1685 under the name of the *Code Noir*, regulating the status of negro slaves in French American colonies; they were classified as being alienable movable property (*biens mobiliers*), but their right to a minimum of respect from their owner was recognised. Although the *Code Noir* was abolished in 1794, it was reintroduced by Napoleon in 1802 at the insistence of colonial landowners, and it was only in 1848 (*décret du 27.4.1848*) that slavery was finally abolished in all French territories.

(ii) Eighteenth century

The major royal ordinances of the eighteenth century, introduced by D'Aguesseau, Chancellor to Louis XV, were the first to deal with matters of private law. The intention (TEXTS, NO. 7) was to harmonise the caselaw of the different *Parlements* in certain areas of private law (whilst retaining the traditional north – south divide). Four *ordonnances* were promulgated to achieve this: the 1731 *ordonnance sur les donations* (gifts; TEXTS, NO. 8); the 1735 *ordonnance sur les testaments* (wills); the 1737 *ordonnance sur les faux* (falsified evidence); and the 1747 *ordonnance sur les substitutions fidéicommissaires* (substitution in succession). The rules set out in these four texts were largely incorporated into the subsequent Civil Code and Codes of Civil and Criminal Procedure. These *ordonnances* represent the last major reforms of civil law during the *Ancien Régime*, as the subsequent reforms of Louis XVI (in 1780 and 1788) were confined to matters of criminal law (the suppression of torture both as a means of proof and as a preliminary punishment to the imposition of the death penalty).

4. Roman law

The French legal system is classified as belonging to the Romano-germanic family of law due to its historical links with both Roman law and Germanic customary law. At the end of the eleventh century, the study of Roman law (in particular the Justinian *Corpus Iuris Civilis*, which until then had been unknown in the Western Empire) was resurrected in the first European universities, primarily at Bologna. Roman public law concepts of imperial power were used by the French king by the end of the twelfth century to assert his authority over the other feudal lords on the basis that as king he was emperor within the kingdom. However, the same concepts were also used to justify a claim of sovereignty over France by the then German emperor on the basis of being the successor to the Carolingian emperor; for this reason, Philippe II persuaded Pope Honorius III to forbid (*Bulla super specula* 1219) the teaching of Roman law at the University of Paris and elsewhere within the kingdom. The ban was brought to an end under Philippe IV with the disappearance of the threat from the German empire. Thereafter, the systematic study of Roman and Canon law was to form the basis of the academic training of would-be continental lawyers; this proved to be of importance in that it made them willing to refer to Roman law concepts when customary law was deficient.

How important then was Roman law as a source of law in France? Two things should be said: firstly, it was never as important in the south as might be thought – as we have seen, although concepts of Roman law in effect constituted the customary law of southern France, it was Roman law as interpreted and adapted to local contemporary conditions by the southern *Parlements*; secondly, it was a true source of law (as *ratio scripta*) in areas of law where both custom and royal legislation were deficient – it was thus of particular importance as a source of the law of obligations (and procedure until the 1667 *ordonnance civile* was passed).

5. Canon law

During the thirteenth century the king sought to assert the sovereignty of the royal courts over not only the *seigneurial* but also the ecclesiastical courts. Each diocese had an *Officialité* presided over by an *official* appointed by the bishop, who sat with assessors. Its jurisdiction extended over lay persons as well as the clergy; it thus had competence in certain civil matters such as the law of benefices, the sacramental nature of the marriage bond (eg annulment, separation and legitimacy), and some areas of the law of contract and succession. Its criminal jurisdiction was exclusive in respect of offences of an ecclesiastic nature (eg heresy, simony) and concurrent (with the lay courts) for offences such as blasphemy, sacrilege and adultery.

It is in the procedure of these diocesan courts, taken from Roman practices, that the roots of the inquisitorial procedure of present-day French courts can be seen. In civil matters, the parties were called before the judge to prove their case by one of a variety of means of proof (such as a statement on oath, and witness statements, procedure being largely written). In criminal cases, the judge personally carried out an investigation into the facts (an *enquête*), interrogating the accused and the witnesses, and obtaining expert evidence where necessary; the accused was given an opportunity to put forward his arguments before judgment was reached and sentence pronounced.

From the early thirteenth century, a series of royal ordinances were promulgated to limit the competence of the *Officialités*; thus cases of heresy and sacrilege were excluded from the jurisdiction of the *Officialités*, as were criminal offences committed by the clergy (apart from offences of a purely spiritual nature, such as the non-respect of a monastic rule). A similar limitation of jurisdiction occurred in civil matters, particularly in matrimonial affairs and the law of contract and succession. The pre-eminence of the royal courts increased during the mid-fifteenth century with the development of the theory of abuse of competence, according to which appeal (*appel comme d'abus*) lay to the royal courts whenever ecclesiastical courts purported to adjudge a matter properly coming within the exclusive jurisdiction of the royal courts. The king also exercised a good deal of political control over the Catholic church, having been recognised under the 1516 Concordat of Bologna as having the authority to appoint bishops and abbots.

The church played an important part in civil life; in 1539 it was given the role of keeping the public register of births, deaths and marriages; in 1685, during the reign of Louis XIV, the *édit de Nantes* of 1598, which had guaranteed the rights of the Protestant Huguenot minority, was revoked. Thereafter Protestants who did not recant their faith were not able to register births, marriages or deaths in the parish register; the non-registration of marriages caused particular problems, as it meant that the children of the marriage were regarded as illegitimate, and thus unable to inherit from their parents. After widespread emigration by Huguenots, discrimination was brought to an end by Louis XVI with the 1787 *édit de tolérance*, which restored the civil rights of Protestants and introduced the civil registration of births, marriages and deaths.

6. Legal writings (la doctrine)

As we have seen, customary law had been largely reduced to writing by the sixteenth century, a fact which only reinforced its provincial nature. Thus in the eighteenth century Voltaire could ironically say that a man could not ride from one province to another without having to change both his horse and his law. Conflicts of law between the differing customs often occurred, and practitioners had to devise conflict rules to overcome these problems; these rules may be seen as being at the source of modern private international law.

Writers commenting on the customs were usually either practising lawyers or judges; because of their education, they were familiar with Roman law concepts, and drew on these in their work. The first commentaries were published soon after the reduction to writing of the customs. Probably the greatest of the commentators was Charles Dumoulin (1500–1566); he published an influential commentary on the Custom of Paris in 1559, to which he annotated all of the customs of France, and which formed the basis of a re-drafting of the Custom of Paris in 1580. He sought to use the Custom of Paris (rather than Roman law) as the basis for an amalgamation of the whole of northern French customary law into one unified custom; he failed because, at the time he was writing, not all customary laws had yet been written down, and the power of the regional *Parlements*, who upheld their own provincial customs, was too strong. Such systematic study, however, did promote the consciousness that all customary laws could be said to have had a common' origin, even if divergence had since occurred. This common foundation of custom was described by the writers as "common customary law" (*droit commun coutumier*; TEXTS, NO. 9(a)–(d)). This should be distinguished from the English notion of common law, a judge-made law created by the judiciary of the Royal Courts of Westminster. The French notion of a common customary law was, in contrast, purely theoretical. However, the identification of a common customary law was to assist practitioners in resisting a wider incursion of Roman law concepts into customary law.

Some of the earliest writings published on the notion of a common customary law were the *Institutions de Droit des Français* by Guy Coquille and the *Institutes Coutumières* by Antoine Loisel, both published in 1607. A writer of particular importance was Jean Domat, whose work *Les Loix Civiles dans leur Ordre Naturel* was posthumously published between 1689 and 1697. Less wide-ranging works on French law included that of Denis le Brun on succession, Philippe de Renusson on dower and matrimonial property, and Jean-Marie Ricard on gifts. Domat did not write on customary laws. Rather he systematically and logically expounded principles of Roman law, holding them out as a coherent body of legal rules. His logical and deductive approach proved to be of great influence on the drafters of the *Code Civil* in 1804.

During the eighteenth century the idea of there being a common customary law gained wider acceptance and resulted in the desire to publish a treatise which would deal systematically with every aspect of private law covering customary law, caselaw, royal ordinances and all other sources of law. A series of treatises of this nature were published by Auguste Poulain-Duparc, a professor of law at Rennes, and by Robert Pothier (1699–1772), professor at Orléans. The influence of Pothier's series of fifteen treatises (embracing the entire body of French private law) on the drafters of the *Code Civil* was to be immense, especially in the area of obligations.

7. Towards codification

As has been examined, positive law in pre-revolutionary France had a variety of sources. Customary law dealt with private law, but covered a restricted subject area, and Roman law principles had to be introduced to complete it. Royal legislation was the primary source of public, criminal and commercial law, as well as civil and criminal procedure; royal legislation drew heavily on Roman-canonical inquisitorial notions of procedure. The work of legal writers in drawing together the various sources of law with a view to the introduction of a national set of legal rules led to the view during the eighteenth century that private law rules should be incorporated into a legislative code, whose principles would be applied throughout the country. For this to happen, the power of the *Parlements* would have to be broken, to end both the customary divergence, and the confusion of legislative and judicial roles enjoyed by the *Parlements*. This would not happen until the Revolution and the subsequent introduction of a judiciary which recognised the supremacy of legislative authority.

C. Revolutionary and post-revolutionary law

The law in force between the Revolution and the Napoleonic codifications is known as "intermediate law" (*droit intermédiaire*). The Revolution gave rise to three desires: to repeal the existing legal system, to enact a codification of civil law, and to define legitimate governmental powers in a written constitution.

1. Repeal of Ancien Droit

(a) Removal of privileges and the introduction of the notion of equality

The legal system of the *Ancien Régime* was abolished in several stages. The first of these was the abolition of feudalism and its associated obligations and privileges. *Ancien Régime* France had a wide-ranging system of privileges; the nobility and the clergy had special status which enabled them to enjoy fiscal exemptions and gave them the right to be judged in a privileged way (the clergy were judged in the *Officialité*, and the nobility were not subject to the lowest level of royal jurisdiction, the *Prévôté*). The right of a local population to be ruled in accordance with its local customary law was itself regarded as a privilege; in addition many individuals and collectivities (*corps*; which included monasteries, hospitals, universities, chambers of commerce, advocates' colleges, royal officers' colleges, trade associations, even individual towns and communities) were accorded special privileges by the king.

During July and August 1789 there were many peasant uprisings (known as the "Great Fear") throughout France against feudal privileges and rights, and in a *décret des 4–11 août 1789*, the nobility in the *Assemblée Nationale* agreed to the abolition of noble status; hereditary nobility was abolished by a *loi des 19–23.6.1790*; servile status, servile tenure of land and all feudal incidents (such as seigneurial taxes) finally disappeared in a *loi du 17.7.1793*. In addition, a series of decrees passed during 1789–1791 restored civic rights to the Protestant and Jewish communities of France.

All citizens were regarded as being equal in status; indeed the revolutionaries accepted the notion (developed by the natural law school of legal philosophers) that the individual had certain inherent rights, which existed in the natural order of things, and did not need to be established by law, merely declared. These inherent rights were thus declared by the *Assemblée Constituante* in the famous *Déclaration des Droits de l'Homme et du Citoyen du 26 août 1789* (TEXTS, NO. 10).

The Declaration sets out what are considered to be the "natural, inalienable and sacred" rights of man. The first article confirms that "men are born and remain free and equal in rights; social distinctions may be founded only on common utility". Thus was accepted the notion of the equality of all citizens before the law. The 1789 Declaration also accepted the principles (*inter alia*) of freedom of conscience, religion, association and expression, the presumption of innocence, and the right not be unjustly arrested. The extent to which these principles have been accepted and applied by the courts as legal norms by which the constitutionality and legality of parliamentary statute and governmental regulations may be judged is examined in Chapter 4.

(b) Laicisation of the law

Another feature of the revolutionary period was the increasing laicisation of the law. The church was reorganised by the *constitution civile du clergé du 19.7.1789*, bishops and priests becoming elected in the same way as other functionaries. This caused much upheaval, with most bishops and many priests refusing to accept the new order, and many going into voluntary exile. Uprisings in western France (especially the *département* of *la Vendée*) were to grow into a serious counter-revolution, which was not suppressed until late 1793. By a *loi du 17.8.1792*, all monasteries and convents were closed, and religious vows declared null. During 1792 and 1793, a policy of dechristianisation was pursued, churches were closed, and place-names with Christian associations were changed; the Gregorian calendar was replaced by a Republican calendar which gave new names to the months of the year, and which increased the number of days in the week to ten, abolishing Sunday and all Christian festivals. The sacramental nature of marriage was also removed, marriage becoming a purely civil contract; divorce was also introduced (*décret du 20.9.1792*). A new civic religion, the cult of the Supreme Being, with its own religious festivals, was introduced in 1794.

A *décret du 21.2.1795* partially separated church from state by enacting that the state would no longer provide premises for church services or pay salaries to the clergy, although it did purport to guarantee freedom of religious belief and freedom of assembly. A relaxation of the relationship between the church and the state occurred under Napoleon with the *concordat* of 1801, whereby the Catholic religion was declared to be that of the majority of the French population, and the salaries of priests became payable by the state once more; Napoleon himself retained the power of nomination of bishops. True separation of church and state did not occur until the passing of the *loi du 9 décembre 1905* (TEXTS CHAPTER 4, NO. 10), which secularised all state education, subjected the holding of religious meetings to administrative control, and brought to an end all state funding of religion (although an exception was made in respect of Alsace-Lorraine).

(c) Reforms to the administration of justice

The administration of justice was completely reorganised by the abolition of the regional *Parlements*, and their replacement (*loi des 27.11–1.12.1790*) by a single appeal court, the *Tribunal de Cassation* (which was to become the *Cour de Cassation* under the reign of

Napoleon). Its role was to ensure the correct and uniform application of legislation throughout France. To enable it to do so, it had the power of *cassation*, to quash the decisions of lower courts in which the law had been improperly applied, or due procedure not followed. In addition, the complex administrative organisation of the *Ancien Régime* was reformed and simplified, the country being divided (*décret des 26.2–4.3.1790*) for administrative purposes into 83 *départements* (there are now 96, including the *départements d'outre-mer*) each controlled by a central government representative (the prefect (*préfet*)). Each *département* was itself divided into circumscriptions known as *districts*, which also served as the jurisdiction of new regional and local courts; this system did not last long, however, and under the reign of Napoleon the present court structure (of local *Tribunaux d'Instance* and departmental *Tribunaux de Grande Instance*) was introduced.

The revolutionaries also took care to enforce the separation of the judiciary from both the legislature and the executive. The subservience of the judiciary to the legislature was enshrined in the 1789 Declaration, which provided (*Art. 7*) that no one could be punished save in accordance with duly promulgated and legally applied legislation; the judiciary was to protect the rights of individuals by applying the law, not by creating it. The judiciary was also separated from the executive; the latter was not to be allowed to be involved in the process of justice in the way that the king had exercised his inherent power as the fount of justice (under the system of *la justice retenue*); final appeal thus lay to the supreme court, the *Tribunal de Cassation*, not to any royal or executive authority.

The other side of this coin was that the executive was not to be subject to the control of the judiciary, which was expressly prohibited (*loi des 16–24.8.1790*) from judging the activities of the executive. The reasons for this are to be found in a long-standing conflict over jurisdiction during the *Ancien Régime* between the royal courts and the regional administrative royal representatives, the *intendants*. The latter had a supervisory role over matters of local administration, finance and the provision of justice; they also acted as first instance judges in fiscal and administrative cases (with appeal to the *Conseil du Roi*). Such a conflict would not have arisen had the king not at the same time been supreme ruler, supreme legislator and supreme judge. The supervisory role of the *intendant* empowered him to remove a case from the *Cour de Bailliage* or *Parlement* if he were of the opinion that the case affected the king's interests; he would then judge minor cases himself and send the more important cases for decision to the *Conseil du Roi*. The *Parlements* resented the interference of the *intendants*, and did their best to hamper them in their task. As we have seen, the *Parlements* also interfered in legislative matters, by refusing to register royal legislation, and by exercising a wide regulatory power through the use of *arrêts de règlement*. *Article 13* of the *loi des 16–24.8.1790* therefore prevented any more interference by the courts in the process of government by providing that "judicial functions are to be distinguished from and will remain separate from administrative functions; judges, under penalty of disciplinary proceedings, may not interfere in any way with the business of administrative bodies, nor summon before them officials in respect of their official functions". This clear delineation between judicial and administrative functions was subsequently confirmed in a series of decrees.

However, it was soon realised that the activities of the executive had to be subject to some sort of legal control; such control came to be exercised by the *Conseil d'Etat*, which had been created by Napoleon in 1799 (by the *Constitution du 22 frimaire an VIII (15.12.1799), Art. 52*) modelled on the old *Conseil du Roi*. The *Conseil d'Etat* would itself formulate a body of principles of administrative law for it to apply to the cases coming before it. In 1872, the *Tribunal des Conflits* was created to settle jurisdictional conflicts between the "ordinary" courts (*tribunaux judiciaires*) and the administrative court (see Chapter 3).

(d) Reforms of procedure and substantive law

The revolutionary *droit intermédiaire* retained existing legal rules where these were not inconsistent with revolutionary ideology, but there were innovations, such as the introduction of the constitutional principle of equality of all citizens before the law, the creation of new legal institutions such as divorce and adoption, the reform of succession laws, and the recognition of the rights of illegitimate children. Two criminal codes were promulgated in succession: the *Code Pénal* of 1791, which was replaced in 1795 by the *Code des Délits et des Peines*. Reforms to criminal procedure were also introduced; there were even attempts to introduce an accusatorial system along Anglo-American lines, with a *jury d'accusation* (grand jury) and *jury de jugement* (petty jury), the notion having been accepted that in a democracy those accused of crime should be accused and judged by their fellow citizens; only the petty jury survived the Napoleonic reforms, which reintroduced the inquisitorial system of criminal justice.

2. Codification of private law

As has been seen, the view developed during the eighteenth century that private law rules should be incorporated into a legislative code having national effect. Codification (which, in its true sense, might be defined as the enactment of a methodical planned collection of legal rules organised in articles expressing the general principles governing a determined branch of the law) became possible with the Revolution and the creation of a judiciary which recognised legislative supremacy.

The 1791 Constitution provided for the drafting of a civil code. The first attempt at codification was carried out by Jean-Jacques Régis de Cambacérès (a practising lawyer who was later to become president of the infamous *Comité du salut public*, then Minister of Justice, and then finally shared the *consulat* with Napoleon during 1799). Cambacérès submitted three draft civil codes (in 1793, 1794, and 1796; TEXTS, NO. 11(a)(b)) all of which were rejected by the legislature on the grounds of being too long, too philosophical, or insufficiently revolutionary.

During the time of the *consulat* (1799 – 1804) Napoleon appointed (*décret du 24 thermidor an 8 (13.8.1800)*) a commission of four practising lawyers to draft a civil code. The commission comprised three senior members of the *Tribunal de Cassation* (Tronchet, Bigot de Préameneu and Malleville), and Portalis (from the *Tribunal des Prises* (maritime courts)). The first two were from the northern customary part of France, the latter two from the Midi. They completed their task in five months, drawing very heavily on the work of doctrinal writers such as Pothier and Domat. The draft was submitted to the *Tribunal de Cassation* and appeal courts for scrutiny and subsequent referral to the *Conseil d'Etat* (which had legislative initiative) and the legislature. The legislature proved to be obstructive, and in 1802 Napoleon had to adjourn the legislative procedure. However, the establishment later that year of Napoleon as consul for life, with wide executive powers (*décret des 14 – 16 thermidor an 10 (4 – 6.8.1802)*) enabled him to introduce a streamlined procedure bypassing legislative resistance.

The different chapters (*titres*) of the code were promulgated by a series of 36 laws passed from March 1803 to March 1804; a final law (*loi du 30 ventôse an 12 (21.3.1804)*) gathered together the 36 laws into a *Code Civil des Français,* having 2,281 articles; it also abolished other sources of law where these conflicted with the provisions of the Code, providing in *Art. 7* that, "Roman law, ordinances, general or local customary laws and other usages or regulations are henceforth without legal force, whether general or special, concerning the areas covered by the said laws constituting the present code".

The Civil Code later became known as the *Code Napoléon*, and rightly so, for Napoleon had been actively involved in seeing through its implementation; he desired to be remembered not just as a general, but also as a lawmaker, and strongly believed in the virtue of legislative codes as a means of uniting the country by ensuring the uniform application of legal rules throughout the territory. He was personally present at about one half of the discussions of the *Conseil d'Etat*, and played a major role in supporting the introduction of certain institutions, especially adoption and divorce. Perhaps his own interests were at stake here; the Empire (a quasi-monarchy, created in 1804) was to be hereditary, and yet his wife Joséphine de Bauharnais was childless – he was to divorce her and marry Marie Louise d'Autriche who produced his son *Napoléon, Duc de Reistadt* (who died aged 19). He also fought successfully for the provisions of the Code to be drafted in language accessible to the ordinary citizen.

The drafters of the Civil Code wanted it to be more practical than theoretical; in this they can be regarded as having been successful. However, the brevity and generality of some of its provisions meant that the courts had to flesh it out in their caselaw; a good example of this can be seen in *Arts. 1382, 1383* which provide simply that, "Every act which causes loss to another obliges the person by whose fault it arose to repair that loss. Everyone is responsible for the loss caused by his acts, negligence and imprudence". The sections have given rise to a substantial body of caselaw clarifying the extent of this tortious liability. The importance of caselaw was anticipated by the Code's authors; in a report accompanying the draft code (*Discours préliminaire*; TEXTS, NO. 12) Portalis made it clear that the commission had been well aware that it would be impossible to foresee every situation that might arise; he said that "the role of the legislator is to set out broadly the general maxims of the law; to establish principles having fertile consequences, and not to descend into the detailed questions which might arise on any given point. It is for the lawyers and judges, being well versed in the law, to direct its application". He went on to say that although it would be desirable to regulate every issue by legislative provision, in the absence of a precise text on every point, a series of well-established court decisions agreeing on a given point would be authoritative.

The Code implements the individualistic liberal philosophy of the Revolution whilst not making a complete break with the past. Its provisions draw from the various sources of *Ancien Droit*: customary law (especially the Custom of Paris), Roman law (in respect of contract and delict) and Canon law (certain areas of family law). As has been seen, the drafting commission relied to a good degree on the efforts of Pothier and Domat; the former's works were particularly important as a source of principles of the law of obligations. However, revolutionary theory did have an impact on the provisions of the Code; examples are the freedom of the individual to own property (property having been recognised in the *1789 Déclaration, Art. 17* as being an "inviolable and sacred right") and to contract as he sees fit (*Code Civil, Art. 1134*); the principle of equality was also incorporated into the law of succession. The structure of the Code follows closely that of François Bourjon, who in 1747 published a general commentary of customary law, taking the Custom of Paris as a model (*Le Droit Commun de la France*).

A *Code Civil* enacted in 1804 might well appear to be unsuited to the needs of a modern society, many aspects of social and economic life having changed since the early nineteenth century. Numerous legislative modifications to the Code have therefore been necessary; furthermore, the courts have not been afraid to update some of its provisions by interpreting them in a way which was not intended by its drafters (see Chapter 2). There was an unsuccessful attempt to carry out a major revision of the Code towards the end of the nineteenth century; finally, in the late 1940s, a commission of twelve lawyers was appointed to carry out a complete revision, and some years later it produced a draft revision of the First Book of the Code (on *les personnes*), which was circulated to the courts and universities for comment. However, the proposed reforms were never implemented; the exercise had taken an unexpectedly long time, and it was realised that it was almost impossible to foresee and plan for all societal developments which might occur, and which might require further reforms of the Code. It was decided that partial modifications to the Code would be carried out as and when necessary. This is done without altering the internal structure of the Code or the numerical order of the articles. Although this is convenient, it does reduce the internal coherence of the Code.

The *Code Civil* was followed by a *Code de Procédure Civile* (1806), a *Code Commercial* and *Code d'Instruction Criminelle* (1808) and a *Code Pénal* (1810); a *Code Forestier* was subsequently promulgated in 1827. In modern French law, there are a multitude of codes; many, however, are codes in name only – they are no more than collections of legislation on a subject, which is not organised to form a coherent ensemble. Although it is true that the law has become more complex, it has also become less clear in the way it is expressed and thus is largely inaccessible to the citizen; this of course is a long way from that which was originally intended by the authors of codification.

3. Introduction of a written constitution

The third main contribution of the Revolution was the promulgation of a written constitution to enforce a strict separation between the legislative, executive and judicial organs of government. In the *Ancien Régime*, there had been a collection of largely unwritten constitutional customs known as the *lois fondamentales du royaume*. These cannot be regarded as a constitution in the true sense, as they dealt only with the nature of royal authority (the king being held to be a "sacred person" (*personne sacrée*) acting with God's authority), the rules of royal succession, and other matters such as the indivisibility of the kingdom (a principle which still applies to the Republic; *1958 Constitution, Art. 2*; see Chapter 4). These constitutional rules did not address at all the central issue of the separation of powers, as no such separation was admitted, all authority residing in the king.

English political and philosophical thought came progressively to France during the eighteenth century; French political thinkers such as Voltaire, Montesquieu and Rousseau were much influenced by John Locke's views on the separation of powers, and the need for an independent legislature. In his famous work, *L'Esprit des Lois* (1748), Montesquieu scrutinised the French political system in the light of other constitutional systems, particularly that of England, and espoused for the first time the theory of separation of powers into executive, legislative and judicial organs.

The desire to have a written constitution clearly separating the different powers and bringing royal absolutism to an end was to be realised during the revolutionary period. On 17 June 1789, the *tiers état* voted to assume legislative power and become the *Assemblée Nationale* (in which it was later to be joined by most of the *clergé* and a few members of the *noblesse*). On 20 June 1789, in response to the king's attempt to suspend the meetings of the different *états* and hold a royal meeting to resolve the conflict, the deputies of the *Assemblée Nationale* took an oath (known as the "tennis court oath" (*serment du jeu de paume*) because the deputies had to meet in a tennis court when the king closed their usual meeting room) to introduce a written constitution. In this they were inspired by the American Declaration of Rights of 1776.

The first written constitution was promulgated, and approved by Louis XVI, in September 1791. The preamble to this constitution incorporated the 1789 *Déclaration des Droits de l'Homme et du Citoyen*, and indeed all subsequent constitutions have expressly referred to its principles. The 1791 constitution was inspired by the English model of partnership between the king and the legislature, royal power being carefully circumscribed. However, it failed because of political crises arising from the use of the royal right of veto, the king having the prerogative power to suspend the implementation of legislation. On 10 August 1792, the monarchy was overthrown, and France became a republic with a new legislative assembly, the *Convention*; the *Convention* drafted a republican constitution in 1793. However, this never came into force, being suspended with the establishment, under the threat of the invasion of France by the Austro-Prussian Empire (war having broken out in April 1792), of the effective dictatorship of the *Comité du salut public* (which had been set up to oversee the war effort) under Robespierre from 1793–4 (the period of *la Terreur*). The present constitution (of the Fifth Republic, 1958) is republican in nature. Since 1789, France has known several different constitutional systems: monarchical (eg *Charte de* 1815 and 1830); imperial (1804, 1852); consular (1799, 1802); directorate (government by a five-man council) (1795); and, of course, republican (1793, 1848, 1875, 1946 and 1958).

Texts and materials

1 Ressorts des Parlements et Conseils Souverains avant 1789

2 France coutumière: seizième – dix-huitième siècles

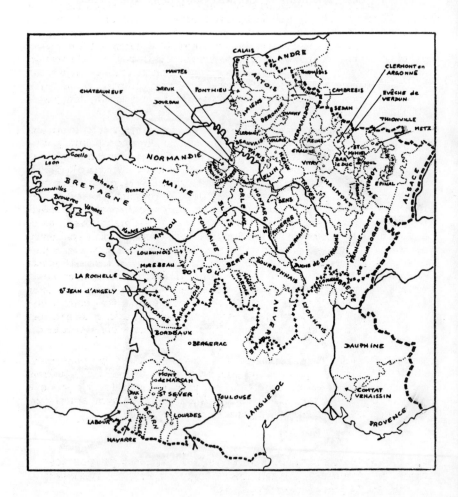

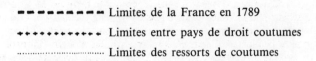

——————— Limites de la France en 1789

+++++++++++ Limites entre pays de droit coutumes

.... Limites des ressorts de coutumes

3 Ordonnance de Montil-lès-Tours (1454), Art.125.

Et que les parties en jugement, tant en nostre Court de Parlement que par devant les autres juges de nostre Royaume, tant nostres qu'autres, proposent et allèguent plusieurs usages, stiles et coustumes, qui sont divers selon la diversité des pays de nostre Royaume, et les leur convient prouver, par quoy les procez sont souventes fois moult allongez et les parties constituées en grands fraiz et despens; et que si les coustumes, usages et stiles des pays de nostre dit Royaume estoient rédigez par escrit, les procez en seroient de trop plus briefz et les parties soublevées des despenses et mises, et aussi les juges en jugeroient mieux et plus certainement; car souventes foys adue les partis prennent coustumes contraires en un mesme pays; et aucunesfois, les coustumes muent et varient à leur appetit, dont grandz dommages et inconveniens adviennent à noz subjectz.

Nous voulans abréger les procez et litiges d'entre noz subjectz et les relever des mises et despens, et mettre certaineté ès jugemens tant faire que ce pourra, et oster toutes matières de variations et contrariétez, ordonnons et décernons, déclairons et statuons que les coustumes, usages et stiles de tous les pays de nostre Royaume, soient rédigez et mis par escrit, accordez par les coustumiers, practiciens et genz de chascun desditz pays de nostre royaume, lesquelz coustumes, usages et stiles ainsi accordez seront mis et escritz en livres, lesquels seront apportez par devers nous, pour les faire veoir et visiter par les genz de nostre grand conseil, ou de nostre Parlement, et par nous les decréter et confermer; et iceux coustumes, usages et stiles ainsi décrétez et confermez, seront observez et gardez ès pays dont ilz seront, et ainsi en nostre Court de Parlement ès causes et procez d'iceux pays; et jugeront les juges de nostre dict Royaume, tant en nostre Court de Parlement, que nos baillifs, séneschaux et autres juges, selon iceux usages, coustumes et stiles, ès pays dont ilz seront, sans en faire autre preuve que ce qui sera escrit audict livre; et lesquelles coustumes, stiles et usages, ainsi éscritz, accordez et confermez, comme dict est, voulons estre observez et gardez en jugement et dehors.

(...) Prohibons et défendons à tous les advocatz de nostre Royaume, qu'ilz n'allèguent ne proposent autres coustumes, usages et stiles que ceux qui seront escritz, accordez et décretez comme dict est; et enjoignons ausdictz juges qu'ils punissent et corrigent ceux qui feront le contraire, et qu'ilz n'oyent ne reçoyvent aucunes personnes à allèguer, proposer, ne dire le contraire.

4 A. Young. Remarques d'un voyageur anglais à propos des arrêts de règlement. Extrait des voyages en France, Deuxième partie. De la Revolution Française.

Il y avait aussi dans la constitution des Parlements, une particularité fort peu connue chez nous, mais qui sous un gouvernement comme celui de la France, apparaissait comme très singulier. Ils avaient le pouvoir dont ils usaient constamment de rendre des édits sans le consentement de la Couronne. Ces édits avaient force de loi dans tout le ressort de leur juridiction, et de toutes les lois, c'étaient les plus sûrement observées, car, comme toute infraction contre eux était portée devant ces Cours elles-mêmes qui les avaient élaborées (horrible système de tyranie!), elle était sûrement punie avec la dernière sévérité. Il peut sembler étrange de voir dans un gouvernement à tant d'égards aussi despotique que celui de la France, les Cours Souveraines faire des lois sans le consentement du Roi, parfois même contre sa volonté. Les Anglais que je recontrai en France en 1789 étaient surpris de voir quelques uns de ces corps prohiber par leurs arrêts la circulation des grains dans le moment même que le Roi, par un organe aussi populaire que M. Necker, décrétait au contraire pleine liberté à ce sujet dans tout le royaume, et ce, à la requête de l'Assemblée Nationale elle-même. Mais il n'y avait rien là que d'ordinaire; telle était leur pratique constante.

5(a) Extrait du discours du Chancelier Maupeou sur le droit de remontrances des Cours Souveraines. Décembre 1770.

...Quand le législateur veut manifester ses volontés vous êtes son organe, et sa bonté permet que vous soyez son conseil; il vous invite à l'éclairer de vos lumières et vous ordonne de lui montrer la vérité. Là finit votre ministère. Le roi pèse vos observations dans sa sagesse; il les balance avec les motifs qui le déterminent; et, de ce coup d'oeil qui embrasse l'ensemble de la monarchie, il juge les avantages et les inconvénients de la loi. S'il commande alors, vous lui devez la plus parfaite soumission. Si vos droits s'étendaient plus loin, si votre résistance n'avait pas un terme, vous ne seriez plus ses officiers, mais ses maîtres; sa volonté serait assujettie à la vôtre; la majesté du trône ne résiderait plus que dans vos assemblées; et, dépouillé des droits les plus essentiels de la couronne, dépendant dans l'établissement des lois, dépendant dans leur exécution, le roi ne conserverait que le nom et l'ombre vaine de la souveraineté.

5(b) Réponse de Louis XV aux remontrances du Parlement de Paris lors de la 'séance de la flagellation' du 3 mars 1766.

Je ne souffrirai pas qu'il se forme dans mon royaume une association qui ferait dégénérer en une confédération de résistance le lien naturel des mêmes devoirs et obligations communes, ni qu'il s'introduise dans la Monarchie un corps imaginaire qui ne pourrait qu'en troubler l'harmonie; la magistrature ne forme point un corps ni un ordre séparé des trois ordres du Royaume; les magistrats sont mes officiers chargés de m'acquitter du devoir vraiment royal de rendre la justice à mes sujets ... Ses vrais ennemis (de la magistrature) sont ceux qui, dans son propre sein, lui font tenir un langage opposé à ses principes; qui lui font dire que tous les parlements ne font qu'un seul et même corps ... que ce corps nécessairement indivisible, est de l'essence de la Monarchie ... qu'il est le siège, le tribunal, l'organe de la Nation; qu'il est le protecteur et le dépositaire essentiel de sa liberté ... qu'il est juge entre le Roi et son peuple; que gardien respectif, il maintient l'équilibre du gouvernement en réprimant également l'excès de la liberté et l'abus du pouvoir; que les parlements coopèrent avec la puissance souveraine dans l'établissement des lois ... qu'ils doivent opposer une barrière insurmontable aux décisions qu'ils attribuent à l'autorité arbitraire et que, s'il en résulte un combat d'autorité, il est de leur devoir d'abandonner leurs fonctions et de se démettre de leurs offices sans que leurs démissions puissent être reçues. Entreprendre d'ériger en principes des nouveautés si pernicieuses c'est faire injure à la magistrature, démentir son institution, trahir ses intérêts et méconnaître les véritables lois fondamentales de l'Etat; comme s'il était permis d'oublier que c'est en ma personne seule que réside la puissance souveraine dont le caractère propre est l'esprit de conseil, de justice, et de raison; que c'est de moi seul que mes cours tiennent leur existence et leur autorité, que la plénitude de cette autorité qu'elles n'exercent qu'en mon nom, demeure toujours en moi et que l'usage n'en peut jamais être tourné contre moi; que c'est à moi seul qu'appartient le pouvoir législatif sans dépendance et sans partage; que c'est par ma seule autorité que les officiers de mes cours procèdent non à la formation mais à l'enregistrement, à la publication, à l'execution de la loi et qu'il leur est permis de me remontrer ce qui est du devoir de bons et utiles conseillers.

6 Introduction aux ordonnances de Louis XIV. Avril 1667. Sur la procédure civile.

Louis, par la grâce de Dieu, Roy de France et de Navarre, à tous présents et avenir − Salut.

Comme la justice est le plus solide fondement de la durée des Etats, qu'elle assure le repos des Familles et le bonheur des Peuples, Nous avons employé tous nos soins pour la rétablir par l'autorité des lois au-dedans de notre Royaume, après lui avoir donné la paix par la force de nos armes. C'est pourquoi, ayant reconnu par le rapport des personnes de grande expérience, que les Ordonnances sagement établies par les Rois nos prédecesseurs pour terminer les Procès, étaient négligées ou changées par le temps et la malice des plaideurs; que même elles étaient observées différemment en plusieurs de nos Cours, qui causait la ruine des Familles par la multiplicité des procédures, les frais des poursuites, et la variété des jugemens, et qu'il était nécessaire d'y pourvoir et rendre l'expédition des affaires plus prompte plus facile et plus sûre, par le retranchement de plusieurs délais et actes inutiles, et par l'établissement d'un stile uniforme dans toutes nos Cours et Sièges (. . .)

(Conclusion)
Voulons que la présente ordonnance soit gardée et observée dans tout notre Royaume, terres et pays de notre obéissance (. . .) Abrogeons toutes Ordonnances, coustumes, lois, statuts, règlements, stiles et usages différents ou contraires aux dispositions y contenues.

7 Mémoire sur les vues générales pour la réformation de la justice. Henri d'Aguesseau. Oeuvres complètes, XIII, Paris 1819, pp 202−5.

Il s'agiroit de reformer les lois anciennes, d'en faire de nouvelles et de réunir les unes aux autres dans un seul corps de législation afin que ceux qui veulent acquérir la science du droit, soit pour défendre les intérêts des plaideurs, soit pour en être les juges, eussent une espèce de code qui devînt le sujet fixe et certain de leur application, au lieu qu'à présent, la multitude et la variété des lois qui sont en usage parmi nous sont si grandes, qu'il arrive souvent qu'on en étudie presque aucune, par la difficulté de les savoir toutes, ou qu'on ne les lit qu'à mesure qu'il se présente une occasion de les appliquer, et qu'il n'est rien de plus rare que de trouver un homme dont on puisse dire qu'il possède parfaitement toutes les parties de la jurisprudence française.

Et une des principales raisons de leur peu d'exécution est qu'elles y sont peu connues, soit par leur multitude et leur variété, soit parce qu'il n'y a aucun receuil où l'on trouve rassemblées toutes celles qui doivent servir de règles dans les jugements.

8 Préambule de l'ordonnance sur les donations, 1731.

Notre amour pour la justice dont nous regardons l'administration comme le premier devoir de la Royauté, et le désir que nous avons de la faire respecter également dans tous nos Etats, ne nous permettent point de tolérer plus longtemps une diversité de jurisprudence qui produit de si grands inconvéniens. Nous aurions pu la faire cesser avec plus d'éclat et de satisfaction pour Nous, si Nous avions différé de faire publier le corps des lois qui seront faites dans cette vue, jusqu'à ce que toutes les parties d'un projet si important eussent été également achevées. Mais l'utilité qu'on doit attendre de la perfection de cet ouvrage, ne pouvait être aussi prompte que Nous désirerions. Notre affection pour nos peuples, dont nous préférons toujours l'intérêt à toute autre considération, Nous a déterminé à leur procurer l'avantage présent, de profiter au moins en partie, d'un travail dont Nous Nous hâterons de leur faire bientôt recueillir tout le fruit. En nous leur en donnons comme les premices, par la décision des questions qui regardent la nature, la forme et les charges ou les conditions essentielles des Donations, matière qui, soit par sa simplicité, soit par le peu d'opposition qui s'y trouve entre les principes du Droit Romain et ceux du Droit Français, Nous a paru la plus propre à fournir le premier exemple de l'exécution du plan que Nous Nous sommes proposé.

9(a) Institution au droict des Françoys. G. Coquille. Paris 1607, p28.

Nos coustumes sont nostre droict civil, de mesme force et vigeur, comme estoit à Rome le droict civil des Romains et selon mon advis, c'est erreur de comparer nos coustumes aux statuts dont parlent tant les Docteurs italiens, car en Italie le droict commun est le droict civil Romain, et si ès villes et territories se trouvent quelques loix particulières qui soient contraires ou diverses au droict civil Romain, ce sont statuts qui sont interprétez estroittement, pour ce qu'ils sont contre ou outre le droict commun. Mais en la France coustumière, le droit civil Romain n'est pas le droict commun, il n'a pas force de loy, ains sert seulement pour la raison et nos coustumes sont nostre vray droict civil, pourquoy n'est besoin d'y faire d'interprétation à l'estroit, comme les Docteurs Italiens font à leurs statuts.

9(b) Charles Dumoulin. Commentarii in consuetudine Parisiensis. Opera omnia, Tomus primus. Paris, 1625. Col.44.45 par.107,109.

Les Francs et les Gaulois eurent toujours des coutumes générales et communes, notamment en matière de successions, heritages, profits matrimoniaux, fiefs, cens, retraits, totalement divergentes du droit commun des Romains auquel les Français ne furent jamais soumis, et ces coutumes générales et communes sont le droit particulier et commun des Francs et des Gaulois; initialement les coutumes locales étaient rares, car l'assemblée suprême, ou le Parlement ambulatoire, était unique pour tout le royaume, et cependant au cours des temps, les coutumes locales se sont multipliées et diversifiées, et ces mêmes droits sont restés le droit général et particulier des Français (. . .) En cas de coutume locale lacunère et douteuse, il ne faut pas recourir au droit romain, mais aux coutumes générales voisines. Ici le droit des Romains n'est aucun usage et ne peut être droit commun si ce n'est dans les lieux régis par le droit écrit où une part encore plus importante du droit écrit est en désuetude (. . .)

Donc les coutumes sont notre droit commun et il est vrai que certaines sont plus générales que d'autres, certaines étant les maitresses, auxquelles il faut se courir. On n'emprunte au droit écrit romain qu'en ultime recours parce qu'il est trouvé conforme à l'équité et à même de régir le contrat.

9(c) Claude Joseph de Ferrière. Dictionnaire de droit et de pratique. Paris 1771. p 540.

Droit commun de la France est sans contredit celui qui est contenu dans les ordonnances de nos Rois, et ensuite ce qui est dans les lois romaines pour les pays de Droit écrit et chaque coutume dans son ressort pour les pays de droit écrit et chaque coutume dans son ressort pour les pays de droit coutumier.

9(d) Jean-Baptiste Denisart. Collection de décisions nouvelles et de notions relatives à la jurisprudence actuelle. Paris 1771. Vol II, p 235 – 7.

On entend par droit commun non seulement les ordonnances et les décisions communes et toutes les coutumes du Royaume, mais encore cette portion de droit Romain qui concerne l'état des personnes, la nature des contrats, l'exécution des testaments et des substitutions que la sagesse de ce droit a fait adopter (. . .) Le droit commun n'établit ordinairement que des règles générales auxquelles une autorité légitime peut apporter des exceptions. Le Droit français est cet assemblage d'ordonnances, édits et déclarations données par nos Rois, et de coutumes rédigées sous leur autorité expresse, par les peuples des provinces qu'ils se sont soumis.

10 Déclaration des Droits de l'Homme et du Citoyen du 26 août 1789.

Les représentants du peuple français, constitués en Assemblée nationale, considérant que l'ignorance, l'oubli ou le mépris des droits de l'homme sont les seules causes des malheurs publics et de la corruption des gouvernements, ont résolu d'exposer, dans une déclaration solennelle, les droits naturels, inaliénables et sacrés de l'homme, afin que cette déclaration, constamment présente à tous les membres du corps social, leur rappelle sans cesse leurs droits et leurs devoirs; afin que les actes du pouvoir législatif et ceux du pouvoir exécutif, pouvant être à chaque instant comparés avec le but de toute institution politique, en soient plus respectés; afin que les réclamations des citoyens, fondées désormais sur des principes simples et incontestables, tournent toujours au maintien de la Constitution et au bonheur de tous.

En conséquence, l'Assemblée nationale reconnaît et déclare, en présence et sous les auspices de l'Etre suprême, les droits suivants de l'Homme et du Citoyen.

Article Premier. Les hommes naissent et demeurent libres et égaux en droits. Les distinctions sociales ne peuvent être fondées que sur l'utilité commune.

Art. 2. Le but de toute association politique est la conservation des droits naturels et imprescriptibles de l'homme. Ces droits sont la liberté, la sûreté et la résistance à l'oppression.

Art. 3. Le principe de toute souveraineté réside essentiellement dans la Nation. Nul corps, nul individu ne peut exercer d'autorité qui n'en émane expressément.

Art. 4. La liberté consiste à pouvoir faire tout ce qui ne nuit pas à autrui: ainsi l'exercice des droits naturels de chaque homme n'a de bornes que celles qui assurent aux autres members de la société la jouissance de ces mêmes droits. Ces bornes ne peuvent être déterminées que par la loi.

Art. 5. La loi n'a le droit de défendre que les actions nuisibles à la société. Tout ce qui n'est pas défendu par la loi ne peut être empêché, et nul ne peut être contraint à faire ce qu'elle n'ordonne pas.

Art. 6. La loi est l'expression de la volonté générale. Tous les citoyens ont droit de concourir personnellement, ou par leurs représentants à sa formation. Elle doit être la même pour tous, soit qu'elle protège, soit qu'elle punisse. Tous les citoyens, étant égaux à ses yeux, sont également admissibles à toutes dignités, places et emplois publics, selon leur capacité et sans autre distinction que celle de leurs vertus et de leurs talents.

Art. 7. Nul homme ne peut être accusé, arrêté ni détenu que dans les cas déterminés par la loi et selon les formes qu'elle a prescrites. Ceux qui sollicitent, expédient, exécutent ou font exécuter des ordres arbitraires doivent être punis; mais tout citoyen appelé ou saisi en vertu de la loi doit obéir à l'instant: il se rend coupable par la résistance.

Art. 8. La loi ne doit établir que des peines strictement et évidemment nécessaires, et nul ne peut être puni qu'en vertu d'une loi établie et promulgée antérieurement au délit, et également appliquée.

Art. 9. Tout homme étant présumé innocent jusqu'à ce qu'il ait été déclaré coupable, s'il est jugé indispensable de l'arrêter, toute rigueur qui ne serait pas nécessaire pour s'assurer de sa personne doit être sévèrement réprimée par la loi.

Art. 10. Nul ne doit être inquiété pour ses opinions, même religieuses, pourvu que leur manifestation ne trouble pas l'ordre public établi par la loi.

Art. 11. La libre communication des pensées et des opinions est un des droits les plus précieux de l'homme; tout citoyen peut donc parler, écrire, imprimer librement, sauf à répondre de l'abus de cette liberté dans les cas déterminés par la loi.

Art. 12. La garantie des droits de l'homme et du citoyen nécessite une force publique; cette force est donc instituée pour l'avantage de tous, et non pour l'utilité particulière de ceux à qui elle est confiée.

Art. 13. Pour l'entretien de la force publique, et pour les dépenses d'administration, une contribution commune est indispensable; elle doit être également répartie entre tous les citoyens, en raison de leurs facultés.

Art. 14. Les citoyens ont le droit de constater, par eux-mêmes ou par leurs représentants, la nécessité de la contribution publique, de la consentir librement, d'en suivre l'emploi, et d'en déterminer la quotité, l'assiette, le recouvrement et la durée.

Art. 15. La société a le droit de demander compte à tout agent public de son administration.

Art. 16. Toute société dans laquelle la garantie des droits n'est pas assurée, ni la séparation des pouvoirs déterminée, n'a point de constitution.

Art. 17. La propriété étant un droit inviolable et sacré, nul ne peut en être privé, si ce n'est lorsque la nécessité publique, légalement constatée, l'exige évidemment, et sous la condition d'une juste et préalable indemnité.

11(a) Discours préliminaire du premier projet de Code Civil de Cambacérès. 1793.

Ce serait se livrer à un espoir chimérique que de concevoir le projet d'un Code qui préviendrait tous les cas. Beaucoup de lois, a dit un historien célèbre, font une mauvaise république, leur multiplicité est un fardeau et le peuple qui en est accablé souffre presque autant de ses lois que de ses vices. Peu de lois suffisent à des hommes honnêtes; il n'en est jamais assez pour les méchants; et lorsque la science des lois devient un dédale où le plus habile se perd, le méchant triomphe avec les armes mêmes de la justice. Une autre difficulté se présente: si la multitude des lois offre des dangers, leur trop petit nombre peut nuire à l'harmonie sociale. Le législateur ne doit pas aspirer à tout dire; mais après avoir posé des principes féconds qui écartent d'avance beaucoup de doutes, il doit saisir des développements qui laissent subsister peu de questions. Quel est donc le principal but auquel nous devons aspirer? C'est l'unité, c'est l'honneur de donner les premiers ce grand exemple aux peuples, d'épurer et d'abréger leur législation. La vérité est une et indivisible. Portons dans le corps de nos lois le même esprit que dans notre corps politique et comme l'égalité, l'unité et l'indivisibilité ont présidé à la formation de la république, que l'unité et l'égalité président à l'établissement de notre Code Civil; que ce soit en un mot par le petit nombre de textes que nous arrivions à cette unité harmonique qui fait la force du corps social, qui en dirige tous les mouvements dans un accord merveilleux, à peu près comme les lois simples de la création président à la marche et á l'harmonie de l'Univers (. . .)

En mesurant l'étendue de ses obligations, le comité n'a point tardé à reconnaître qu'un bon code devait embrasser les principes généraux et les éléments indicatifs de ces principes. Le législateur travaille pour le peuple; il doit surtout parler au peuple; il a rempli sa tâche lorsqu'il en est entendu. L'esquisse que nous vous offrons contient des articles dont l'application sera facile aux cas qui se reproduisent avec fréquence dans le cours de la vie civile; elle contient aussi des précautions destinées à prévenir les procès qui naissent presque toujours de l'obscurité des textes ou de leur contradiction. Si notre travail peut obtenir votre suffrage, nous le compléterons par un livre particulier contenant des règles simples pour l'exercice des actions civiles, et par de nouvelles vues sur les lois pénales et sur la justice criminelle.

11(b) Discours préliminaire du troisième projet de Code Civil de Cambacérès rapporté au Conseil des Cinq Cents. 1795.

La nécessité d'une réforme dans la législation civile n'est point équivoque; demandée depuis des siècles par les bons esprits, elle avait dû trouver des obstacles dans nos institutions, dans nos moeurs, dans nos habitudes, dans l'esprit du gouvernement, peut-être dans le sentiment toujours actif de l'intérêt personnel. Ces causes ne subsistent plus. Aujourd'hui que tout est changé dans l'ordre politique, il est indispensable de substituer aux lois anciennes un code de lois simples, dont la rédaction facilite l'intelligence, et qui soit tout à la fois le principe du bonheur social et la sauvegarde de la morale publique. C'est dans cet esprit que fut rédigé le premier projet de Code Civil. En le discutant, la Convention nationale ne tarda point à découvrir en lui diverses imperfections, effet inévitable de la rapidité avec laquel l'ouvrage avait été conçu et éxécuté. Pour les faire disparaître, le Comité de législation s'attacha singulièrement à séparer les principes des développements, les règles des corollaires, et à réduire l'ouvrage en un recueil de préceptes où chacun peut trouver les règles de sa conduite dans la vie civile. Quelque avantage que puisse représenter cette méthode, elle ne saurait remplir ni l'attente de la nation, ni les vues du corps législatif. Là où les juges ne sont point législateurs, il ne suffit pas d'assurer l'autorité des lois par la justice; il faut encore qu'elles soient disposées de manière à en écarter le doute par la clarté, à en prévenir les exceptions par la prévoyance. Ainsi, sans aspirer à tout dire, le législateur doit poser des principes féconds qui puissent d'avance résoudre beaucoup de doutes, et saisir des développements qui laissent subsister peu de questions (...)

Loin de nous la ridicule présomption de présenter un ouvrage fini! N'est-ce pas avoir fait un grand pas vers le progrès de la législation, si sortant de la route des préjugés sans abandonner celle des principes, nous parvenons à porter l'attention du législateur sur tous les points qui doivent le fixer, et si nous plaçons sous ses yeux une suite de règles qui laissent peu de doutes à résoudre et peu de difficultés à craindre? C'est à l'expérience, à la sagesse, à la méditation, qu'il appartient de compléter notre ouvrage, ou plutôt de lui donner une vie nouvelle. A Athènes on plaçait une copie de la loi au pied de la statue des dix héros afin qu'elle fût examinée par tout le monde et que chacun pût exposer ses réflexions au Sénat. Cet exemple ne sera point perdu pour nous: nous soumettons avec confiance et avec résignation le résultat de notre travail à la censure des deux Conseils, et à celle de tous les citoyens, nous les invitons à en faire l'objet de leurs méditations. Le devoir commande aux représentants du peuple de faire cesser cette bigarrure étrange qui place sous des lois si différentes les habitants d'un même état, et il leur prescrit de substituer à un système vicieux un système plus régulier et surtout plus conforme aux institutions républicains.

12 Discours préliminaire du Code Civil de 1804 par Portalis.

Quelle tâche que la rédaction d'une législation civile pour un grand peuple!
L'ouvrage serait au-dessus des forces humaines, s'il s'agissait de donner à ce
peuple une institution absolument nouvelle et si, oubliant le premier rang qu'il
occupe parmi les nations policées, on dédaignait de profiter de l'expérience
du passé et de cette tradition de bon sens, de règles et de maximes, qui est
parvenue jusqu'à nous, et qui forme l'esprit des siècles.

Les lois ne sont pas de purs actes de puissance; ce sont des actes de sagesse, de
justice et de raison. Le législateur exerce moins une autorité qu'un sacerdoce.
Il ne doit point perdre de vue que les lois sont faites pour les hommes et
non les hommes pour les lois; qu'elles doivent être adaptées au caractère, aux
habitudes, à la situation du peuple pour lesquelles elles sont faites; qu'il faut
être sobre de nouveautés en matière de législation, parce que s'il est possible
dans une institution nouvelle de calculer les avantages que la théorie nous
offre, il ne l'est pas de connaître tous les inconvénients que la pratique seule
peut découvrir; qu'il faut laisser le bien si l'on en est en doute du mieux; qu'en
corrigeant un abus, il faut encore voir les dangers de la correction même; qu'il
serait absurde de se livrer à des idées absolues de perfection dans les choses
qui ne sont susceptibles que d'une bonté relative; qu'au lieu de changer les
lois, il est presque toujours plus utile de présenter aux citoyens de nouveaux
motifs de les aimer; que l'histoire nous offre à peine la promulgation de deux
ou trois bonnes lois dans l'espace de plusieurs siècles; qu'enfin, il n'appartient
de proposer des changements, qu'à ceux qui sont assez heureusement nés pour
pénétrer, d'un coup de génie, et par une sorte d'illumination soudaine, toute
la constitution d'un état (...)

A l'ouverture de nos conférences, nous avons été frappés de l'opinion, si
généralement répandue, que dans la rédaction d'un Code Civil, quelques
textes bien précis sur chaque matière peuvent suffire, et que le grand art
est de tout simplifier en prévoyant tout. Tout simplifier est une opération
sur laquelle on a besoin de s'entendre. Tout prévoir est un but qu'il est
impossible d'atteindre. Il ne faut point de lois inutiles; elles affaibliraient
les lois nécessaires; elles compromettraient la certitude et la majesté de la
législation. Mais un grand Etat comme la France, qui est à la fois agricole
et commerçant, qui renferme tant de professions différentes, et qui offre tant
de genres divers d'industrie, ne saurait comporter des lois aussi simples que
celles d'une société pauvre ou plus réduite (...)

Nous n'avons pas cru devoir simplifier les lois au point de laisser les citoyens
sans règle et sans garantie sur leurs plus grands intérêts. Nous nous sommes
également préservés de la dangereuse ambition de vouloir tout régler et tout
prévoir. Qui pourrait penser que ce sont ceux mêmes auxquels un code paraît
toujours trop volumineux, qui osent prescrire impérieusement au législateur la
terrible tâche de ne rien abandonner à la décision du juge? Quoi que l'on fasse,
les lois positives ne sauraient jamais entièrement remplacer l'usage de la raison
naturelle dans les affaires de la vie. Les besoins de la société sont si variés, la
communication des hommes est si active, leurs intérêts sont si multipliés, et leurs
rapports si étendus, qu'il est impossible au législateur de pourvoir à tout. Dans
les matières mêmes qui fixent particulièrement son attention, il est une foule de
détails qui lui échappent, ou qui sont trop contentieux et trop mobiles pour
pouvoir devenir l'objet d'un texte de loi (...) Un code, quelque complet
qu'il puisse paraître, n'est pas plutôt achevé, que mille questions inattendues

viennent s'offrir au magistrat. Car les lois, une fois redigées, demeurent telles qu'elles ont été écrites. Les hommes, au contraire, ne se reposent jamais; ils agissent toujours, et ce mouvement, qui ne s'arrête pas, et dont les effets sont diversement modifiés par les circonstances, produit à chaque instant, quelque combinaison nouvelle, quelque nouveau fait, quelque résultat nouveau. Une foule de choses sont donc nécessairement abandonnées à l'empire de l'usage, à la discussion des hommes instruits, à l'arbitrage des juges.

L'office de la loi est de fixer, par de grandes vues, les maximes générales du droit; d'établir des principes féconds en conséquences, et non de descendre dans le détail des questions qui peuvent naître sur chaque matière. C'est au magistrat et au jurisconsulte, pénétré de l'esprit général des lois, à en diriger l'application. De là, chez toutes les nations policées, on voit toujours se former, à côté du sanctuaire des lois, et sous la surveillance du législateur, un dépôt de maximes, de décisions et de doctrines qui s'épure journellement par la pratique et par le choc des débats judiciaries, qui s'accroît sans cesse de toutes les connaissances acquises, et qui constamment est regardé comme le vrai supplément de la législation.

On fait à ceux qui professent la jurisprudence le reproche d'avoir multiplié les subtilités, les compilations et les commentaires. Ce reproche peut être fondé. Mais dans quel art, dans quelle science, ne s'est-on pas exposé à le mériter? (...) Si l'on peut pardonner à l'intempérence de commenter, de discuter et d'écrire, c'est surtout en jurisprudence. On n'hésitera point à le croire, si l'on réfléchit sur les fils innombrables qui lient les citoyens, sur le développement et la progression successive des objets dont le magistrat et le jurisconsulte sont obligés de s'occuper, sur le cours des évènements et des circonstances qui modifient de tant de manières les relations sociales; enfin sur l'action et la réaction continue de toutes les passions et de tous les intérêts divers. Tel blâme les subtilités et les commentaires, qui devient, dans une cause personnelle, le commentateur le plus subtil et le plus fastidieux.

Il serait, sans doute, désirable que toutes les matières pussent être réglées par des lois. Mais à défaut de texte précis sur chaque matière, un usage ancien, constant et bien établi, une suite non interrompue de décisions semblables, une opinion ou une maxime reçue, tiennent lieu de loi. Quand on n'est dirigé par rien de ce qui est établi ou connu, quand il s'agit d'un fait absolument nouveau, on remonte aux principes du droit naturel. Car si la prévoyance du législateur est limitée, la nature est infinie; elle s'applique à tout ce qui peut intéresser les hommes. Tout cela suppose des compilations, des recueuils, des traités, de nombreux volumes de recherches et de dissertations. Le peuple, dit-on, ne peut dans ce dédale démêler ce qu'il doit éviter, ou ce qu'il doit faire pour avoir la sûreté de ses possessions et de ses droits. Mais le Code, même le plus simple, serait-il à la portée de toutes les classes de la société? Les passions ne seraient-elles pas perpétuellement occupées à en détourner le vrai sens? Ne faut-il pas une certaine expérience pour faire une sage application des lois? Quelle est d'ailleurs la Nation à laquelle des lois simples et en petit nombre aient longtemps suffi? Ce serait donc une erreur de penser qu'il pût exister un corps de lois qui eût d'avance pourvu à tous les cas possibles, et qui cependant fût à la portée du moindre citoyen.

Dans l'état de nos sociétés, il est trop heureux que la jurisprudence forme une science qui puisse fixer le talent, flatter l'amour-propre, et réveiller l'émulation. Une classe entière d'hommes se voue dès lors à cette science, et cette classe, consacrée à l'étude des lois, offre des conseils et des défenseurs aux citoyens qui ne pourraient se diriger et se défendre eux-mêmes, et devient comme le séminaire de la magistrature. Il est trop heureux qu'il y ait des recueuils et une tradition suivie d'usages, de maximes et de règles pour que l'on soit, en quelque sorte, nécessité à juger aujourd'hui, comme on a jugé hier, et qu'il n'y ait d'autres variations dans les jugements publics, que celles qui sont amenées par le progrès des lumières et par la force des circonstances. Il est trop heureux que la nécessité où est le juge de s'instruire, de faire des recherches, d'approfondir les questions qui s'offrent à lui, ne lui permette jamais d'oublier que, s'il est des choses qui sont arbitraires à sa raison, il n'en est point qui soient purement à son caprice ou à sa volonté (. . .)

Sur le fondement de la maxime que les juges doivent obéir aux lois et qu'il leur est défendu de les interpréter, les tribunaux, dans ces dernières années, renvoyaient par des référés les justiciables au pouvoir législatif, toutes les fois qu'ils manquaient de loi, ou que la loi existante leur paraissait obscure. Le tribunal de cassation a constamment réprimé cet abus comme un déni de justice. Il est deux sortes d'interprétations: l'une par voie de doctrine, l'autre par voie d'autorité. L'interprétation par voie de doctrine consiste à saisir le vrai sens des lois, à les appliquer avec discernement et à les suppléer dans les cas qu'elles n'ont pas réglés. Sans cette espèce d'interprétation, pourrait-on concevoir la possibilité de remplir l'office de juge? L'interprétation par voie d'autorité consiste à résoudre les questions et les doutes par voie de règlements ou de dispositions générales. Ce mode d'interprétation est le seul qui soit interdit au juge. Quand la loi est claire, il faut la suivre; quand elle est obscure, il faut en approfondir les dispositions. Si l'on manque de loi, il faut consulter l'usage ou l'équité. L'équité est le retour à la loi naturelle, dans le silence, l'opposition ou l'obscurité des lois positives. Forcer le magistrat de recourir au législateur, ce serait admettre le plus funeste des principes; ce serait renouveler parmi nous la désastreuse législation des rescrits. Car lorsque le législateur intervient pour prononcer sur des affaires nées et vivement agitées entre particuliers, il n'est pas plus à l'abri des surprises que les tribunaux. On a moins à redouter l'arbitraire réglé, timide et circonspect d'un magistrat qui peut être réformé, et qui est soumis à l'action en forfaiture, que l'arbitraire absolu d'un pouvoir indépendant qui n'est jamais responsable.

Les parties qui traitent entre elles sur une matière que la loi positive n'a pas définie, se soumettent aux usages reçus ou à l'équité universelle, à défaut de tout usage. Or, constater un point d'usage et l'appliquer à une contestation privée, c'est faire un acte judiciaire et non un acte législatif. L'application même de cette équité ou de cette justice distributive, qui suit et qui doit suivre dans chaque cas particulier, tous les petits fils par lesquels une des parties litigentes tient à l'autre, ne peut jamais appartenir au législateur, uniquement ministre de cette justice ou de cette équité générale qui, sans égard à aucune circonstance particulière, embrasse l'universalité des choses et des personnes. Des lois intervenues sur des affaires privées seraient donc souvent suspectes de partialité, et toujours elles seraient rétroactives et injustes pour ceux dont le litige aurait précédé l'intervention de ces lois. De plus, le recours au législateur entraînerait des longueurs fatales au justiciable; et, ce qui est pire, il compromettrait la sagesse et la sainteté des lois. En effet, la loi statue sur tous; elle considère les hommes en masse, jamais comme particuliers; elle ne doit point se mêler des faits individuels ni des litiges qui divisent les citoyens. S'il en était autrement, il faudrait journellement faire de nouvelles lois; leur multitude étoufferait leur dignité et nuirait à leur observation. Le jurisconsulte serait sans fonctions, et le législateur, entraîné par les détails, ne serait bientôt plus que jurisconsulte. Les intérêts particuliers assiégeraient la puissance législative; ils la détourneraient, à chaque instant, de l'intérêt général de la société. Il y a une science pour les législateurs, comme il y en a une pour les magistrats, et l'une ne ressemble pas à l'autre. La science du législateur consiste à trouver, dans chaque matière, les principes les plus favorables au bien commun; la science du magistrat est de mettre ces principes en action, de les ramifier, de les étendre, par une application sage et raisonnée, aux hypothèses privées; d'étudier l'esprit de la loi quand la lettre tue; et de ne pas s'exposer au risque d'être tour à tour esclave et rebelle et de désobéir par esprit de servitude. Il faut que le législateur veille sur la jurisprudence; il peut être éclairé par elle, et il peut, de son côté, la corriger; mais il faut qu'il y en ait une. Dans cette immensité d'objets divers, qui composent les matières civiles, et dont le jugement, dans le plus grand nombre des cas, est moins l'application d'un texte précis, que la combinaison de plusieurs textes qui conduisent à la décision bien plus qu'ils ne la renferment, on ne peut pas plus se passer de jurisprudence que de lois. Or, c'est à la jurisprudence que nous abandonnons les cas rares et extraordinaires qui ne sauraient entrer dans le plan d'une législation raisonnable, les détails trop variables et trop contentieux qui ne doivent point occuper le législateur, et tous les objets que l'on s'efforcerait inutilement de prévoir, ou qu'une prévoyance précipitée ne pourrait définir sans danger. C'est à l'expérience à combler successivement les vides que nous laissons. Les codes des peuples se font avec le temps, mais à proprement parler, on ne les fait pas (...).

Chapter 2

Modern sources of law

A. Introduction

As has been seen in the previous chapter, the legal system of the pre-revolutionary *Ancien Régime* was characterised by its great diversity. Not only were there differences in respect of the rules of private law which were applicable (there being some 60 regional and 300 local customs), but the law was also inegalitarian, individuals being treated differently depending on their social status (nobleman, clergy or commoner (*roturier*)), and denominational, Canon law thus regulating the sacramental nature of the matrimonial bond. This diversity was brought to an end by the Revolution, firstly through its affirmation of political principles such as freedom of conscience and the equality of status of individuals, and secondly with the abolition of the greater part of the differing customary laws and their subsequent replacement by a code of civil law applicable throughout the country.

The principal source of contemporary French law is parliamentary statute (*lois*, ie statutes passed by the *Assemblée Nationale* and *Sénat* and promulgated by the President of the Republic). However, since the institution of the 1958 Constitution of the Fifth Republic, Parliament has in effect shared its legislative function with the government, the latter now having its own autonomous power to enact law by means of regulations (*règlements autonomes*), as well as being able to issue regulations in application of parliamentary statute (*règlements d'application*). Customary law, although to a large extent abolished during the revolutionary period, retains a place as a minor source of law. Caselaw (*la jurisprudence*) and doctrinal writings (*la doctrine*), although not theoretically recognised as formal sources of law, are of persuasive value. Finally, fundamental and general principles of law have been derived by the courts (particularly in administrative and constitutional law) from written law (these are examined below under statutory interpretation; see also Chapter 4).

B. Legislation

In this section we will briefly outline the hierarchy of the differing categories of legislation in the French legal system. Each of these is examined in more detail in the context of the 1958 Constitution of the Fifth Republic in Chapter 4.

1. Loi and règlement

The French word *loi* has both a general and a technical meaning. In a general sense it refers to legal rules enacted by an authorised agent of the state (eg parliamentary statutes and government regulations), in contrast to legal rules of customary origin. However, in a technical sense it refers to parliamentary statute as opposed to government regulation. Before 1958, Parliament was competent to pass legislation on any matter, regulations issued by the government being essentially by way of implementation of such legislation. However, for reasons which are examined in Chapter 4, the 1958 Constitution (TEXTS, CHAPTER 4, NO. 1) restricted the competence of Parliament to pass statutes (*lois*) to those matters set out in *Art. 34* of the Constitution ("*C.1958*"); by *Art. 37* the government is entitled to enact law in its own right by way of autonomous regulations (*règlements autonomes*) in all other fields. Parliament is competent in matters concerning fundamental civil rights and individual liberties (see below). However, even in these areas it is possible for the Prime Minister to use his regulation-making power to issue regulations to implement and even complete parliamentary statutes. Furthermore, it is possible for Parliament to authorise the Prime Minister to enact law (by means of *ordonnances*) for a given period in respect of matters within the parliamentary field of competence.

2. Hierarchy of texts

Legislation can be classified into three main categories: parliamentary *lois*, government *ordonnances* and government *règlements*. We will first outline the different categories of *lois* in decreasing order of authority; the way in which the conformity of the norms lower in the hierarchy to those which are higher is ensured by means of the twin doctrines of constitutionality and legality is examined in Chapter 4.

(a) La loi

(i) Constitutional laws

Constitutional law is superior to ordinary parliamentary statute in that if the latter contradicts the former, it may be held to be unconstitutional. To ensure that Parliament legislates only within its field of competence, the 1958 Constitution created the Constitutional Council (*le Conseil Constitutionnel*) whose original role was to strike down (before promulgation) on the grounds of unconstitutionality any parliamentary statutes which dealt with matters within the government's field of competence. However, the *Conseil Constitutionnel* has extended its role to that of controlling the constitutionality of parliamentary statute by reference not only to the provisions of the Constitution as a whole, but also to norms to which the *Conseil Constitutionnel* ascribes constitutional value, such as the broad rights and principles set out in the 1789 Declaration (TEXTS, CHAPTER 1, NO. 10) and the Preamble to the 1946 Constitution (TEXTS, CHAPTER 4, NO. 7), both of which are incorporated into the 1958 Constitution by reason of the Preamble to the latter. This control of the constitutionality of *lois* is examined in detail in Chapter 4.

As might be expected, the text of the Constitution may be repealed or amended only in accordance with special procedures, which are set out in *C.1958, Art. 89*. Both the legislature and the executive (the President acting on the proposition of the Prime Minister) may initiate amendments. The reform bill must be passed in identical terms by both houses of Parliament. It must then be ratified; this is done in one of two ways. The President may have the proposals ratified directly by the people by way of referendum. Alternatively, in the case of a government bill, the proposals may be submitted by the President to both houses sitting together. Approval must be by a majority of three-fifths of the votes cast. Following ratification, the constitutional law will be promulgated by the President. The republican form of government is sacrosanct (as is the integrity of the French territory), and may not be the subject of an amendment.

(ii) International treaties

By *C.1958, Art. 55*, duly ratified or approved treaties and agreements are accorded authority superior to that of parliamentary statute. Thus, if confronted with provisions of a treaty and a statute which are incompatible, the courts (ordinary and administrative) will apply the treaty provisions (see Chapter 4).

(iii) Organic laws

Organic laws (*lois organiques*) are the means by which some of the detail of constitutional law is enacted. Organic laws (*C.1958, Art. 46*) are those which are so described in the Constitution, such as those dealing with the status of judges (*C.1958, Art. 64*). They are subject to particular procedural requirements, of which the most important is the need for them to be submitted before promulgation to the *Conseil Constitutionnel* for their conformity to the Constitution to be confirmed.

(iv) Ordinary parliamentary statutes

We have seen that in the Fifth Republic Parliament is not sovereign, and may legislate only on the matters listed in *C.1958, Art. 34*. In certain matters (local government, the general organisation of national defence, social security, labour law, civil and commercial obligations, property rights and education) fundamental principles at least must be determined by parliamentary statute. The procedure for the passing of a statute (*loi*) is examined below. It is possible for a bill to become law (ie *loi*) without being passed by Parliament if it has been approved by the people in a referendum. A referendum may be called by the President (*C.1958, Art. 11*) on any bill affecting the organisation of public powers or approving a treaty which would affect the functioning of the institutions of the Republic. If it is approved, it will become law on promulgation by the President.

(b) Ordinances and presidential decisions

There are two ways in which the executive may enact laws within the parliamentary field of competence of *C.1958, Art. 34*. The first is where Parliament passes an enabling Act (*loi d'habilitation; C.1958, Art. 38*) expressly authorising the government to enact such laws for a limited period by means of ordinances (*ordonnances*); the latter are passed in the Council of Ministers, after obtaining the advice of the *Conseil d'Etat*, and are signed by the President (*C.1958, Arts. 13, 38*). Once ratified, the ordinances have the force of parliamentary statute. The second occurs where in a time of crisis the President of the Republic uses the emergency powers granted to him by *C.1958, Art. 16* to legislate directly by means of decisions (*décisions*) in order to re-establish the normal and regular functioning of constitutional organs. He must consult the Prime Minister, the president of both houses and the *Conseil Constitutionnel*.

(c) Government regulations

(i) Le pouvoir réglementaire

The generic name for government regulations is *règlements*. The government has a general power to issue regulations which is shared by the President (*C.1958, Art. 13*) and Prime Minister (*C.1958, Art. 21*); essentially this *pouvoir réglementaire* is exercised by the Prime Minister (with the countersignature of the relevant ministers) unless it deals with matters discussed in the Council of Ministers, which is chaired by the President whose signature is therefore required. Other administrative authorities also have certain powers to issue regulations (see Chapter 4). The form in which regulations are issued depends on the identity of the administrative authority from which they emanate; this will be in the form of a *décret* if issued by the President or Prime Minister, or an *arrêté* if by a minister, prefect or mayor. It should be noted that the terms *décret* and *arrêté* are also used to describe decisions having individual rather than general effect issued by the said administrative authorities. The various categories of *règlement* are, in decreasing hierarchical order, as follows: *règlements autonomes, règlements d'application, arrêtés ministériels, arrêtés préfectoraux* and *arrêtés municipaux*.

(ii) Règlements autonomes

As has been seen, except in the fields reserved to Parliament by *C.1958, Art. 34*, the government is recognised as having the power to enact law by means of autonomous regulations under *C.1958, Art. 37*. In practice, the competence of the Government to issue such regulations is not as wide as might be expected, but is recognised as covering several fields, such as the internal organisation of administrative services and the creation of the least serious criminal offences (*contraventions de police; Code Pénal, Art. R.25*).

(iii) Règlements d'application

The Prime Minister is given the general commission of ensuring the execution of parliamentary statutes (*C.1958, Art. 21*). In consequence, he has the right to issue *règlements d'application*. Such regulations are countersigned by the ministers charged with implementing them (*C.1958, Art. 22*). A statute may provide that its provisions will be implemented by *règlement*. In such a case this can be by *décret en Conseil d'Etat*, if so provided by statute. However, the government's right to issue *décrets d'application* is not dependent on such an express provision in a statute, as is recognised by the breadth of the commission granted to the Prime Minister by *C.1958, Art. 21*.

(iv) Arrêtés ministériels

Apart from the matters in respect of which the power to pass regulations is expressly or impliedly accorded to a minister in a statute or decree, a minister does not have power to issue regulations other than those dealing with the internal running of his department, a power which he enjoys by reason of his position as the *chef du service*; this he will do by way of *arrêtés*. Ministers also issue circulars giving an official view on, for example, the proper interpretation of a rule of law. Although these must be followed within the administration, as having hierarchical authority, they generally are not binding on persons outside the administration.

(v) Arrêtés préfectoraux

The prefect is the representative of central government in a *département* and hence has delegated power to issue *arrêtés préfectoraux* (prefectoral orders). The president of the *conseil général* (the departmental council) acting as executive of the council also has certain powers to issue regulations.

(vi) Arrêtés municipaux

The mayor (*maire*), who is elected by the members of the local council (*conseil municipal*) from amongst their number, has, as local representative of the state, a power to issue by-laws (*arrêtés municipaux*), particularly in respect of matters of local policing (see Chapter 4).

(vii) Other regulations

Some official bodies are entitled to issue regulations where authorised by a public authority; eg *décisions* of the Banque de France, *arrêtés* of the presidents of universities, and *décisions* of the *conseil supérieur de l'audiovisuel*. It should also be noted that certain professional bodies (eg *ordres des médecins/avocats*) are recognised as having power to issue regulations binding the members of their profession.

In accordance with the principle of legality (*la légalité*; see Chapter 4) each category of regulation must conform to superior norms on the same subject within the hierarchy outlined above, or risk being annulled. Whereas *lois* may only be held unconstitutional before promulgation by the *Conseil Constitutionnel, règlements* may be annulled by the administrative courts after being passed.

3. Parliamentary statutes (lois)

(a) Procedure for adoption

The procedure for the adoption of parliamentary statutes is laid down in *C.1958, Arts. 10, 39–51, 69–70*. Government bills (*projets de loi*) are vetted by the *Conseil d'Etat* before being discussed by the Council of Ministers. Government bills of an economic or social nature must, and other bills (or even draft *ordonnances* and *décrets*) may, be submitted for advice to the Economic and Social Council, a consultative body of some 230 members comprising representatives of organised groups (including the professions, employees, employers, farming organisations) and government appointees. The bill will be laid before one of the two houses, the National Assembly and the Senate, finance bills being laid first before the former.

Private members' bills (*propositions de loi*) may be set down by *députés* in the National Assembly or *sénateurs* in the Senate, but are restricted to matters which do not result in a charge on the public purse (as are private members' amendments to government bills). A further obstacle facing a private member's bill is getting on to the order of business, which is controlled by the government.

Having been laid before the house, the bill will be examined by committee (either standing or special), the membership of which is representative of the house. The report of the committee will then be presented to the house in a full debate on the bill, both in regard to its general principles and to the detailed provisions. The government can insist that the house should vote on the bill or merely a part of the bill, retaining only the amendments acceptable to it (*le vote bloqué*).

If the bill is passed, it will then be sent for debate to the other house with a view to both houses passing a text in identical terms. Where the houses cannot agree on a text the government can, after two readings in each house (or just one in the case of urgency), require the setting up of a committee of both houses to draw up a text acceptable to both. If this too is unsuccessful, the National Assembly will have the last word. It should be noted that a bill may be referred at any time before promulgation to the *Conseil Constitutionnel* for a ruling on its constitutionality under *C.1958, Art. 61*; see Chapter 4. The bill will finally be promulgated by the President of the Republic.

(b) Commencement and operation

The decree of the President promulgating a statute (*décret de promulgation*) will include an order for the statute to be executed. In principle, a statute (and for that matter a regulation) comes into effect on publication, in conformity with the principle that *nemo censetur ignorare legem* (no one may be taken to be ignorant of the law). Publication consists of an insertion in the *Journal officiel*. Unless otherwise provided, a *loi* or *décret* will come into force in Paris one clear day after publication, and in the provinces one clear day after the arrival of the *Journal officiel* (*décret-loi du 5.11.1870*). *Arrêtés* become effective either by publication in the *Journal officiel* or by being brought to the attention of the persons they affect (in the case of municipal by-laws, usually by the display of a notice in the town, or by publication in the local press).

Code Civil, Art. 2 sets out the general principle that legislation does not have retroactive effect, although in respect of private law matters the legislature may expressly provide that a statute be retroactive; this power to provide for retroactive effect does not apply in respect of criminal law (cf *Déclaration de 1789, Art. 8*).

In principle, statutes are of mandatory effect, applying regardless of the wishes of individuals affected by their provisions. Statutes having this mandatory nature are described as "imperative" or "public order" statutes (*lois impératives, lois d'ordre public*); their operation cannot be excluded, even expressly. However, it is accepted, at least in private law, that a statute may be of effect only in the absence of expressed contrary intention; where the operation of a statute may be excluded in this way it is known as a statute suppletive to individual intention (*loi supplétive de volonté*). To illustrate the distinction from some family law examples: *Code Civil, Art. 1388* provides that spouses may not derogate from the provisions of the Civil Code in respect of the obligations and rights of marriage, nor may they derogate from the rules relating to parental authority. These provisions are thus imperative. In contrast, *Code*

Civil, Art. 1400, referring to the provisions setting out the rules for the matrimonial community of property regime, states that the community property regime will apply to spouses "in the absence of a contract or declaration to the contrary". In other words, these provisions are suppletive, and the spouses may opt out of the community regime, choosing instead, for example, a regime of separation of property. In the examples given, the legislator has clearly specified the imperative or suppletive nature of the legal rule; this, however, is not always so, in which case the issue will be one for the courts to determine.

(c) Duration

Unless repealed, legislation does not cease to have effect through lapse of time or through having become obsolete (by way of exception Finance Acts, which set out the annual budget, are of one year's duration). Repeal (*abrogation*) may be either express, new legislation formally repealing earlier provisions, or implied (*tacite*) when the provisions of the new law are inconsistent with those of the old. However, repeal may be effected only by measures of the appropriate hierarchical value; thus the provisions of a *loi* may generally be repealed only by *loi*, those of a *décret autonome* by *décret, décret d'application* by *loi* or *décret* etc.

(d) Codified legislation

As defined in the previous chapter, codification is the enactment of a methodical planned collection of legal rules organised in articles expressing the general principles governing a determined branch of the law. Codification is used to give an intellectual cohesion and style to rules originating from different sources; furthermore, it makes a set of legal rules more accessible. The best example of codification in this classical sense is the 1804 *Code Civil*.

However, since 1804 many of the codifications which have been carried out are little more than compilations of legislative texts. Modern codes may be divided into several parts, containing parliamentary *lois* (Art . . . or Art.L . . .), *décrets* (Art.D . . .), and *règlements* (Art.R . . .). There may follow a final part, setting out, in chronological order, non-codified texts which relate to the area of law dealt with in the code. The body of the Social Security Code, for example, comprises only 781 articles (some 203 pages), to which are annexed some 1,000 pages of *lois* and *règlements* dealing with such matters as the administrative and financial organisation of the social security system. This modern form of codification results at least partly from the multiplication of texts since the end of the Second World War dealing with increasingly complex and technical legal issues. The number of codes has grown well beyond the original six of the early nineteenth century, and now includes the following: *Code du Travail* (1973), *Code de l'Urbanisme* (1954), *Code Rural et Forestier* (1955), *Code de la Sécurité Sociale* (1955, 1985), *Code de la Santé Publique* (1953), and *Code des Impôts* (1981).

Other unofficial *codes* are published, collecting together provisions on a particular subject. These take a variety of forms, and include the *Code Administratif, Code des Sociétés, Code de la Copropriété,* and the *Code de l'Environnement*.

4. Interpretation of legislation

(a) Introduction

As we have seen, the primary source of legal rules in France is parliamentary statute, which is often found in the form of codes. The legal rules set out in the statutes may be formulated in a rather general abstract way (an example (examined in Chapter 1) being *Code Civil, Arts. 1382, 1383* which set out in very broad terms the principles of civil delictual responsibility). These abstract rules have to be applied by the courts to real facts. Moreover, at times the ambit of the rule will not be clear, or the factual situation confronting the judge will not be one which was foreseen by the legislature. Hence the need for the judge to interpret the legal rule so as to be able to apply it to the case before him in accordance with the intention of the legislature. That this interpretive role of the judge was clearly foreseen, and approved of by the drafters of the Civil Code, is clear from the report of Portalis, one of its drafters, which accompanied the draft code (*Discours préliminaire*; CHAPTER 1 TEXTS, NO. 12) and in which he stated that it was the role of the legislature to lay down the broad principles on any given matter, and that of the judge to apply these principles with wisdom to individual cases. When the text is clear, it is simply to be applied; if not, it will first need to be interpreted. The interpretation given to a text by the judge could not, however, be regarded as binding other judges faced with similar facts in the future.

(b) Theoretical foundations

The methods of statutory interpretation of the courts have been influenced by the work of academic writers; two distinct schools of thought may be identified. During the nineteenth century, the dominant view was that of the "school of exegesis" (*l'école de l'exégèse*). According to this view written law (*loi*), as the expression of the general will, was regarded as being the only true source of legal rules in the subject matter covered. A careful study of the text was therefore thought sufficient to reveal the solution to any situation which might arise. The role of the judge was thus to clarify the meaning of the text in order that it might be applied to the case before him. This narrow view of interpretation mirrored the limited role that the judge was recognised as having; that of simply executing the will of the legislature as expressed in the words used.

Towards the end of the nineteenth century, the view was expressed that the rigid adherence to the text of the codes expounded by the school of exegesis made less sense the greater the time that had elapsed since the texts were enacted, it eventually becoming somewhat artificial to attempt to ascertain the intention of the legislature, particularly when applying the text to a situation the legislature could not have foreseen. Such rigid adherence, it was argued, could only hamper the proper development of the law so as to enable it to meet the needs of an increasingly industrialised society. Writers such as François Gény (a member of the so-called "school of free scientific research" (*l'école de la libre recherche scientifique*)) in his 1899 work *La Méthode d'Interprétation et Sources du Droit Privé Français* argued that the drafters of the codes had not in fact foreseen every situation that might arise, and where faced with a situation to which the provisions of the codes provided no answer, the judge should adopt a more creative role, and starting from the spirit of the provisions of the code, should construct a solution which was in conformity with notions of equity and justice and was appropriate to societal needs and mores of the day. In this way, although continuing to give the appearance of respecting the authority of the written law, its provisions could be brought up to date.

Portalis and the other drafters of the Civil Code would have approved of these broader techniques of interpretation, recognising as they did (*Discours préliminaire,* above) that "positive law will never entirely replace the use of natural reason in the affairs of life", and that as society moves on and unforeseen situations arise "a number of things will necessarily be left to the domain of usage . . . and the arbitration of the judge".

(c) Modern techniques of interpretation of legislation

Although the courts have in their approach towards statutory interpretation undoubtedly been influenced by the call to move away from a strict adherence to the statutory text, the methods of interpretation that are adopted appear to remain based largely on the interpretation and construction of the words of the text in accordance with the intention of the legislature. Let us now identify some of the techniques used.

The judge will adopt a literal interpretation where a statutory provision is clear and addresses the point in issue. In such a case it has been held (eg *Riom, 21.10.1946, D.1947, 90* (TEXTS, NO. 1)) that the judge may not refuse to adopt a literal interpretation on the ground that the wording of the provision appears not to accord with the intention of the legislature. However, where a literal interpretation leads to an absurd result, or the text is capable of bearing more than one meaning, the judge may interpret the text in accordance with the perceived intention of the legislature. Professor Mazeaud (*Leçons de Droit Civil, T.1,V.1, para. 110*) gives the example, in respect of absurdity, of a decree which made it an offence for train passengers to board or alight a train "when the train had come to a standstill". Perhaps not surprisingly, the courts had little difficulty in upholding the convictions of passengers who boarded or alighted a train which was still in motion.

Article 4 of the Civil Code (below; TEXTS, NO. 8) confirms that the judge cannot refuse to reach a decision on the grounds of the silence, obscurity or insufficiency of the written law. Furthermore, Portalis (above) recognised that the judge has a broad role of interpretation and application, stating in the *Discours préliminaire* that the broad principles set down by the legislature were to be applied by judges "steeped in the general spirit of written laws" in accordance with the "spirit of the law, when the letter kills"; furthermore, where the written law is unclear or deficient, its provisions should be "augmented by reference to usages and equity". In other words, the judge, in seeking to apply the written law in accordance with the intention of the legislature, should draw on his general knowledge and understanding of the law.

It is natural in practice, however, for the judge first to seek the legislative intention from an examination of the relevant provisions in the context of the text as a whole, examining the vocabulary used, and the structure of the text. Where this proves to be insufficient guidance, further assistance may be sought from the legislative history of the text. The documents that may be referred to for this purpose (collectively known as *les travaux préparatoires*) include draft bills (and the explanatory notes which are often issued with them), committee reports on the bill presented to Parliament, and even the parliamentary debates themselves, although the latter are recognised as being of limited assistance. This approach to interpretation is of course more difficult in respect of government *règlements*, which will not have been the subject of parliamentary debate, although the government does sometimes issue explanatory guidelines.

The courts have developed rules of logic which guide them in interpreting statutes. Firstly, there are a number of general maxims of interpretation, such as: *exceptio est strictissimae interpretationes* (exceptions are to be strictly interpreted); *specialia generalibus derogant* (specific provisions take precedence over general provisions); *ubi lex non distinguit nec nos distinguere debemus* (no distinctions may be made which are not made by the statute); and *poenalia sunt restrigenda* (penal laws must be restrictively interpreted).

Furthermore, particularly in cases where the statutory provisions do not appear to cover the point in issue, the courts have had recourse to techniques of logical interpretation favoured by the school of exegesis, such as reasoning by analogy (the extension of the rule of law set out in the text to similar situations not expressly provided for), *a fortiori* (the extension of the rule of law to similar situations where the principle on which the rule is based applies with even more reason) or *a contrario* (where the text sets out an exhaustive list of the situations to which it applies, it does not apply to other situations).

Another technique which has been used is a process of induction and deduction; a general principle is drawn by induction from a number of texts of particular application to a given subject, and that general principle is then applied by deduction to the novel situation at issue in the case. In this way the courts have been able to identify and formulate "general principles" (*principes généraux*) from the general spirit of the written law, which they have then applied. Many general principles have thus been derived by the *Conseil d'Etat* in administrative law (and in a similar fashion *principes fondamentaux* have been derived by the *Conseil Constitutionnel*; see Chapter 4). Although there has been less need for recourse to general principles in private law than in administrative law, thanks to provisions of the *Code Civil*, there are some examples: one which is quoted by some authors is that of the principle of unjust enrichment (*enrichissement sans cause*), which has been recognised by the *Cour de Cassation* (*Req., 15.6.1892, D, 1892, I, 596*; TEXTS, NO. 2).

Interpretation based on the perceived intention of the legislature is the usual technique of statutory interpretation employed. This is perhaps appropriate in respect of modern legislation, as the intention of the legislature will be readily discernible, and will still correspond to current social conditions. However, the older the text, the less true this is, and indeed perhaps the less relevant the original intention of the legislature is to the application of the text in modern conditions.

It is on this basis that the courts have on occasion shown a willingness to adopt freer techniques of interpretation, particularly where older legislative provisions are concerned. Two examples of this are firstly the "teleological technique" (*l'interprétation téléologique*), by which the court will seek to identify the objective social purpose of the enactment when it was introduced, and will interpret its provisions in a way which best enables that purpose to be most effectively achieved in modern society. The second is the "evolutive technique", by which it is recognised that in seeking to apply a provision of, say, the 1804 Civil Code, it may be futile in the light of the societal changes that have occurred to seek the intention of the legislature; the court is thus in effect entitled to adapt the provisions to the current needs of society. The usual example which is given of a legislative text which has been adapted to modern situations is *Code Civil, Art. 1384(1)* (TEXTS, NO. 3). This states that "A person is responsible not only for the damage caused by his own action but also for that caused by the actions of other persons for whom he is answerable, or of things in his care". In a 1930 case (*Chambres réunies, 13.2.1930, D.P.1930, I, 57* TEXTS, NO. 4) the *Cour de Cassation* held that on the basis of this article a person having a motor vehicle in his care could be strictly liable to the victim of a road accident that involved the vehicle, the victim thus not having to prove fault. The article was in this way extended to cover a situation which its drafters could not have foreseen.

It is clear from the above that there is a good degree of flexibility in the way the French courts interpret and apply legislative texts. There are no "canons of interpretation" as in English law. Also, the brevity and formalism of court judgments sometimes make it difficult actually to identify the techniques of interpretation used by the courts. It should finally be noted that the courts adopt essentially the same techniques of interpretation in respect of government regulations as they do for parliamentary statutes; the right of the ordinary (as opposed to administrative) courts to interpret regulations of general effect has been recognised by the *Tribunal des Conflits* (*T.C., 16.7.1923, Septfonds, S.1923, 3, 49*).

C. Caselaw (la jurisprudence)

1. Introduction

In French the word *jurisprudence* refers not only to the philosophy of law, but more strictly to the caselaw of the courts. In the latter sense it may refer either to caselaw in general, or to the body of decisions of the courts on any given subject. Professor Carbonnier (*Droit Civil, Introduction, 1990, para. 142*) in this sense defines *la jurisprudence* as being "the solution generally given by the courts to a question of law". Unlike legislative law and custom, caselaw is not formally recognised as a source of law in the French legal system; it cannot be, because of the separation of powers in the Constitution in which the role of the legislature is to pass law and that of the judiciary to apply it. Moreover, the revolutionary legislature, wary of the power of the judiciary, introduced provisions making it impossible for the decisions of the courts to be formally binding in subsequent cases. Furthermore, as has been seen, the primary source of law in France is statute, and many of the rules of law which in England and Wales are the creation of the common law or equity are set out in the codes, in broad terms at least.

Although important, the role of caselaw is therefore subsidiary. As caselaw does not formally constitute a source of law, the courts cannot base their decisions on previous cases, and therefore their judgments (whether those of the ordinary or administrative courts) do not contain detailed analyses of the relevant cases as do those of the English and Welsh courts. However, caselaw is of persuasive value, particularly where there is a series of cases confirming a particular point. In private law this will usually be an interpretation of a provision of the codes; in administrative law, however, fewer of the rules of substantive law are found in legislative texts, and the role of the judges has therefore, of necessity, been more creative. Moreover, caselaw is of great importance in practice; the decisions of the *Cour de Cassation, Conseil d'Etat* and *Conseil Constitutionnel* are extensively reported, are both consulted and cited in court by practising lawyers, and are the subject of critical analysis by academic writers. Indeed, as well as examining the codes, the French law student will spend much of his time reading casebooks, like his British counterpart. Caselaw may be seen, particularly in civil law, as a supplement to the written law, the means by which the latter is completed and applied to actual situations.

2. Is caselaw a source of law?

(a) Role of the judiciary

(i) Historical perspective

One of the strongest reasons for denying that the judges make law is the constitutional position of the judiciary. As was seen in Chapter 1, in the *Ancien Régime* the king had legislative, executive and judicial powers, the latter being delegated to the courts (such as the regional *Parlements*). However, the *Parlements* had taken upon themselves the right, in effect, to make law in areas which were not regulated by custom or royal ordinance. This they did by way of judgments having the effect of regulations (*arrêts de règlement*) which had binding authority within the jurisdiction of the *Parlement*. The Revolution brought about the separation of powers with the formation of a legislative body to enact legislation. The role of the courts was limited to that of applying to individual cases the legal rules emanating from the legislature. To prevent any interference by the judiciary in the field of competence of the legislature, the *loi des 16–24.8.1790 (Titre II, Art. 12*; TEXTS, NO. 5) provided that no decisions of the court could have regulatory effect.

Furthermore, the statute introduced the laborious procedure of legislative reference (*le référé législatif*), according to which whenever a statutory provision needed to be interpreted, the court had to refer the case to the legislative body for an interpretation, which would then be implemented on reference back to the court. This system, which confused the legislative role of law making and the judicial role of applying the law, was in time abolished as unworkable; to prevent abuses by the judiciary of their power of interpretation, the system that was eventually settled on (*loi du 1.4.1837*) was that the interpretation of a text by the *Cour de Cassation* would be definitive only when it heard a case on a second appeal, sitting as a full court (*assemblée plénière*; see Chapter 3).

(ii) Role of the courts

The role of the courts is thus essentially one of interpreting and applying legal rules which emanate from a source other than the courts themselves; in effect, statute and custom. In respect of civil law, the source of the legal rules is the Civil Code, and the dependence on statute is shown by the fact that a decision of the *Cour de Cassation* will invariably refer expressly to a legislative provision on which it purportedly rests. The principle is also true of administrative law, despite the fact that few of its major principles are to be found in statutory provisions.

(b) Non-binding nature of decisions

That a decision of the court cannot constitute a binding precedent is confirmed by *Code Civil, Art. 5* (TEXTS, NO. 6), which provides that the judges are forbidden from making general or regulatory decisions in respect of the cases coming before them. This article, confirming the prohibition on the use of *arrêts de règlement*, makes it clear that the rule of *stare decisis* has no place in French law. This is underlined by the principle of the relative effect of a judgment, *Code Civil, Art. 1351* (TEXTS, NO. 7) providing (in the context of the law of obligations) that a judgment has binding authority only for the parties to the action (thus preventing them from litigating on the same matter in the future).

As a result, an earlier decision, even of the *Cour de Cassation*, may not be used as justification for reaching a later decision. No court may give as the reason for reaching a decision the fact that it was "bound" by authority; if it does, its decision will be quashed by the *Cour de Cassation* (eg *Crim., 3.11.1955, D, 1956.I.557*). Nor does the failure of a court to follow earlier authority, again even of the *Cour de Cassation*, constitute sufficient grounds for an appeal against that decision. However, this can appear to be a little artificial. Let us suppose that a case involves the interpretation of a provision of the Civil Code, and that a *Cour d'Appel* refuses to apply a recent interpretation of the provision by the *Cour de Cassation*. Although it is true that any appeal (by way of *recours en cassation*; see Chapter 3) to the *Cour de Cassation* against the decision of the *Cour d'Appel* may not be based on the fact that the interpretation of the *Cour de Cassation* was not followed but rather on the grounds, for example, of *violation de la loi*, it is likely that on appeal the decision of the *Cour d'Appel* will be quashed for *violation de la loi* for in effect failing to follow the interpretation of *la loi* which the *Cour de Cassation* set out in its earlier judgment (unless of course the latter can be persuaded to change its interpretation).

The non-binding nature of precedents means that there is an inherent instability in caselaw. This is contrasted by some authors with the principle of *stare decisis* according to which a single decision may be binding. It is certainly the case that a court may refuse to follow any precedent, even that of the highest courts (with the limited exception of a decision of the *assemblée plénière* of the *Cour de Cassation*; see above). However, precedents will in practice usually be followed, and there is therefore a greater degree of security in caselaw than might be thought.

3. The authority of caselaw

(a) The persuasive value of caselaw

Although Article 5 of the Civil Code prevents caselaw from becoming a formal source of law, the effect of Article 4 (TEXTS, NO. 8) is to underline the persuasive value of caselaw. The article sets out the important principle that a judge will be in breach of the obligations of his office if he fails to reach a decision on the grounds of the silence, lack of clarity or insufficiency of the written law. In such cases (which are not unusual, bearing in mind the breadth and imprecision of many of the provisions of the Civil Code) the judge will want to base his decision on rational grounds, and it will therefore be natural for him to seek guidance and inspiration from caselaw, although he will not expressly refer to earlier cases in his judgment. The fact that all judgments must be reasoned (*loi du 16−24.8.1790, Titre 8, Art. 208*; also *Nouveau Code de Procédure Civile, Art. 455*) further increases the authoritative value of caselaw. Cases of the *Cour de Cassation* have indeed been reported from as early as 1799.

Adherence to caselaw not only provides a rational basis for a decision in the absence of clear statutory guidance; it also accords with notions of justice in treating like cases in the same way, and provides security to business relationships which would be threatened if the courts were too ready to abandon a settled interpretation of statutory provisions. Moreover, a court will be aware on a practical level that if it refuses to follow the precedents of higher courts, its decisions are likely to be overturned on appeal, which it will be keen to avoid.

When examining the issue of the persuasive value of caselaw, the role of the *Cour de Cassation* should be borne in mind. The role is essentially that of ensuring the uniform interpretation and application of the law throughout France. In view of the fact that there are some 30 regional *Cours d'Appel*, for this uniformity to be achieved the decisions of the *Cour de Cassation* have to have a certain persuasive value. It also means that the *Cour de Cassation* is unlikely to overrule its own settled caselaw (especially decisions of the *assemblée plénière*) without good reason.

(b) Determining the persuasive value of caselaw

A variety of factors determine the persuasive value of caselaw. These should not however be regarded as a series of rules to be strictly applied as in England and Wales, where the principle of *stare decisis*, according to which the legal rule of a precedent is binding to the extent that it relates to the material facts of the case, has led to the technique of "distinguishing" cases and the development of a series of techniques for weighing the respective value of precedents. In France, the principles for weighing the persuasive value of cases are more flexible, the role of the courts, as has been seen, being essentially one of interpreting and adapting legal rules which have emanated from a source other than the courts themselves. The authority of the decisions of the superior courts is lessened by the sheer volume of cases (over 26,000 heard by the *Cour de Cassation* in 1989) and the brevity and formal style of their judgments, which have been the subject of some criticism in recent years. The case notes, which are written by academic writers and are printed with the judgments in reports such as those of *Dalloz* and *La Semaine Juridique*, are often essential in helping the reader come to an understanding of the true import of a case.

Caselaw (*une jurisprudence*) becomes increasingly authoritative as a particular interpretation or principle is confirmed in a series of cases, especially where these emanate from the supreme court. The part of the judgment that is authoritative is that part in which the court formally expresses its reasoning (*les motifs de droit*). A judgment is regarded as being particularly authoritative where the court clearly sets out its position on the principle of law it is applying; such a decision is known as an *arrêt de principe* (in contrast to an *arrêt d'espèce*, a judgment reached in consideration of the particular facts of the case, and which is therefore of limited authoritative value).

A decision of the *Cour de Cassation* sitting *en assemblée plénière* on a second appeal on a given point of law is binding on the *Cour d'Appel* (or other court) to whom the case is subsequently referred for implementation (see Chapter 3). Apart from this, it is rare for a single decision, even of the *Cour de Cassation*, to be authoritative until confirmed in subsequent cases; indeed the word *jurisprudence* usually refers to a series of cases on a particular point or interpretation. The lower courts are far less likely to refuse to follow a settled line of authority (known as *une jurisprudence assise*, as opposed to *une jurisprudence controversée*). However, the position in the court hierarchy of the court from which the decision emanates is obviously an important factor; a decision of the *Cour de Cassation* or the *Conseil d'Etat* carries much greater weight than those of lower courts.

Another factor which is particular to France is that of the regional impact of a decision. A decision of a *Cour d'Appel* (or *Cour Administrative d'Appel*) is bound to be of greater authoritative value to the first instance courts within the appeal court's jurisdiction, as a refusal to follow a decision of the latter is likely to be reversed on appeal to the same. The age of the decision is also of relevance; essentially, the more recent the case, the more weight it carries, greater authority being accorded, for example, to the latest interpretation by the *Cour de Cassation* of a legislative provision. This underlines the role of French cases as being interpretive of statute law; where caselaw itself is a source of law, as in England and Wales, the greater the age of a precedent, the greater its authority.

4. Form and presentation of decisions

A judgment is always expressed according to a formal, logical structure; the judge is not free to adopt his own method of reasoning and expression. Indeed, despite the fact that in all higher courts there is more than one judge, there is only one judgment, and no dissenting opinions are expressed. This results from the theory of unity; on the basis that the written law is one (*la loi est une*), a judgment made in application of the law can be expressed only in the form of a single majority decision. The practice originated in the *Ancien Régime*, in which the written law was one, being the expression of the king as sole legislator; the judgments of the *Parlements* were therefore expressed in the same form.

The judgments of the lower courts are fairly expansive. However, those of the *Cour de Cassation* are succinct; usually the judgment will first quote (in the *visa*) the relevant statutory provisions (eg *Vu l'Art. 1134, Code Civil . . .*), particularly where the decision is one quashing the decision of the lower court. Then will be set out in outline the relevant facts of the case, the decision of the lower court against which appeal by way of *cassation* has been made and the arguments (*moyens*) put forward on behalf of the parties. The reasoning of the court is then expressed in a way which refers both to the extent to which the parties' *moyens* were justified, and to the legal provisions that the court is applying. The final part of the judgment, the *dispositif*, sets out the conclusion of the court, and is introduced by the phrase *par ces motifs . . .* (or *décide . . .* in the administrative courts). This rigidity of structure and the use of specialist, rather inaccessible, language are a result of both the influence of Cartesian reasoning and of judicial traditions regarding the appropriate language for use in judgments.

The decisions of the *Conseil d'Etat* are generally structured similarly to those of the *Cour de Cassation*. They therefore contain *visas, motifs* introduced by "*considérant que . . .*", and *dispositifs* divided into numbered articles.

5. Law reports

There are both official and private reports of judgments. The official reports of the decisions of the *Cour de Cassation* (*Bulletin des arrêts de la Cour de Cassation*) are published in two sets, one covering criminal decisions (*Bull. crim.*) and the other, civil (*Bull. civ. 1–5*, depending on the division). These contain all decisions of the full court (*assemblée plénière*) and those of mixed divisions (*chambres mixtes*), and a selection of the rest. Cases of the administrative courts and the *Conseil Constitutionnel* are reported in the *Recueil des décisions du Conseil d'Etat, du Tribunal des Conflits, des Cours Administratives d'Appel et des jugements des Tribunaux Administratifs* and the *Recueil des Décisions du Conseil Constitutionnel* (both *Rec.*).

The most long-standing of the private reports, published since 1791, are those of *J-B. Sirey* (*Recueil général des lois et arrêts*), reporting not just cases but also legislative texts; *Sirey* was merged in 1965 with the reports of *Dalloz*, a similar collection dating back to 1845. The *Recueil Dalloz Sirey* (*D.*) is published every week, and is divided into three main sections, the first containing doctrinal articles (*Chronique*), the second caselaw (*Jurisprudence*) with case notes written by academic writers (some cases are reported in summary form only (*Informations rapides*)), and the third legislative texts (*Législation*). Other similar journals are the weekly *Jurisclasseur Périodique* (*J.C.P.*, also known as *La Semaine Juridique*) first published in 1927, and the *Gazette du Palais* (*G.P.*), published several times per week, and dating from 1881. In all these journals, it is usual for the decisions of only the appeal courts and above to be published. Additionally, different series of casebooks are published, such as the "*Grands Arrêts*" series of *Sirey* (eg *Les Grands Arrêts de la Jurisprudence Administrative*) and the "*Grandes Décisions de la Jurisprudence*" series of *Presses Universitaires de France* (eg *Les Grandes Décisions de la Procédure Pénale*).

D. Legal writings (la doctrine)

1. Definition and role

The word *doctrine* is used to refer to legal writing in all its forms, such as case notes, articles and books. Doctrine is not regarded as a source of law, although it influences the interpretation of the written law by judges and lawyers. Indeed, doctrinal writers, in pointing out deficiencies in the law, sometimes propose solutions which are subsequently implemented by the courts (although no reference to doctrine will be found in the decision, even if inspired by it) or the legislature. An example may be found in the decision of the *Cour de Cassation* of *13.2.1930* (above; TEXTS, NO. 4), which marked an important extension of the application of *Code Civil, Art. 1384(1)*; in his submission to the court (*conclusions*), the *procureur général* referred to the works of such academics as *Josserand* and *Capitant* favouring such an extension.

2. Form

The opinions of legal writers are expressed in many forms such as books, academic articles, and case notes (often published with the case report). Another important source (in administrative law) is to be found in the *conclusions* of the *commissaire du gouvernement* (see Chapter 3), in which a synthesis of the law is followed by proposals for the appropriate decision for the court to take.

Immediately after the promulgation of the *Code Civil*, there was a revival of legal study: the *loi du 22 ventôse An XII* (1804) re-established the law faculties of Paris, Aix-en-Provence, Caen, Dijon, Grenoble, Poitiers, Rennes, Strasbourg and Toulouse, following the abolition of the pre-revolutionary universities during the revolutionary period. The first task of these law schools was to comment upon the new Civil Code, and there subsequently appeared a number of *commentaires* such as those by Maleville, Toullier et Duvergier, Delvincourt, Duranton, Troplong and Marcadé, in which the Code was analysed article by article. Other authors published *traités* in which the provisions of the codes were examined by subject matter (eg Aubry et Rau, Demolombe, and Planiol et Ripert). More recently published are the less detailed works known as *manuels* written essentially as student textbooks (eg in civil law, Carbonnier, Weil et Terré and Mazeaud). Several *traités* and many *manuels* are now published on a wide range of fields of law. Additionally, many legal journals and reviews are published, from the long-established and wide-ranging *Revue Trimestrielle de Droit Civil* and *Revue de Droit Public et de la Science Politique* to specialist journals such as the *Revue de Droit Bancaire et de la Bourse* and the *Revue de Droit Sanitaire et Social*.

E. Custom

1. Introduction

Although the codifications of the early nineteenth century greatly reduced the role of customary law, it still remains a subsidiary source of law.

2. Continuing importance of custom

Since the time of the Revolution, the prevalent view has been that parliamentary legislation, being an expression of the will of the nation (see *C.1958, Art. 3* and Chapter 4), is the only true source of law. Nevertheless custom is still important.

Article 7 of the law which promulgated the Civil Code (*loi du 30 ventôse an XII (21.4.1804)*) provides that, "As from the date of the coming into force of (the Civil Code), Roman law, (royal) ordinances, general and local customs, (municipal) statutes and other regulations shall cease to have general or particular effect in the areas which are within the scope of the said (Civil Code)." The effect of this provision, which is still in force, is that the entire body of *Ancien Droit* was abrogated to the extent that it was supplanted by the provisions of the Civil Code. Outside the scope of the Civil Code, both customary law and royal legislation continued to have effect; indeed, an early nineteenth century compilation of subsisting royal legislation and customs, published as a complement to the Civil Code, was more voluminous than the latter, and included such matters as the policing of rivers and canals, the issuing of planning and building permits, and maritime law. In time, many of these areas have become regulated by modern legislative provisions. However, a very limited amount of pre-codification legislation remains in force; an example is the *loi du 29.12.1790* dealing with ground rents. Another is in relation to the protection of coastal zones. Until a reform introduced by a *loi du 3.1.1986* this matter was regulated (in part at least) by the 1681 *ordonnance maritime*.

Subsisting customary rules fall into three categories: those that have been expressly retained by statute, those that act as a supplement to statute, filling in its lacunae, and those which act in a way which contradicts statute. Let us examine each of these in turn. Firstly there are customs expressly retained by the Civil Code. A small number of local customs in matters of land law are expressly retained by *Code Civil, Arts. 645*, 663*, 671, 674* (eg on water rights and party walls) presumably because of their diversity and hence the difficulty of codifying them. In other matters (especially leaseholds (*ibid., Arts. 1736*, 1745, 1753, 1754, 1757*, 1758*, 1777*) and usufructs (*ibid., Arts. 590, 591, 593*)) the general principles of civil law are stated to be subject to local variation. Furthermore, the Civil Code expressly preserves certain customs which help in the interpretation of contracts; in some articles it is therefore provided that contracts are to be interpreted according to local customs, and/or that they are to be taken to contain all terms which are usual in the trade (*Code Civil, Arts. 1135*, 1159*, 1160*; articles marked with * are reproduced in TEXTS, NO. 9).

Further to instructions issued by the Minister of the Interior in 1844, departmental councils (*conseils généraux*) collated and published collections of local usages, a process which continued into the 1930s. An example is the *Usages Locaux de Nantes* (TEXTS, NO. 10), published in 1910, which deals essentially with parol leases. This remains in force.

The second group are customs which act as a supplement to the written law, filling in its lacunae. The usual example given is the custom by which a married woman adopts the surname of her husband, a matter which is not regulated by statute.

Thirdly, custom may in a few rare cases actually contradict statute. Two examples: by *Code Civil, Art. 931*, donations must, to be legal, be made by notarial deed; however, the courts have repeatedly upheld the validity of the practice of making "donations by hand" (*dons manuels*), ie the making of a gift by the transfer of possession. The second example is an instance where the custom which was contrary to a statutory provision eventually led to the latter being amended. By *Code Civil, Art. 55*, the registration of the birth of a child had to be effected by physical presentation of the child to the registrar. However, in practice, registrars registered births on simple declaration, and in 1919 the article was amended to bring it in line with practice.

Customs are also found in the form of legal maxims and adages. Some of these have been translated into provisions of the Civil Code; thus *Art. 312* (TEXTS, NO. 11), in affirming the presumption of paternity during marriage, is simply enacting the old adage *pater is est quem nuptiae demonstrant* (the father is that which is shown by the marriage). Another example is *Art. 2279*, which enacts a maxim originating in the caselaw of the Parisian Châtelet court, that *en fait de meuble, possession vaut titre* (in respect of movable property, possession is equivalent to title).

Many old systems of customary law, including French law, were replete with such maxims, and many are still invoked by the courts (especially the *Cour de Cassation*) even though not incorporated into the Civil Code; an example is the maxim *contra non valentem agere non currit praescriptio* (the limitation period runs in favour of only him who enjoys user as of right). Indeed, a 1979 survey (H. Roland & L. Boyer, *Locutions Latines et Adages du Droit Français Contemporain*) found 307 such maxims or adages which had either been incorporated into the provisions of the written law or had been invoked in the decisions of the courts.

Texts and materials

1 Riom, 21 octobre 1946, D.1947, 90

(Dame Fournet, épouse Chevalon *C*. Chevalon.) – ARRÊT.

Attendu que par jugement en date du 16 mai 1946, le tribunal de première instance de Cusset, statuant sur la demande de Chevalon, a converti en divorce la séparation de corps prononcée le 2 nov. 1943, par jugement du même tribunal, au profit de la dame Chevalon; – Attendu que la dame Chevalon a régulièrement interjeté appel de cette décision; – Attendu que le tribunal a fait application de l'art. 4 *ter* ajouté à l'ordonnance du 12 avr. 1945 par la loi du 18 mars 1946, qui dispose que tous jugements ou arrêts de séparation de corps, même devenus définitifs avant la promulgation de l'ordonnance du 12 avr. 1945, seront de droit convertis, à la demande de l'un des époux, en jugements ou arrêts de divorce, à condition qu'ils se réfèrent à des instances introduites entre le 13 avr. 1941 et le 13 avr. 1945; – Attendu que la dame Chevalon soutient à l'appui de son appel que cette disposition légale n'est pas applicable à la demande formée par son mari; qu'en effet ce texte a un caractère exceptionnel et ne vise que les jugements, ou arrêts rendus à la suite d'instances introduites sous le régime de la loi du 2 avr. 1941, qui imposait un délai de trois ans à dater de la célébration du mariage pour que puisse être introduite une demande en divorce; que le législateur avait donc eu uniquement pour but de remédier à la situation des époux qui, ne remplissant pas les conditions exigées par la loi du 2 avr. 1941 pour demander le divorce, avaient dû se résigner à demander la séparation de corps, et non à ceux qui, comme elle et son mari, pouvaient former une demande en divorce, se trouvant dans les délais prévus par la loi; qu'en conséquence, la demande formée par son mari devait être soumise aux dispositions de l'art. 310 c. civ. maintenu en vigueur; – Mais attendu que la cour se trouve en présence d'un texte dont la clarté et la précision ne lui permettent pas, même s'il est vraisemblable que sa rédaction ne corresponde pas à l'intention véritable du législateur, de l'interpréter comme le demande la dame Chevalon; – Attendu, en effet, que les mots «tous jugements» ont une portée générale et que, sans violer le texte de l'ordonnance du 12 avr. 1945, on ne saurait admettre que certains jugements font exception à la règle impérative qu'elle a formulée; – Attendu que reconnaître aux tribunaux la possibilité, sous prétexte de l'interpréter, de modifier ou restreindre la portée d'un texte de loi qui ne comporte aucune ambiguité et se suffit à lui-même, serait autoriser le pouvoir judiciaire à se substituer au législatif; – Attendu que le jugement ayant prononcé la séparation de corps entre les époux Chevalon rentre dans le cadre des décisions judiciaires visées à l'art. 4 *ter* de l'ordonnance du 12 avr. 1945 (L. 18 mars 1946); que c'est donc à bon droit que les premiers juges ont déclaré bien fondée la demande introduite par Chevalon; – Par ces motifs, confirme.

2 Cour de Cassation, Req., 15 juin 1892, D.1892, I, 596

(Julien Patureau-Miran *C*. Boudier.) – ARRÊT.

LA COUR; – Vu la connexité, joint les causes et statuant par un seul et même arrêt sur les deux pourvois:

Sur le premier moyen du premier pourvoi tiré de la violation de l'art. 1165 c. civ., de l'art. 2102 du même code et de la fausse application des principes de l'action *de in rem verso*;

Sur la première et la deuxième branches tirées de la violation des art. 1165 et 2102 c. civ.: − Attendu que s'il est de principe que les conventions n'ont d'effet qu'entre les parties contractantes et ne nuisent point aux tiers, il est certain que ce principe n'a pas été méconnu par le jugement attaqué; qu'en effet, cette décision n'a point admis, comme le prétend le pourvoi, que le demandeur pouvait être obligé envers les défendeurs éventuels à raison d'une fourniture d'engrais chimiques faite par ces derniers à un tiers, mais seulement à raison du profit personnel et direct que ce même demandeur aurait retiré de l'emploi de ces engrais sur ses propres terres dans des circonstances déterminées; d'où il suit que, dans cette première branche, le moyen manque par le fait qui lui sert de base; − Attendu qu'il en est de même en ce qui concerne la seconde branche prise de la violation de l'art. 2102 c. civ.; − Qu'en effet, la décision attaquée a eu soin de spécifier que la créance du vendeur d'engrais ne constituait qu'une simple créance chirographaire ne lui conférant aucun privilège sur le prix de la récolte, et que, dès lors, l'article susvisé n'a pas été violé;

Sur la troisième branche, relative à la fausse application des principes de l'action *de in rem verso*: − Attendu que cette action dérivant du principe d'équité qui défend de s'enrichir au détriment d'autrui et n'ayant été réglementée par aucun texte de nos lois, son exercice n'est soumis à aucune condition déterminée; − Qu'il suffit, pour la rendre recevable, que le demandeur allègue et offre d'établir l'existence d'un avantage qu'il aurait, par un sacrifice ou un fait personnel, procuré à celui contre lequel il agit; − Que, dès lors, en admettant les défendeurs éventuels à prouver par témoins que les engrais par eux fournis à la date indiquée par le jugement avaient bien été employés sur le domaine du demandeur pour servir aux ensemencements dont ce dernier a profité, le jugement attaqué (Trib. civ. de Châteauroux, 2 dec. 1890) n'a fait des principes de la matière qu'une exacte application;

Sur le deuxième moyen pris de la violation des art. 1341 et 1348 c. civ.; − Attendu que le jugement attaqué déclare en fait qu'il n'a pas été possible aux défendeurs éventuels de se procurer une preuve écrite de l'engagement contracté à leur profit par le demandeur, devant les experts et à l'occasion du compte de sortie réglée par ces derniers entre le fermier et le propriétaire; − Qu'en admettant la preuve testimoniale dans ce cas excepté nommément par l'art. 1348 c. civ., ledit jugement a fait une juste application dudit article et, par suite, n'a pu violer l'art. 1341 du même code;

Sur le premier moyen du deuxième pourvoi pris de la violation de l'art. 262 c. proc. civ. et des règles sur les formes des enquêtes: − Attendu qu'il résulte des qualités du jugement attaqué (Trib. civ. de Châteauroux, 27 janv. 1891) «qu'au moment où le témoin Foucret allait commencer sa déposition, le demandeur a fait remarquer que ledit témoin était resté dans la salle d'audience durant les dépositions sur son reproche des sieurs Belleau et Nichié et qu'un jugement a donné acte de ce fait»; − Attendu que vainement le pourvoi prétend tirer de ce fait la conséquence que la déposition dudit Foucret serait entachée d'une nullité absolue et que le jugement qui a retenu cette déposition comme élément de décision manquerait de base légale; − Attendu, en effet, que si, aux termes de l'art. 262 c. pr. civ., les témoins doivent être entendus séparément, rien dans les qualités précitées du jugement attaqué ne révèle que cette prescription légale n'ait pas été observée à l'égard du témoin susnommé lorsqu'il a été appelé à déposer sur les faits mêmes du procès; que si ce témoin a assisté aux dépositions des sieurs Belleau et Michel, il est constant, d'après lesdites qualités, que ces derniers n'ont été appelés que pour déposer exclusivement sur les faits allégués en reproche par le demandeur contre le témoin Foucret; d'où il suit que ce dernier n'ayant été présent à l'audience à aucun moment de l'enquête proprement dite, le premier moyen du pourvoi manque par le fait qui lui sert de base;

Sur le deuxième moyen pris de la violation et fausse application de l'art. 548 c. civ. et des règles de l'action *de in rem verso*: − Attendu qu'il en est de même en ce qui concerne la première branche de ce deuxième moyen tirée de la violation et fausse application de l'art. 548 c. civ.; − Attendu, en effet, que le jugement attaqué déclare formellement que le droit des défendeurs éventuels n'est pas fondé sur cet article, lequel n'est mentionné qu'à titre d'exemple et comme constituant une des applications du principe consacré virtuellement par le code que nul ne peut s'enrichir au détriment d'autrui;

Sur la deuxième branche tirée de la fausse application des règles de l'action *de in rem verso*: − Attendu que la solution, précédemment donnée sur la troisième branche du premier moyen dans le premier pourvoi, rend inutile l'examen de celle-ci, qui n'en est que l'exacte reproduction;

Sur le troisième moyen pris de la violation de l'art. 1165 c. civ. et de la règle *res inter alios acta aliis neque nocere, neque prodesse potest:* − Attendu que, par une série de constatations et d'appréciations souveraines résultant des enquêtes et des documents de la cause, le jugement arrive à déclarer que le demandeur a pris l'engagement implicite mais formel de payer la dette contractée envers les défendeurs éventuels; qu'une semblable déclaration, qui ne saurait d'ailleurs être révisée par la cour, n'implique aucune violation de l'article ni de la règle susvisée;

Sur le quatrième moyen pris d'un excès de pouvoir et de la fausse application de l'art. 130 c. pr. civ.: − Attendu, d'une part, qu'en ordonnant le dépôt au greffe d'une pièce qui lui paraissait constituer un des éléments utiles du débat et à l'égard de laquelle aucunes conclusions n'avaient été prises pour l'en faire écarter, le juge du fond, loin d'excéder ses pouvoirs, n'en a fait, au contraire, qu'un usage des plus légitimes; − Attendu, d'autre part, qu'en condamnant le demandeur à payer les frais d'enregistrement de cette pièce, et ce, au besoin, à titre de dommages-intérêts, à raison du préjudice causé et d'après les faits et circonstances de la cause, alors que ledit demandeur succombait sur tous les points de l'instance, le jugement attaqué n'a fait également de l'art. 130 c. pr. civ. qu'une exacte application;

Par ces motifs, rejette.

3 Code Civil, Art. 1384(1)

On est responsable non seulement du dommage que l'on cause par son propre fait, mais encore de celui qui est causé par le fait des personnes dont on doit répondre, ou des choses que l'on a sous sa garde. (. . .)

4 Cour de Cassation, Chambres réunies, 13 février 1930, D.P. 1930, I, 57

Veuve Jand'heur c. Soc. des Galeries belfortaises.

Mme veuve Jand'heur s'est pourvue en cassation contre l'arrêt du 7 juillet 1927 (rapporté Gaz. Pal. 1927.2.398 — S. 1927.2.106) par lequel la Cour de Lyon, statuant comme cour de renvoi à la suite de l'arrêt de cassation du 21 février 1927 (Gaz. Pal. 1927.1.407 — S. 1927.1.137 — D. 1927.1.97), s'était prononcée en sens contraire de cet arrêt, appliquant à la cause les mêmes principes que la Cour de Besançon dont l'arrêt du 29 décembre 1925 avait été cassé.

Moyen unique du pourvoi: «Fausse application de l'art. 1382 C. civ., violation de l'art. 1384 du même Code et 7 de la loi du 20 avril 1810, en ce que l'arrêt attaqué a mis à la charge de la victime d'un accident causé par automobile la preuve d'une faute imputable au conducteur, alors que la faute du conducteur devait être présumée».

M. le procureur général Paul Matter a présenté les conclusions suivantes:

MONSIEUR LE PREMIER PRÉSIDENT,
MESSIEURS.

Aux termes de l'art. 1384 C. civ. dans son 1er alinéa, chacun est responsable du dommage causé par la chose dont il a la garde. Cette prescription est-elle applicable aux accidents causés par les automobiles en marche? Telle est la question, très brève et nette, posée à votre haute juridiction. Elle se présente devant vous, d'ailleurs, en fait, dans les conditions les plus simples:

Une enfant, la jeune Jand'heur, a été renversée par un camion automobile appartenant à la Société des Galeries belfortaises. Sa mère et tutrice, Mme Jand'heur, demande réparation, au principal en se fondant sur l'art. 1384 C. civ, et, par conclusions subsidiaires, en se réclamant des dispositions de l'art. 1382 et en demandant à être autorisée à prouver la faute du chauffeur de l'automobile.

Le Tribunal civil de Belfort admet la demande principale et, par conséquent, l'applicabilité de l'art. 1384 C. civ., mais, avant faire droit, autorise la Société à prouver, par témoins, que l'accident est dû à l'imprudence de la jeune victime.

Appel, naturellement, par la Société des Galeries belfortaises. Le 16 juillet 1925, la Cour de Besançon rejette l'application de l'art. 1384, n'admet que le jeu de l'art. 1382, c'est-à-dire la nécessité, pour la demanderesse, de prouver la faute du conducteur, et ordonne une enquête permettant d'établir cette faute, si faute a été commise.

Mme Jand'heur forme un premier pourvoi qui trouve sa solution devant la Chambre civile, le 21 février 1927. Votre Chambre civile a cassé l'arrêt attaqué, en se fondant sur ce motif principal que, pour l'application de la présomption qu'elle édicte, la loi ne distingue pas suivant que la chose qui a causé le dommage était ou non actionnée par la main de l'homme; qu'il suffit qu'il s'agisse d'une chose soumise à la nécessité d'une garde, en raison même du danger qu'elle peut faire courir à autrui.

Votre Chambre civile a renvoyé l'affaire devant la Cour d'appel de Lyon. Le 7 juillet 1927, par un arrêt dont je m'empresse de reconnaître qu'il est fortement charpenté et vigoureusement motivé, la juridiction de renvoi a nettement contredit la théorie de la Chambre civile, et un nouveau pourvoi a été formé.

La contradiction entre les deux arrêts, l'arrêt de la Chambre civile et l'arrêt de la Cour de Lyon, était telle, il y avait si complète identité de parties, de qualités et de moyens, qu'aux termes de l'art. 1er de la loi du 1er avril 1837, seules les Chambres réunies pouvaient donner à cette affaire sa solution définitive. (. . .)

Mais nous sommes en présence d'une question qui, à raison de son caractère, doit être prise tout entière. Il ne faut pas, comme le faisait hier la défense, s'en tenir à deux ou trois arguments: il faut reprendre toute la question dans son intégrité, et je crois que, pour l'examiner toute entière, il est indispensable de rechercher d'abord les origines de l'article 1384, premier alinéa, dans notre ancien droit; puis d'analyser, jusqu'en son tréfonds, le texte même de cet article; encore de suivre l'évolution jurisprudentielle, dont les décisions en matière d'automobiles ne sont qu'un dernier aboutissement; enfin, reprendre, l'un après l'autre, tous les arguments du pourvoi (. . .).

I. – Tout d'abord, les origines du 1er alinéa de l'art. 1384, portant, en termes généraux: «Responsabilité du fait des choses dont on a la garde». (. . .)

Un principe général, en effet, existe dans la législation coutumière de notre ancienne France. Dans notre ancien droit, le maître répondait, d'une manière générale, des choses inanimées qui lui appartenaient (. . .).

Qu'est, je vous prie, cette pratique de l'ancien droit, la responsabilité des choses, de toutes les choses inanimées, poursuivie d'abord contre la chose elle-même, ensuite contre son propriétaire, mieux, contre son gardien, – sinon les dispositions de l'art. 1384, § 1, C. civ., et est-il présomptueux de penser qu'ici, comme dans tant d'autres matières, les législateurs de 1804, les Tronchet, les Bigot de Préameneu, les Cambacérès, fins connaisseurs de notre ancien Droit, n'ont fait qu'adapter, dans une formule lapidaire, ce qu'ils avaient trouvé dans notre Droit coutumier?(. . .).

II. – Après les dispositions préparatoires, le texte maintenant. Toutes les fois que vous avez un texte à appliquer, toutes les fois que vous êtes en présence d'une difficulté de texte, la première chose à faire et votre premier devoir, c'est d'examiner ce texte lui-même, de le scruter, de l'analyser et de voir tout ce qui en peut être tiré.

Aux termes de l'art. 1384 C. civ., on est responsable, non seulement du dommage que l'on cause par son propre fait, mais encore de celui qui est causé par le fait des personnes dont on doit répondre ou des choses dont on a la garde. Ainsi faut-il immédiatement relever la généralité de cette expression: «le fait des choses», sans aucune limitation. C'est ce qu'a vu, c'est ce qu'a dit, c'est ce qu'a exposé parfaitement un jurisconsulte, M. Saleilles (note au Rec. Dalloz 1897.1.437):

«Vouloir restreindre cet article aux dommages causés par les animaux et aux dégâts provenant d'immeubles, c'est en méconnaître simplement et complètement l'esprit et la portée. L'art. 1384 donne une formule très générale, inspirée par une idée de raison et de justice. Cette formule, c'est l'idée de garde. Qui donc prétendrait qu'on ne peut avoir sous sa garde que des animaux ou des bâtiments? L'idée de garde a une bien autre extension; elle se rallie à cette idée de justice que se servir d'une chose dans son intérêt, à son profit, c'est en assumer la surveillance d'abord et les risques ensuite. Rien n'est plus juste.

«Or, nous ne pensons pas que l'on puisse restreindre l'application d'un principe aussi équitable et aussi rationnel à certaines catégories de choses étroitement délimitées, car plus il est juste, plus il est rationnel, plus il faut l'étendre.»

Certains adversaires de ces idées si saines ont proposé un autre raisonnement, que l'on retrouve à la base de l'arrêt attaqué et même de la défense, quoiqu'elle l'ait soigneusement dissimulé. Le voici: Le 1er § de l'art. 1384 n'est autre chose qu'une tête de chapitre, une indication des exceptions qui, ensuite, surviendront, des exceptions au principe général des art. 1382 et 1383, exceptions que soit l'art. 1384, soit l'art. 1385, soit l'art. 1386, énuméreront et de façon limitative. De telle manière que, toutes les fois que l'on sortira de cette énumération limitative, on sera en dehors du champ d'application de l'art. 1384, même dans son 1er alinéa. Et l'on ajoute: A quoi bon cette énumération des personnes, – enfants, domestiques, élèves, – des animaux, des bâtiments tombés en ruines, si le principe général les englobe dans le fait générateur de responsabilité? Il n'était pas nécessaire de porter en tête de l'article un principe général, si ce n'était autre chose que l'annonce de ce qui allait être précisé par la suite.

Messieurs, cette critique, dans la forme tout au moins, s'adresse moins à l'esprit du principe qu'à la façon dont il est présenté. C'est, en effet, une critique adressée à un mode de rédaction vicieux, fréquemment employé par les rédacteurs de notre Code. (...)

L'article 1384, après avoir posé dans son 1er alinéa, le principe que chacun doit répondre des personnes et des choses dont il a la garde, donne une longue énumération, simplement énonciative, comprenant certaines de ces personnes et choses, en fixant les modalités spéciales sous lesquelles cette responsabilité est encourue, et, remarquez ceci, Messieurs, en fixant ces modalités pour étendre la responsabilité, ou, tout au contraire, la restreindre.

Ne nous occupant que des choses, je relèverai la responsabilité du propriétaire de l'animal. Elle s'étend même lorsque le propriétaire n'a plus l'animal en main, puisque l'art. 1385 ajoute: « ... soit que l'animal fût sous sa garde, soit qu'il fût égaré ou échappé.»

Dans l'art. 1386, le Code précise, au contraire, que le propriétaire d'un bâtiment est responsable du dommage causé par sa ruine, mais d'une façon restreinte: seulement lorsqu'elle est arrivée par suite du défaut d'entretien ou par le vice de sa construction.

Ainsi, l'énumération n'est point limitative, elle est énonciative, et ce qui le démontre bien, c'est que, précisément, il donne cette énonciation pour accroître, dans un cas, et pour restreindre dans l'autre, la responsabilité du propriétaire de l'animal ou du bâtiment en ruine. Ce sont là deux cas-types de responsabilité des choses, mais rien, dans notre 1er §, ne vient restreindre ces prescriptions à ces deux cas seulement.

Il ne serait vraiment pas nécessaire de poser un principe général si c'était pour lc limiter, immédiatement, à deux cas spécialement prévus et qui ne sont point les plus fréquents: le cas des animaux et le cas des bâtiments en ruine. (...)

J'arrive maintenant à examiner l'évolution de la doctrine et de la jurisprudence.

III. – Les premiers interprètes de notre Code civil n'ont pas donné cette large compréhension au § 1er de notre art. 1384. Au milieu du XIXe siècle, le plus brillant des commentateurs du Code civil, Demolombe (t. XXI, n° 559), n'admettait la présomption légale de faute que pour «ceux des quasi-délits que la loi a spécialement prévus», ce qui excluait, par là même, la responsabilité des choses autres que les animaux et les immeubles en ruines.

La rédaction d'Aubry et Rau et de différents auteurs que j'ai sous les yeux n'était pas plus large, et elle se bornait, en général, à reproduire, purement et simplement, le texte même de notre 1er alin. de l'art. 1384.

Pareillement, à cette époque, la jurisprudence était très peu extensive. (...)

Enfin, le Conseil d'Etat, dans un arrêt du 21 juin 1895 (D. 96.3.66), et sur de fortes conclusions de M. Romieu, fondées, je le reconnais, plus sur des considérations de service public que sur des raisonnements de droit civil, le Conseil d'Etat reconnaissait la responsabilité du propriétaire d'une machine par le seul fait de sa détention.

A ce moment-là, la Chambre civile prononçait un arrêt décisif: c'est l'arrêt du 11 juin 1896 (D. 97.1.433 – S. 97.1.17 – Gaz. Pal. 96.2.91), par lequel elle s'engageait nettement dans une voie nouvelle. Dans un navire, une machine a fait explosion, causant la mort du mécanicien, ce que nous appellerions, actuellement, un «accident du travail». Le tribunal, puis la cour d'appel, déclarent responsable, sur la base de l'art. 1384 § 1er C. civ., le propriétaire du bateau. Pourvoi. (...)

La Cour rejette le pourvoi. Sans doute, elle relève que l'explosion de la machine est due à un vice de construction, mais elle ajoute: «qu'aux termes de l'art. 1384 C. civ., cette constatation, qui exclut le cas fortuit et la force majeure, établit, vis-à-vis de la victime de l'accident, la responsabilité du remorqueur, sans qu'il puisse s'y soustraire en prouvant soit la faute du constructeur de la machine, soit le caractère occulte du vice incriminé.»

C'était, d'un coup, ébranler toute la théorie sur la spécialité des dérogations des art. 1384 à 1386, dresser fortement le système nouveau de la généralité des termes du 1er alin. de l'art. 1384, la responsabilité du fait des choses, quelles que fussent ces choses.

Cet arrêt eut un grand retentissement et, encore plus, la note qui l'accompagne, non au Sirey, mais au Dalloz, une note de M. Saleilles; elle comporte exactement quatorze colonnes. Elle exposait en termes vigoureux toute la doctrine à laquelle vous alliez, désormais, être entraînés. Elle donnait au gardien de la chose une responsabilité pleine et entière, quelle que soit cette chose, et ajoutait: «C'est la pensée qui a inspiré l'art. 1384. C. civ. Il suffit de lui donner tout le développement qu'elle comporte, et c'est la mission qui appartient à la jurisprudence.»

Ces paroles étaient prophétiques: A cette mission, vous n'avez point manqué.

Cet arrêt était intervenu en matière d'accidents du travail, avant la loi de 1898, avant que ne fussent posés les principes nouveaux du risque du patron (...)

Mais la jurisprudence continue, sans doute point avec une absolue fermeté, avec des hésitations, des retours, suivis de marche en avant, si bien que, chaque progrès étant plus fort que le recul, dans l'ensemble, c'est une avance permanente de la jurisprudence des deux Chambres civiles de la Cour de cassation (...)

L'évolution lente et sûre, arrivée à ce point, a sa conclusion inévitable. Dans le courant des années 1919 et 1921, à quatre reprises, vos deux Chambres civiles vont avoir l'occasion de proclamer hautement qu'elles reconnaissent au 1er alin. de l'art. 1384, une portée générale et absolue; que la responsabilité pour le gardien de la chose est entière; que la présomption légale atteint tous les dommages causés par toutes les choses. (...)

Dans ces quatre arrêts, une même idée reparaît, sans doute formulée dans des termes non identiques, mais toujours la même au fond, et que j'emprunte à l'arrêt du 21 janvier 1919, qui expose en ces termes la généralité de la prescription du 1er alin. de l'art. 1384: «La présomption de faute édictée par cet alinéa, à l'encontre de celui qui a sous sa garde la chose inanimée qui a causé le dommage, ne peut être détruite que par la preuve d'un cas fortuit ou de force majeure ou d'une cause étrangère qui ne lui soit pas imputable. Il ne suffit pas de prouver qu'il n'a commis aucune faute, ni que la cause du dommage est restée inconnue.» (. . .)

Il ne restait plus qu'une dernière sanction: c'était l'approbation législative. Elle a été donnée sous forme implicite, mais très nette. L'émotion avait été vive dans les compagnies d'assurances lorsque furent rendus les arrêts des deux Chambres civiles en date des 26 novembre 1920 et 15 mars 1921; elles firent remarquer qu'elles seraient, désormais, obligées d'augmenter les primes. Elles comprenaient peut-être mal l'esprit même qui avait dicté ces deux arrêts, mais elles voulurent restreindre l'application de l'art. 1384, en excluant les cas d'incendie. Ce fut ce que vota le Parlement et qui devint un paragraphe spécial de l'art. 1384 C. civ. Il est ainsi conçu: «Toutefois . . . (remarquez bien ce «toutefois»; nous en tirerons parti dans un instant) . . .«Toutefois, celui qui détient, à un titre quelconque, tout ou partie de l'immeuble ou des biens immobiliers dans lesquels un incendie a pris naissance, ne sera responsable, etc . . .»

«Toutefois!» ce mot est là pour poser une restriction, une exception au principe général du 1er alin., tel qu'il a été développé par la jurisprudence nouvelle; c'était adopter, accepter cette jurisprudence, sauf sur un point, en ce qui concerne les incendies d'immeubles ou de biens mobiliers, et c'était, par ce «toutefois», confirmer toute votre jurisprudence (. . .)

Tel était l'état de l'opinion doctrinale, jurisprudentielle, législative, sur la portée de l'art. 1384 dans son alinéa, 1er, avant même que vous n'ayez eu à envisager l'application de ces dispositions aux accidents d'automobile. (. . .)

IV. – Chose curieuse, la jurisprudence ne se porta point, tout d'abord, sur ce terrain. Un premier arrêt de la Chambre des requêtes, du 22 mars 1911 (D. 1911 1.354 – Gaz. Pal. 1911.1.427), semblait se rallier, tout au contraire, à la théorie opposée, en décidant qu'au cas d'accident d'automobile «il s'agit, non de la responsabilité de la chose, dans les termes de l'art. 1384, mais de la responsabilité résultant du fait du préposé auquel elle était confiée et que, par suite, il incombait à la victime ou à ses ayants cause de prouver la faute». Mais, quelques années après, survenaient les arrêts dont je parlais tout à l'heure, si nets, de 1919 et de 1920, qui donnaient à la théorie extensive sa formule définitive, et la Chambre civile allait en faire application en matière d'accidents d'automobile.

Par un premier arrêt, en date du 29 juillet 1924 (D. 1925.1.5 – S. 1924.1.321 – Gaz. Pal. 1924.2.385), au rapport de M. le conseiller Lénard, et sur les conclusions conformes de M. l'avocat général Langlois, la Chambre civile a, dans son arrêt Bessières, purement et simplement repris la formule de son arrêt du 21 janvier 1919, pour en faire l'application à l'accident causé par une voiture automobile. (. . .)

Depuis lors, vos deux Chambres civiles sont demeurées fidèles à cette doctrine. Sans doute, on a pu, dans leurs arrêts, examinés à la loupe, signaler quelques nuances que les arrêtistes n'ont point manqué de souligner. D'une part, tantôt ces arrêts ont fait reposer la présomption de responsabilité sur la simple détention de la chose, introduisant ainsi dans la loi la notion du risque matériel; tantôt, au contraire, ils se sont fondés, et beaucoup plus juridiquement à mon gré, sur la présomption de faute ou, pour parler plus exactement, sur la présomption de responsabilité que je relevais tout à l'heure dans les travaux préparatoires du Code civil, et ils ont ainsi rattaché l'art. 1384 à l'art. 1382, comme la Chambre civile l'avait déjà fait fortement dans ses arrêts sur la responsabilité de l'art. 1385, contre le maître de l'animal.

D'autre part, parmi ces arrêts, les uns, précisant, restreignant le sens de l'article, ont parlé de choses dangereuses parce que, seules, elles nécessitent une garde, et l'on retrouve ici l'influence de M. le professeur Ripert, qui, sous l'arrêt de 1924, donna une longue note au Dalloz, où il soutenait vigoureusement qu'on doit fonder la présomption de responsabilité sur le caractère dangereux de la chose qui est sous la garde de l'homme, telle qu'une automobile. Les autres, au contraire, ont reproduit le mot employé par notre paragraphe: «les choses», tout simplement, tout uniquement, sans plus, puisque la loi ne distingue pas et que toute chose peut porter dommage à autrui, peut devenir dangereuse (...)

Mais, dans leur ensemble, tous ces arrêts se rapportent à une même conclusion: la responsabilité du conducteur de l'automobile en marche est la même pour tout accident causé par sa voiture, sauf à lui à prouver l'existence d'un cas fortuit ou d'une force majeure ou d'une cause étrangère qui ne lui soit pas imputable; le plus souvent la faute même de la victime. (...)

Telle est, dans ses origines, dans son texte, dans son développement, la doctrine contre laquelle s'est prononcée la grande Cour de Lyon, par une argumentation vigoureuse et serrée.

V. – Il me reste maintenant à étudier les arguments de l'arrêt attaqué et de la défense. (...)

Ces arguments, je les grouperai en quatre postulats (. ...)

B. – Deuxième argument, et c'est le principal, la pierre d'angle de l'édifice lyonnais, sur lequel la Cour revient, à plusieurs reprises: La présomption de l'art. 1384, applicable si la lésion a été réalisée directement par la chose: l'explosion du moteur, l'éclatement d'un pneu, la rupture d'un frein ou du volant, bref, un vice qui rendait dangereux l'usage normal de la chose, est inadmissible au cas où la machine est sous la conduite de l'homme où (je cite l'arrêt attaqué): « ... le fait de l'automobile dirigée se confond nécessairement avec celui de l'homme.»

Et l'arrêt de développer très fortement cette argumentation: dans les actes du conducteur, il n'y a plus seulement fait de la chose, mais responsabilité personnelle d'un agent, car alors il y a conduite, acte de volonté et non simple garde.

Présentée avec luxe par l'arrêt attaqué, cette argumentation paraît se tenir, mais il y a longtemps qu'on en a fait raison; elle se heurte, en effet, à trois objections inséparables: d'une part, elle repose sur une distinction que notre alinéa ne comporte nullement. Or, il est une règle d'interprétation essentielle dans l'art d'interpréter les lois, ce que, je crois, on appelle à l'Ecole, un peu pédantesquement: l'herméneutique. Cette règle, elle est exprimée dans une formule latine, que nous avons apprise dès notre première année de Droit: *Ubi lex non distinguit, nec nos distinguere debemus.*» Aussi, les interprètes sont-ils d'accord pour opposer, à la distinction proposée par la Cour de Lyon, une exception catégorique, et M. Ripert, dans sa note de 1922 (D. 1922.1.26), disait déjà, et à juste titre: «Cette distinction ne peut se justifier.»

D'autre part, elle est jugée et condamnée, par les conséquences mêmes, tout à fait extraordinaires, auxquelles elle aboutit. Elle a été mise à mal, de la manière la plus forte, par M. Josserand, dans ce récent article de la *Chronique* du Dalloz: «Il serait surprenant, en vérité, que la responsabilité du gardien fût atténuée par la mise en marche du véhicule, c'est-à-dire au moment précis où son utilisation devient vraiment dangereuse. On ne distingue pas, pour les dommages causés par une machine, que la locomotive soit arrêtée ou non, qu'une batteuse soit en mouvement ou pas; on ne voit pas pourquoi on traiterait autrement les accidents de locomotion automobile. En réalité, c'est là une distinction factice et presque byzantine. Une automobile n'est jamais autant sous la garde de son propriétaire que lorsque celui-ci est au volant.» Et M. Josserand de conclure: «La cause est entendue.»

Et le pourvoi, hier, résumait toute cette théorie dans une formule excellente, que je vous rappelle: «Cette théorie rend l'homme responsable de sa passivité et non de son activité.»

Enfin, et surtout, on l'a déjà remarqué, dans tous les cas de responsabilité du fait de la chose, aussi bien dans ceux formellement prévus par les art. 1384 à 1386 que ceux acceptés par la doctrine et par la jurisprudence, toujours, sous le fait de la chose, apparaît l'acte de l'homme (. . .).

Mais c'est qu'il y a toujours un fait personnel sous le dommage causé par la personne ou la chose dont on répond. Dans la responsabilité de l'art. 1384 de l'instituteur, du père, du commettant, ne peut-on relever une faute originaire du père qui a mal élevé son enfant; du commettant qui a mal choisi son commis; du maître ou de l'instituteur qui a mal surveillé les élèves confiés à sa garde? (. . .)

Il en est de même dans les nombreuses espèces où, antérieurement à la jurisprudence sur les automobiles, les Chambres civiles se sont prononcées. S'agit-il d'une machine qui fait explosion? Arrêts du 11 juin 1896 et du 21 janvier 1920. Mais c'est le fait du mécanicien, qui l'a mal soignée, ou du conducteur qui l'a mal établie. S'agit-il de l'explosion de grenades à mains? Arrêt du 28 juin 1920. C'est, soit le fait des ouvriers qui les ont maniées, soit de l'entrepositaire qui les a mal conservées, ou du constructeur qui les a mal préparées. (. . .)

Il en est de même, dirons-nous, pour l'automobile. Sous le fait de la voiture en marche, ayant même son dynamisme propre, c'est l'action du conducteur mal maître de sa machine, et M. l'avocat général Langlois de dire: «L'automobiliste perd le contrôle de sa voiture qui échappe à la main qui la conduit et recèle en elle des causes d'accident.» (21 février 1927, aff. Jand'heur, Gaz. Pal. 1927.1.407).

J'en ai assez dit pour démontrer tout ce que la distinction, admise par la Cour de Lyon, a d'arbitraire, contraire à la loi, fondé sur des principes inexacts, donc inadmissibles (. . .)

D. – La Défense s'est bien gardée de reprendre, en sa forme tout au moins, la dernière objection de l'arrêt attaqué. Je le cite textuellement: «La doctrine à laquelle s'est attachée la juridiction du premier degré (et, par conséquent, la Chambre civile) se heurte à l'autorité de la tradition. Elle apporte une modification au système du Code civil, alors qu'il n'appartient qu'au pouvoir législatif d'ajouter des présomptions de faute à celles édictés expressément ou d'une façon virtuelle par notre grande charte civile.» (. . .)

La tradition? Quelle tradition? Comme le disait spirituellement M. l'avocat général Langlois, jusqu'en 1896, il n'y a point eu de tradition, il n'y a eu que des contradictions. C'est depuis 1896, lentement, sûrement, pas à pas, comme vous le faites, avec prudence et sagesse, qu'une tradition jurisprudentielle s'est formée (. . .) 25 arrêts peut-être de vos deux Chambres civiles, – et j'en trouverais des traces dans des arrêts de la Chambre criminelle, – formant un véritable corps de jurisprudence.

Cette jurisprudence dépasse-t-elle les termes de la loi? Nullement. Dans son texte même, elle a cherché son principe et sa base. Tout au plus peut-on dire qu'elle a adapté à des besoins nouveaux un texte dont les arrêts précédents n'avaient pas envisagé toute la portée, et cela encore est dans vos traditions.

Peut-être conviendrait-il ici de vous rappeler les phrases qu'à ce sujet consacrait justement un grand magistrat quand il disait que la jurisprudence opère une oeuvre créatrice; qu'en présence de tous les changements opérés dans les idées, dans les moeurs, dans les institutions, dans l'état économique de la France, on doit adapter libéralement, humainement, le texte aux réalités et aux exigences de la vie moderne (. . .)

Si quelques arrêtistes s'en sont indignés, cette règle de droit est entrée maintenant dans les moeurs judiciaires. Où est la proposition faite pour la contester? Où sont les protestations actuelles? Tout le monde l'accepte maintenant et, pourtant, c'est en trois ans que s'est faite cette modification profonde.

Le 1er alinéa de l'art 1384 a été édicté à une époque bien ancienne, au temps des diligences et des coucous, mais au temps aussi où l'on savait rédiger un texte, non point seulement pour l'heure actuelle, pour les besoins du moment, mais pour l'avenir. Ces textes empruntés les uns à notre ancien droit, au droit romain les autres, au droit coutumier ceux-ci, au droit écrit ceux-là, ces textes ont cet immense avantage de poser des principes généraux, et toutes les fois qu'on en parle avec un jurisconsulte étranger, toutes les fois qu'on discute avec lui sur la portée de tel article de notre Code civil, spécialement dans son titre «Des Obligations», il ne manque pas de dire l'admiration profonde qu'il a pour des écrits qui contiennent des formules si souples et si précises en même temps, si larges et si compréhensives que, formulées au temps du cabriolet, elles sont aussi bien applicables à l'automobile ou même à l'avion (. . .)

M. le professeur Saleilles terminait sa grande note de 1897 par ceux-ci: «L'article 1384 est fondé sur une idée simple, équitable, que celui qui a le fonctionnement d'une entreprise doit en emporter les risques. C'est la pensée qui a inspiré l'art. 1384. C'est la mission de la jurisprudence de donner à la loi toute la vitalité progressive d'un principe qui opère et qui agit.»

Belles paroles et que je vais simplement m'approprier. Non, il n'est point exact que, depuis 1896, arrêt après arrêt doivent tomber sous le coup d'une faux implacable. Non, il n'est point exact que vous ayez erré depuis trente-quatre ans: J'ai recherché les origines lointaines de cet art. 1384, j'ai scruté son texte, j'ai examiné l'évolution de votre jurisprudence, j'ai étudié les critiques qui lui sont adressées et, maintenant, je crois que je suis autorisé à dire: cette jurisprudence est humaine, elle répond bien aux besoins de l'heure actuelle; elle est juste, parce qu'elle repose sur un texte précis; son adaptation, mettons, si vous le voulez, l'extension de ce vieux texte, large et souple, à des situations nouvelles, ne dépasse point la portée de ses termes.

La jurisprudence de la Chambre civile et de la Chambre des requêtes doit être approuvée.

Je conclus à la cassation.

Arrêt (ap. délib. en ch. du conseil):

LA COUR,

Sur le moyen du pourvoi:

Vu l'art. 1384, alinéa 1er, C. civ.;

Attendu que la présomption de responsabilité établie par cet article à l'encontre de celui qui a sous sa garde la chose inanimée qui a causé un dommage à autrui ne peut être détruite que par la preuve d'un cas fortuit ou de force majeure ou d'une cause étrangère qui ne lui soit pas imputable; qu'il ne suffit pas de prouver qu'il n'a commis aucune faute ou que la cause du fait dommageable est demeurée inconnue;

Attendu que, le 22 avril 1925, un camion automobile appartenant à la Société «Aux Galeries belfortaises» a renversé et blessé la mineure Lise Jand'heur; que l'arrêt attaqué a refusé d'appliquer le texte susvisé par le motif que l'accident causé par une automobile en mouvement, sous l'impulsion et la direction de l'homme, ne constituait pas, alors qu'aucune preuve n'existe qu'il soit dû à un vice propre de la voiture, le fait de la chose que l'on a sous sa garde dans les termes de l'art. 1384, § 1er, et que, dès lors, la victime était tenue, pour obtenir réparation du préjudice, d'établir à la charge du conducteur une faute qui lui fût imputable;

Mais attendu que la loi, pour l'application de la présomption qu'elle édicte, ne distingue pas suivant que la chose qui a causé le dommage était ou non actionnée par la main de l'homme; qu'il n'est pas nécessaire qu'elle ait un vice inhérent à sa nature et susceptible de causer le dommage, l'art. 1384 rattachant la responsabilité à la garde de la chose, non à la chose elle-même;

D'où il suit qu'en statuant comme il l'a fait, l'arrêt attaqué a interverti l'ordre légal de la preuve et violé le texte de loi susvisé;

Par ces motifs,

Casse ...

5 Loi des 16−24 août 1790

Titre II, Art.12. Ils (les juges) ne pourront point faire des règlements, mais ils adresseront leurs représentations au Corps législatif toutes les fois qu'ils croient nécessaire, soit d'interpréter une loi, soit d'en faire une nouvelle.

6 Code Civil, Art. 5

Il est défendu aux juges de prononcer par voie de disposition générale et réglementaire sur les causes qui leur sont soumises.

7 Code Civil, Art. 1351

L'autorité de la chose jugée n'a lieu qu'à l'égard de ce qui a fait l'objet du jugement. Il faut que la chose demandée soit la même; que la demande soit fondée sur la même cause; que la demande soit entre les mêmes parties, et formée par elles et contre elles en la même qualité.

8 Code Civil, Art. 4

Art. 4 – Le juge qui refusera de juger, sous prétexte du silence, de l'obscurité ou de l'insuffisance de la loi, pourra être poursuivi comme coupable de déni de justice.

9 Code Civil, Arts. 645, 663, 1135, 1159, 1736, 1757, 1758

Art. 645. – S'il s'élève une contestation entre les propriétaires auxquels ces eaux peuvent être utiles, les tribunaux, en prononçant, doivent concilier l'intérêt de l'agriculture avec le respect dû à la propriété; et, dans tous les cas, les règlements particuliers et locaux sur le cours et l'usage des eaux doivent être observés.

Art. 663. – Chacun peut contraindre son voisin, dans les villes et faubourgs, à contribuer aux constructions et réparations de la clôture faisant séparation de leurs maisons, cours et jardins assis ès dites villes et faubourgs: la hauteur de la clôture sera fixée suivant les règlements particuliers ou les usages constants et reconnus, et, à défaut d'usages et de règlements, tout mur de séparation entre voisins, qui sera construit ou rétabli à l'avenir, doit avoir au moins trente-deux décimètres de hauteur, compris le chaperon, dans les villes de cinquante mille âmes et au-dessus, et vingt-six décimètres dans les autres.

Art. 1135. – Les conventions obligent non seulement à ce qui y est exprimé, mais encore à toutes les suites que l'équité, l'usage ou la loi donnent à l'obligation d'après sa nature.

Art. 1159. – Ce qui est ambigu s'interprète par ce qui est d'usage dans le pays où le contrat est passé.

Art. 1736. – Si le bail a été fait sans écrit, l'une des parties ne pourra donner congé à l'autre qu'en observant les délais fixés par l'usage des lieux.

Art. 1757. – Le bail des meubles fournis pour garnir une maison entière, un corps de logis entier, une boutique, ou tous autres appartements, est censé fait pour la durée ordinaire des baux de maisons, corps de logis, boutiques ou autres appartements, selon l'usage des lieux.

Art. 1758. – Le bail d'un appartement meublé est censé fait à l'année, quand il a été fait à tant par an;

Au mois, quand il a été fait à tant par mois;

Au jour, s'il a été fait à tant par jour.

Si rien ne constate que le bail soit fait à tant par an, par mois ou par jour, la location est censée faite suivant l'usage des lieux.

10 Extrait des Usages Locaux de Nantes

Des Baux et de leur durée

Avant de traiter les questions subsidiaires, il est nécessaire de savoir pendant combien de temps on peut jouir d'un appartement ou d'un immeuble concédé à titre de location soit verbale, soit écrite.

Dans le premier cas, le contrat n'est pas sans aléa et peut devenir la source de contestations fort désagréables et sans nombre pour les propriétaires qui pourraient souvent les éviter si les conventions étaient fixées en un acte sous seing privé.

Depuis longtemps l'usage du «Denier à Dieu» qui consistait en la remise d'une petite somme d'argent scellant le contrat intervenu entre propriétaire et locataire, est tombé en désuétude et de cette coutume on n'en retrouve guère la trace que dans les locations de chambres pour lesquelles on stipule parfois que le paiement aura lieu un ou trois mois d'avance.

En tout cas, à moins de conventions spéciales, les locations verbales sont faites pour un an et à partir du 24 juin, au gré des deux parties qui peuvent d'un commun accord et avant le 24 mars à midi donner congé par huissier (jugement du tribunal civil de Nantes, 12 mars 1903). Toute location pour une année prend fin sans donner congé, à l'expiration de cette année. Si le locataire reste dans les lieux et commence ainsi une nouvelle année, il devra alors donner congé trois mois avant la fin de la dite année.

Il est d'usage lorsque le locataire entre en jouissance à la Noël que le bail soit contracté pour dix-huit mois.

Si avant les dates sus-mentionnées aucune des parties n'a donné congé à l'autre, la location se poursuit tacitement pour une nouvelle année et continue ainsi jusqu'à congé régulier.

L'usage à Nantes est que les locations verbales vont de la Saint-Jean à la Saint-Jean, et à la campagne de la Toussaint à la Toussaint (cantons de Carquefou, de Saint-Mars-la-Jaille, de Ligné) ou de Noël à la Noël.

Pour les locations écrites, ordinairement de trois, six ou neuf années, il y a lieu, lorsqu'une clause du contrat donne la faculté au preneur et au propriétaire de révoquer la location à l'expiration de l'une des deux premières périodes triennales, de signifier congé trois mois avant la fin de la période en cours, sauf convention expresse insérée dans le bail. Mais pour les locations à usage de commerce, la coutume veut que le locataire informe le propriétaire six mois à l'avance et réciproquement de son désir de ne plus continuer à occuper les lieux loués.

Lorsque le bail est en cours et que la dernière période vient à expiration, il n'est pas nécessaire de donner congé.

Chambres garnies

Les locations sont faites au mois. Pour donner congé on doit prévenir huit jours avant l'expiration du mois (...)

Du paiement du loyer

L'article 1728, qui contraint le preneur «d'user de la chose louée en bon père de famille», l'oblige également à payer le prix du bail aux «termes convenus» ou, à défaut de convention spéciale, aux époques fixées par l'usage des lieux, c'est-à-dire tous les six mois, à la Saint-Jean et à la Noël, le terme étant exigible «dès le lendemain de son échéance».

Un locataire ne peut valablement se refuser à payer le loyer échu qu'il doit pour toute la durée de la jouissance, alors même qu'il n'aurait pas occupé les lieux faisant l'objet de la location, le fait seul de n'en avoir pas joui indiquant amplement la liberté qu'il avait d'en disposer à son gré. Il ne saurait également baser son refus sur ce que le propriétaire n'a pas fait de réparations jugées nécessaires au moment de sa prise en possession; alors même que le preneur aurait fait des dépenses de gros entretient nécessaires à la conservation de la chose, il ne serait pas fondé, à la fin du bail, à opposer au bailleur la compensation des termes de loyer échus avec les impenses par lui faites à l'immeuble loué.

A partir du jour où l'action en paiement est intentée, les sommes dues pour loyer produisent intérêts, le bailleur conservant toujours, d'après l'article 2102 du Code civil, un privilège sur les meubles garnissant les locaux. En même temps qu'on intente des poursuites contre le locataire, on peut demander la résiliation du bail et l'expulsion.

Si à expiration de jouissance, le preneur, en plus du prix, refusait de faire les réparations dites locatives, il pourrait être sommé d'avoir à les exécuter; faute par lui de se conformer à cet acte, le juge, sur assignation en référé, condamnerait, par provision, le locataire sortant à les effectuer, autorisant, pour garantie, la saisie des meubles.

Après cinq ans, aucune action en paiement n'est possible, la prescription étant acquise.

On considère à Nantes que le montant des loyers est payable au domicile du propriétaire, si les parties n'en ont pas convenu autrement.

Un locataire peut-il valablement se libérer en acquittant le prix entre les mains du concierge de l'immeuble? Un jugement récent déclare que si le concierge est en possession de quittances faites par le propriétaire, le preneur peut sans aucun risque lui remettre l'argent contre reçu signé du bailleur; il serait également libéré si la personne à qui il verse le montant de la location avait une procuration enregistrée; mais il ne doit en aucun cas accepter de s'acquitter entre les mains d'un concierge qui n'aurait aucun pouvoir à cet effet, alors même qu'il lui établirait un reçu provisoire; le locataire pourrait être contraint au paiement du prix déjà versé.

Aucune formule n'est imposée par la loi pour le libellé des reçus de loyer qui doivent indiquer le montant de la somme et l'époque pour laquelle elle est due.

Une quittance donnée sans réserve fait présumer le paiement des termes précédents, et le juge, en cas de contestation, doit pouvoir de ce fait établir la libération du preneur pour les années antérieures. (. . .)

11 Code Civil, Art. 312

L'enfant conçu pendant le mariage a pour père le mari. Néanmoins, celui-ci pourra désavouer l'enfant en justice, s'il justifie de faits propres à démontrer qu'il ne peut pas en être le père.

Chapter 3

The court system, the judiciary and the legal professions

A. The court system

1. General principles

(a) Separation of ordinary and administrative courts

(i) Introduction

In Chapter 1 we examined the reasons why the revolutionaries determined to avoid the jurisdictional conflicts of the *Ancien Régime* by removing (by the *loi du 16–24 août 1790*) the jurisdiction of the courts in respect of administrative activity. Some control of such activity of course became necessary, and soon came to be exercised by the *Conseil d'Etat*. This body was created in 1799 as a government advisory body. However, the fact that the civil courts were not competent to deal with litigation involving the administration soon led ministers to turn to the *Conseil d'Etat* for its advice. However, in this latter role the *Conseil* did not initially act in a truly judicial fashion, for although from as early as 1806 a special judicial committee (*la commission du contentieux*) sat to hear such cases, it only made recommendations, the final decision being taken by the head of state or his ministers (known as the system of *la justice retenue*). It did not have authority to make decisions (the system of *la justice déléguée*) until the passing of the *loi du 24.5.1872*, which provided (*Art. 9*; TEXTS, NO. 1) that the *Conseil d'Etat* had sovereign power to pronounce judgment in administrative cases. Up until the passing of the 1872 law, there had been a good deal of debate on the judicial role of the *Conseil d'Etat*, many commentators taking the view that all litigation, even that involving the administration, should come within the jurisdiction of the ordinary courts. However, in 1872 the jurisdiction of the *Conseil d'Etat* was confirmed, and since then the *Conseil* has taken it upon itself to elaborate the basic principles of French administrative law. As will be seen, the administrative court system has been extended in recent years, and now comprises regional first instance courts (*Tribunaux Administratifs*) and appeal courts (*Cours Administratives d'Appel*), with the *Conseil d'Etat* in Paris at the summit of the system.

This administrative court system operates in parallel with a system of ordinary courts (*juridictions judiciaires*) which deal with both criminal and civil cases. In respect of the latter, first instance civil cases are heard before local *Tribunaux d'Instance* or *Tribunaux de Grande Instance*, depending on the amount of the claim, with appeal to the regional *Cour d'Appel* and appeal on a point of law to the supreme *Cour de Cassation*. This duality of court systems presents the obvious difficulty for the would-be litigant in knowing in which set of courts he should commence his action. The issue is particularly important because of the fact that over the years the *Conseil d'Etat*, on the basis that rules designed to regulate relationships between private individuals or corporations are not always appropriate for relationships involving the state or public bodies, has developed principles of administrative law, particularly in the fields of the law of contract and tortious responsibility, in a way that differs from the civil law of contract and tortious responsibility as set out in the Civil Code; these distinctive principles of administrative law apply if the case comes within the jurisdiction of the administrative courts.

(ii) Rules for determining competence

A set of rules has been developed for determining the cases for which the administrative courts have competence; any conflicts of jurisdiction between the two court systems are resolved by a court specially created for this purpose in 1872, the *Tribunal des Conflits* (see below), comprising an equal number of judges from the two supreme courts.

It is obviously in the interests of litigants that the rules for determining competence should be straightforward and clear-cut. Unfortunately, they are complex and, indeed, are the subject of much academic debate. There is no legislative text defining the basis of the competence of the administrative courts, as the revolutionary texts on which the lack of competence of the judicial courts is based pre-date the creation of the *Conseil d'Etat* and are silent on the matter. There are only a few limited texts dealing with a small number of specific types of litigation. It has thus been left to the *Tribunal des Conflits* and the *Conseil d'Etat* to delimit for themselves the jurisdiction of the administrative courts.

The distinctive principles of administrative law are appropriate essentially to cases involving the activities of the state and administrative bodies. One of the ways administrative activity was distinguished from private activity in the early caselaw of the *Conseil d'Etat* was by the nature of the powers which were being exercised, in particular the use of prerogative powers (*prérogatives de puissance publique*) by the administration. However, in the 1873 case of *Blanco (T.C., 8.2.1873,* Rec., 1er, 61) the *Tribunal des Conflits* introduced a test which concentrated more on the activity being undertaken – the test of "public service" (*service public*) – the administrative courts having jurisdiction for cases connected with the organisation and functioning of public services (ie activities carried out in the general interest intended to meet a public need), whether local, regional or national. The two tests of *prérogatives de puissance publique* and *service public* frequently combine, and there has been a good deal of debate over their relative importance. Furthermore, the growth during the twentieth century of the range of public services, and the introduction of public services of an industrial or commercial nature, have clouded the distinction between administrative and private activity. The courts have therefore drawn a distinction between, on the one hand, traditional administrative activities, to which the principles of administrative law are applicable and which come within the competence of the administrative courts, and, on the other hand, public services which are of an industrial or commercial nature to which principles of private law apply, the ordinary courts having jurisdiction. There are, however, several exceptions to this general approach.

It should be noted *en passant* that all activities in the nature of a public service (*service public*) must conform to certain principles (known as *les lois de Rolland* after the academic writer Louis Rolland) of which there are three: the principle of the continuity of public service (*la continuité du service public*) according to which the provider of a *service public* is under an obligation to continue to provide that service; the principle of equality in the provision of the service (*l'égalité devant le service public*) according to which persons in equivalent positions must in principle be treated in the same way in the provision of a public service; finally, the principle of the adaptation or mutability of public service (*l'adaptation* or *la mutabilité du service public*) according to which the provision of a public service must in the light of the general interest be adapted to the changing needs of the recipients of the service.

The test of *service public* is now best regarded as giving rise to no more than a presumption of the competence of the administrative courts. The modern *prima facie* test may be stated as follows: the administrative courts have competence to hear cases which arise from an activity of the administration which is an activity involving the provision of a *service public*. However, even where the case does involve the functioning of a *service public*, it is now accepted, as we have seen, that in certain cases the ordinary courts should have competence; at the heart of the modern test is the issue of which set of legal rules, that of administrative or civil law, is more appropriate to any given case.

Activity of the administration: We will now examine the two parts of the test in more detail. Let us first consider the statement that the administrative courts are competent only where the activity which is the subject of the litigation is an activity of the administration. The administrative courts are not in principle competent to deal with disputes between private individuals or bodies, to which civil law rules more naturally apply.

However, difficulties arise where private bodies are involved in the provision of public services. Disputes involving members of the public in respect of the services provided by such bodies are generally subject to civil law. However, they may by way of exception be subject to the rules of administrative law; eg litigation in respect of "public works" (*travaux publics*), and cases where in exercising its functions the private body has recourse to *les prérogatives de puissance publique*.

Furthermore, the administrative courts are the judge of the activities of the executive, not those of the other organs of state. The administrative courts thus have no jurisdiction in respect of matters relating to the legislative function of the state. The *Conseil d'Etat* therefore cannot hold a parliamentary statute to be unconstitutional; only the *Conseil Constitutionnel* may do so (see below). The *Conseil d'Etat* may, however, adjudge the legality of regulations issued by the government. Furthermore, certain executive activities have traditionally been regarded as being outside the control of the courts (both administrative and ordinary), and such *actes de gouvernement* encompass not only international relations, but also activities of the executive connected with the functioning of Parliament, such as a decision by the President of the Republic to refer a bill directly to the people by referendum under Article 11 of the 1958 Constitution (see Chapter 4).

Nor may the administrative courts adjudge judicial activity; a party to an action in the ordinary courts cannot therefore refer a decision of those courts to the administrative courts for review. Although cases relating to the functioning of the ordinary courts are thus outside the jurisdiction of the administrative courts, those connected with their organisation are not.

Activity in the nature of a public service: As we have seen, the notion of *service public* is not the sole criterion for determining the competence of the administrative courts. Furthermore, it should be noted that litigation in respect of certain types of public service activity has been traditionally recognised by the administrative courts as coming within the competence of the ordinary courts or has been specifically assigned to the ordinary courts by statute.

Firstly, the administrative courts will not have competence where the activity of the administrative body is of a private nature. This is the case where the administrative body carries out a public service of an industrial or commercial nature; any litigation arising from such activity will thus be heard in the ordinary courts, who will apply the relevant principles of private law. It is felt that the interests of justice are best served by applying the one set of rules to activities carried out in analogous conditions, whether by private or public bodies.

Contracts in which at least one of the parties is an administrative body may be administrative, and thus subject to the rules of administrative law, or private. Some contracts are classified by statute as being administrative (eg contracts for public works (*loi du 28 pluviôse an VIII*)). Such cases aside, the *Conseil d'Etat* has accepted that a contract may have the characteristics of an administrative contract. This may be the case where the contract involves a private contractor participating in the carrying out of a *service public*, or where the respective obligations of the parties as set out in the contract reveal the inequality of their position, as will be the case where there are *clauses exorbitantes* (ie clauses of a nature that one would not expect to find in a similar private law contract). Alternatively the contract may be of a private law nature, in which case any disputes are to be dealt with in the ordinary courts in accordance with the principles of private law.

Secondly, both statute and caselaw have recognised that particular categories of litigation which would otherwise be within the competence of the administrative courts should be assigned to the ordinary courts. Statute does so in respect of, *inter alia*, litigation relating to loss caused by motor vehicles belonging to the administration or used in the execution of public works (*loi du 31.12.1957*); there is obviously interest in ensuring that litigation involving road traffic accidents is subject to one set of legal principles, whether the vehicle is driven by an agent of an administrative body or a private individual. Matters of indirect taxation (eg *taxe sur la valeur ajoutée*) (cf VAT)) and customs duties are also assigned to the ordinary courts, the administrative courts remaining competent to deal with direct taxation.

There is also a general principle which the *Conseil d'Etat* has derived (from some early nineteenth century texts) that the ordinary courts alone are entitled to deal with matters involving individual liberty, private property or an individual's personal status. When the texts were passed, the *Conseil d'Etat* had not yet proved its independence from government, and the ordinary courts were regarded as being the best guarantor of individual liberties (now see 1958 Constitution, Art. 66; CHAPTER 4, TEXTS, NO. 1). The ordinary courts thus deal with all cases involving personal status (*état des personnes*) such as marriage, affiliation, domicile, civic capacity and nationality. They are also involved in determining the quantum of compensation to be paid by a public authority for the expropriation of private real property; in the case of a legal expropriation (eg in furtherance of a compulsory purchase order), statute often specifically gives this role to the ordinary courts; where the expropriation is illegal (known as an *emprise*), the ordinary courts are recognised as having jurisdiction without the need for statutory authority, because of their role as guarantor of individual rights. Furthermore, by the doctrine of *voie de fait*, where a public authority, in the execution of a public service, acts in a way which is not merely illegal, but is flagrantly or grossly illegal, thereby harming individual liberties or property rights, the administrative courts lose jurisdiction for actions for compensation by the injured party in favour of the ordinary courts (eg *C.E., 18.11.1949, Carlier,* CHAPTER 4 TEXTS, NO. 30).

The question of the constitutional basis of the division of competence between the administrative and "ordinary" courts was fully addressed only during the 1980s. The 1958 Constitution of the Fifth Republic makes no reference to the administrative court system. However, in a 1980 decision (*C.C., 22.7.1980, D.1981, IR, 356*) the *Conseil Constitutionnel* recognised the independence of the *Conseil d'Etat* as a fundamental constitutional principle. Furthermore, by a decision of *23.1.1987 (D.1988, 117)* the *Conseil Constitutionnel* impliedly recognised the existence of the separate administrative courts, and confirmed that cases in respect of the annulment or modification of decisions taken by administrative authorities are within the competence of the administrative courts.

Preliminary reference: Having examined in outline the rules used to determine which set of courts is competent to deal with any given case, rules which are applied in case of dispute by the *Tribunal des Conflits* (see below), there remains the issue of what occurs when in a matter before, say, the ordinary courts, a point of administrative law requires interpretation, or vice versa. Usually in such circumstances the proceedings will have to be adjourned for a preliminary reference (*question préjudicielle*) on this point to the other set of courts. However, there are exceptions to this principle. The ordinary courts are always competent to interpret, without a preliminary reference, administrative regulations having general effect (but not decisions having individual effect). They cannot, however, determine the legality of such regulations (*T.C., 16.6.1923, Septfonds, Rec., 498*); the only exception to this is that where, in a criminal trial, the question of the legality of administrative regulations is raised (minor offences (*contraventions*) being regulated by government regulations under Articles 34 and 37 of the 1958 Constitution), the criminal court may deal with the issue there and then (*T.C., 5.7.1951, Avranches et Desmarets, Rec., 638*). This *exception d'illégalité* is permitted so as to avoid undue delays in the criminal process.

(b) Regionalisation and specialisation of the courts

A feature of the court system is the degree of regionalisation. Although the supreme courts of the ordinary (*Cour de Cassation*) and administrative (*Conseil d'Etat*) systems are located in Paris (as well as the *Tribunal des Conflits* and the *Conseil Constitutionnel*), lower courts, both first instance and appeal, are located throughout the country. There are thus in metropolitan France some 175 *Tribunaux de Grande Instance* and 30

Cours d'Appel, and in the administrative court system 26 *Tribunaux Administratifs* and 5 *Cours Administratives d'Appel*.

Courts are also classified according to whether their competence is general or special. Courts of general jurisdiction, having competence to deal with cases which are not specifically assigned to another court, are known as *juridictions de droit commun*, for example, the higher first instance civil courts (*Tribunaux de Grande Instance*) and the first instance administrative courts (*Tribunaux Administratifs*). In contrast, the courts of special competence (*juridictions d'exception*; also known as *juridictions spécialisées*) are competent to hear only those categories of cases which are assigned to them by statute. Such courts include the *Tribunaux d'Instance*, the *Tribunaux de Commerce* and the *Conseils de Prud'hommes*.

(c) Second level of jurisdiction; appel

A central feature of the organisation of the ordinary courts is that there are two levels of jurisdiction (*le principe du double degré de juridiction*). This system was introduced by the revolutionaries in an endeavour to ensure that justice was done in any given case. As a result of this principle, appeal (ie *appel*) from a decision of the first instance court, whether civil or criminal, takes the form of a rehearing by the *Cour d'Appel*. This is a guarantee against not only errors of law but also errors of fact by the trial court. A similar principle also applies in the administrative court system.

In the ordinary court system, appeal lies from all first instance courts to the *Cour d'Appel*, but only where the case involves more than 13,000 FF (currently 18,200 FF for appeals from the *Conseil de Prud'hommes*). Where no appeal lies, the first instance courts thus act as courts of first and last resort (*premier et dernier ressort*); however, appeal by way of *pourvoi en cassation* may still lie to the *Cour de Cassation* (see below). No such monetary limits apply to appeals in the administrative court system; depending on the type of case, appeal from a decision of a *Tribunal Administratif* lies either to a *Cour Administrative d'Appel* or directly to the *Conseil d'Etat* (see below).

2. Ordinary courts

(a) First instance civil courts

(i) Tribunaux de grande instance

There are a total of 175 *Tribunaux de Grande Instance* in metropolitan France, at least one in each of the 96 *départements*. In principle, a civil action is started in the *Tribunal de Grande Instance* of the jurisdiction where the defendant resides or, in the case of a corporation, where it is registered or has its registered office (*Nouveau Code de Procédure Civile*,

Arts. 42, 43: TEXTS, NO. 2).There are exceptions to this principle.

The *Tribunal de Grande Instance* has competence for civil claims exceeding 30,000 FF which are not by statute expressly assigned to other courts (*Code de l'Organisation Judiciaire, Art.R. 311–1*). However, the *Tribunal* has exclusive competence, whatever the amount involved, in respect of certain civil matters, such as real property, intellectual property, and cases on personal status (*l'état des personnes*) such as nationality, adoption, affiliation, and divorce.

Some *Tribunaux de Grande Instance* have a very large number of judges (eg 80 in Marseille, 200 in Paris). The *"TGI"* deals not just with civil matters, but also with criminal matters (intermediate offences, *délits*), sitting as the *Tribunal Correctionnel* (see below). In the smaller courts, the same judges deal with both civil and criminal cases. In the larger courts, there are several specialised criminal divisions (*chambres correctionnelles*). Furthermore, it is from the ranks of the *Tribunaux de Grande Instance* judges that examining magistrates (*juges d'instruction*: see Chapter 5) are drawn. Where a *TGI* has more than five judges, it will be divided into divisions (*chambres*), each having a certain degree of specialisation.

Unless otherwise provided, three judges sit. However, a single judge is appointed to deal with certain cases involving minors (*le juge des enfants*), and another to deal with divorce and separation cases (*le juge délégué aux affaires matrimoniales (JAM)*). Additionally, a single judge (known as *le juge de la mise en état*) will oversee the pre-trial procedure of a civil case; interlocutory matters are dealt with by a single judge, *le juge des référés* or *le juge de la mise en état*; see Chapter 6. Furthermore, the president of the court may decide (*Code de l'Organisation Judiciaire, Art.L. 311–10*) that a case (with some exceptions, such as a case relating to *l'état des personnes* (see above)) be tried by a sole judge. This he might do, for example, where he considers the case to be insufficiently complex to justify trial by the full court. However, the parties can always insist on trial by a full court of three judges. It should also be noted that a single judge (*le juge de l'exécution*) deals with matters of execution of judgments (*Code de l'Org. Jud., Art.L. 311–12; loi du 9.7.1991*).

The court generally sits in public (*en audience publique*) although it may decide to sit behind closed doors (*en chambre du conseil*) in sensitive cases such as divorce and affiliation cases. Appeal lies to the *Cour d'Appel*, as with all first instance civil courts, but generally only where the case involves more than 13,000 FF. In 1989, 460,022 cases were heard by the *Tribunaux de Grande Instance*.

(ii) Tribunaux d'Instance

Since 1958, small civil claims have been dealt with by the *Tribunaux d'Instance*. These courts replaced the earlier system of civil justices of the peace (*juges de paix*). The latter were often drawn from the ranks of respected members of the local community rather than being trained lawyers; indeed, a legal qualification was not a requirement until 1926. The *Tribunaux d'Instance* also sit as the *Tribunaux de Police* to deal with minor criminal offences (*contraventions*); again, in small courts the same judges exercise civil and criminal functions, although there is more specialisation in the larger courts. There are a total of some 470 *Tribunaux d'Instance*.

Judges are appointed to the *Tribunaux d'Instance* for a three-year renewable period from the ranks of the judiciary of the local *Tribunaux de Grande Instance*. A differing number of judges are appointed to each *Tribunal d'Instance* depending on the work-load of the court. Cases are heard by a judge sitting alone; this is an exception to the general principle that judgments should be collegiate.

The *Tribunaux d'Instance* are competent to hear civil claims not exceeding 30,000 FF not specifically assigned by statute to another jurisdiction. In addition, the *TI* have been given specific competence by statute for many particular matters (for example, residential leaseholds). A typical work-load includes contract cases, and minor claims in delict. 480,624 cases were dealt with by the *Tribunaux d'Instance* in 1989. Appeal lies to the *Cour d'Appel*, usually only where the case involves more than 13,000 FF.

(iii) Tribunaux de Commerce

The *Tribunaux de Commerce*, which hear commercial cases (defined below), are the longest standing courts in the French legal system, having been introduced in 1563. Of all the courts of the *Ancien Régime*, they alone managed to survive the Revolution, being retained by the *loi du 16–24.8.1790*. The members of the bench are not professional judges, but are members of the business community elected to the position by their fellows on an unpaid basis for a limited period. They are often known as *juges consulaires*. Within Alsace-Lorraine a different system applies, commercial cases being heard by a special division of the *Tribunal de Grande Instance* (*chambre commerciale*), with a judge assisted by business people acting as assessors. A court of mixed composition such as this is known as a system of *échevinage* (cf the *scabini* of the Middle Ages).

Tribunaux de Commerce have over the years been set up in areas which, due to the level of business activity, have needed them; there is therefore no uniform system throughout France. Major commercial centres have several tribunals (thus in the *département* of Loire-Atlantique, there are tribunals both in Nantes and St. Nazaire). In other areas (eg the *département* of Haute-Savoie) there are none; where this is so, any commercial matters will be heard by the local *Tribunal de Grande Instance*. There are some 230 *Tribunaux de Commerce* in metropolitan France, with a total of over 2,500 judges. The *Tribunaux* are classified as either minor or major; only the latter are competent to deal with cases of insolvency of large businesses (ie those having more than 50 employees or a turnover exceeding 20 million FF).

The *Tribunaux* are competent to hear "commercial" matters; these are defined (*Code de Commerce, Art. 631*) as including: (i) litigation between traders (*commerçants*) relating to their commercial activities; (ii) disputes relating to activities and transactions of a commercial nature (*actes de commerce*). Some instruments, eg bills of exchange (*lettres de change*), are regarded as inherently commercial by nature; therefore any disputes relating to a bill of exchange are dealt with by the commercial court, regardless of the status of the parties. What happens if the *acte* is commercial for one of the parties only – for example, a contract between a *commerçant* and a non-*commerçant*? If the *acte* is commercial for the plaintiff only, he can sue the defendant only in the ordinary civil courts. Where, however, the *acte* is commercial for the defendant only, the plaintiff may sue either in the ordinary courts or in the *Tribunal de Commerce*; (iii) litigation involving the shareholders of a commercial corporation (*société commerciale*); (iv) matters relating to the judicial supervision, receivership and winding up (*liquidation*) of artisans, *commerçants* and commercial corporations. Where the corporation involved is non-commercial (eg *sociétés civiles*), such cases are heard by the *Tribunal de Grande Instance*. Recourse to arbitration, rather than the *Tribunaux de Commerce*, is possible by means of an arbitration clause (see Chapter 6).

The number of judges in each *Tribunal de Commerce* is fixed by decree, and depends on the level of economic activity of the region (thus in the Paris *Tribunal* there are over 140). At least three judges sit when trying a case, although interlocutory matters may be dealt with by the president sitting alone *en référé*, or by a *juge rapporteur* (see Chapter 6). Judges are elected by an electoral college of representatives (known as *délégués consulaires*) elected by *commerçants*, heads of business, and past and present members of the *Tribunaux de Commerce* and Chambers of Commerce. Anyone over 29 years of age who has carried out a commercial activity for at least five years and who is on the list of voters for *délégués consulaires* is eligible for election as a *juge consulaire*. Election is for an initial term of two years, then for renewable terms of four years (although, after fourteen years' continuous service, a sabbatical of twelve months must be taken).

Disciplinary matters are dealt with, since a *loi du 16.7.1987*, by a national disciplinary council. *Juges consulaires* do not have the status of professional judges or the guarantee of independence and prospect of advancement that go with it. An advantage of lay judges is their expertise in commercial and economic activity. This is particularly useful when having to make decisions not strictly based on legal considerations (eg when determining the best way to supervise a company in financial difficulty). However, it does mean that their knowledge of commercial law may be limited, there being no requirement of having had a legal education. The *juges consulaires* do however have the assistance of the clerk of the court (*greffier*) who in addition to his secretarial function organises the *Registre du Commerce et des Sociétés* (on which traders register, whether sole or corporate traders) and other commercial registers.

The *Tribunaux de Commerce* heard 190,275 cases in 1989. Appeal (*appel*) lies to the *Cour d'Appel* in the normal way (if the case involves more than 13,000 FF).

(iv) Conseils de Prud'hommes

These courts deal largely with disputes relating to contracts of employment and apprenticeship. They have a double role of conciliation and judgment. Their judges (known as *conseillers prud'hommes*) are elected by management and workers. The courts were created in 1806, on the initiative of Napoleon himself, taking as a model a similar jurisdiction which had existed in the *Ancien Régime* (originating amongst the silk traders of Lyon) and which had been abolished during the Revolution.

Conseils de Prud'hommes were set up whenever and wherever the economic activity of the area required them; they therefore covered only about one-fifth of the territory of France. In 1979, a reform (*loi du 18.1.1979*) provided that there should be at least one *Conseil de Prud'hommes* attached to every *Tribunal de Grande Instance*. In some industrial areas, however, there are several; currently the total number is 282. A system of *échevinage* (see above) particular to Alsace-Lorraine was abolished in 1982. A *conseil supérieur de la prud'homie* has an advisory and consultative role (reporting particularly to the Ministry of Justice and the Ministry of Employment) in respect of the functioning of the courts and the appointment of the *conseillers prud'hommes*.

The competence of the *Conseils de Prud'hommes* was widened by the 1979 statute. Earlier rules limiting competence to certain defined sectors have been abolished. The *Conseils* now have sole competence (no recourse to arbitration being permitted) to deal with all disputes relating to contracts of employment and apprenticeship, whatever the amount involved, both in the private sector and the public sector (where there are private sector conditions of work). They thus hear cases relating to unfair dismissal (*licenciement*), redundancy (*licenciement pour motif économique*), and individual salary disputes. They do not have competence in respect of collective disputes (such as strikes or collective bargaining) or matters relating to employee participation in management, which are dealt with by the ordinary civil courts.

All *conseillers prud'hommes* are directly elected for a renewable five-year term. As a *tribunal paritaire*, a *Conseil de Prud'hommes* is composed of different but equal elements. An equal number of *conseillers prud'hommes* are thus elected (by proportional representation) by two separate electoral colleges: a college of employers (which includes managers exercising the responsibilities of an employer) and a college of employees (and apprentices aged at least 16). Any French national who is over 21 years of age and who is enrolled on the voting list for *conseillers prud'hommes* (whether as employer or employee) is eligible to stand for election as *conseiller prud'homme*.

Employee *conseillers prud'hommes* are given statutory protection from dismissal for being absent from the workplace to fulfil their judicial functions. Nor do they suffer any loss of pay, the state compensating the employer for the lost man-hours. They are also entitled to two weeks' study leave each year to attend training courses. Employer *conseillers prud'hommes* receive financial compensation for time spent attending to their judicial activities.

Each *Conseil de Prud'hommes* is divided into five autonomous specialist sections (each comprising at least four employer and four employee *conseillers prud'hommes*) covering the range of business activity (ie management, industry, commerce, agriculture and miscellaneous). This enables the specialist knowledge that the *conseillers prud'hommes* have of differing customs and practices to be used to best effect. Their specialist knowledge also increases the authority of their decisions.

A case is initially referred to a *bureau de conciliation* of the relevant section, comprising one employer *conseiller* and one employee *conseiller*, in an attempt to resolve the matter by conciliation (see Chapter 6). If conciliation proves to be impossible, the matter is referred to the *bureau de jugement*, comprising two employer *conseillers* and two employee *conseillers*, which will try the case at a public hearing. The parties may be represented at either stage. Where the *bureau de jugement* cannot reach a majority verdict, a *juge d'instance* is brought in to sit with the *bureau de jugement* and break the deadlock. Interlocutory matters may be dealt with by a *formation de référée*, although the *ureaux de conciliation* have certain important interlocutory powers.

The *Conseils de Prud'hommes* dealt with 148,970 cases in 1989. Appeal lies to the *Cour d'Appel*, but only where the case involves more than 18,200 FF (1992 figures).

(v) Tribunaux des Affaires de Sécurité Sociale

General social security matters are heard by *Tribunaux des Affaires de Sécurité Sociale*, of which there are some 110 throughout France. These courts are an example of the *échevinage* system, comprising a president, who is a *juge du Tribunal de Grande Instance* (appointed by the *Cour d'Appel* for a three-year term), and two lay assessors, one representing salaried employees, the other the self-employed and employers. The assessors are appointed for a three-year term by the president of the *Cour d'Appel* from a list approved by the social security authorities, the candidates' names having been put forward by organisations representing employers and employees, and social security organisations. Assessors are given the statutory right to attend to their judicial functions during working hours. The *Tribunaux des Affaires de Sécurité Sociale* dealt with 109,465 cases in 1989. Appeal is to the *Cour d'Appel* for cases involving more than 13,000 FF.

Certain technical social security matters, such as the assessment of the degree of invalidity and capacity to work, are dealt with by *commissions régionales* of the regional social security authorities, comprising the regional director (as chairman), medical experts and representatives of both employers and employees. Appeals are heard by a *commission nationale technique* whose president is a judge.

(vi) Tribunaux Paritaires des Baux Ruraux

These courts have jurisdiction for agricultural tenancy cases. There is, in theory, one attached to each of the 470 *Tribunaux d'Instance*; however, some of the latter have exclusively urban jurisdictions, and therefore the total number of *Tribunaux Paritaires des Baux Ruraux* is only 412. They are presided over by a *juge du Tribunal d'Instance* who sits with four assessors elected for a five-year term, two representing agricultural landlords (*bailleurs*), two agricultural tenants (*preneurs*). As with the *Conseils de Prud'hommes*, there is an obligation for the court to call the parties to attend with a view to conciliation before proceeding to a full hearing of the issue. The court does not sit in permanent session, but only when business requires it to do so. The existence of a special court to deal solely with agricultural tenancies, when there are a far greater number of disputes in relation to residential and business leases, which are heard by the ordinary courts, has been much criticised.

(b) First instance criminal courts

(i) Introduction

Depending on their seriousness, offences are tried in one of three different criminal courts. Minor offences (*contraventions*) are tried before a single judge in the *Tribunal de Police* (in effect this is the *Tribunal d'Instance* exercising criminal jurisdiction). Intermediate offences (*délits*) are tried before a panel of three judges of the *Tribunal de Grande Instance* sitting as the *Tribunal Correctionnel*. Serious offences (*crimes*) are tried by a panel of three judges and a jury of nine in the *Cour d'Assises* (which has no direct civil equivalent, comprising judges from the *Cour d'Appel* and *Tribunaux de Grande Instance*). Appeal (*appel*) lies against decisions of the *Tribunaux de Police* and *Tribunaux Correctionnels* to the *Cour d'Appel*, where the case will be retried, but the jury decisions of the *Cour d'Assises* are not subject to appeal in this way, although appeal on a point of law (*pourvoi en cassation*) may lie to the *Cour de Cassation*.

When examining the criminal court structure, the inquisitorial nature of French criminal procedure should be borne in mind (see Chapter 5).

With regard to *crimes* and certain *délits*, after initial police enquiries have been carried out, the case will be passed on to an examining magistrate, the *juge d'instruction*, who will question the accused and witnesses and collate all the evidence, and determine whether or not to send the matter for trial. In respect of *crimes*, the case will then be sent by the *juge d'instruction* for a second level of *instruction* to the *chambre d'accusation* of the *Cour d'Appel* before proceeding to trial in the *Cour d'Assises*. The examining magistrate will not participate in the trial itself, the functions of *instruction* and *jugement* being separate. The *juridictions d'instruction* (ie the *juge d'instruction* and the *chambre d'accusation*) are usually considered in France in the context of criminal jurisdictions; however, they will be studied not in this chapter but in the context of criminal procedure (see Chapter 5).

(ii) Tribunaux de Police

As has already been stated, these are the *Tribunaux d'Instance* sitting to hear minor criminal cases, *contraventions*. In certain courts, the judges deal partly with civil, and partly with criminal cases. However, in most *Tribunaux d'Instance* certain judges specialise in criminal matters.

(iii) Tribunaux Correctionnels

The *Tribunal Correctionnel* is in effect the criminal division of a *Tribunal de Grande Instance*; it has jurisdiction to try intermediate offences (*délits*). In the larger *Tribunaux de Grande Instance*, one or more *chambres correctionnels* are created specifically to exercise this criminal jurisdiction. There is also one *Tribunal Correctionnel* within the jurisdiction of each *Cour d'Appel* which is designated to have exclusive jurisdiction in respect of certain offences involving complex financial dealings (*Code de Procédure Pénale, Arts. 704, 705*); these include cases concerned with fraud, tax, customs, banking and company law offences − judges specialising in financial and economic matters try such cases.

The *Tribunal Correctionnel*, in accordance with the collegiate principle, normally comprises three judges. However, in an endeavour to increase the efficiency of the court, recourse may be had to a single judge in respect of particular offences, such as those relating to cheques, motor vehicle insurance and the offence of causing death whilst driving a vehicle (*ibid., Arts. 398, 398−1*). Within each *Tribunal Correctionnel*, a judge is designated (for a three-year renewable period) to act as *juge de l'application des peines*, dealing with matters relating to the execution of sentences of imprisonment.

(iv) Cours d'Assises

The *Cour d'Assises* tries serious offences (*crimes*). There is one for Paris and for each *département*, sitting usually in the chief town or city (*chef-lieu*). It must sit at least once every three months, each session lasting for as long as the work-load requires. In Paris the court is practically in permanent session. Those selected to serve as jurors serve for a session. The bench is designated every three months by the president of the *Cour d'Appel*; it comprises a president (a judge of the *Cour d'Appel*) and two assessors (judges of the *Cour d'Appel* or the *Tribunal de Grande Instance*). The bench of three and jury of nine together determine both culpability and sentence. The selection of the jury, court procedure and appeals are examined in Chapter 5.

(v) First instance criminal courts of special jurisdiction (juridictions pénales spécialisées)

Juvenile courts (Tribunaux pour Enfants; Cours d'Assises des Mineurs): Offenders under the age of 18 are dealt with in special juvenile courts. These are usually the *Tribunaux pour Enfants*, but serious cases involving older juveniles are dealt with in the *Cours d'Assises des Mineurs. Instruction* is carried out (in respect of a wider range of offences than is the case for adult offenders) either by an examining magistrate or by a *juge des enfants* (see below), a second level of *instruction* taking place before the *chambre d'accusation* in respect of *crimes*.

The proceedings of the juvenile courts take place in camera. The sanctions which the courts are empowered to impose on juvenile offenders depend on the age of the offender. No criminal penalties can be imposed on those under 13, only "educational measures". Criminal sanctions are available in respect of those aged between 13 and 18 where required by the circumstances of the offence and the background of the offender; even here, if the offender is under 16 years of age, the maximum penalties are one half of those which can be imposed on an adult. Where the offender is aged between 16 and 18, the court has a discretion as to whether or not to limit the sentence in this way.

There is at least one *Tribunal pour Enfants* in each *département*; the current total is 129. They are autonomous courts, although related administratively to the *Tribunaux de Grande Instance*. They are competent to hear all cases involving juveniles aged under 16 (at the date of the commission of the offence) whatever the seriousness of the offence, and cases of *contraventions* (of Class 5, the most serious; lesser *contraventions* are dealt with by the *Tribunal de Police*) and *délits* for juveniles aged 16–18. The bench of three judges comprises a *juge des enfants* (who is a *juge du Tribunal de Grande Instance*) and two assessors who are not professional judges, but lay persons who are appointed to the position (by the Ministry of Justice on a four-year term) being French nationals of at least 30 years of age who have displayed an interest in issues affecting juveniles.

The *juge des enfants* also has a certain civil jurisdiction in respect of minors; for example, by Article 375 of the Civil Code, where the health, safety or morality of a minor is endangered or the conditions of his education are seriously compromised, the judge may take appropriate measures to protect the child.

The *Cour d'Assises des Mineurs* tries juveniles aged 16 to 18 who are charged with having committed a *crime*. It is essentially the same body as the ordinary *Cour d'Assises*, with a bench of three judges (a president and two assessors) and a jury of nine. However, the assessors will normally be *juges des enfants*.

(vi) Haute Cour de Justice

This is a political court of constitutional origin (*Constitution de 1958, Arts. 67, 68;* CHAPTER 4 TEXTS, NO. 1) whose role is to try cases of high treason (which is not defined) by the President of the Republic, and *crimes* and *délits* committed by members of the government in the exercise of their functions. A prosecution is commenced not by the prosecution service (*le ministère public*), but by motion passed in identical terms by both houses of Parliament; for the motion to be put to the vote in the first place it needs to be signed by at least one-tenth of the members of the chamber. *Instruction* is then carried out by a commission of five judges of the *Cour de Cassation*. The 24 judges of the *Haute Cour de Justice* are appointed, by both houses of Parliament, from the ranks of the parliamentarians of the National Assembly and the Senate. They determine both culpability and sentence. The proceedings of the court may be ordered to take place in camera. No appeal against the decisions of the court is possible. No case has ever actually proceeded to trial in the *Haute Cour de Justice*.

(c) Cours d'Appel

As has been seen above, the appeals system is designed to weed out both errors of law and errors of fact committed by the first instance courts; this is achieved by appeals to the *Cour d'Appel* taking the form of a rehearing of the case, the court hearing the evidence for itself. The *Cours d'Appel* have jurisdiction to hear appeals (by way of *appel*), where they lie, from civil and criminal first instance courts. Grounds of appeal and the way in which the court rehears the case are examined in more detail in the context of criminal and civil procedure (see Chapters 5 and 6).

There are currently 30 *Cours d'Appel* in metropolitan France, often situated in the towns where the *Parlements* of the *Ancien Régime* sat. The jurisdiction of each almost always straddles several *départements*; there is thus only one *Cour d'Appel* for Brittany, sitting at Rennes, the jurisdiction of which covers the *départements* of Loire-Atlantique, Ille-et-Vilaine, Morbihan, Côtes-du-Nord and Finistère.

The *Cour d'Appel* hears appeals from civil and criminal first instance courts within its territorial jurisdiction. There are, however, exceptions.

Firstly, in respect of criminal matters, no appeal (*appel*) lies against the decisions of the *Cour d'Assises*, the sanctity of jury decisions being respected (although *pourvoi en cassation* may lie to the *Cour de Cassation*; see below). Also by way of exception, no appeal in principle lies in a civil case against decisions of the first instance courts where small claims are involved; in 1989 the minimum figure was 13,000 FF (18,200 FF for appeals from decisions of the *Conseils de Prud'hommes* (1992 figures)). Below this figure the first instance court is a court of "first and last resort", although *pourvoi en cassation* to the *Cour de Cassation* may be available.

The appeal court judges are experienced career judges who have risen through the ranks; they are known as *conseillers* (as were the judges in the *Parlements* of the *Ancien Régime*). Each *Cour d'Appel* has at least three judges (two *conseillers* and a *premier président*) and will usually have several divisions (*chambres*), each having its own president; that of Paris has 25 *chambres* and a total complement of over 180 judges.

There is usually at least one civil and one criminal division, and one *chambre sociale* dealing with social security appeals and with appeals from the *Conseils de Prud'hommes*. There may also be a *chambre commerciale*. A judge may belong to more than one division concurrently. The criminal division includes a *chambre d'accusation*, and a *chambre des appels correctionnels*. Criminal appeals from decisions of the *Tribunaux de Police* and the *Tribunaux Correctionnels* are heard by the *chambre des appels correctionnels*, appeals from juvenile courts by the *chambre spéciale*. The *chambre d'accusation* consists of a president and two *conseillers*, and carries out a second tier of *instruction* into *crimes* before they are sent for trial in the *Cour d'Assises*, and also hears appeals against certain orders of *juges d'instruction*. In addition, its jurisdiction includes matters of extradition and disciplinary cases involving judicial police functions (see Chapter 5).

When dealing with ordinary appeals, the *Cour d'Appel* consists of three judges (*en audience ordinaire*). However, when sitting to hear a case which has been referred to it after *cassation* by the *Cour de Cassation* (see below), the court sits more formally (*en audience solonnelle*), with a bench of five judges from two divisions. The first president of the *Cour d'Appel* has the power, sitting alone, to make decisions on certain interlocutory matters (see Chapter 6).

The *Cours d'Appel* heard 163,973 civil and 43,683 criminal appeals in 1989.

(d) Cour de Cassation

The *Cour de Cassation*, which sits in Paris, is the supreme court of the "ordinary" court hierarchy. It was instituted in 1790 as the *Tribunal de Cassation*, being the successor of the *Conseil des Parties* (a division of the *Conseil du Roi*), which had heard appeals from decisions of the

Parlements of the *Ancien Régime*. It hears civil and criminal appeals on a point of law only (by way of *pourvoi en cassation*) from courts of "last resort" (see *Nouveau Code de Procédure Civile, Art. 605*); ie from the decisions of the *Cours d'Appel* (in civil and criminal matters) and the *Cours d'Assises* (in respect of *crimes*). However, it also includes reference from decisions of first instance civil courts against which no *appel* lies to the *Cours d'Appel*; ie decisions involving less than 13,000 FF (18,200 FF in cases from the *Conseils de Prud'hommes*). As there are a substantial number of *Cours d'Appel* (30 in metropolitan France), the *Cour de Cassation* has a particular role in ensuring the uniform interpretation and application of the law throughout France, thereby upholding the constitutional principle of the equality of all citizens before the law.

A *pourvoi en cassation* lies in criminal matters on the grounds that the decision of the lower court was contrary to the law (*violation de la loi; Code de Procédure Pénale, Art. 591*). *Article 593* goes on to specify that a decision will be quashed if it is not reasoned, or the reasons are insufficient to enable the *Cour de Cassation* to exercise its control and determine whether or not the law has been respected. Criminal *pourvois en cassation* are examined in more detail in Chapter 5. In civil matters *pourvoi en cassation* lies (*Nouveau Code de Procédure Civile, Art. 604*) on the grounds that the judgment of the lower court does not conform to the law (see Chapter 6). A *pourvoi en cassation* must be lodged within five days of the notification of the judgment in criminal matters (*Code de Procédure Pénale, Art. 568*) or within two months of the judgment complained of in civil matters (*Nouveau Code de Procédure Civile, Art. 612*).

If the *Cour de Cassation* is of the opinion that the lower court correctly applied the law, it will reject the appeal (*rejet du pourvoi*). If not, the decision of the lower court will be quashed (*cassation* or *censure*). However, the *Cour* cannot substitute its own decision for the decision that it has quashed; it therefore usually refers the matter back (*renvoi*) for reconsideration not to the court from which the *pourvoi* originated, but to a different court of the same type and level in the hierarchy (*Code de l'Organisation Judiciaire, Art.L. 131 – 4*). *Cassation* without *renvoi* is possible in certain exceptional circumstances (*ibid, Art.L. 131 – 5*), for example where the reason for *cassation* was that a claim had become statute barred.

When a case is referred down following *cassation*, usually in practice to a *Cour d'Appel*, the latter will retry the case on both facts and law in respect of the issues raised at *cassation* (see *Nouveau Code de Procédure Civile, Art. 638*); indeed, the parties may even raise new arguments (*moyens; ibid, Art. 632*). It should be noted that the court retrying the case (known as the *juridiction de renvoi*) is not bound to apply the interpretation of the law set out in the decision of the *Cour de Cassation*. This may of course lead to a second *pourvoi en cassation*, which will be heard by the *Cour de Cassation* sitting more formally (*en assemblée plénière*). If it again decides to quash the decision of the lower court on the same grounds as before, the matter will be sent to a third court of equivalent status, which this time, although still accorded liberty in respect of its appreciation of the facts, is bound to implement the interpretation of the law as set out by the *Cour de Cassation*. As will be seen in Chapters 5 and 6, recourse may also be had to the *Cour de Cassation* by way of *pourvoi en révision*, a procedure which enables a decision to be reviewed; in criminal procedure this permits the review of allegedly wrongful convictions.

The organisation of the *Cour de Cassation* has been the subject of several reforms designed to enable it to deal with the increasing number of cases referred to it in recent years (in 1990 it heard 18,613 civil and 7,338 criminal appeals; compared with a 1976 total of 10,598 cases). The *Cour* is divided into six divisions (*chambres*): one criminal and five civil. Of the latter, three are *chambres civiles*, each of which specialises in a particular aspect of civil law (the first in contract, insurance, the law of persons and international law, the second in delict, divorce and civil procedure, and the third in the law of property). There is also a *chambre commerciale et financière* and a *chambre sociale*.

The *Cour de Cassation* currently comprises a total of 128 judges: a first president (who, in addition to his judicial and administrative functions, presides in the *Conseil supérieur de la magistrature* when dealing with disciplinary matters), 6 divisional presidents, 84 *conseillers*, and 37 *conseillers référendaires* (who are assistant judges appointed for a non-renewable term of up to ten years). There are also some 18 *auditeurs*, who are young judges with purely administrative responsibilities. The *loi organique du 25.2.1992 (Art. 36)* has created (*inter alia*) the post of *conseiller à la Cour de Cassation en service extraordinaire*. *Conseillers* are appointed to act for a non-renewable term of five years.

The usual composition of the *Cour de Cassation* when hearing a case is five judges. It is possible, however, for the first president or the divisional president to refer cases which appear straightforward to a bench of three judges (*la formation restreinte*), although this happens only rarely. The *Cour* will sit *en chambre mixte* where a case raises a question of law which comes within the competence of more than one division, or where the question has been or might be answered differently by different divisions (*Code de l'Organisation Judiciaire, Art.L. 131–2*). The *chambre mixte* comprises representation (the divisional president and three *conseillers*) from at least three divisions, presided over by the first president (ie a minimum of 13 judges). A decision to send the case before the *chambre mixte* may be taken either by the first president, or by the divisional president, or by the *procureur général*. The most formal composition of the *Cour de Cassation* is the *assemblée plénière*, comprising a total of 25 judges: the *premier président* and four representatives (including the divisional presidents) from each of the six divisions. Recourse is had to the *assemblée plénière* when a case involves a question of principle (usually where an issue which has given rise to a divergence of opinion between the different *Cours d'Appel* needs to be resolved) or when a case which has previously come before the *Cour de Cassation* is subject to a second *pourvoi* (see above).

Where a lower court is faced with a novel point of law (eg the interpretation of a new statute) which is likely to present serious difficulties and which has arisen in several cases, it may (*loi du 15.5.1991; Code de l'Org. Jud., Arts. L. 151 – 1 to 151 – 3;* also *décret du 12.3.1992*), before giving its judgment, refer the matter to the *Cour de Cassation* for advice. (Such a reference is not permitted from the criminal courts.) The question will be examined, within three months, by the *Cour de Cassation* comprising the first president, the divisional presidents, and two *conseillers* from the divisions which are particularly concerned. The court from which the reference came is not in theory bound to follow the opinion given by the *Cour de Cassation*, but in practice its opinion is likely to be followed.

A special formation of the *Cour de Cassation*, the *Commission nationale d'indemnisation en matière de détention provisoire*, deals with claims for compensation for unjustified detention pending a trial resulting in an acquittal (see Chapter 5).

3. Administrative courts

(a) Introduction

We have already seen that the *Conseil d'Etat* has both judicial and administrative functions. In the former role it is the supreme court of the administrative court system. In the latter (acting through its administrative, rather than judicial divisions), it acts as the legal adviser to the government, and is involved in the process of drafting government bills. For many years it was the administrative court with general competence (*juridiction de droit commun*) to deal with administrative cases. However, its increasing work-load (giving rise to an average waiting list of some four years in the early 1950s) led to the transformation in 1953 of the *Conseils de Préfecture* into first instance administrative courts of general competence, becoming the *Tribunaux Administratifs*. In 1989 an intermediate level of court was introduced, the *Cours Administratives d'Appel*. There are also specialised administrative jurisdictions (see below). The *Conseil d'Etat* therefore now exercises the role of the supreme court of the administrative court system; however, it continues to act as a first instance court in respect of some types of administrative cases.

(b) Tribunaux Administratifs

There are 26 *Tribunaux Administratifs* in metropolitan France. Their territorial jurisdiction covers several *départements*, and is sometimes based on the administrative regions; the Nantes *Tribunal Administratif*, for example, has competence for cases originating in five *départements*: Loire-Atlantique, Vendée, Maine-et-Loire, Sarthe and Mayenne, together comprising the region of the *Pays de la Loire*.

The *Tribunaux Administratifs* perform essentially judicial functions; although they may be consulted on legal matters by the prefect, in practice this rarely happens. More importantly, they have general jurisdiction to hear at first instance any administrative case (defined above) where jurisdiction is not by statute conferred on another court.

The judges are known as *conseillers*. The majority are appointed from the graduates of the *Ecole nationale d'administration* (see below). A certain number are recruited directly from the ranks of experienced civil servants. Each *Tribunal Administratif* comprises at least one president and two *conseillers*. The more important *Tribunaux* have between two and five divisions, each with three judges. A case is usually dealt with by one division, but all divisions may sit together (*en formation plénière*) to hear important cases. The president of the *Tribunal* is empowered to deal with interlocutory matters alone as *juge des référés administratifs*; in addition, a few minor cases (such as some tax matters) may be dealt with by a *conseiller délégué*. The *Tribunal Administratif* of Paris has 14 divisions (arranged in 7 sections) to deal with its large case-load; cases are heard either by a division, or by a section (comprising a section president and four *conseillers*), or by the *formation plénière* of the president of the *Tribunal* and all 7 section presidents.

In 1991 the *Tribunaux* heard 70,819 cases. Appeal is either to the *Cours Administratives d'Appel* or directly to the *Conseil d'Etat*, depending on the type of action involved; in addition, appeal by way of *recours en cassation* lies to the *Conseil d'Etat* (see below).

(c) Cours Administratives d'Appel

The backlog of cases waiting to be heard by the *Conseil d'Etat* (there was a waiting list of some two years by the mid-1980s) led to the creation by the *loi du 31.12.1987* of a set of interregional administrative courts of appeal to which certain appeals from the *Tribunal Administratif* are now directed.

Each of the five *Cours Administratives d'Appel* (situated at Paris, Bordeaux, Lyon, Nancy and Nantes) has a wide territorial jurisdiction extending over several regions; for example, that of Nantes hears appeals from the *Tribunaux Administratifs* of Nantes, Rennes, Orléans, Caen and Rouen, a total of 20 *départements*.

These courts are competent to hear certain appeals (by way of *appel*) from the *Tribunaux Administratifs*. Although there is no requirement that the case must involve more than a certain pecuniary amount as there is in the ordinary courts – certain categories of *appel* continue to be made directly to the *Conseil d'Etat* from the *Tribunaux Administratifs*. These categories are appeals in respect of disputes in local elections (municipal and cantonal) and those relating to the category of administrative action known as *recours pour excès de pouvoir* in respect of regulations of general effect. The *Cours Administratives d'Appel* have jurisdiction to hear appeals in respect of matters other than those made directly to the *Conseil d'Etat*; for example, *recours pour excès de pouvoir* in respect of administrative decisions of individual effect, actions for damages (*recours de pleine juridiction*), and decisions in respect of certain "highway" offences (*contraventions de grande voirie*) on public property (*le domaine public*) other than roads; as to the different types of administrative action (*recours*), see Chapter 6. The jurisdiction of the *Cours Administratives d'Appel* is being progressively extended to include appeals in respect of *recours pour excès de pouvoir*.

The judges of the *Cours Administratives d'Appel*, also known as *conseillers,* are appointed from the *conseillers* of the *Tribunaux Administratifs*. The *Cours* of Nantes, Nancy and Bordeaux have three divisions, those of Lyon and Paris four. Cases are usually heard by a division comprising the divisional president, two *conseillers* of that division and one *conseiller* of another. More important cases go before a full court of the president of the *Cour* (who is *conseiller d'Etat*) and five other *conseillers*, including the divisional presidents. Interlocutory matters are heard by the president of the *Cour* sitting alone.

As with the civil appeal courts, appeal takes the form of a rehearing, the appeal court having the same powers as the first instance court. It is seized of the case as a whole (*plénitude de juridiction*), although the appellant may decide to limit the *appel* to certain issues.

There is no appeal as such (ie *appel*) from decisions of the *Cours Administratives d'Appel* to the *Conseil d'Etat*, although *recours en cassation* to the *Conseil* does lie. The 1987 law also permits references from a *Cour Administrative d'Appel* to the *Conseil d'Etat* when the former finds itself confronted by a "new question of law presenting a serious difficulty and being raised in numerous cases"; the *Cours*, before announcing its judgment, obtains the opinion of the *Conseil* on the point; it is not bound by this opinion, but is likely to follow it (or risk its judgment being overturned on a *recours en cassation*).

(d) Le Conseil d'Etat

(i) Introduction

The *Conseil d'Etat* occupies a central position within the administrative system. Not only is it the supreme administrative court, but it is also adviser to the government; for this reason it is divided into administrative and judicial sections (see below). As government adviser it has a particular role in the drafting of government legislation; its advice must be sought (although not necessarily followed) in respect of government bills (*Constitution de 1958, Art. 39*; CHAPTER 4 TEXTS, NO. 1). It must also be consulted in respect of certain types of government regulations: *ordonnances* passed by the government by a delegation from Parliament under *ibid, Art. 38*; delegated legislation which in the enabling Act is specified as having to take the form of *décret pris en Conseil d'Etat*; and decrees modifying texts in the form of parliamentary statutes dealing with matters within the competence of government (*textes de forme législative*) under *ibid, Art. 37*. See Chapter 4. It may be consulted in respect of other forms of government regulation.

Also in its advisory function it receives requests from the different government departments for its advice on particular points of law, and may even offer unsolicited advice on matters it considers to be in the general interest. Moreover, it must be consulted in respect of certain administrative decisions, for example as to whether or not to grant status similar to charitable status (*reconnaissance d'utilité publique*) to an association or foundation.

(ii) Judicial function

In its judicial function, it acts as a first instance court, an appeal court, and as a court of *cassation*. Despite the *Tribunaux Administratifs* having been given general first instance competence, certain administrative litigation is still dealt with at first and last instance (*en premier et dernier ressort*) by the *Conseil d'Etat*; this is known as its *compétence directe*. The cases it hears in this way are principally: *recours en annulation* against decrees (*décrets*), ordinances issued under 1958 Constitution, Art. 38 (before ratification) and ministerial regulations (eg *arrêté ministériel*); *recours en annulation* against administrative decisions of bodies with national competence (such as the *Conseil national de l'ordre des médecins*, and the boards of public corporations (*établissements publics*) such as *Electricité de France*, and *Société nationale des chemins de fer*); litigation within the jurisdiction of more than one *Tribunal Administratif*; litigation in respect of elections to regional councils and the European Parliament; litigation in respect of civil servants (*fonctionnaires*) appointed by decree of the President of the Republic (eg litigation relating to the appointment, career advancement or discipline of a prefect).

The *Conseil d'Etat* also acts as an appeal court. Despite the creation in 1989 of the *Cours Administratives d'Appel*, the *Conseil d'Etat* continues to hear appeals (by way of *appel*) directly from decisions of the *Tribunaux Administratifs* in the matter of *recours pour excès de pouvoir* in respect of regulations of general effect and litigation relating to local (ie municipal and cantonal) elections; however, a *décret du 17.3.1992* now provides for the progressive extension of the jurisdiction of the *Cours Administratives d'Appel* to hear appeals in respect of certain *recours pour excès de pouvoir* (ie for decisions having individual rather than general effect: *actes non réglementaires*). The *Conseil d'Etat* in effect retries the case on appeal, the *Conseil*, like the *Cour Administrative d'Appel*, having full jurisdiction (*plénitude de juridiction*) on appeal. The *Conseil d'Etat* does not hear appeals (ie *appel*) from the *Cours Administratives d'Appel* or from the specialist jurisdictions (such as the *Cours des Comptes* (see below), some of which have their own appeal structures); however in such cases appeal by way of *cassation* may lie.

The *Conseil d'Etat*, in addition to its role as an appeal court, acts as a court of *cassation*, adjudging the legality of decisions of cases from inferior administrative courts and specialist jurisdictions such as the *Cours des Comptes*. A *recours en cassation* is available (unless statute expressly excludes it) from any judgment of a lower court from which no *appel* lies (ie *décision en dernier ressort*) within two months of notification of the judgment. A *Commission d'admission des pourvois en cassation* of the *Conseil d'Etat*, consisting of three judges, filters out *recours en cassation* which are inadmissible or have no serious legal foundation; no appeal lies against a decision not to admit a *recours*. The control exercised by the *Conseil d'Etat* when acting *en cassation* is essentially to carry out a review of the principles of law applied by the inferior court.

If the *Conseil d'Etat* quashes a decision of the inferior jurisdiction, it has several options open to it; these are wider than those enjoyed by the *Cour de Cassation*. It may, although it rarely does so, refer the matter back to a different jurisdiction of equivalent status to implement its decision (if the latter fails to implement the decision this may lead to a second *recours en cassation*, at which point the *Conseil d'Etat* will make a final ruling). Alternatively, and more usually, it will refer the case back to the same jurisdiction from which it came, the latter then being obliged to implement the decision of the *Conseil d'Etat*. Finally, it may, on the grounds of the good administration of justice, decide that a reference is not appropriate, and make a final ruling itself.

(iii) Organisation

A particular feature of the organisation of the *Conseil d'Etat* is that although it is divided into 6 sections, 5 administrative and 1 judicial, with only the latter dealing with judicial matters, there is a good deal of cross-fertilisation between the two sides. The members of the *Conseil*, amounting to more than 250 in total, are divided into 3 categories: *auditeurs* on the bottom rung, *maîtres de requêtes*, and *conseillers d'Etat* at the summit. In addition, each *section* has a president, and the *Conseil* itself is in effect presided over by its vice-president, the Prime Minister as head of the government being the nominal president. Most of the personnel are recruited from the *Ecole nationale d'administration*, but a certain proportion of the higher echelons (one-quarter of the *maîtres de requêtes* and one-third of the *conseillers d'Etat*) are recruited from the ranks of experienced civil servants (recruitment by *tour extérieur*). In addition, 12 senior civil servants are appointed to serve as *conseillers d'Etat en service extraordinaire* for a term of 4 years; they exercise exclusively administrative functions.

There are 5 administrative sections of the *Conseil d'Etat*; the *sections des finances, des travaux publics, de l'intérieur; la section sociale* and *la section du rapport et des études*. The different categories of personnel are represented in each section. An advisory opinion of the *Conseil* will be given by the relevant section (or sometimes, for example in more important matters, by an *assemblée générale*).

The judicial function of the *Conseil* is exercised by the *section du contentieux* which is subdivided into 10 *sous-sections*, each having 3 *conseillers d'Etat* (one of whom acts as *président de sous-section*) and several *maîtres de requêtes* and *auditeurs*. A case is initially referred to 1 *sous-section* to carry out an investigation (*instruction*); thereafter judgment will be reached either by that *sous-section* comprising at least 5 members or, if it is a more complex or important case, by 2 (or 3) *sous-sections* sitting together as the *section du contentieux en formation de jugement* numbering 17 judges, or in the most important cases by the *assemblée du contentieux*, which is the most formal formation of the *Conseil*, comprising 13 of its most senior members.

A cross-fertilisation between the administrative and judicial functions of the *Conseil* has been deliberately instituted on the basis that this leads to each of the functions being exercised in a more informed way, and its decisions are likely to carry greater respect. The overlap mainly shows itself in two ways: firstly, all members of the *Conseil* (apart from those presiding over *sections* or *sous-sections*) are attached to both an administrative and a judicial section (known as the principle of "mixing" − *le brassage*). Secondly, some of its units are structured in such a way as to ensure representation from both branches; thus the *assemblée du contentieux* includes the presidents of five administrative sections.

(e) Juridictions administratives spécialisées

In addition to the administrative courts there are some 50 specialised administrative tribunals (*juridictions administratives spécialisées*), all of which are the creation of statute and are subject to the control of the *Conseil d'Etat* in that *pourvoi en cassation* (usually − although sometimes *appel*) lies to the *Conseil d'Etat* from their decisions. The functions of these tribunals are varied. Some deal with administrative matters, such as the *Commission centrale d'aide sociale* (supplementary benefit appeals) and the *Commission de recours des réfugiés*, which deals with requests for refugee status. Others have disciplinary functions, for example the disciplinary committees of a variety of professional orders (such as the *Conseil national de l'ordre des médecins*). Of particular importance are the tribunals whose role is to exercise control over public expenditure, from the annual parliamentary budget to the expenditure of local collectivities: the *Cour des Comptes* and the 22 *Chambres régionales des comptes*.

There are wide variations in the ways in which these different tribunals are organised; their personnel are often made up of a combination of a judge or judges seconded from the administrative (or even ordinary) courts, specialised assessors, and representatives of interested bodies. With some, judgments are at first and last instance; with others, appeal lies to a higher jurisdiction within the hierarchy (eg from the *Chambres régionales des comptes* to the *Cour des Comptes*).

(f) Tribunal des Conflits

This court was created by the *loi du 24.5.1872* to resolve conflicts of jurisdiction between the ordinary and administrative courts. No such court was necessary before then, because under the earlier system in which the *Conseil d'Etat* merely advised the head of state (*la justice retenue*), the latter (acting in *Conseil d'Etat*) determined any conflicts of jurisdiction. The rules of competence of the administrative courts that have developed have been examined above.

The *Tribunal des Conflits* comprises the Minister of Justice (who, although nominally the president, does not normally sit), three *conseillers d'Etat* and three judges of the *Cour de Cassation* (all of whom are appointed by their colleagues), and two other judges elected by the six who have been appointed; in practice this means one additional representative of each of the supreme courts. Appointment is for a renewable three-year term. The quorum for the court is five. The Minister of Justice will sit only to break a deadlock where the other judges are unable to reach a majority decision. The court is otherwise chaired by its vice-president, elected by the other members of the court.

A conflict may be referred to the *Tribunal des Conflits* in one of several ways; it is clear, however, that the essential function of the *Tribunal* is to implement the principle of the 1790 statute that the ordinary courts may not interfere with the activities of the administration. This is clear from the first type of conflict that may arise, the *conflit positif*. When a civil case has been brought in the ordinary courts (but not the *Cour de Cassation*) which the prefect considers properly comes within the competence of the administrative courts, he may at any time before judgment is pronounced, as representative of the administrative authority and guardian of the public interest, instruct the *ministère public* to request (by means of a *déclinatoire de compétence*) that the court declare itself incompetent to continue to try the case. Should the court refuse to do so, the prefect will refer the case to the *Tribunal des Conflits* by an *arrêté de conflit* which automatically suspends the proceedings of the ordinary court. It should be noted that it is not possible for the ordinary courts to intervene in this way in a case being heard before the administrative courts.

A *conflit négatif* arises where a plaintiff seeks to commence an action in each set of courts in turn, both of which refuse to accept jurisdiction. He may then refer the matter to the *Tribunal des Conflits*; however he will not usually have to do so himself, for where a court of one of the systems declines competence in a judgment against which no further appeal lies, a court of the other system which is subsequently seized of the matter must, if similarly minded to declare its own incompetence, refer the case directly to the *Tribunal*. Furthermore, rules to deal with potential conflicts (*conflits éventuels*), and thus to reduce the delay in resolving jurisdictional disputes, were introduced in 1960; these permit either of the sovereign courts (ie the *Cour de Cassation* or the *Conseil d'Etat*), when hearing a case which raises serious difficulties, to refer the matter directly to the *Tribunal* where there is a potential conflict of jurisdiction.

The role of the *Tribunal des Conflits* in most cases is simply to decide which set of courts is competent to hear a particular case. However, it may actually have to try a case (*jugement sur le fond*) where the case has given rise to two conflicting judgments; this might arise where, for example, one of the parties brings a case in, say, the *Tribunal Administratif*, and the other party does likewise in the *Tribunal de Grande Instance*, and both parties obtain judgments in their own favour.

No appeal (by way of *appel* or *cassation*) is possible against the decisions of the *Tribunal des Conflits*. It heard 58 cases in 1988.

4. Le Conseil Constitutionnel

The *Conseil Constitutionnel* was created by the 1958 Constitution (*Arts. 56–63*) primarily to control the division of legislative power between Parliament and the government set out in the Constitution (*Arts. 34, 37*; see Chapter 4); its particular role is to ensure that Parliament does not stray outside its authorised legislative domain. However, it has extended this role to that of adjudging the constitutionality of parliamentary statutes by reference to a broad range of constitutional norms, including general principles drawn from constitutional documents such as the 1789 *Déclaration des Droits de l'Homme et du Citoyen*.

The *Conseil* can be seized only before a bill has been promulgated, and then only by the President, the Prime Minister, the president of either house or (since a 1974 reform) a group of 60 members of the *Sénat* or *Assemblée Nationale*, and not by an individual. The *Conseil* is also competent to hear litigation relating to the holding of presidential and parliamentary elections and referenda. In an advisory capacity it advises on the compatibility with the Constitution of international treaties, and must be consulted by the President when he is minded to exercise emergency powers in times of grave threat under *Art. 16* of the 1958 Constitution.

The nine judges of the *Conseil Constitutionnel* are all political appointees, three each being appointed for a nine-year non-renewable mandate by the President of the Republic and the president of each of the two houses; every three years one-third of the membership of the *Conseil* is renewed. In practice, senior lawyers or experienced politicians have been appointed. In addition, former Presidents of the Republic are in principle entitled to sit. On appointment, certain public functions are prohibited, such as being a member of Parliament or the government. The quorum for the *Conseil* is seven. Its judgments, which must be reasoned and must be reached within one month of the *Conseil* being seized of the matter, are binding on all legislative, executive and judicial bodies (*Constitution de 1958, Art. 62*) and cannot be the subject of *appel* or a *recours en cassation*.

The grounds upon which the *Conseil Constitutionnel* may be seized to adjudge the constitutionality of a parliamentary statute, and the norms of constitutionality that it applies, are examined in detail in Chapter 4.

B. The judiciary

1. Introduction

The French judiciary, unlike its counterparts in England and Wales, is not appointed from the ranks of experienced advocates. This is perhaps not surprising, as the inquisitorial nature of French procedure requires the judiciary to exercise skills differing from those which are necessary for judging an accusatorial trial. The French judiciary is essentially a career judiciary, with law graduates studying at judicial training school before commencing a career on the lowest rung of the profession. Those seeking to become judges of the ordinary courts (or *magistrats du parquet*; see below) attend the *Ecole nationale de la magistrature* in Bordeaux. Similarly, most members of the administrative court are graduates of the *Ecole nationale d'administration*, which has been based in Paris but which is to move to Strasbourg.

As has been seen, however, not all judges are appointed in this way; in particular, a certain proportion are drawn from the ranks of the civil service to ensure a cross-fertilisation between administrative practice and the administrative courts. Even in the ordinary courts a certain number of the judicial appointments are made from those who have experience as legal practitioners, academic lawyers or civil servants. Furthermore, in the ordinary courts, particularly the specialised courts, there is a long tradition of using non-professional judges with expertise in the particular field of law that the court deals with, sitting either without a professional judge (eg *Tribunaux de Commerce, Conseils de Prud'hommes*) or as assessors with a professional judge (eg *Tribunaux des Affaires de Sécurité Sociale, Tribunaux Paritaires des Baux Ruraux*).

The President of the Republic is the guarantor of the independence of the judiciary (*Constitution de 1958, Art. 64*; CHAPTER 4 TEXTS, NO. 1); independence is also ensured by a national commission on the judiciary, the *Conseil supérieur de la magistrature*. It should however be noted that *magistrats* are divided into two categories, the judges who actually try cases (*juges du siège*, from whose ranks are also drawn examining magistrates (*juges d'instruction*)) and those who act as prosecutors (*magistrats debouts*, also known as *magistrats du parquet*). Although the latter are *magistrats*, they do not have the same degree of independence as trial judges. The functions and status of the *magistrats du parquet* are examined in the context of criminal procedure in Chapter 5.

The members of the administrative courts, whose functions, as has been seen, are not only judicial but also include acting as legal adviser to the executive, have the status of civil servants (*fonctionnaires*) and do not enjoy the constitutional guarantee of independence, although members of the lower administrative courts have been effectively recognised as independent by the *loi du 6.1.1986* (see below). Moreover, the *Conseil d'Etat* has over the years proved its impartiality in the way it has exercised its judicial function.

2. Recruitment and training

(a) Ordinary courts

In the early days of the Revolution judges were elected, but soon they came to be appointed by the head of state. The present system is one of appointment by the executive coupled with a constitutional guarantee of independence. Most judges are appointed after graduating from the *Ecole nationale de la magistrature*, which was instituted (under a different name) in 1958 operating under the supervision of the Ministry of Justice. Entry to the school is open to French nationals who have either the equivalent of a university masters' degree or four years' experience as a civil servant. Furthermore the candidates must either pass an entry examination (*concours*), which is usually taken after a year of study at a centre of judicial studies attached to a law faculty, or show that they have certain legal experience (eg practice as an *avocat* for at least three years); no more than one-third of the annual entry may be by this latter route. On enrolment at the *ENM*, the student acquires the status of *auditeur de justice*. He will be paid during his 27 months' training period, comprising periods of study and a one-year attachment to a court, during which the *auditeur* will play an active role, working with *juges du siège, juges d'instruction* and *magistrats du parquet*. Final examinations are sat and the candidates are classified according to merit.

A small proportion of judges are appointed not following graduation from the *ENM*, but directly from a career in the law (*recrutement latéral*); eg *avocats, notaires*, civil servants and academic lawyers with several years' experience. Those with greater experience may be appointed directly to a high position in the court hierarchy (*loi organique du 25.2.1992*).

Appointment as a *juge du siège* is by decree (of the President of the Republic on the proposition of the Minister of Justice) taken with the advice of the *Conseil supérieur de la magistrature*. On taking up appointment, the judge is sworn in before the *Cour d'Appel*.

(b) Administrative courts

Most members of the administrative courts are graduates of the *Ecole nationale d'administration*, which was created in 1945 to train high-calibre students for a career in the administration. Entry to the *ENA* is by entry examination which is open to those with a degree or with prescribed experience in the civil service (or in trade unions, non-profit associations, etc). The course (during which the student enjoys the status of civil servant and receives a salary) lasts for three years, and includes periods of practical training. The candidates' performance in the final examinations determines their career; the best are offered positions in the *Conseil d'Etat*, those ranking lower elsewhere, eg in the inferior courts, administrative jurisdictions or administrative bodies. As has been seen above, one-quarter of the *maîtres de requêtes* and one-third of the *conseillers d'Etat* are recruited from the ranks of public servants (civil or military) with at least ten years' experience (*le tour extérieur*). In addition, a dozen senior civil servants are given short-term appointments (four years) to exercise administrative functions as *conseillers d'Etat en service extraordinaire*. Appointees to the *Cours Administratives d'Appel* and *Tribunaux Administratifs* include graduates of the *ENA*, entrants from the *tour extérieur* and those with prescribed experience as a civil servant who pass an examination. Appointment to the administrative courts is by decree of the President of the Republic.

3. Independence

(a) Independence from the executive

Article 64 of the 1958 Constitution states that the President of the Republic is the guarantor of the independence of the judiciary and that *magistrats du siège* cannot be removed. Indeed they cannot be moved to another position (even if a promotion) without their consent (*ordonnance du 22.12.1958, Art. 4*). This constitutional protection extends only to *magistrats du siège* of the ordinary courts, not to *magistrats du parquet*, or to members of the administrative courts. In respect of members of the administrative courts, the prestige of the *Conseil d'Etat* has resulted in effective freedom from political interference; furthermore, the *Conseil Constitutionnel* has affirmed (*C.C., 22.7.1980*) that the independence of administrative judges is a fundamental principle recognised by the laws of the Republic. This has been bolstered by the *loi du 6.1.1986*, which provides that the members of the *Cours Administratives d'Appel* and *Tribunaux Administratifs* cannot be moved without their consent, even if this amounts to a promotion.

In principle, the executive plays no role in matters of career advancement (or discipline) of the judiciary. In such matters the role of the *Conseil supérieur de la magistrature (CSM)* and the *Conseil supérieur des Tribunaux Administratifs et Cours Administratives d'Appel* should be noted. The *CSM* has as its president the President of the Republic. However it is usually the vice-president of the *CSM* (the Minister of Justice) who presides at the meetings. There are nine other members, all of whom are appointed by the President of the Republic for a four-year term. Of these, six are judges of the ordinary courts (whose names are put forward by the *Cour de Cassation*) and one is a *conseiller d'Etat*). The *Conseil supérieur des Tribunaux Administratifs et Cours Administratives d'Appel* is presided over by the vice-president of the *Conseil d'Etat*. Its twelve other members are four senior administrative judges and officials (ex officio), five administrative judges elected by their colleagues and one nominee of the President of the Republic and each of the two houses of Parliament.

The role of the *CSM* is to assist the President of the Republic in guaranteeing the independence of the judiciary, with particular responsibilities in respect of appointment, advancement and discipline. It thus advises the President on who should be appointed as a judge (indeed, it proposes the names in respect of appointments to the higher echelons of the judiciary). A similar system exists within the administrative court structure.

(b) Restrictions

By way of a safeguard of judicial independence, judges are forbidden from practising any other profession or business. They are, however, allowed to carry out activities of a literary, scientific, artistic or educational nature. Members of the administrative courts may also hold certain administrative posts. A judge, ordinary or administrative, may not become a member of Parliament or of the European Parliament. Nor may he hold a position on his local departmental or municipal council, although he may stand in other constituencies. Overt political activity (such as taking part in a demonstration) is prohibited. Ordinary judges are specifically denied the right to strike (*ordonnance du 22.12.1958, Art. 10(3)*), although it is not forbidden to join a trade union.

Should a judge not do so spontaneously, a party to an action may request that the judge step down for potential partiality where, for example, the judge or his spouse has a personal interest in the case (a procedure known as *la récusation*).

4. Discipline

(a) Ordinary courts

A judge may be disciplined for failing to comply with the obligations of his position or with the appropriate standards of honour, modesty and dignity. The disciplinary measures which may be taken include reprimand, suspension, demotion, forced early retirement and the loss of pension rights. Matters of discipline of *juges du siège* are dealt with by the *Conseil supérieur de la magistrature* (presided over for this purpose by the first president of the *Cour de Cassation*). In principle, no appeal lies against its decision. Disciplinary charges against *magistrats du parquet* are heard before a *Commission de discipline du parquet* (chaired by the *procureur général* of the *Cour de Cassation*), although the final decision is taken and the penalty pronounced by the Minister of Justice. Judicial review (*recours pour excès de pouvoir*) lies to the *Conseil d'Etat* against the decision of the Minister.

(b) Administrative courts

As a general principle, members of the administrative courts are answerable in matters of discipline to the government, as are other civil servants. However, in recent years particular disciplinary procedures have been introduced. In respect of members of the *Conseil d'Etat* this was by a *décret du 30.7.1963*. Minor cases are dealt with by the vice-president of the *Conseil d'Etat*, who is empowered to take such measures as issuing a warning. However, more serious penalties may be imposed only by the Minister of Justice after the matter has first been referred to a disciplinary commission. By a *loi du*

31.12.1987 disciplinary matters relating to judges of the *Tribunaux Administratifs* and the *Cours Administratives d'Appel* are referred to the *Conseil supérieur des Tribunaux Administratifs et Cours Administratives d'Appel* which makes a recommendation to the Minister, with whom the final decision rests.

C. The legal professions

1. Introduction

Professor René David (*English Law and French Law*, 1980, Chapter 4) maintains that "there is no general concept of a legal profession in France". Traditionally, monopolies of certain functions (eg advocacy, real property transfers) have been recognised in favour of particular legal professions (*avocats* and *notaires* respectively); other people have been able to hold themselves out as legal advisers, provided that they do not interfere with such monopolies. However, in recent years there has been increasing regulation of those giving legal advice. This trend culminated in the *loi No. 90–1259 du 31 décembre 1990* (modifying the *loi No. 71–1130 du 31 décembre 1971*, referred to in this chapter as *loi 1971*, and completed by the *décret No. 91–1197 du 27 novembre 1991*) which ensures that those who give legal advice are members of regulated professions. The statute also introduced major reforms in the legal professions; the intention of the reforms was to modernise the professions so as to make them more competitive in the single market. The reforms came into operation on 1 January 1992.

2. The legal professions before the 1990 reform law

The various types of lawyers are collectively known as *auxiliaires de justice*. Before the 1990 reforms there were not two, but three main professions: the *avocat*, the *conseil juridique*, and the *notaire*. A fourth profession is that of the *huissier de justice*. We will examine the role and regulation of these different categories of lawyer before moving on to look at the impact of the reforms, which merged the professions of *avocat* and *conseil juridique* to create a new fused profession of *avocat*.

(a) Avocats

The *avocat* has traditionally had exclusive rights of audience in all courts of general jurisdiction (ie *Tribunaux de Grande Instance, Cours d'Appel, Tribunaux Administratifs, Cours Administratives d'Appel*) and all criminal courts; however, parties may appear on their own behalf. In the *Tribunaux d'Instance*, representation is permitted by a family member (and in the case of an employer, by someone from his business); in the *Conseils de Prud'hommes* by a family member, work colleague or union representative, and in the *Tribunaux de Commerce* by any person of the party's choice who is so empowered (which includes a *conseil juridique* and a *huissier de justice*).

Before the reforms, *avocats* also had the exclusive right to conduct litigation and to carry out the formal pre-trial procedural steps for a client (known as *la représentation* or *la postulation*) in a civil case before the *Tribunal de Grande Instance*. This function used to be carried out by a separate specialised profession, that of the *avoué*. In a 1971 reform the functions of both *avoués* and *avocats* became exercisable by *avocats*, and the profession of *avoué* was largely abolished; it now exists only for proceedings before the *Cours d'Appel*. An *avocat* is also entitled to give legal advice for reward, but has no monopoly of this function, sharing it with other advisers such as *conseils juridiques*.

The profession of *avocat* is a liberal independent profession, and an *avocat* is entitled to refuse to represent a client (unless a case has been assigned to him by the *bâtonnier* (see below)). Independence is at least partly assured by an immunity from action for defamation for anything said or produced in writing before the court; unlike the English and Welsh barrister, however, the *avocat* may be liable for the negligent carrying out of any of his functions, including the conduct of a case − professional negligence insurance must be carried.

Avocats must belong to a local Bar Association (*barreau*), of which there is one for each local *Tribunal de Grande Instance*. Until the reforms, there was no formal national representative body for *avocats*, although there was a *Conférence des bâtonniers* (at which the *barreau de Paris* was not however represented). The Bar Council (*Conseil de l'ordre*) of each *barreau* is elected for three years (in thirds) by the *avocats*. Its functions are administrative (admission to pupillage (*stage*) and to the roll (*tableau*), and vetting the professional accounts of the members of the Bar), disciplinary (with appeal lying to the *Cour d'Appel*), and representative. It also has the role of maintaining "probity, impartiality, moderation and confraternity" within the profession. It is presided over by a *bâtonnier*, who is elected for a two-year period. In 1989 there were some 17,500 *avocats*, approximately 7,000 of whom were practising in Paris.

There is a separate body of *avocats aux conseils* who have exclusive rights of audience in the *Cour de Cassation, Conseil d'Etat* and *Tribunal des Conflits*. They have their own *ordre*. Their office is a *charge*, as is the case with *notaires* (see below); there are 60 *charges*. They are regulated by a *décret du 28 octobre 1991*; they are largely unaffected by the reforms.

(b) Conseils juridiques

As already mentioned, the profession of *conseil juridique* was merged with that of *avocat* as from 1 January 1992. Before 1972 no control was exercised over those who gave legal advice for reward, if they were not members of the regulated professions of *avocat* or *notaire*; such advisers usually called themselves *conseils juridiques* (legal counsel). Regulation was introduced by the *loi 1971* (as completed by the *décret No. 72–670 du 13 juillet 1972* ("*décret 1972*")), the right to give advice or draft legal documents as *conseil juridique* being limited to those who were registered as such with the *procureur de la République*. The functions of the *conseil juridique* were defined (*décret 1972, Art. 47*) as the giving of advice, the drafting of private signed documents (*actes sous seing privé*; to be contrasted with the more formal notarial deeds (*actes authentiques* – see below) and the carrying out of all associated formalities. They could also assist their clients in the drafting of declarations, statements and responses to public or private bodies or organisations, and they could represent them before these bodies or organisations as well as before any jurisdiction which permits the parties to be represented by the person of their choice (eg *Tribunaux de Commerce*). The role that the profession assumed was that of corporate adviser. Other persons were able to give legal advice for a fee (eg trade unions) as long as they did not hold themselves out as *conseils juridiques*; such advisers were subject to the disciplinary supervision of the *procureur*.

The profession of *conseil juridique* was recognised (*loi 1971, Art. 56*) as being a liberal independent profession; to safeguard such status, it was forbidden for the *conseil juridique* to carry out commercial activities other than those related to his profession. He had to observe, in all circumstances, "an attitude compatible with the dignity and independence of the profession" (*décret 1972, Art. 59*). Professional negligence insurance had to be carried. *Conseils juridiques* were under a statutory duty to act prudently and diligently so as to safeguard the interests of clients, and to refrain from acting for parties with opposing interests in any given case. Statute did not require the same degree of supervision and control over the activities of *conseils juridiques* as the *barreaux* exercised over *avocats*, although most *conseils juridiques* belonged to regional professional bodies (*Commissions régionales des conseils juridiques*) representing the interests of the profession and involved in the provision of professional training. There was a *Commission nationale des conseils juridiques*.

Discipline was exercised by the prosecutor, who could commence disciplinary proceedings in the *Tribunal de Grande Instance* for behaviour contrary to honour, probity or good morality, or for contravention of the statutory practice rules. The court had wide disciplinary powers, with appeal lying to the *Cour d'Appel*. There were some 4,800 registered *conseils juridiques* in 1990.

(c) Notaires

The profession of *notaire* has been mostly untouched by the 1990 reform law. Like that of *avocat*, the profession has been regulated by statute since the revolutionary period (now by the *ordonnance du 2.11.1945* and *décret du 5.7.1973* as amended). The work undertaken by *notaires* appears at first sight to parallel the non-contentious work of the British solicitor, but there are major differences between the two, as will be seen.

The function of a *notaire* is to give authenticity to documents which require such formality (*ordonnance 1945, Art. 1*) and to give related legal advice. It is thus necessary to employ a *notaire* to attend to such matters as the transfer of real property, the drafting of a marriage contract (*régime matrimonial*), and the creation of certain charges on realty (*hypothèque*), as such instruments must take the form of a notarial deed known as an *acte authentique*. Facts attested by the *notaire* in such a deed are presumed to be true unless disproved by a particularly formal procedure (*l'inscription de faux*); the *notaire* will also keep the *acte* in his custody and issue certified copies. Other legal documents may be attested by the *notaire*; it is thus usual to employ a *notaire* in the making of a will and the winding up of a deceased person's estate. In addition, a *notaire* may attend to certain enforced sales of property (*ventes judiciaires*) in civil procedure.

Notaires are public officers (*officiers publics*) in the sense that an attestation of a document by a *notaire* is regarded as that of a public authority, hence the presumption of truth. They are not, however, civil servants as such, their fees being paid by their clients. They are (formally) appointed by the Minister of Justice, usually on the retirement of another member of the profession, as the number of *notaires* in any area is limited by reference to the size of the local population. The office (*charge*) of *notaire* is purchased by the appointee from the retiring *notaire* or is inherited on death (eg where the son of a deceased *notaire* is also a *notaire*). On appointment, the *notaire* swears a professional oath before the local *Tribunal de Grande Instance*.

Notaires may practise as sole practitioners, or in partnership, but only with other *notaires*. They may not exercise any functions deemed incompatible with their office, such as commercial or banking activities. Nor may they be *avocats*. A national body, *le Conseil supérieur du notariat*, represents the profession and ensures proper practice, but leaves to local *chambres des notaires* in each *département* (and the *Conseil régional des notaires* attached to each *Cour d'Appel*) matters of internal regulation, discipline and training. Training consists of an academic stage, professional examinations, and two years as an articled clerk (*notaire stagiaire*). The existing monopolies of *notaires* have not been affected by the 1990 reform law, but the practice structures are extended in a way similar to those of *avocats*, enabling for the first time the emergence of salaried *notaires*; indeed, it may become possible for *notaires* and *avocats* to practise together in a new type of corporate practice structure, the *société d'exercice libéral* (see below). In 1987, there were 7,334 *notaires*.

(d) Huissiers de justice

Huissiers de justice have a monopoly of certain functions; firstly, they execute the service (*la signification*) of writs (*assignations*) and other formal documents of civil procedure (*actes de procédure*). Secondly, they play a role in the execution of judgments, particularly in effecting seizures (*saisies*); see Chapter 6. Such functions are analogous to those of bailiffs. However, *huissiers* (particularly *huissiers-audienciers*) also act as court ushers. In addition to these monopolies, *huissiers* may discharge other functions, such as the carrying out of investigations of fact (*constats*), either for the court, or for one of the parties, and effecting the recovery of debts. The profession is currently actively seeking to expand its role in the recovery of debts.

The *chambres départementales d'huissiers* have certain supervisory and disciplinary functions over the profession. There are also regional *chambres* and a national *chambre d'huissiers*. To become a *huissier* it is necessary to have a degree in law (*licence en droit*), work for two years as a *stagiaire*, and pass professional examinations. *Huissiers* practise as sole practitioners, or collectively either in a *société civile professionnelle* (in which case the practice has the *charge* of *huissier*), or retaining their own *charge* but sharing resources in a *société d'huissiers de justice*.

Having concluded this outline of the pre-reform structure of the legal professions, let us proceed to examine the reasons for the reforms, and how they affect the professions.

3. Why reform?

The seeds of the 1990 reform were planted in the *loi 1971*, which provided (*Art. 78*) for the creation of a commission to advise the Minister of Justice on "the measures appropriate for the merger of the professions of *avocat* and *conseil juridique*", the argument having been accepted at the time that the functions of giving legal advice and conducting proceedings are closely related, and that a client should be able to obtain a comprehensive service from the one lawyer. By 1989 the profession of *conseil juridique* had carved out a niche for itself in the legal services market, and reform was put once more on the government agenda, the catalyst being the impending single market and a determination that the traditions of the legal professions should not be allowed to shackle them in competing for legal work after 1992. The *Commission Saint Pierre* reported on reform in June 1989. The aims of the reforms were not only to modernise the legal professions but also to ensure that legal advice is given, and legal documents drafted, only by properly regulated professionals carrying indemnity insurance.

4. Impact of the 1990 reforms

The new law creates a new profession of *avocat*, comprising all those practising before the reforms as *avocats* or *conseils juridiques*, the two professions being fused into a new merged profession. As has been seen, many of the practice rules of the two professions were brought into line in the 1971 reforms, thus preparing the way for fusion. What effect do the reforms have on legal practice?

(a) Authorised activities

The right to conduct litigation (*la représentation*) and the rights of audience in the courts (*la plaidoirie*) which were enjoyed by *avocats* are now exercisable by all members of the merged profession (ie *avocats* and ex-*conseils juridiques*).

In return, *avocats* are formally recognised as sharing the rights of *conseils juridiques* to give legal advice or to draft legal documents for reward. *Article 54* of the amended 1971 law ("amended *loi 1971*"; TEXTS, NO. 3(a)) provides that no one may, on a habitual basis, give legal advice or draft private signed documents for reward unless so permitted by the law. Unauthorised activities constitute the commission of a criminal offence. Such rights to give advice and draft legal documents for reward are recognised by the statute as being exercisable by members of the new merged profession of *avocat*, as well as the *avocats aux conseils, notaires*, and *avoués*; also by members of certain auxiliary professions, such as liquidators and judicial administrators, to the extent permitted by their professional regulations (a minimum qualification of a degree (*licence*) in law is required for all legal advisers and drafters; *amended loi 1971, Art. 54(1)*). It is further specified (*ibid, Art. 55*) that all legal advisers and drafters must carry professional liability insurance.

Other regulated professions such as accountants and insurance agents (and non-regulated professions whose members hold certain recognised qualifications) are entitled, subject to their own professional regulations, to give legal advice and draft legal documents, but only in respect of matters relating to their principal activities. Public service bodies such as chambers of commerce may also give legal advice as part of their services, as may law lecturers of higher education establishments. Lawyers employed by a company or business may continue to give advice to and draft deeds and documents for their employer in respect of matters connected with the employer's activities. Limited rights to give legal advice are also recognised in favour of such bodies as trade unions and certain associations.

The reforms affect foreign lawyers operating in France. Under the 1971 law, only French nationals could become *avocats* (*loi 1971, Art. 11(1)*), a limitation which did not extend to *conseils juridiques*. Lawyers from non-member states of the EC had to register as *conseils juridiques*, and confine their advice to overseas or international law, conditions which did not apply to those from EC member states. By the *amended loi*

1971, Art. 11, a foreign lawyer may enrol as an *avocat* if he is from a state which allows French lawyers unrestricted access to legal practice (or is a recognised refugee or a stateless person), and has either obtained the qualifications of an *avocat* (ie by obtaining the *certificat d'aptitude à la profession d'avocat (CAPA)*) or has passed a series of examinations on French law (as specified in regulations). Henceforth, lawyers from EC member states who wish to practise in France may do so only by registering as an *avocat* with a *barreau*. Regulations have been introduced (*décret du 27.11.1991*; see TEXTS, NO. 3 (b)) which determine the precise conditions within which such registration is permitted. These are as follows. The lawyer must fulfil the conditions required for practice in his home country. He must also pass a series of examinations (specified by regulation) if his education and training is "substantially different" from that of a French *avocat*, or if the profession is not regulated in his home country. The examinations will be conducted by the *Centres de formation professionnelle des avocats*. The *Conseil national du barreau* may determine that in view of a candidate's initial education and training he should be examined in particular subjects. There are, however, transitional provisions to the effect that any lawyer qualified in an EC member state practising in France before 1992 but not registered as *conseil juridique* is entitled, within two years of the implementation of the reforms, to enrol with a local *barreau* as *avocat*, on condition that he has been in continual practice for three years, at least eighteen months of which must have been spent in France, giving legal advice or drafting legal documents (*amended loi 1971, Art. 50(viii)*). Foreign lawyers enrolled before 1992 as *conseils juridiques*, as well as firms of foreign lawyers who have practised in France since before 1 July 1971, are automatically entitled to become members of the new profession. Other foreign firms operating in France before 1992 are able, within two years, to enrol with the local *barreau* if they show that they have had appropriate experience of legal work and that all of their representatives in France are enrolled with a *barreau*.

The net result of the reforms is that any lawyer qualified in a foreign jurisdiction is henceforth entitled to practise in France only if enrolled as *avocat*. This is consistent with one of the aims of the reforms, that of ensuring the proper regulation of all lawyers practising in France.

(b) Forms of practice

The reform laws broaden the permitted practice structures. Before the reforms, *avocats* were required to practise either as sole practitioners, or with other *avocats* in an association (overheads being shared, but each *avocat* remaining personally responsible for his clients), *société civile professionnelle* (a type of incorporated partnership; the clients (and profits) are those of the *SCP*, not of any individual *avocat*. Its *avocats* are personally responsible without limit for their own professional negligence; furthermore, however, the *SCP* itself is jointly liable in respect of loss caused by the professional activities of its *avocats*), or collaborative practice (where one *avocat* gives some or all of his time to the practice of another *avocat* without being the salaried assistant of the latter). There is a good deal of regulation of all such practices: the partnership deed must contain certain specified provisions, be approved by the local *barreau*, and be lodged with the *Tribunal de Grande Instance*. However, a good proportion of *avocats* still practise on their own account, official figures for 1988 revealing that 52 per cent of all French *avocats* practised as sole practitioners. The 1990 reforms are likely to lead to a reduction in the number of those practising as sole practitioners.

Less control was exercised over the formation of practices of *conseils juridiques*; thus the only ground on which the *procureur* could refuse to register a partnership deed was a failure to comply with the general provisions relating to professional partnerships. *Conseils juridiques* could be sole practitioners, or in an incorporated partnership (*société civile professionnelle*), or could be a salaried assistant lawyer of either, or a collaborator with other *conseils juridiques*. In the case of an incorporated partnership, it was the partnership itself that was registered as exercising the functions of *conseil juridique*. The major difference from the practices of *avocats* was that *conseils juridiques* could practise through the medium of a company (public or private). Although outside investment in such a company was possible, control was retained by the enrolled *conseils juridiques* themselves, as such persons had to hold the majority of the shares and control the board of directors. In 1990 there were some 650 corporations of *conseils juridiques* of one form or another.

Reform to practice structures was introduced by a second *loi du 31.12.1990 (No. 90–1258; loi relatif à l'exercice sous forme de sociétés d'exercice libéral des professions soumises à un statut législatif ou réglementaire)*. This enables the members of the new fused profession to practise by means of new types of corporate structure. Such a corporation is known as a *société d'exercice libéral à responsabilité limitée* (*SELARL*) when taking the form of a private company, a *société d'exercice libéral à forme anonyme* (*SELAFA*) when public (there must be a minimum of three members), and a *société d'exercice libéral en commandite par actions* (*SELCA*) when taking the form of a *société en commandite par actions* (a type of incorporated public commercial limited partnership which has legal personality but in which the executive partners (*commandités*) have unlimited liability). Such companies and any group practices can include *avocats* from different *barreaux*, but can only carry out the preparatory work of cases (*la représentation*) in areas where they have a member of the company registered with the local *Tribunal de Grande Instance*. These new practice structures are available to all of the liberal professions, not just lawyers, potentially enabling the creation of multi-disciplinary practices; however, such a company will only be able to carry out the professional activities for which its members are duly qualified.

119

Avocats are also permitted to practise in the form of economic interest groups, European economic interest groups and joint venture groups (*sociétés en participation*). The pre-existing practice structures remain available, although the pre-1992 corporations of *conseils juridiques* must comply with the new law within five years (*Loi 90–1258 du 31.12.1990, Art. 18*).

The government has recognised the right of the professions to be consulted in determining the extent to which the provisions of the new law apply to their own members, it being provided (*ibid, Art. 21*) that regulations would be introduced to implement these provisions only after obtaining the advice of the representative organisations of the different professions.

When the new forms of corporate practice were first mooted, *avocats* argued that to preserve the independence of the profession, the majority of the share capital should be held by *avocats* alone. The reform law does not do this. Rather, it provides (*loi 90–1258 du 31.12.1990, Art. 5*) that more than one-half of the shareholding (and voting rights) must be held by liberal professionals (or corporations of liberal professionals) practising within the company. Liberal professionals also control the management of the company, as they must constitute at least two-thirds of the membership of the board. The remainder of the shareholding must in principle be held by other liberal professionals (whether still practising or retired) and their next of kin.

However, by way of exception, to enable those professions that so desire to bring in outside investment, it is provided that regulations may be introduced, in respect of each profession, permitting up to one-quarter of the share capital to be owned by non-professionals. However, following pressure exerted on the *Sénat* by *avocats*, who argued that this would pose a serious threat to professional independence, this facility of recourse to external capital is expressly stated not to apply to the legal professions.

These new forms of corporate structure for liberal professionals do not fall neatly into existing categories of corporation. Perhaps the most unusual characteristic is that corporate personality does not prevent the professional members from being personally liable for negligence in respect of their professional activities. Such liability is expressly retained, the company being jointly liable with the professionals. Another change from commercial practice is that litigation in respect of such companies is to be dealt with by the ordinary courts, and not, as might be expected, by the commercial courts.

A further innovation of the reform law is to permit for the first time an individual to practise as a salaried *avocat* of another *avocat* or a practice (*amended loi 1971, Art. 7*). To allay fears that a salaried *avocat* may lack professional independence, it is expressly provided that in respect of his own case-load, the salaried *avocat* is independent (although the clientele is regarded as that of the practice, not of him

120

personally) and he is subordinate to his employer only in respect of matters of work conditions. Nor may the contract of employment, which must be in writing, contain a covenant restricting the employee's freedom of establishment on the expiry of the contract. Any disputes relating to the contract are referred to the arbitration of the *bâtonnier*, rather than the court usually competent to deal with employment matters, the *Conseil de Prud'hommes*. Appeal is to the *Cour d'Appel*.

(c) Organisation of the profession

All members of the new merged profession of *avocat*, including those who previously practised as *conseils juridiques*, must belong to one of the pre-existing *barreaux*, who exercise regulatory and disciplinary control over their members. A National Bar Council (*Conseil national du barreau*) has been created (*amended loi 1971, Art. 21 – 1*), having 60 members elected for a three-year term by an electoral college whose membership is designed to be a fair representation of the different Bar associations. It is responsible for representing the profession before public authorities, overseeing the harmonisation of the regulations and customs of the profession, and supervising the provision of professional training offered by regional Bar schools.

(d) Training

Under the reform law, the training requirements of entrants to the common profession follow closely, *mutatis mutandis*, the earlier requirements for the training of *avocats*. These comprise (*amended loi 1971, Art. 12*) an academic stage (obtaining a master's degree in law, or an equivalent diploma), a professional stage (one year spent at a regional Bar school (*Centre de formation professionnelle*; an entry examination must first be passed), and a two-year period as a pupil (*avocat stagiaire*) before admission to the roll. All would-be *avocats* must follow this training programme. Before 1992, trainee *conseils juridiques*, although they had to complete an academic stage, did not have to attend a *Centre de formation professionnelle* (although they did attend 200 hours of professional education classes organised by the regional commission of *conseils juridiques*), and there was a compulsory three-year period of articles. The *Centres* also provide continuing education courses for practising *avocats*, and oversee pupillages (*amended loi 1971, Art. 14*).

(e) Specialisation and advertising

Conseils juridiques had a greater tradition of specialisation than *avocats*; indeed, it was possible for a *conseil juridique* to be granted the title of specialist. In recent years, the *barreaux* recognised the need to identify specialisms, and indeed started to advertise the "dominant activities" of their members in local directories of *avocats*.

Under the reforms (*amended loi 1971, Art. 12 – 1; décret du 27.11.91,*

121

Arts. 88–91) the regional Bar schools are empowered to grant specialisation certificates to those who show that they have been active in a specialism for at least four years, and who have passed a test of competence. *Conseils juridiques* who had obtained the title of specialist may continue to use the title without the need to obtain a specialisation certificate. Specialisation is likely to increase in the light of the potential growth in the size of firms.

D. Costs and legal aid

1. Introduction

The *loi du 16–24 août 1790* introduced the principle of *la gratuité de la justice*; it might thus be thought paradoxical to speak of the cost of justice. However, nowadays the principle of gratuity signifies only that the parties do not pay the judges, or the court officials, whose salaries are paid by the state. Before 1790 judges, who bought their office from the king, received their income from fees paid to them by the litigants.

The major costs which have to be borne by the parties to a court action are the fees of the different professionals who participate in the legal process, such as *avocats, avoués* (in the *Cour d'Appel*) and expert witnesses (*experts*).

2. Costs

In French law a distinction is made between two categories of costs (*frais*). Firstly, there are costs known as *dépens*, comprising among other things (*Nouveau Code de Procédure Civile, Art. 695*) witnesses' expenses and certain fees (*émoluments*) determined either by reference to a scale (for example, the scale fees of an *avoué* or a *huissier* for carrying out procedural steps in an action), or by the judge in accordance with an assessment of the importance of the case and the difficulty of the function (eg the fees of an *expert*). In principle (*NCPC, Art. 696*) the *dépens* of the two parties are borne by the party who is eventually unsuccessful, unless the judge determines otherwise. It is rare for the judge not to order such costs to follow the event, but it might happen for example where the successful party carried out unnecessary procedural steps.

The second category of costs (ie apart from *dépens*) consists essentially of the fees (*honoraires*) of the parties' *avocats*. The amount of these fees is agreed between the *avocat* and his client. Such fees are not subject to taxation by the court. In principle, each party pays the *honoraires* of his own *avocat*, the unsuccessful party not bearing both sets of fees as might be expected. However, the unjustness of this principle is alleviated for civil proceedings by *NCPC, Art. 700* which provides that where it appears inequitable for a party to pay the fees of his own *avocat*, the judge may order the other party to pay such amount as is determined by him. In their submission to the court, *avocats* almost systematically ask the judge to condemn the other side to such costs under *NCPC, Art. 700* (also *loi du 10.7.1991, Art. 75–1*). In practice, the judge will order the loser to pay a sum (2,000–5,000 FF in an average *Tribunal de Grande Instance* case) towards the cost of the *honoraires* of the winner's *avocat*. The same rule now applies to administrative and criminal cases (*loi du 10.7.1991, Art. 75*).

3. Legal aid

(a) Introduction

The *loi du 22.1.1851* introduced a system of legal aid which was known as *assistance judiciaire*. However, aid was given only to a party to an action who was totally without resources. Moreover, the lawyer who acted for such a litigant received no payment for his work. This situation can perhaps be understood in the context of a time when legal practitioners often had a private income, thus enabling them to carry out some unremunerated work. However, the system was clearly inappropriate for a modern legal system, and was replaced in 1972 (*loi du 3.1.1972*) by a system of legal aid known as *l'aide judiciaire*. This system not only extended aid to those of moderate income, but also provided for the payment of fees to participating lawyers. Originally, the scheme did not cover criminal proceedings; if a defendant was without resources, an *avocat* was appointed by the *bâtonnier* (known as a *commission d'office*) to act without remuneration. However, a *loi du 31.12.1982* provided for the payment of *avocats* assigned to represent a criminal client in this way.

The legal aid scheme was much criticised, particularly by *avocats*, on two fronts: firstly on the basis that it covered only representation in respect of a court action, not the giving of legal advice; secondly, it was argued that the level of payment for legal aid work was actually below the costs incurred in representing a client. The system was again reformed by a *loi du 10.7.1991*, responding to these criticisms. We will examine how the system under the 1972 law operates, and the effect of the 1991 reforms, which largely came into effect on 1 January 1992.

(b) Legal aid

(i) Eligibility

Legal aid may be granted to a plaintiff or defendant to cover the costs of civil, criminal or administrative proceedings. It is available to individuals who are of French nationality or foreigners habitually resident in France. Companies may not benefit. The proposed action must not be "manifestly inadmissible or without foundation". To be granted legal aid, the applicant must, of course, comply with certain financial limits, which are regularly reviewed.

(ii) Procedure

The 1991 reform law has retained many of the features of the 1972 law. An award of legal aid is made by the appropriate legal aid office (known as *bureaux d'aide juridictionnelle* under the reforms); these are organised around the *Tribunaux de Grande Instance, Cour de Cassation, Conseil d'Etat,* and *Commission des Recours de Réfugiés.* Each *bureau* is composed of civil servants and representatives of the judiciary and the legal professions. Appeal lies against the decisions of the *bureaux* to the president of the relevant court (in certain cases only through the *procureur de la République*).

(iii) Consequences of an award

The legally aided party is entitled to the services of an *avocat* and, where appropriate, other legal professionals such as a *huissier* or *avoué*. It is for the assisted party to choose which lawyer he wishes to represent him. However, where the lawyer who is chosen refuses to act, or where the assisted party cannot make a choice, a lawyer will be appointed by the *bâtonnier* (or president of the appropriate local professional body). In practice, junior members of the legal profession often take legal aid cases.

What is the liability of the legally aided party for *honoraires* and *dépens*? Firstly, *honoraires*: if he is in receipt of full legal aid he will not have to pay the *honoraires* of his *avocat*; these will be met out of the legal aid funds. If, however, he had obtained only partial legal aid, he will pay only a proportion depending on his financial resources. Secondly, in respect of the *dépens*, liability depends on the outcome of the case. If the legally aided party is successful, he will not pay for the *dépens*, all of which will normally be borne by the loser; in such a case the legal aid fund will recover from the loser the costs of the successful assisted party (ie *dépens* and *honoraires*) already borne by the fund, unless either the loser is himself legally aided, or the judge determines otherwise. If on the other hand the legally aided party is unsuccessful, he will *prima facie* be liable for the *dépens* of both parties. The legal aid fund will cover the cost of his own *dépens*; however, he remains liable to pay the *dépens* (but not in principle the *honoraires*) of his successful adversary. The effect of this surprising rule is mitigated somewhat by the fact that in such a case the court may excuse the legally aided party from paying a proportion of the *dépens* of the winner, which will then be paid for by the legal aid fund.

The lawyer acting for the fully legally aided party is not paid directly by his client, but receives a payment (*une indemnité*) from the legal aid fund; in the case of a partial award, the client will, as we have seen, pay a proportion of the *honoraires*. The level of the *indemnité* varies with the nature of the case and the court in which the case is brought. Constant criticism from the legal profession about the low level of these payments was the major factor which led the government to introduce the 1991 reforms.

(c) The 1991 reform law

A bill was published by the French government in April 1991; its proposals were implemented by the *loi du 10.7.1991* (as completed by the *décret du 19.12.1991*). The system of legal aid for representation, under the new name of *aide juridictionnelle,* has been improved. The maximum income which qualifies for legal aid has been increased considerably; this ceiling is 4,400 FF per month for an award of full legal aid (ie approximately the minimum wage (*SMIC*) equivalent) and 6,600 FF for partial legal aid. The number of households eligible for full legal aid has thus increased from 4.8 million to 6 million. There has also been a marked increase in the remuneration paid to participating lawyers; by 1994 this will have doubled for certain types of work.

Furthermore, the management of the legal aid system has been reformed; a National Council of Access to the Law and Justice will monitor the system, a function carried out at a local level by departmental public interest groups with representatives of the local authorities and legal professions. *Avocats* themselves, through the *barreaux*, will have an increased role in operating the system.

A second aspect of the reform law is that legal aid becomes available not just for contentious matters but also for the obtaining of legal advice. It is known as *l'aide à l'accès au droit* (see *circulaire du 12.3.1992*). To pay for this extension of the legal aid scheme, the statute provides for funding from a variety of sources, such as the state, local collectivities, social security organisations, and professional organisations of the legal professions, including the *barreaux*. The latter will contribute through the *Caisses des réglements pécuniaires des avocats (CARPA)*. These organisations are controlled by one or more *barreaux*. Damages awarded in court are paid from the loser's to the winner's *avocat*; all such sums pass through a *CARPA*. The interest which accrues is used by the *barreaux* for a variety of purposes of common interest to the profession. A proportion of these sums will be available for legal advice payments.

The government envisages that the reforms will cause the legal aid budget to increase from 411 million FF in 1991 to 1,500 million FF.

Texts and materials

1 Loi du 24 mai 1872, Art. 9

Art 9. Le Conseil d'Etat statue souverainement sur les recours en matière contentieuse administrative et sur les demandes d'annulation pour excès de pouvoir formées contre les actes des diverses autorités administratives.

2 Nouveau Code de Procédure Civile, Arts. 42, 43

Art. 42 – La juridiction territorialement compétente est, sauf disposition contraire, celle du lieu où demeure le défendeur.

S'il y a plusieurs défendeurs, le demandeur saisit, à son choix, la juridiction du lieu où demeure l'un d'eux.

Si le défendeur n'a ni domicile ni résidence connus, le demandeur peut saisir la juridiction du lieu où il demeure ou celle de son choix s'il demeure à l'étranger.

Art. 43 – Le lieu où demeure le défendeur s'entend:

– s'il s'agit d'une personne physique, du lieu où celle-ci a son domicile ou, à défaut, sa résidence;

– s'il s'agit d'une personne morale, du lieu où celle-ci est établie.

3(a) Loi N° 71–1130 du 31 décembre 1971 (modifiée par la Loi N° 90–1259 de 31 décembre 1990 et la Loi N° 91–647 du 10 juillet 1991) portant réforme de certaines professions judiciaires et juridiques (extraits)

TITRE 1er. – CRÉATION ET ORGANISATION
DE LA NOUVELLE PROFESSION D'AVOCAT.

CHAPITRE 1er. – *Dispositions générales*

Art. 1er. – Une nouvelle profession dont les membres portent le titre d'avocat est substituée aux professions d'avocat et de conseil juridique. Les membres de ces professions font d'office partie, s'ils n'y renoncent, de la nouvelle profession. Les conseils juridiques, inscrits sur la liste dressée par le procureur de la République à la date d'entrée en vigueur du titre 1er de la loi n° 90–1259 du 31 décembre 1990 portant réforme de certaines professions judiciaires et juridiques, sont inscrits au tableau du barreau établi près le tribunal de grande instance auprès duquel ils sont inscrits comme conseil juridique avec effet à la date de leur entrée dans la profession, s'ils l'exerçaient avant le 16 septembre 1972, ou de leur inscription sur la liste.

Les membres de la nouvelle profession exercent l'ensemble des fonctions antérieurement dévolues aux professions d'avocat et de conseil juridique, dans les conditions prévues par le titre 1er de la présente loi.

La profession d'avocat est une profession libérale et indépendante.

Le titre d'avocat peut être suivi, le cas échéant, de la mention des titres universitaires, des distinctions professionnelles, de la profession juridique réglementée précédemment exercée, d'un titre dont le port est réglementé à l'étranger et permet l'exercice en France des fonctions d'avocat ainsi que de celle d'une ou plusieurs spécialisations.

Les avocats inscrits à un barreau et les conseils juridiques, en exercice depuis plus de quinze ans à la date d'entrée en vigueur du titre 1er de la loi n° 90-1259 du 31 décembre 1990 portant réforme de certaines professions judiciaires et juridiques et qui renoncent à faire partie de la nouvelle profession sont autorisés à solliciter l'honorariat de leur activité professionnelle. Il en va de même pour ceux qui entrent dans la nouvelle profession, lors de la cessation de leur activité si elle intervient après vingt ans au moins d'exercice de leur profession antérieure et de la nouvelle profession. (. . .)

Art. 3. Les avocats sont des auxiliaires de justice.

Ils prêtent serment en ces termes: "Je jure, comme avocat, d'exercer mes fonctions avec dignité, conscience, indépendance, probité et humanité"

Ils revêtent, dans l'exercice de leurs fonctions judiciaires, le costume de leur profession.

Art. 5. Les avocats exercent leur ministère et peuvent plaider sans limitation territoriale devant toutes les juridictions et organismes juridictionnels ou disciplinaires, sous les réserves prévues à l'article précédent.

Ils exercent exclusivement devant le tribunal de grande instance dans le ressort duquel ils ont établi leur résidence professionnelle les activités antérieurement dévolues au ministère obligatoire de l'avoué auprès de ce tribunal. Toutefois, les avocats exercent ces activités devant tous les tribunaux de grande instance près desquels leur barreau est constitué. (. . .)

Art. 6. Les avocats peuvent assister et représenter autrui devant les administrations publiques, sous réserve des dispositions législatives et réglementaires.

Ils peuvent, s'ils justifient de sept années d'exercice d'une profession juridique réglementée, remplir les fonctions de membre du conseil de surveillance d'une société commerciale ou d'administrateur de société. Le conseil de l'ordre peut accorder une dispense d'une partie de cette durée.

Art. 6. *bis*. Les avocats peuvent recevoir des missions confiées par justice.

Art. 7. L'avocat peut exercer sa profession soit à titre individuel, soit au sein d'une association, d'une société civile professionnelle, d'une société d'exercice libéral ou d'une société en participation prévues par la loi n° 90-1258 du 31 décembre 1990 relative à l'exercice sous forme de sociétés des professions libérales soumises à un statut législatif ou réglementaire ou dont le titre est protégé, soit en qualité de salarié ou de collaborateur non salarié d'un avocat ou d'une association ou société d'avocats. Il peut également être membre d'un groupement d'intérêt économique ou d'un groupement européen d'intérêt économique.

Le contrat de collaboration ou le contrat de travail doit être établi par écrit. Il doit préciser les modalités de la rémunération.

Le contrat de collaboration indique également les conditions dans lesquelles l'avocat collaborateur pourra satisfaire aux besoins de sa clientèle personnelle.

L'avocat salarié ne peut avoir de clientèle personnelle. Dans l'exercice des missions qui lui sont confiées, il bénéficie de l'indépendance que comporte son serment et n'est soumis à un lien de subordination à l'égard de son employeur que pour la détermination de ses conditions de travail.

Le contrat de collaboration ou le contrat de travail ne doit pas comporter de stipulation limitant la liberté d'établissement ultérieure du collaborateur ou du salarié.

En aucun cas, les contrats ou l'appartenance à une société, une association ou un groupement ne peuvent porter atteinte aux règles déontologiques de la profession d'avocat, et notamment au respect des obligations en matière d'aide judiciaire et de commission d'office, et à la faculté pour l'avocat collaborateur ou salarié de demander à être déchargé d'une mission qu'il estime contraire à sa conscience ou susceptible de porter atteinte à son indépendance.

Les litiges nés à l'occasion d'un contrat de travail sont soumis à l'arbitrage du bâtonnier, à charge d'appel devant la cour d'appel siégeant en chambre du conseil.

Art. 8. Tout groupement, société ou association prévu à l'article 7 peut être constitué entre avocats, personnes physiques, groupements, sociétés ou ssociations d'avocats appartenant ou non à des barreaux différents.

L'association ou la société peut postuler auprès de chaque tribunal par le ministère d'un avocat inscrit au barreau établi près ce tribunal.

Art. 8–1. Sans préjudice des dispositions de l'article 5, l'avocat peut établir un ou plusieurs bureaux secondaires, après déclaration au conseil de l'Ordre du barreau auquel il appartient.

Lorsque le bureau secondaire est situé dans le ressort d'un barreau différent de celui où est établie sa résidence professionnelle, l'avocat doit en outre demander l'autorisation du conseil de l'Ordre de barreau dans le ressort duquel il envisage d'établir un bureau secondaire. Le conseil de l'Ordre statue dans les trois mois à compter de la réception de la demande. A défaut, l'autorisation est réputée accordée.

L'autorisation ne peut être refusée que pour des motifs tirés des conditions d'exercice de la profession dans le bureau secondaire. Sans préjudice des sanctions disciplinaires pouvant être prononcées par le conseil de l'Ordre du barreau auquel appartient l'avocat, elle ne peut être retirée que pour les mêmes motifs.

Dans tous les cas, l'avocat disposant d'un bureau secondaire doit y exercer une activité professionnelle effective sous peine de fermeture sur décision du conseil de l'Ordre du barreau dans lequel il est situé.

Art. 8–2. Par dérogation aux dispositions de l'article 8–1, les avocats inscrits au barreau de l'un des tribunaux de grande instance de Paris, Bobigny, Créteil et Nanterre ne peuvent ouvrir un bureau secondaire dans le ressort de l'un de ces tribunaux de grande instance autre que celui du barreau auquel ils appartiennent.

Art. 9. L'avocat régulièrement commis d'office par le bâtonnier ou par le président de la cour d'assises ne peut refuser son ministère sans faire approuver ses motifs d'excuse ou d'empêchement par le bâtonnier ou par le président.

Art. 10. La tarification de la postulation et des actes de procédure est régie par les dispositions sur la procédure civile. Les honoraires de consultation, d'assistance, de conseil, de rédaction d'actes juridiques sous seing privé et de plaidoirie sont fixés en accord avec le client.

A défaut de convention entre l'avocat et son client, l'honoraire est fixé selon les usages, en fonction de la situation de fortune du client, de la difficulté de l'affaire, des frais exposés par l'avocat, de sa notoriété et des diligences de celui-ci.

Toute fixation d'honoraires, qui ne le serait qu'en fonction du résultat judiciaire, est interdite. Est licite la convention qui, outre la rémunération des prestations effectuées, prévoit la fixation d'un honoraire complémentaire en fonction du résultat obtenu ou du service rendu.

CHAPITRE II. – *De l'organisation et de l'administration de la profession*

Art. 11. Nul ne peut accéder à la profession d'avocat s'il ne remplit les conditions suivantes:

1° Etre Français, ressortissant d'un Etat membre des Communautés européennes ou ressortissant d'un Etat ou d'une unité territoriale n'appartenant pas à ces communautés qui accorde aux Français la faculté d'exercer sous les mêmes conditions l'activité professionnelle que l'intéressé se propose lui-même d'exercer en France, sous réserve des décisions du conseil des Communautés européennes relatives à l'association des pays et territoires d'outre-mer à la Communauté économique européenne ou avoir la qualité de réfugié ou d'apatride reconnue par l'Office français de protection des réfugiés et apatrides;

2° Etre titulaire, sous réserve des dispositions réglementaires prises pour l'application de la directive C.E.E. n° 89–48 du Conseil des communautés européennes du 21 décembre 1988, et de celles concernant les personnes ayant exercé certaines fonctions ou activités en France, d'au moins une maîtrise en droit ou de titres ou diplômes reconnus comme équivalents pour l'exercice de la profession par arrêté conjoint du garde des sceaux, ministre de la justice, et du ministre chargé des universités;

3° Etre titulaire du certificat d'aptitude à la profession d'avocat, sous réserve des dispositions réglementaires mentionnées au 2°, ou, dans le cadre de la réciprocité, de l'examen prévu au dernier alinéa du présent article;

4° N'avoir pas été l'auteur de faits ayant donné lieu à condamnation pénale pour agissements contraires à l'honneur, à la probité ou aux bonnes moeurs;

5° N'avoir pas été l'auteur de faits de même nature ayant donné lieu à une sanction disciplinaire ou administrative de destitution, radiation, révocation, de retrait d'agrément ou d'autorisation;

6° N'avoir pas été frappé de faillite personnelle ou d'autre sanction en application du titre VI de la loi n° 85–98 du 25 janvier 1985 relative au redressement et à la liquidation judiciaires des entreprises ou, dans le régime antérieur à cette loi, en application du titre II de la loi n° 67–563 du 13 juillet 1967 sur le règlement judiciaire, la liquidation des biens, la faillite personnelle et les banqueroutes. (...)

L'avocat ressortissant d'un Etat ou d'une unité territoriale n'appartenant pas aux communautés européennes, s'il n'est past titulaire du certificat d'aptitude à la profession d'avocat, doit subir, pour pouvoir s'inscrire à un barreau français, les épreuves d'un examen de contrôle des connaissances en droit français selon des modalités fixées par décret en Conseil d'Etat. Il en est de même d'un ressortissant d'un Etat membre des communautés européennes qui aurait acquis la qualité d'avocat dans un Etat ou une unité territoriale n'appartenant pas à ces communautés.

CHAPITRE VI. – *Dispositions transitoires et diverses*

Art. 50. – (...)

VII. – Toute personne peut, dans un délai de deux ans à compter de la date d'entrée en vigueur du titre 1er de la loi no 90–1259 du 31 décembre 1990 portant réforme de certaines professions judiciaires et juridiques, sur sa demande, bénéficier de plein droit de son inscription à un barreau à condition qu'elle remplisse les conditions prévues aux 1o, 2o, 4o, 5o et 6o de l'article 11 et qu'elle justifie de l'exercice effectif, continu, exclusif et rémunéré en France, pendant au moins cinq ans à cette même date, d'activités de consultation ou de rédaction d'actes en matière juridique, soit à titre individuel, soit en qualité de membre d'une personne morale ayant pour objet principal l'exercice de cette activité, soit en qualité de salarié d'une personne morale de ce type, soit en qualité de membre ou de salarié ou de collaborateur d'un groupement constitué sous l'empire d'une législation étrangère et ayant le même objet. Il en est de même de tout Français ou de tout ressortissant d'un autre Etat membre de la Communauté économique européenne qui, remplissant les mêmes conditions, aurait exercé les mêmes activités hors de France.

VIII. – Les ressortissants de l'un des Etats membres de la Communauté économique européenne autre que la France ou de l'un des Etats ou unités territoriales visés au 1o de l'article 11, membres d'une profession juridique réglementée dans l'un des pays dont ils sont ressortissants, qui ne seraient pas inscrits sur une liste de conseils juridiques à la date d'entrée en vigueur du titre 1er de la loi no 90–1259 du 31 décembre 1990 portant réforme de certaines professions judiciaires et juridiques, peuvent, dans un délai de deux ans à compter de cette date, sur leur demande, bénéficier de plein droit de leur inscription à un barreau français à condition qu'ils justifient de l'exercice effectif, continu, exclusif et rémunéré pendant au moins trois ans, dont dix-huit mois en France à cette même date, d'activités de consultation ou de rédaction d'actes en matière juridique, soit à titre individuel, soit en qualité de membre d'une personne morale ayant pour objet principal l'exercice de ces activités, soit en qualité de salarié d'une personne morale de ce type, soit en qualité de membre ou de salarié ou de collaborateur d'un groupement constitué sous l'empire d'une législation étrangère et ayant le même objet.

XIII. – Les groupements constitués sous l'empire d'une législation étrangère installés en France le 31 décembre 1990 peuvent, dans un délai de deux ans à compter de la date d'entrée en vigueur du titre 1er de la loi no 90–1259 du 31 décembre 1990 portant réforme de certaines professions judiciaires et juridiques, sur leur demande, bénéficier de plein droit de leur inscription au barreau de leur choix s'ils justifient de l'exercice effectif et régulier en France, à titre exclusif, d'activités de consultation et de rédaction d'actes en matière juridique et à condition que tous les membres ayant le pouvoir de représenter le groupement en France soient inscrits à un barreau.

TITRE II. – RÉGLEMENTATION DE LA CONSULTATION EN MATIÈRE
JURIDIQUE ET DE LA RÉDACTION D'ACTES SOUS SEING PRIVÉ

CHAPITRE 1er. – *Dispositions générales.*

Art. 54. Nul ne peut, directement ou par personne interposée, à titre habituel
et rémunéré, donner des consultations juridiques ou rédiger des actes sous
seing privé, pour autrui:

1° S'il n'est titulaire d'une licence en droit ou d'un titre ou diplôme reconnu
comme équivalent par arrêté conjoint du garde des sceaux, ministre de la
justice, et du ministre chargé des universités;

2° S'il a été l'auteur de faits ayant donné lieu à condamnation pénale pour
agissements contraires à l'honneur, à la probité ou aux bonnes moeurs;

3° S'il a été l'auteur de faits de même nature ayant donné lieu à une sanction
disciplinaire ou administrative de destitution, radiation, révocation, de retrait
d'agrément ou d'autorisation;

4° S'il a été frappé de faillite personnelle ou d'autre sanction en application
du titre VI de la loi n° 85–98 du 25 janvier 1985 précitée ou, dans le régime
antérieur à cette loi, en application du titre II de la loi n° 67–563 du 13
juillet 1967 précitée;

5° S'il ne répond en outre aux conditions prévues par les articles suivants du
présent chapitre et s'il n'y est pas autorisé au titre desdits articles et dans les
limites qu'ils prévoient. (...)

Art. 55. Toute personne autorisée par le présent chapitre à donner des consultations juridiques ou à rédiger des actes sous seing privé, pour autrui,
de manière habituelle et rémunérée, doit être couverte par une assurance
souscrite personnellement ou collectivement et garantissant les conséquences
pécuniaires de la responsabilité civile professionnelle qu'elle peut encourir au
titre des activités.

Elle doit également justifier d'une garantie financière, qui ne peut résulter que
d'un engagement de caution pris par une entreprise d'assurance régie par le
code des assurances ou par un établissement de crédit habilités à cet effet,
spécialement affectée au remboursement des fonds, effets ou valeurs reçus à
ces occasions.

En outre, elle doit respecter le secret professionnel conformément aux
dispositions de l'article 378 du Code pénal et s'interdire d'intervenir si elle
a un intérêt direct ou indirect à l'objet de la prestation fournie.

Les obligations prévues à l'alinéa précédent sont également applicables à toute
personne qui, à titre habituel et gratuit, donne des consultations juridiques ou
rédige des actes sous seing privé.

Art. 56. Les avocats au Conseil d'Etat et à la Cour de cassation, les avocats
inscrits à un barreau français, les avoués près les cours d'appel, les notaires,
les huissiers de justice, les commissaires-priseurs, les administrateurs judiciaires
et les mandataires-liquidateurs disposent concurremment, dans le cadre des
activités définies par leurs statuts respectifs, du droit de donner des consultations juridiques et de rédiger des actes sous seing privé pour autrui.

Art. 58. Les juristes d'entreprise exerçant leurs fonctions en exécution d'un contrat
de travail au sein d'une entreprise ou d'un groupe d'entreprises peuvent, dans

l'exercice de ces fonctions et au profit exclusif de l'entreprise qui les emploie ou de toute entreprise du groupe auquel elle appartient, donner des consultations juridiques et rédiger des actes sous seing privé relevant de l'activité desdites entreprises.

Art. 59. Les personnes exerçant une activité professionnelle réglementée peuvent, dans les limites autorisées par la réglementation qui leur est applicable, donner des consultations juridiques relevant de leur activité principale et rédiger des actes sous seing. privé qui constituent l'accessoire direct de la prestation fournie.

Art. 60. Les personnes exerçant une activité professionnelle non réglementée pour laquelle elles justifient d'une qualification reconnue par l'Etat ou attestée par un organisme public ou un organisme professionnel agréé peuvent, dans les limites de cette qualification, donner des consultations juridiques relevant directement de leur activité principale et rédiger des actes sous seing privé qui constituent l'accessoire nécessaire de cette activité.

Art. 61. Les organismes chargés d'une mission de service public peuvent, dans l'exercice de cette mission donner des consultations juridiques.

Art. 63. Les associations reconnues d'utilité publique, (...) les fondations reconnues d'utilité publique, les associations agréées de consommateurs, les associations agréées exerçant leur activité dans les domaines de la protection de la nature et de l'environnement et de l'amélioration du cadre de vie et du logement, les associations habilitées par la loi à exercer les droits de la partie civile devant la juridiction pénale, les associations familiales et les unions d'associations familiales régies par le Code de la famille et de l'aide sociale, les centres et associations de gestion agréés, les groupements mutualistes régis par le Code de la mutualité peuvent donner à leurs membres des consultations juridiques relatives aux questions se rapportant directement à leur objet.

Art. 64. Les syndicats et associations professionnels régis par le Code du travail peuvent donner des consultations juridiques et rédiger des actes sous seing privé au profit des personnes dont la défense des intérêts est visée par leurs statuts, sur des questions se rapportant directement à leur objet.

Art. 65. Les organismes constitués, sous quelque forme juridique que ce soit, entre ou par des organisations professionnelles ou interprofessionnelles ainsi que les fédérations et confédérations de sociétés coopératives peuvent donner des consultations juridiques et rédiger des actes sous seing privé au profit de ces organisations ou de leurs membres, sur des questions se rapportant directement à l'activité professionnelle considérée.

Art. 66. Les organes de presse ou de communication audiovisuelle ne peuvent offrir à leurs lecteurs ou auditeurs de consultations juridiques qu'autant qu'elles ont pour auteur un membre d'une profession juridique réglementée.

Art. 66−1. Le présent chapitre ne fait pas obstacle à la diffusion en matière juridique de renseignements et informations à caractère documentaire.

Art. 66−2. Sera puni des peines prévues à l'article 72 quiconque aura, en violation des dispositions du présent chapitre, donné des consultations ou rédigé pour autrui des actes sous seing privé en matière juridique.

CHAPITRE II – *Dispositions diverses.*

Art. 66–5. Les consultations adressées par un avocat à son client et les correspondances échangées entre le client et son avocat sont couvertes par le secret professionnel.

Art. 66–6. Les modalités d'application du présent titre sont précisées par un décret en Conseil d'Etat.

3(b) Décret N° 91–1197 du 27 novembre 1991 organisant la profession d'avocat (extraits)

CHAPITRE II – *Le tableau*

Section 1

L'inscription au tableau

Sous-section 1. – *Conditions générales d'inscription*

Art. 93. – Peuvent être inscrits au tableau d'un barreau:

1° Les avocats possédant le certificat de fin de stage; (. . .)

3° Les personnes ayant acquis la qualité d'avocat dans un Etat ou une unité territoriale n'appartenant pas à la Communauté économique européenne et qui ont subi avec succès le certificat d'aptitude à la profession d'avocat ou l'examen de contrôle des connaissances prévu au dernier alinéa de l'article 11 de la loi du 31 décembre 1971 précitée;

4° Les sociétés civiles professionnelles, les sociétés d'exercice libéral d'avocats; (. . .)

Sous-section 3. – *Conditions particulières d'inscription au barreau des ressortissants de la Communauté économique européenne*

Art. 99. – Peuvent être inscrites au tableau d'un barreau sans remplir les conditions de diplômes, de stage ou d'examens professionnels prévues aux articles 11 et 12 de la loi du 31 décembre 1971 précitée les personnes qui ont suivi avec succès un cycle d'études d'une durée minimale de trois ans ou d'une durée équivalente à temps partiel dans une université ou un établissement d'enseignement supérieur ou dans un autre établissement de même niveau de formation et, le cas échéant, la formation professionnelle requise en plus de ce cycle d'études et qui justifient:

1. De diplômes, certificats ou autres titres permettant l'exercice de la profession dans un Etat membre des communautés européennes délivrés:

a) Soit par l'autorité compétente de cet Etat et sanctionnant une formation acquise de façon prépondérante dans la Communauté;

b) Soit par un pays tiers, à condition que soit fournie une attestation émanant de l'autorité compétente de l'Etat membre qui a reconnu les diplômes, certificats ou autres titres, certifiant que leur titulaire a une expérience professionnelle de trois ans au moins dans cet Etat;

2. Ou de l'exercice à plein temps de la profession pendant deux ans au moins au cours des dix années précédentes dans un Etat membre qui ne réglemente pas l'accès ou l'exercice de cette profession, à condition que cet exercice soit attesté par l'autorité compétente de cet Etat.

L'intéressé doit subir devant le jury prévu à l'article 69 un examen d'aptitude dont le programme et les modalités sont fixés par arrêté du garde des sceaux, ministre de la justice, après avis du Conseil national des barreaux:

1° Lorsque sa formation porte sur des matières substantiellement différentes de celles qui figurent aux programmes de l'examen d'accès à un centre régional de formation professionnelle et du certificat d'aptitude à la profession d'avocat;

2° Ou lorsqu'une ou plusieurs des activités professionnelles dont l'exercice est subordonné à la possession de ces diplômes et examens ne sont pas réglementées dans l'Etat membre d'origine ou de provenance ou sont réglementées de manière différente et que cette différence est caractérisée par une formation spécifique requise en France portant sur des matières substantiellement différentes de celles couvertes par le diplôme dont le demandeur fait état.

A la réception du dossier complet de l'intéressé, le Conseil national des barreaux lui délivre un récépissé. Il se prononce par décision motivée dans un délai de quatre mois à compter de la date de délivrance du récépissé.

La décision du Conseil national des barreaux par laquelle est arrêtée la liste des candidats admis à se présenter à l'examen d'aptitude précise, le cas échéant, les matières sur lesquelles les candidats doivent être interrogés compte tenu de leur formation initiale.

Nul ne peut se présenter plus de trois fois à l'examen d'aptitude.

Sous-section 4. – *Conditions particulières d'inscription au barreau des personnes ayant acquis la qualité d'avocat dans un Etat ou une unité territoriale n'appartenant pas à la Communauté économique européenne*

Art. 100. – Les modalités et le programme de l'examen de contrôle des connaissances prévu au dernier alinéa de l'article 11 de la loi du 31 décembre 1971 précitée pour l'inscription au tableau d'un barreau français des personnes ayant acquis la qualité d'avocat dans un Etat ou une unité territoriale n'appartenant pas à la Communauté économique europénne sont fixés par arrêté du garde des sceaux, ministre de la justice, après avis du Conseil national des barreaux.

L'examen est subi devant le jury prévu à l'article 69, qui peut, au vu des travaux universitaires ou scientifiques du candidat, dispenser celui-ci de certaines épreuves.

Nul ne peut se présenter plus de trois fois à l'examen de contrôle des connaissances.

TITRE V. – LA LIBRE PRESTATION DE SERVICES EN FRANCE PAR LES AVOCATS DES ETATS MEMBRES DES COMMUNAUTES EUROPEENNES

Art. 200. – Le présent titre est applicable aux avocats ressortissants d l'un des Etats membres des communautés européennes établis à titre permanent dans l'un de ces Etats autres que la France et venant accomplir, en France, une activité professionnelle occasionnelle.

Cette activité est librement exercée dans les conditions prévues ci-après. Elle ne peut toutefois s'étendre au domaine qui relève de la compétence exclusive des officiers publics ou ministériels.

Art. 201 – Pour l'application du présent titre, sont reconnus en France comme avocats les ressortissants des Etats membres des communautés européennes qui exercent dans l'un de ces Etats autres que la France leurs activités professionnelles sous l'une des dénominations suivantes:

- en Belgique: avocat ou advocaat;
- au Danemark: advokat;
- en Allemagne: Rechtsanwalt;
- en Espagne: abogado;
- en Grèce: dikigoros;
- en Irlande: barrister, solicitor;
- en Italie: avvocato;
- au Luxembourg: avocat-avoué;
- aux Pays-Bas: advocaat;
- au Portugal: advogado;
- au Royaume-Uni: advocate, barrister, solicitor.

Les personnes mentionnées au premier alinéa font usage, en France, de l'un de ces titres, exprimé dans la ou l'une des langues de l'Etat où elles sont établies, accompagné du nom de l'organisme professionnel dont elles relèvent ou de celui de la juridiction auprès de laquelle elles sont habilitées à exercer en application de la législation de cet Etat.

Le procureur général près la cour d'appel dans le ressort de laquelle est assurée la prestation de services, le bâtonnier de l'ordre des avocats territorialement compétent, le président et les membres de la juridiction ou de l'organisme juridictionnel ou disciplinaire ou le représentant qualifié de l'autorité publique devant lequel se présente l'avocat peuvent lui demander de justifier de sa qualité.

Art. 202 – Lorsqu'un avocat mentionné à l'article 201 assure la représentation ou la défense d'un client en justice ou devant les autorités publiques, il exerce ses fonctions dans les mêmes conditions qu'un avocat inscrit à un barreau français.

Il respecte les règles professionnelles françaises, sans préjudice des obligations non contraires qui lui incombent dans l'Etat dans lequel il est établi.

Il doit notamment se soumettre aux prescriptions de l'article 158.

En matière civile, lorsque la représentation est obligatoire devant le tribunal de grande instance, il ne peut se constituer qu'après avoir élu domicile auprès d'un avocat établi près le tribunal saisi et auquel les actes de la procédure sont valablement notifiés. Devant la cour d'appel, il doit agir de concert avec un avoué près cette cour d'appel ou un avocat habilité à représenter les parties devant elle.

Art. 203 – Pour l'exercice, en France, des activités autres que celles prévues à l'article 202, les avocats restent soumis aux conditions d'exercice et aux règles professionnelles applicables à leur profession dans l'Etat dans lequel ils sont établis.

Ils sont aussi tenus au respect des règles qui s'imposent, pour l'exercice de ces activités, aux avocats inscrits à un barreau français, notamment celles concernant l'incompatibilité entre l'exercice, en France, des activités d'avocat et celui d'autres activités, le secret professionnel, les rapports confraternels, l'interdiction d'assistance par un même avocat de parties ayant des intérêts opposés et la publicité. Ces règles ne leur sont applicables que si elles peuvent être observées alors qu'ils ne disposent pas d'un établissement en France et dans la mesure où leur observation se justifie objectivement pour assurer, en France, l'exercice correct des activités d'avocat, la dignité de la profession et le respect des incompatibilités.

Art. 204 – En cas de manquement par les avocats aux dispositions du présent décret, ceux-ci sont soumis aux dispositions des articles 180 et suivants relatifs à la discipline des avocats inscrits à un barreau français. Toutefois, pour l'application de l'article 184, les peines disciplinaires de l'interdiction temporaire et de la radiation du tableau ou de la liste du stage sont remplacées par la peine de l'interdiction provisoire ou définitive d'exercer, en France, des activités professionnelles. L'autorité disciplinaire française peut demander à l'autorité compétente de l'État d'origine communication des renseignements professionnels concernant les avocats intéressés. Elle informe cette dernière autorité de toute décision prise. Ces communications ne portent pas atteinte au caractère confidentiel des renseignements fournis.

Art. 285 – Le présent décret entrera en vigueur le 1er janvier 1992, à l'exception des articles 246, 250, 251, 261 et 263, qui sont immédiatement applicables.

Chapter 4

The constitutional framework

A. Introduction

The word constitution in a restrictive and formal sense refers to a text having supreme legal value which has been adopted in accordance with a special procedure and which describes the organisation and functioning of the state. However, in a broad sense it describes the body of rules relating to the organisation and exercise of power. In the French system, both of these meanings are applicable. Since the 1789 Revolution, France has had an unbroken tradition of written constitutions. However, the entire body of constitutional law is not to be found within these written constitutions. Recourse has been had, especially since the establishment of the Third Republic in 1875, to various rules of a constitutional nature. Some of these rules have legal constitutional value, such as the caselaw of the Constitutional Council (*Conseil Constitutionnel*), some not. Some are closely related to the constitutional texts, some not. All, however, are part of a broad framework describing how power is exercised in France.

This wide definition of constitutional rules leads us in this chapter to an examination of certain rules and institutions which are not normally dealt with in the context of constitutional law in French textbooks, such as the principles of administrative proceedings for the annulment of illegal administrative decisions or regulations (*recours pour excès de pouvoir*). These are dealt with in the context of constitutional law because they are all a product of French political and legal history, and are rooted in the basic principles which form the core of public law. Such rules and institutions, taken together with the constitutional texts themselves, form a coherent whole, and this coherence is one of the main characteristics of the French constitutional system. The origin of this system can be traced back to 1789. It has been developed with great continuity since 1875 under the Third (1875–1940), Fourth (1946–58) and Fifth (1958–) Republics. The establishment of the Fifth Republic in 1958 (*Constitution de 1958;* TEXTS, NO. 1) brought with it certain innovations, but, to be properly understood, these (as well as the growing impact of EC law) should be seen in the light of this constitutional continuity. French constitutional rules are best explained when seen within a framework based on three foundational notions − France as a Republic, a Nation and an *Etat de droit* (literally "State of law") − and therefore they will now be examined within this framework.

B. The Republic

1. The notion of "République"

La République is the official designation of France used in legal documents ranging from the *Journal officiel* (the official journal in which all legislation and parliamentary debates are published) to the identity card (*carte d'identité*) which all citizens are encouraged to carry with them. It is also traditional for the *Président de la République* to finish his political speeches with the phrase, "*Vive la République, vive la France*".

What is meant by *la République*? It has several meanings. In a negative sense, the Republic is to be contrasted with the monarchy, and the inheritability of public functions. In a positive sense, it refers to a particular form of political organisation which is a product of history and is bound up with the related notions of nation, democracy and *l'Etat de droit*. There is also an ideological aspect to *la République*; there is a republican programme and a republican ethic. The so-called republican tradition (*la tradition républicaine*), the existence of which has been acknowledged by the *Conseil d'Etat (Avis du C.E., 6.2.53;* TEXTS, NO. 2), is a mixture of political practices and basic political and legal principles. The content of this republican tradition has, like any other tradition, varied with time, and is therefore a little vague. This fact should not be considered to be too important, however, as the true significance of the notion of *la tradition républicaine* is as a reference to a political sensitivity; the notion is invoked by politicians as an appeal to authority, and as a means of bringing to an end all debate on an issue. The *Conseil Constitutionnel* has even granted legal constitutional force to some of the elements of this tradition as being part of the "fundamental principles recognised by the laws of the Republic" (*C.C., 16.7.1971; J.O., 18.7.1971, 7114;* TEXTS, NO. 3).

2. The continuity of the Republic

The preamble to the Constitution of the Second Republic of 1848 declared the republican form of government to be the definitive form of government of France. However, following the 1851 *coup d'état* of

Louis-Napoléon Bonaparte, the Empire was re-established in 1852, and lasted until the defeat of the French army at the hands of the Prussians in 1870. The *Assemblée Nationale* which was elected in 1871 had the task of drawing up a new constitution, which it did by adopting three constitutional laws in 1875. Despite being largely in favour of the restoration of the monarchy, the *Assemblée Nationale* was paralysed by divisions amongst the ranks of the royalists; the Republic was finally reinstated impliedly with the adoption by a single vote (on 30 January 1875) of an amendment to the text of a constitutional law (known as *l'amendement Wallon*) which referred to the head of state as being *le Président de la République (Loi du 25.2.1875, Art. 2;* TEXTS, NO. 4). The increasing influence of the republicans enabled them to introduce a revision of the Constitution in 1884 which inserted a provision that the republican form of government could not be changed (*Loi du 14.8.1884;* TEXTS, NO. 5).

Following the collapse of the French army in 1940, a constitutional law of 10 July 1940 granted power to Marshal Pétain to produce a new constitution. This led to the creation of a new political regime; that of the "French State" (*L'État français*) in which power was effectively exercised by the head of state. General de Gaulle, following an appeal on 18 June 1940 to continue the struggle (broadcast from London), became the leader of the Free French, and in due course the head of the provisional government of the French Republic. De Gaulle, in an ordinance passed soon after liberation (*ordonnance du 9.8.1944;* TEXTS, NO. 6), proclaimed that the Republic had never officially ceased to exist; this enabled legislation which had been passed during the Vichy regime and which was contrary to *la tradition Républicaine* (such as the *loi constitutionnelle du 10.7.1940*) to be declared null and void.

The 1958 Constitution of the Fifth Republic (*Art. 89;* TEXTS, NO. 1) reiterates the principle that the republican form of government cannot be changed.

3. The republican programme

(a) Introduction

The first ideological source of the republican programme was the *1789 Déclaration des Droits de l'Homme et du Citoyen* (CHAPTER 1 TEXTS, NO. 10), the value of which has increased greatly during the Fifth Republic due particularly to the fact that the *Conseil Constitutionnel* has accorded legal force to its provisions (see below).

The official motto of *liberté, égalité, fraternité* may be regarded as a concise summary of the republican programme. The addition of *fraternité* to *liberté* and *égalité* in the Constitution of the Second Republic in 1848 signified the Republic's awakening concern with social preoccupations. This concern was to find formal expression in the preamble to the 1946 Constitution, which was reaffirmed in the preamble to the 1958 Constitution.

(b) The ideological basis of the republican programme

The revolutionaries of 1789 gave universal value to the idea of the natural inherent rights of the individual by identifying these rights and proclaiming them in the *Déclaration* of that year. The authors of the text, and many since, have felt that it opened a new chapter in political history; Tocqueville expressed this view in his seminal work *L'Ancien Régime et la Révolution* (1856) when he stated that the Revolution was not merely political in nature, but quasi-religious. The *Déclaration* marks the foundation of an ideology of human rights in French political history. Since then each new regime has felt obliged, on coming into power, to affirm its own legitimacy by declaring an adherence to the notion of human rights. Such adherence has been affirmed in different ways. In 1793, it was by the proclamation of a new official *Déclaration des Droits de l'Homme*, issued with the constitution of that year. With the restoration of the monarchy under Louis XVIII, it took the form of a political proclamation (*la Déclaration Royale de St-Ouen du 2.5.1814*). In the Constitutions of 1946 (TEXTS, NO. 7) and 1958 (TEXTS, NO. 1) the rights of the individual were mentioned in the preamble. Additionally, there are instances of references to such rights in the provisions of constitutional texts themselves; for example the 1958 Constitution (*Art. 66*) expressly affirms the right of an individual not to be arbitrarily detained.

(c) Foundational principles of the Republic

These are set out in the 1958 Constitution which states (*Art. 2*) that "France is an indivisible, lay, democratic and social Republic". Let us examine each element in turn.

(i) Indivisible

The indivisibility of the Republic is a strong principle expressing in ideological terms the unity of the Republic, and in particular of its territory. It was a tenet of the ideology known as Jacobinism, which stood for a strongly centralised state. Although the roots of this notion of unity may be found in the *Ancien Régime*, it was during the revolutionary period that it was developed in its modern sense. Indeed, it was Napoleon who gave the notion systematic form both in respect of the legal system, implementing the *Code Civil* throughout the country, and in respect of the administrative institutions, by increasing the degree of centralisation and by creating uniform administrative territorial units throughout the country, such as the *départements*.

Indivisibility, however, has long been regarded as compatible with the existence of a certain number of "territorial collectivities" (*collectivités territoriales de la République; Constitution de 1958, Art. 72;* TEXTS, NO. 1) such as *communes, départements,* overseas *départements (départements d'outre-mer;* eg Martinique, Guadeloupe, Guyane, La Réunion), and overseas territories (*territoires d'outre-mer;* eg La Nouvelle Calédonie). The Constitution (*Art. 72*) permits the creation of new territorial collectivities by statute. On this basis, one of the decentralisation laws of the early 1980s (*loi du 2.3.1982*) conferred upon the regions (*régions*) the status of a new type of territorial collectivity, and special status has been granted to two overseas territories (Mayotte and St Pierre et Miquelon).

The indivisible nature of the Republic theoretically prevents the dismemberment of its territory. However, this principle has had to be compromised with the granting of independence to colonial possessions. Algeria, which gained independence in 1962 following eight years of military conflict, posed particular difficulties, as part of it had acquired the status of *départements* (known as *les départements français d'Algérie*). The subsequent granting of independence to colonial territories, such as the Comoros Islands, occurred without armed conflict. Indeed, the constitutionality of the statute which granted independence to the islands was confirmed by the *Conseil Constitutionnel (C.C., 30.12.75; Rec., 26;* TEXTS, NO. 8). However, some uncertainty remains, as the *Conseil* did so in terms which have generally been interpreted as recognising that the *territoires d'outre-mer* have a right to independence but the *départements d'outre-mer* do not.

The indivisibility of the territory of the Republic has also often been regarded as an obstacle to the recognition of the linguistic rights of minority groups such as Bretons, Alsatians, and Corsicans. However, there have been gradual and cautious changes. The decentralisation laws of the 1980s introduced true local government structures in a way that had not before been known in an over-centralised France. The role of the prefect, the representative of central government in a *département*, nowadays consists more in controlling the legality of local administrative decisions than in actually taking substantive decisions himself. Indeed, the recent tendency has been to transfer power from centrally appointed government representatives such as the prefect to locally elected representatives of the people; in particular, the *régions* (of which there are 26, including overseas regions) have been given a major role in administering the territory of the Republic.

The *Conseil Constitutionnel* has shown a certain resistance to this drift from the traditional concept of the indivisible Republic. Thus, an attempt by the government to grant special status to Corsica in a 1990 bill, by granting the island strong autonomous powers and expressly recognising the existence of the "Corsican people", partly failed. The *Conseil Constitutionnel* accepted as constitutional the new powers granted to the region, but refused to recognise the legal existence of a particular people-group within France, saying that the Constitution recognised only the French people without distinction of origin, race or religion (*C.C., 9.5.1991; D. 1991, 624;* TEXTS, NO. 9).

(ii) Secular

That France is a secular state results from the *loi du 9.12.1905* (TEXTS, NO. 10) which separates church from state, and which was passed despite strong opposition from the Catholic church. Being a secular state implies that the Republic should be neutral in matters of religion and ideology (apart from the need to retain republican ideology). This neutrality has gradually achieved wide consensus in French public opinion, as have the legal implications of such neutrality, such as freedom to exercise a creed, and freedom from religious discrimination in the workplace. The one exception appears to be the question of schooling. France has for decades been divided on the issue of whether or not *écoles libres* (ie private, usually religious, usually Catholic schools) should be publicly funded. The *loi Debré* of 1959 (*loi du 31.12.59;* TEXTS, NO. 11) started a new phase in the debate by granting state moneys to such schools at the same time as introducing measures to ensure effective state control. This law represented a workable compromise, and gradually gained acceptance with many sectors of French society. However, the government which came to power in 1981, and which was led by the socialists, sought in December 1982 to modify the law by increasing state control. This led to great public opposition, and the reform bill had to be withdrawn.

The religious rights of minorities have been another source of controversy in this area. In 1989 the question arose as to whether or not Muslim girls could be authorised, on the grounds of their religious beliefs, to wear Islamic headcoverings at school, and to refuse to participate in certain school activities such as sport. The issue caused much public debate and political division. The government sought the opinion of the *Conseil d'Etat*. In a balanced opinion (*C.E., Avis du 27.11.89;* TEXTS, NO. 12) the *Conseil d'Etat*, whilst recognising the right of pupils to express their religious beliefs in school, also recognised the right of the headteacher of a school to refuse admission to a pupil who distinguishes him or herself from the other pupils in any way which constitutes an act of "pressure, provocation, proselytisation or propaganda" or which would be likely to cause trouble in the school.

(iii) Democratic

The Republic represents itself as the government of the people by the people and for the people (*Constitution de 1958, Art. 2*); this motto is based on the twin principles of liberty and equality. The French people have in the past tended to show more concern for equality than for liberty, but the motto nevertheless confirms the adherence

142

of the Republic to the principles of political liberalism. One aspect of this is that access to political positions may be determined only by democratic election. All those of age are entitled to vote. The age of majority was fixed at 18 by *loi du 5.7.1974*. Although universal suffrage for men was introduced in 1848 (*Constitution de 1848, Art. 25*), women had to wait until 1944 (*ordonnance du Général de Gaulle du 21.4.1944*). The Maastricht agreement on the European Union establishes a citizenship of the Union entailing, *inter alia*, the right of a citizen to vote and stand as a candidate in municipal elections in the member state in which he resides. This is one of the provisions of the treaty which resulted in the need to modify the constitution (see below).

Various public liberties are legally guaranteed and protected. Although these public liberties derive from the *Déclaration de 1789*, many were legally recognised only during the Third Republic. The main liberties are: freedom to hold public meetings (*loi du 30.6.1881*); freedom of the press (*loi du 29.7.1881*); freedom to create associations and societies (*loi du 1.7.1901*); freedom to create and join a trade union (*loi du 21.3.1884*); and freedom of religion (*loi du 9.12.1905*, see above). Political parties obtained constitutional recognition in the 1958 Constitution (*Art. 4*). However, the issue of the financing of political parties caused much controversy and scandal during the late 1980s, and has yet to be properly resolved.

A recurrent theme of French political life is democratisation. This notion bears two distinct but closely related meanings, one emphasising equality, the other liberty. It refers firstly to a process towards greater equality, a good example of which is the democratisation of education, by which is meant the widening of access to all levels of education for all classes of society. Secondly, however, democratisation also refers to the move towards greater participation in the exercise of all forms of power, for example the decentralisation laws of the 1980s which increased local democracy.

(iv) Social

The social ambitions of the Republic, which were declared in the preamble to the Constitution of the Second Republic in 1848, were to become a major characteristic of the Fourth Republic in the years after the Second World War. It drew its inspiration at least in part from the social programme which had been proposed during the War by the *Conseil National de la Résistance*. The Republic, although it has a social programme, is not a socialist Republic. The preamble to the 1946 Constitution (TEXTS, NO. 7) clearly states that "the French people solemnly reaffirm the human rights and liberties set out in the 1789 Declaration and the fundamental principles recognised by the laws of the Republic"; the social programme of the Republic is therefore firmly set within this framework.

By way of implementation of this programme, the preamble to the 1946

Constitution recognised certain political, economic and social rights regarded as being (*para. 2*) "particularly necessary in our times", especially in the fields of social security (the state guaranteeing to all citizens, and particularly to children, mothers and senior citizens health protection, material security, and the right to rest and leisure); sexual equality (women being guaranteed equal rights to men in all fields); and the workplace (such as the right to work, and the right to strike). Furthermore the provisions of the preamble also legitimised the policy of nationalisation of broad areas of essential economic activity which was implemented immediately after the War. State intervention in the economy continued into the Fifth Republic. However, it was greatly reduced as a consequence of the extensive programme of privatisation carried out by the government of Jacques Chirac during the so-called period of cohabitation (March 1986 to May 1988). A major step in the implementation of new social rights was made in 1982 with the passing of legislation (known as the *lois Auroux*) which extended the rights of employees (ie *loi du 4.8.82* on employees' freedoms and rights in the workplace; *loi du 28.10.82* on employees' representative institutions; *loi du 13.11.82* on collective disputes; and *loi du 23.12.82* on Hygiene, Safety and Work Conditions Committees). It should be noted that EC competition rules have had quite an impact on the French public sector.

The rights set out in the preamble to the 1946 Constitution, like those of the 1789 Declaration, have constitutional value. This is confirmed in the preamble to the 1958 Constitution, which provides that "the French people solemnly proclaim their adherence to the rights of man and the principles of national sovereignty as defined in the 1789 Declaration and confirmed and completed by the preamble to the 1946 Constitution".

4. The institutions of the Republic

The Republic is organised in accordance with the principle of the separation of powers. The Fifth Republic possesses the elements of a parliamentary regime, although the position of the President gives the French system a particular character.

(a) The separation of powers

(i) Theoretical basis

The doctrine of the separation of powers was, as we have seen (Chapter 1) elaborated in France by Montesquieu in his book *L'Esprit des Lois* in 1748. Montesquieu distinguished three functions of the state: "that of creating law, that of executing public decisions, and that of judging crimes or disputes between individuals". He went on to say that should these three powers be concentrated in the hands of one body, "there is no liberty", and "everything would be lost". In accordance with these ideas, the 1848 Constitution (*Art. 19*) provided that "the separation of powers is the first condition of a free government". The Republic, adhering to the principles of a liberal democracy, has respected this separation of powers in the three constitutions since 1875.

The reality is, however, more complex and indeed more subtle. The need for the state to act with one voice requires co-operation between the powers and the imposition of limits on their separation; sometimes one of the institutions needs to be given the last word on an issue. In the Fifth Republic, the role of the President of the Republic does blur the position, as his role of overseeing the constitution means that his functions straddle all three powers: the executive (he chairs meetings of the Council of Ministers (*Conseil des Ministres*) and signs their ordinances); the legislature (eg promulgating parliamentary statutes); and the judiciary (he appoints the members of the body with responsibility for the advancement and discipline of the judiciary (*le Conseil supérieur de la magistrature*)). Nor are the three powers of the same relative strength; the dominance of executive power is underlined by the weakened position of the legislature and the judiciary. Let us now examine the roles of the legislature and the judiciary vis-à-vis the executive.

(ii) Legislative power

During the Third Republic, the government exercised increasingly wide powers to legislate by means of regulation rather than parliamentary statute. This practice originated during the economic crises of the inter-war years, when it was used to enable the government to push through urgent or unpopular measures. Increasingly, the legislature delegated, by means of enabling acts (*lois d'habilitation*), its legislative power to the executive, which then enacted law by means of regulations known as *décrets-lois*. The 1946 Constitution sought to prevent this practice by providing (*Art. 13*) that "only the National Assembly may pass laws, and cannot delegate this right". However, this provision proved to be unworkable, and in 1953 the government sought the opinion of the *Conseil d'Etat* on the legality of the practice of executive law-making by delegation. The *Conseil d'Etat (C.E., Avis du 6.2.1953*; TEXTS, NO. 2) impliedly upheld the practice, but limited it by saying that in accordance with the republican tradition certain matters, such as the basic principles of individual liberties, could only be legislated on by Parliament. The legislature's practice of delegating its legislative function to the executive shows the decline of the institution of Parliament, and led to an innovation in the Constitution of the Fifth Republic (*C. 1958, Arts. 34, 37*) which divided legislative power between Parliament and the government (see below).

(iii) Judicial authority

In France, political history has played a large role in the way relations between the institutions are organised in the written constitutions.

145

The Republic has always traditionally been wary of the power of the judiciary. This distrust is rooted in the way the *Parlements* of the *Ancien Régime* abused their position and interfered in politics; the judiciary is thus readily suspected of seeking *gouvernement des juges*. As a result, the judiciary has tended throughout republican history to be in a weak position. As was noted in Chapter 2, an indication of this subordinate position of the judiciary is given in the 1958 Constitution (*C.1958, Art. 64*), which refers not to judicial power (*le pouvoir judiciaire*) but merely to judicial authority (*l'autorité judiciaire*). Moreover, the article makes it clear that the judiciary is not inherently independent of the other institutions, with its provision that "the President of the Republic is the guarantor of the independence of the judicial authority".

It should be noted that the ideas of General de Gaulle on the supremacy of the President of the Republic were not in conformity with the traditional doctrine of the separation of powers. In a well-known press conference in 1964, (TEXTS, NO. 13), he expressed the view that he considered all power to be enjoyed subject to the power of the President, and made it clear that he placed judicial authority no higher than the level of ministerial or military power.

(b) The parliamentary regime

The 1958 Constitution displays the elements of a parliamentary regime, although the prominent role of the President of the Republic gives the French regime a particular character. We will examine in turn the Parliament and the government.

(i) Parliament

Bicameralism: France has had a bicameral parliamentary system since 1875, now confirmed in the 1958 Constitution (*C.1958, Art. 24*). The upper house, the *Sénat*, plays a minor and rather conservative role compared with the lower house, the *Assemblée Nationale*. This is partly as a result of its members (*sénateurs*; only individuals aged at least 35 are eligible) being indirectly elected by an electoral college comprising persons who themselves are elected delegates. Thus in each *département* those entitled to vote include the *députés*, and members of the regional and departmental councils, and representatives of the municipal councils. The number of *sénateurs* representing each *département* depends on the size of its population. In 1989 there were a total of 322 *sénateurs* (of which 296 represented metropolitan France). They are elected in tranches of one-third every three years for a nine-year term. Under *C.1958, Art. 45*, although the *Sénat* can delay the promulgation of a bill, it cannot at the end of the day block it. Where a bill is not adopted by both houses, the Prime Minister may set up a commission comprising an equal number of parliamentarians from the two houses to propose a compromise draft of the bill. If this draft is not approved, the government can submit the bill (in its original or modified form) to the *Assemblée Nationale* which has the last word. The upper house has survived attempts to reform it (a reform bill was put to a referendum by President de Gaulle on 27.4.1969) or even abolish it (*projet de constitution du 19.4.1946*, again put to a referendum).

The *députés* of the National Assembly are elected by direct universal suffrage for a five-year term. They total 577, of which 555 represent metropolitan France.

The powers of Parliament: The 1958 Constitution has markedly reduced the power and influence of Parliament, and increased those of the government. The most noticeable feature of this is, as was seen in Chapter 2 (see also below), that the legislative function has effectively been parcelled out between Parliament and the government, Parliament's legislative power being restricted largely to the fields set out in *C.1958, Art. 34*. Despite the reduction in the power of Parliament, its essential functions remain: it passes laws within the field of its competence; it adopts the budget; it can bring down the government by a motion of censure. It should also be noted that the supremacy of EC law over national legislation has the effect of reducing the power of Parliament.

(ii) Government

The government determines and implements national policy (*C.1958, Art. 20*). It is led by a Prime Minister appointed by the President of the Republic. The Prime Minister is granted power (*C.1958, Art. 37*) to make law by regulation in the fields not exclusively reserved for Parliament under *C.1958, Art. 34*.

As one would expect in a parliamentary system, the government is answerable to Parliament (*C.1958, Arts. 20, 50*); a motion of censure of the government can thus be set down by one-tenth of the members of the *Assemblée Nationale* (*C.1958, Art. 49(2)*) and, if it is passed, the government must tender its resignation (*C.1958, Art. 50*). However, this answerability to Parliament is balanced by the fact that the government has a good degree of control over Parliament. The government determines the order of business of Parliament (*C.1958, Art. 48*). Under *C.1958, Art. 41*, if the government is of the opinion that Parliament is exceeding its competence (which is limited by *C.1958, Art. 34*) it may challenge Parliament's right to discuss a bill; if Parliament resists the challenge, the matter will be resolved by the *Conseil Constitutionnel*.

Furthermore, *C.1958, Art. 49(3)* enables the government to push through the adoption of a *loi* without the express vote of Parliament. This article, the use of which is a form of political brinkmanship, is sparingly employed, and operates as follows. The Council of Ministers will make a bill the subject of a vote of confidence. The bill will automatically be adopted at the end of 24 hours, without debate, unless within that time the opposition puts down a motion of censure, which (*C.1958, Art. 49(2)*) if adopted, will lead to the resignation of the government. The use of this procedure has become more frequent in recent years, pointing not only to a decline in the authority of Parliament, but also to the political weakness of the government, which has not been able to steer bills through Parliament in the normal way. The procedure has been criticised as being undemocratic.

The government does, however, share governmental powers with the President. In Republics before the Fifth Republic he played a minor role. Since 1958 he has become the central figure of the political system.

(c) The President of the Republic

(i) Introduction

In the Fourth Republic, the predominance of Parliament coupled with deep political divisions led to governmental instability. The Constitution of the Fifth Republic represents a reaction against parliamentary supremacy, and provides the President of the Republic with a strong position. The definition of his powers under *C.1958, Art. 5* makes it clear that his role is to uphold the Constitution and to act as referee and arbitrator between the different public powers so as to ensure the effective functioning of the state. Since 1958 he has been regarded as the "cornerstone" of the Constitution. President de Gaulle, desiring to prevent a drift back towards the parliamentary system of the Fourth Republic with all its weaknesses, sought to reinforce the central role of the presidency for his successors with the introduction of direct elections for the presidency (*référendum du 28.10.1962*). The traditional seven-year term of the presidency has been criticised as being too long in the light of the increased powers of the President under the Fifth Republic. The position of President has been held successively by De Gaulle (1959–1969), Pompidou (1969–1974), Giscard d'Estaing (1974–1981) and Mitterrand (1981–).

The President is the head of state. He has a certain number of traditional functions. He thus appoints the head of the government and chairs meetings of the Council of Ministers. He also appoints, in collaboration with the government, a wide range of senior civil servants (including *conseillers d'Etat*) and members of the armed forces (*C.1958, Art. 13*). He is entitled to grant amnesties (*le droit de grâce; C.1958, Art. 17*); thus, in July 1991 President Mitterrand granted an amnesty to some 1,200 prisoners, as is commonly done on the national day of 14 July. Furthermore, he has ceremonial functions such as receiving visiting heads of state and accrediting foreign ambassadors (*C.1958, Art. 14*). A second aspect of his role is that of ensuring the proper functioning of the state. This is perhaps best shown by his power to intervene in times of grave crisis to take "whatever measures are required by the circumstances" with a view to restoring the normal functioning of constitutional authorities (*C.1958, Art. 16*).

(ii) Presidential powers

Many of the presidential powers reveal the supervisory role that the President has in the functioning of the different institutions of state. Turning firstly to his relationship with the government, it is provided by *C.1958, Art. 8* that the President appoints the Prime Minister. The article does not lay down any limitations on the President's choice; indeed, there is no need for the Prime Minister to be a member of Parliament. However, as the Prime Minister is the head of the government and it is through him that the government is responsible to Parliament, the President in practice appoints a Prime Minister from the ranks of the party or coalition which has achieved a parliamentary majority. This led to the socialist President Mitterrand, following the defeat of the socialists in the 1986 parliamentary elections at the hands of the right-wing RPR-UDF alliance, appointing his political opponent, Jacques Chirac, as Prime Minister. Article 8 of the 1958 Constitution provides that the President accepts the resignation of the Prime Minister; it is now accepted that the Prime Minister cannot stay in office without enjoying the confidence of the President. It is also for the President, upon the proposition of the Prime Minister, to appoint (and accept the resignation of) the members of the government. In practice, the Prime Minister negotiates with the President and an agreed list of ministers is produced.

The President participates in the regulation-making power of the government. He chairs meetings of the Council of Ministers (*C.1958, Art. 9*) and signs ordinances and decrees of the Council (*C.1958, Art. 13*). This function has traditionally been regarded as being formal, but during the period of cohabitation President Mitterrand showed himself willing to refuse to sign ordinances of the cabinet of Prime Minister Chirac that he disagreed with, basing such action on the role given to him by *C.1958, Art. 5* as guarantor of the proper functioning of institutions of the Republic.

One area in which the President has particular authority is foreign relations and defence. Under *C.1958, Art. 52*, in principle the President negotiates and ratifies treaties, although many important treaties will be ratified only following parliamentary authorisation (*C.1958, Art. 53*). He is informed of other international agreements, ie those of lesser importance, which are negotiated by the government. The President's authority in matters of defence is confirmed by his position as the Commander in Chief of the armed forces and chairman of the national defence committee (*C.1958, Art. 15*). Furthermore, by a *décret du 14.1.1964*, France's nuclear forces (the so-called *"force de frappe"*) are under the control of the President. It has become clear during the course of the Fifth Republic that matters of defence are regarded as matters of presidential prerogative, the Prime Minister's role being essentially one of implementation of presidential policies, despite the reference in

C.1958, Art. 21 to the Prime Minister having responsibility for national defence.

Turning next to the relationship between the President and the legislature, one of the greatest political weapons that the President holds is the power to dissolve the *Assemblée Nationale* before the end of its five-year term, a power which according to *C.1958, Art. 12* is to be exercised by the President after simple consultation with the Prime Minister and the presidents of both houses; parliamentary elections must be held within 20–40 days following dissolution. There is little limitation on the exercise of this power, apart from the fact that the *Assemblée Nationale* cannot be dissolved when the President intervenes during a time of crisis and legislates directly under *C.1958, Art. 16*. Nor may dissolution be decreed within twelve months of a previous dissolution. The fact that the power of dissolution belongs to the President shows that he is the key player in the political game. The power has been used several times during the Fifth Republic.

The President is entitled to communicate with Parliament by means of messages. This procedure is not frequently used. The message is delivered by the president of the house. It is not followed by a debate. As to the role of the President in the legislative process, he does not have the power to initiate legislation directly (although see *C.1958, Art. 89* in respect of the revision of the Constitution), such power of initiative belonging to the Prime Minister, *députés* and *sénateurs* (*C.1958, Art. 39*). A statute which has been passed by both houses of Parliament must within 15 days be promulgated by the President (*C.1958, Art. 10*). Promulgation is a process by which he confirms that a statute has been adopted in accordance with due procedure. Before promulgation, the President may refer the statute to the *Conseil Constitutionnel*. Moreover, he may within the 15 day period require Parliament to re-examine the statute or particular articles; it is rare that this happens, but occurred in 1985, for example, in respect of the statute dealing with the status of New Caledonia.

A referendum may (under *C.1958, Art. 11*) be called by the President on a bill affecting the organisation of public powers or approving certain treaties of particular importance (see below). Although in principle the initiative for calling a referendum lies with either the government or both houses acting together, in practice the President has the political authority needed to determine to call a referendum. There have been six referenda in the Fifth Republic (up until 1992). Four of these were during the presidency of General de Gaulle; we have already noted two of these, the referendum of 27 April 1969 and that relating to the introduction of direct elections for the presidency (28 October 1962) – it should be noted that the use of a referendum under *C.1958, Art. 11* on these two occasions by General de Gaulle was at the time criticised as being unconstitutional, as each involved modifications to the constitution for which *C.1958, Art. 89* provides the more appropriate mechanism, an issue that surfaced again in

1992 in relation to the ratification of the Maastricht treaty: although President Mitterrand opted in May 1992 for the parliamentary procedure of *C.1958, Art. 89* for the necessary revision of the constitution (the resulting reform bill, approved at a joint session of the *Assemblée Nationale* and the *Sénat* on 23 June 1992, is reproduced in the Appendix), he announced on 3 June 1992 that the matter of the actual ratification of the treaty would be the subject of a referendum. The other two (of 8 January 1961 and 8 April 1962) related to the Algerian crisis, the latter indeed approving the agreement (*les accords d'Evian*) which brought the conflict to an end. In a referendum of 23 April 1972 President Pompidou successfully sought support for the accession of the UK, the Republic of Ireland and Denmark to the EC, and by a referendum of 6 November 1988 the people approved an agreement (*les accords de Matignon*) on self-determination for New Caledonia.

The 1958 Constitution also deals with the relationship between the President and the judiciary. He is the guarantor of the independence of the judiciary, and is the titular president of the *Conseil supérieur de la magistrature*, whose members he appoints (*C.1958, Art. 65(2)*), and which has responsibility for the appointment, advancement and discipline of members of the judiciary (see Chapter 3). This influence extends to the administrative court system, *conseillers d'Etat* being appointed by the President.

(iii) The importance of presidential powers

The powers accorded to the President enable him to direct the broad trends of French political life. A feature of the presidency is that he is not legally responsible (particularly to Parliament) for the acts carried out in the exercise of his functions, such as the appointment of the Prime Minister, recourse to a referendum or to the emergency powers of *C.1958, Art. 16*, or a reference to the *Conseil Constitutionnel* or a decision to dissolve the *Assemblée Nationale*. This absence of responsibility, which is confirmed in *C.1958, Art. 68*, explains why normally (see *C.1958, Art. 19* for exceptions) the powers of the President can be exercised only with the counter-signature of the Prime Minister and (usually) the appropriate ministers, who of course do not benefit from the privilege of absence of responsibility.

The President may, however, be responsible for his acts in the case of high treason, when he will be tried by the *Haute Cour de Justice* comprised of parliamentarians (*C.1958, Art. 68*; see Chapter 3). Furthermore, being directly elected, he is politically answerable to the electorate, either in the septennial presidential elections (assuming that he stands again), or when putting a matter to the electorate by way of a referendum. Indeed, General de Gaulle's resignation from the presidency in 1969 followed the rejection of his proposals to reform the Senate and the regions in the *référendum du 27.4.1969*.

(iv) A presidential regime?

The regime of the Fifth Republic cannot be regarded as a presidential regime in the usual sense, power being shared by the President with the government which is answerable to Parliament. The sharing of executive powers in this way means that the 1958 Constitution is capable of being interpreted and indeed used in different ways, depending on whether emphasis is put on the position of the President or of the government. This will of course depend on the characters of the individual politicians of the time, and above all on the prevailing political conditions. A central issue is whether or not the President has the support of the majority of the *Assemblée Nationale* (*la majorité presidentielle*) and of the government. If he does, any potential rivalry between the President and the Prime Minister will not surface, and the President will dominate political life. However, this will not be the case where there is no political unity between the President and the government, as happened in the two-year period of cohabitation following the 1986 elections. Also, the President's powers, although substantial in respect of executive matters, are limited vis-à-vis Parliament (he cannot for example dissolve the *Sénat*) and the judiciary (of whose independence he is the guarantor).

5. The defence of the Republic

(a) Introduction

The state naturally endeavours to protect itself against those who seek to overthrow its institutions. This is primarily achieved through recourse to normal legal procedures such as public order offences, and by cases of spying and treason being dealt with in the courts. However, in times of crisis, it has been considered necessary to introduce particular protective measures. For example, during the Third Republic, the activities of extreme right-wing organisations were regarded as constituting a threat to the Republic and led to the introduction of the *loi du 10.7.1936* which banned groups who undermined the republican form of government. The principle has thus been accepted that the Republic must be free (at least up to a certain point) to wage war on its enemies, and that laws and institutions established for normal situations may not be adequate for such purposes. Normal principles of legality may therefore in such circumstances be put aside and special powers granted to the authorities. This principle has been applied by the creation of a series of emergency powers.

(b) State of siege

The first of these is the state of siege (*état de siège*). This was first regulated by the *loi du 9.8.1849* (since amended). A state of siege may be declared by the Council of Ministers in respect of a *département*, *commune* or *arrondissement* where a perilous situation has arisen due to a foreign conflict or an armed insurrection. The consequence of the declaration is, in effect, the suspension of individual liberties, and the military authorities' acquisition of the powers of policing and maintenance of public order which are normally exercised by the civilian authorities; they can take whatever measures are required to deal with the situation by means of a series of broad powers (eg of search and seizure, arrest, curfew, banning of meetings, requisition and conscription). Furthermore, the military courts acquire competence to deal with a large number of criminal offences. After a period of twelve days, parliamentary authorisation must be obtained if the state of siege is to continue to apply (*C.1958, Art. 36*).

(c) State of emergency

The power to declare a state of emergency (*état d'urgence*) was introduced (in order to facilitate the conduct of military operations in Algeria) by a *loi du 3.4.1955* (modified by an *ordonnance du 15.4.1960*) and can be used where a situation of imminent peril arises due to a serious threat to public order or to an event which has the characteristics of a public calamity. The declaration of a state of emergency by the Council of Ministers (in respect of all or a specified area of metropolitan France or an overseas territory or *département*) has the effect of endowing the civil authorities with extraordinary powers. For example the Minister of the Interior may impose a variety of confinement and curfew measures and the prefect of the affected *département* may make regulations, for example excluding persons and traffic from certain areas or districts. Either may also forbid the holding of meetings, order the closure of public meeting places, and authorise the carrying out of searches and seizures and the imposition of controls on the media. Parliament must approve any extension beyond twelve days, and then for a specified period. The jurisdiction of the courts is not necessarily suspended during a state of emergency (although the military courts may be authorised to deal with certain serious offences), and indeed a person affected by the emergency measures may commence an action in the administrative courts for the measures to be annulled on the grounds of their being illegal (*recours pour excès de pouvoir*). A state of emergency was declared several times during the Algerian crisis, and in 1961 in mainland France during the attempted *coup d'état* of 21 April 1961. Its last use was in 1985 in respect of the overseas territory of New Caledonia.

(d) Exceptional circumstances

The *Conseil d'Etat* has developed the doctrine (*la théorie des circonstances exceptionnelles*) that where there is a grave crisis, public authorities are to be recognised as having increased powers which are not subject to the normal principles of legality. This principle was first applied by the *Conseil d'Etat* in a case relating to the functioning of the civil service during the First World War (*C.E., 28.6.1918, Heyriès, Rec., 651*), and has been used since in times of crisis such as the Second World War, and the Algerian conflict. The doctrine states that where there are "exceptional circumstances" (see the comments of *commissaire du gouvernement Letourneur* in *C.E., 16.4.1948, Laugier, S.1948, III, 36*; TEXTS, NO. 14), public authorities may carry out acts required by the circumstances which would otherwise be illegal. An example is the decision of the *Conseil d'Etat* of 10.12.1954 (*Desfont, Rec., 657*) in which a decree of the Minister for Foreign Affairs forbidding even French citizens from entering French Indo-China in the interests of order and security was held to be justified in the exceptional circumstances prevailing at the time.

(e) Presidential rule under Article 16, 1958 Constitution

As has been seen, this article provides that in times of grave crisis, when the institutions of the Republic or the integrity of its territory or its ability to carry out its international obligations are threatened in a grave and immediate fashion, and the proper functioning of the constitutional public authorities has been interrupted, the President may intervene and take "whatever measures are required by the circumstances" with a view to restoring the normal functioning of the constitutional authorities within as short a time as possible. This article thus empowers the President to rule (by *décision*) in a quasi-dictatorial way. Many authors are of the opinion that while he is so doing, the law-making powers of Parliament and the government are temporarily suspended, at least in matters which are the subject of presidential *décision*. This wide power is tempered by the fact that the *Assemblée Nationale* remains entitled to sit (and may thus debate the exercise of the powers). Nor may the Constitution be amended. Furthermore, the President must, before exercising the power, officially consult (although he is not bound to follow the advice of) the Prime Minister, the presidents of both houses and the *Conseil Constitutionnel*; the latter's opinion must be reasoned and will be published in the *Journal officiel*. The nation must also be informed of the situation by the President. In effect, control of the exercise of the use of these powers is political rather than judicial. It is possible, however, in the event of abuse for the President to be arraigned by Parliament for high treason before the *Haute Cour de Justice*.

President de Gaulle used these powers following a military rebellion in Algeria in April 1961; the procedure set out in *C.1958, Art. 16* was duly followed, and the advice of the *Conseil Constitutionnel*, which agreed that recourse to the emergency powers was justified, was obtained. He ruled directly in this way until September of that year even though the rebellion was put down by the end of April.

The question arises as to the legal value to be ascribed to the measures (*décisions*) taken by the President in furtherance of his powers. These may regulate matters normally coming within the field of competence of Parliament under *C.1958, Art. 34* or the government under *C.1958, Art. 37*. The issue came before the *Conseil d'Etat* in a case of 2 March 1962 (*Rubin de Servens, D.1962, 307*; TEXTS, NO. 15), where it was held that the legal value of the *décisions* depends on their subject matter; if they deal with matters usually within parliamentary competence, they are to be accorded the value of parliamentary statute; if on the other hand their subject matter is normally within the competence of the government, they have the value of government regulations. As the subject matter of many *décisions* is likely to be in the parliamentary field of competence, it is unlikely that the *décisions* will be subject to judicial review. Such was the case in *Rubin de Servens* itself, where the *Conseil d'Etat* held that a *décision* of President de Gaulle issued under *C.1958, Art. 16* creating a military court with special juris-diction and procedure would normally be within parliamentary competence, and therefore the *Conseil* was incompetent to adjudge its legality. Moreover, the initial decision of the President to have recourse to his powers under *C.1958, Art. 16* (and indeed to bring them to an end) was held to be an *acte de gouvernement* and therefore not subject to the scrutiny of the courts.

C. The nation

1. Theoretical basis

The idea of "nation" plays an important role in the French political system. It is rooted in the French Revolution, and paradoxically is particularly strong because of its abstraction. In this tradition, the nation expresses the notion of the political community as a whole, and must therefore be one. The nation is necessarily regarded as being sovereign. The state is regarded as being legitimate because it is founded on, and acts for and in the name of the nation. The nation thus provides a strong ideological basis for the state. National sovereignty implies state sovereignty and vice versa. The notion of national sovereignty has since 1789 been understood in this context. It has precise constitutional, political and legal implications which, as will be seen, have undergone a substantial degree of modification with the inauguration of the Fifth Republic.

2. National sovereignty

(a) The concept of national sovereignty

The revolutionaries justified their actions by the principle of national sovereignty. It meant that political legitimacy no longer rested on the divine right to rule of a monarch. National sovereignty was not, however, based on the sovereignty of the people as a concrete social reality (*la souveraineté populaire*) − the view being held that the people were not always capable of acting in the general interest − but was based rather on an abstraction, the nation. This is confirmed by Article 3 of the 1789 Declaration (TEXTS, CHAPTER 1, NO. 10) which provides that "the principle of sovereignty resides essentially in the nation. No body or individual may exercise authority except where the same emanates expressly from the nation".

As sovereignty resided not in the people as a collection of individuals but in the nation as a whole, voting could be regarded as being not a right to be enjoyed by the individual but, rather, as a function to be accorded to those who had shown themselves capable of exercising it properly. Thus the distinction was introduced in the 1791 Constitution between citizens who by reason of their participation (by paying a minimum amount of taxes) were regarded as having capacity to vote (*citoyens actifs*) and those who were not (*citoyens passifs*). This distinction has of course gone with democratisation, but the idea of the nation remains of fundamental ideological importance.

The principle of national sovereignty has always been closely linked to the notion of individual liberties. National sovereignty is expressed by the nation's representatives' passing of statutes which are an expression of the general will (*la volonté générale; Déclaration de 1789, Art. 6*), and it is clear from Article 4 of the *Déclaration* that the bounds of individual liberties may be determined only by parliamentary statute.

The revolutionary conception of national sovereignty reinforced the state in that it permitted no place or function for organisations or bodies which did not derive their authority from the state. The concept of nation recognised the right of the citizen to participate in the process of expressing the general will only by means of his representatives passing statutes, not by entitling him to participate in any interest groups. Thus as early as 1791 the *loi le Chapelier (loi du 14.6.1791;* TEXTS, NO. 16) was passed, abolishing all professional organisations and forbidding the creation of all types of professional and workers' unions, associations and societies. The effect of this was to deprive the working class of the means of defending its collective interest. The right to form unions was not formally recognised until the passing of the *loi du 21.3.1884.* Furthermore, in its French conception, national sovereignty implies a unitary state; therefore the revolutionaries abolished the administrative structures of the *Ancien Régime*, such as *provinces*, and replaced them by new structures (eg the *départements*), strengthening at the same time the powers of central administration.

This conception of unitary national sovereignty has acted as a brake on the political development of the EC, in that it does not readily admit the possibility of a transfer of sovereignty away from the nation to the EC institutions. This was shown in a 1976 case (under *C.1958, Art. 54*) on the constitutionality of the introduction of the principle of the election of members of the European Parliament by universal suffrage, in which the *Conseil Constitutionnel* took up a conservative position, holding that because national sovereignty is unitary and cannot be divided, no transfer of sovereignty is possible; on the facts it held that no such transfer occurred in any event (*C.C., 30.12.1976, D.1977, 201*; TEXTS, NO. 17). This position was confirmed in a 1991 case in which the *Conseil Constitutionnel* was asked to determine the constitutionality of a statute authorising the ratification of the Schengen agreement (entered into by certain EC member states, removing cross-border formalities). The *Conseil (C.C., 25.7.1991; J.O. 27.7.1991, 10001)* held that the agreement complied with the Constitution, because (*inter alia*) its provisions did not imply a transfer or abandonment of sovereignty. However in, respect of the ratification of the Maastricht agreement, the *Conseil Constitutionnel* took a less rigid position. It held (*C.C., 9.4.1992; J.O. 11.4.1992, P.5354;* APPENDIX) that ratification required the modification of the Constitution, but accepted that transfers of competence were possible in the context of the development of the European Community. However, in a parliamentary debate after this decision, the Minister of Justice insisted on the distinction between transfers of competence and transfers of sovereignty. He expressed the traditional point of view that French sovereignty is "*inalienable, imprescriptible, incessible et indivisible*", and that accordingly a transfer of sovereignty was not possible.

(b) The traditional implications of the principle of national sovereignty

(i) The role of Parliament

As has been seen, the nation can express itself only through its representatives. It is traditionally the role of Parliament to represent the nation, and to express its will. Members of Parliament are the representatives of the nation, expressing the national will in the statutes that they pass. As such, they must act independently. A *député* therefore does not in the exercise of his parliamentary functions represent the people who voted for him, or the constituency for which he was elected, or *a fortiori* private interests, but rather he represents the national interest. It is therefore provided (*C.1958, Art. 27*) that any imperative mandate by which the electors instruct their *député* as to how to vote on any particular issue is illegal. This principle might appear to be contradicted somewhat by the existence of a whip system imposed by political parties on their parliamentarians, but such sanctions as there are for disobedience are of a political and not legal nature. By passing statutes, the representatives of the nation express the general will which, like the nation, is sovereign, and which cannot be limited. Sovereignty of the nation thus leads to sovereignty of Parliament and to the supremacy of parliamentary statute.

Before the inauguration of the Fifth Republic, *la loi* was defined by its organic origin; ie a text adopted by both houses of Parliament and promulgated by the President. *La loi* could not be submitted to any form of control as no institution could substitute its will for that of Parliament. Under the 1958 Constitution, although this organic definition remains, it has been restricted by the addition of a criterion which limits the competence of Parliament to defined fields.

(ii) Citizenship

The concepts of citizenship (*citoyenneté*) and nationality are synonymous in the French tradition, all French nationals thus being French citizens with the advantages and obligations that this implies. It was felt to be democratic that all nationals should, as members of the nation, be able to participate in political life, in particular by voting in the elections which determine the nation's representatives. For this reason, the right to vote cannot be granted to non-nationals; this political principle is enshrined in *C.1958, Art. 3*. In a decision of 18 November 1982 (*Rec., 66*; TEXTS, NO. 18) the *Conseil Constitutionnel* showed that it was prepared to enforce this principle strictly, holding, in respect of elections to municipal councils, that it was unconstitutional to impose a maximum quota of 75% of candidates of either gender. It is therefore not surprising that recent proposals to give the right to vote in local elections to immigrants long established in France without the need for them to obtain French nationality gave rise to much controversy, and appeared not to command the support of the majority of the French people. The provisions of the Maastricht agreement in respect of the voting rights of EC nationals in municipal elections have resulted in the need to amend *C.1958, Art. 3*.

3. Amendments to the principle of national sovereignty in the 1958 Constitution

The traditional significance of the principle of national sovereignty has been considerably changed by the 1958 Constitution (*Art. 3*) both in the matter of representation of the nation and in how national sovereignty is expressed.

(a) Representation of the nation

The question that arises in the Fifth Republic is, given the imprecision of the wording used in *C.1958, Art. 3* to refer to national sovereignty and the actual distribution of powers in the Constitution, whether or not the category of representatives of the nation should now include not only Parliament but also the President of the Republic. As we have seen, the 1958 Constitution gives the President certain important powers exercisable on his own initiative, without having to obtain the counter-signature of the Prime Minister (*C.1958, Art. 19*), and he is not responsible to the government or Parliament for such acts. The granting of such powers to the President may itself be sufficient to justify his being regarded as a representative of the nation. That he is a representative has in any event been effectively unarguable since the introduction in 1962 of direct universal elections for the presidency, which has conferred democratic legitimacy on the central constitutional position of the President. President de Gaulle went so far as to say (above; TEXTS, NO. 13) that "the indivisible authority of the state is conferred wholly on the President by the people who have elected him". There is now therefore a duality of national representation, which is effectively shared between Parliament and the President. At times this may result in rivalry, as was witnessed during the period of cohabitation.

(b) The expression of national sovereignty

The 1958 Constitution has also made important changes in the way that the will of the nation is expressed, firstly by the introduction of the referendum, the nation thereby expressing itself directly without the intervention of Parliament, and secondly by restricting the fields within which Parliament may legislate.

(i) Referendum

The introduction of the referendum in the Fifth Republic may be regarded as a sign of the decline of Parliament and of some of the traditional notions of earlier Republics. As has been seen above, a referendum may (under *C.1958, Art. 11*) be called by the President, on the initiative of the government or the two houses of Parliament, on a bill affecting the organisation of public powers or approving a treaty which affects the functioning of the institutions of the Republic; it can also be used as part of the procedure for amending the Constitution under *C.1958, Art. 89*. A referendum enables the people to express the general will (*la volonté générale*) directly. Because a referendum enables the President to consult the people in this way, it has in practice been used by Presidents as a technique for reinforcing their legitimacy or for seeking support for a particular policy; the classic example of this is the referendum of 27 April 1969 in which President de Gaulle sought the support of the people on his proposals to reform the Senate and the regions; when he failed to obtain their support, he resigned.

(ii) Parliamentary competence: loi and règlement

As has been seen, according to early revolutionary theory, Parliament alone, as the representative of the nation, was regarded as being entitled to pass statutes as an expression of the general will. Parliamentary power to legislate (*le pouvoir législatif*) was superior to governmental power to issue regulations (*le pouvoir réglementaire*) in implementation of parliamentary statute, and regulations are subordinate to parliamentary statute. However, as has already been mentioned, from the end of the First World War, due to increasing economic and political difficulties, the practice grew of Parliament effectively delegating broad powers to the government to enact law by means of *décret-lois* having the force of parliamentary statute. The Constitution of the Fifth Republic gives constitutional recognition to this evolution by granting autonomous power to the government to enact law; it therefore restricts the competence of Parliament (*le domaine de la loi*) to a number of defined areas (set out mainly in *C.1958, Art. 34*) – other matters are regarded as coming within the competence of the government (*C.1958, Art. 37*) which may legislate by autonomous regulation.

The matters of parliamentary competence are wide, and in accordance with the republican tradition include fundamental rights and individual liberties. They thus include, for example, the imposition by the state of liabilities on the individual (such as taxes, conscription and requisition); matters of criminal responsibility (such as the regulation of serious criminal offences (*crimes* and *délits*) and criminal procedure); the provision of certain basic safeguards for individual liberties (eg the creation of new jurisdictions; the status of *magistrats*); and the status of the individual (eg nationality and civic status, matrimonial property laws, and succession law). Furthermore *C.1958, Art. 34* provides that, in respect of certain other matters, the general principles at least must be determined by parliamentary statute; this includes many of the rules by which private relationships are organised, such as the fundamental principles of property law, civil and commercial obligations, employment and union law. Other provisions of the 1958 Constitution assign particular matters to the competence of Parliament (eg the approval of certain treaties before ratification, the declaration of war, matters of individual liberties; *C.1958, Arts. 53, 35, 66*).

It should however be noted that even the areas which are stated by *C.1958, Art. 34* to be within Parliamentary competence may be the subject of government regulations. Firstly the government may use its powers under *C.1958, Art. 21* to issue regulations in application and implementation of parliamentary statutes passed under *C.1958, Art. 34*. Furthermore, *C.1958, Art. 38* may be used by the government to obtain from Parliament authority (in the form of an enabling

Act; *loi d'habilitation*) to enact law for a given period by means of government regulations known as *ordonnances* in respect of subject matter which would normally come within parliamentary competence.

The fundamental innovation of the 1958 Constitution is that parliamentary supremacy is constitutionally restricted; this restriction of Parliament is enforced by the *Conseil Constitutionnel*, which was created primarily to ensure that Parliament does not stray into the *domaine réglementaire* of the government. By *C.1958, Art. 41*, if the government is of the opinion that a private member's bill (*proposition de loi*) which is before Parliament properly comes within the *domaine réglementaire*, it can request that the progress of the bill be suspended. If Parliament does not agree to do so, the matter will be referred to the *Conseil Constitutionnel* which will determine whether the bill comes within the competence of Parliament or the government; its decision is binding on all authorities (*C.1958, Art. 62*). The fact that Parliament is not sovereign in the Fifth Republic has provided the constitutional setting for the *Conseil Constitutionnel* to extend its control of a parliamentary statute beyond ensuring compliance with *C.1958, Art. 34* to adjudging its constitutionality in the light of broad constitutional norms, including, for example, the wide principles set out in the 1789 Declaration; such control is exercised when a statute is referred to the *Conseil* under *C.1958, Art. 61*. This development of a general control of the constitutionality of parliamentary statute was a logical step for the *Conseil Constitutionnel* to take, but it was only in 1971 that it did so. This control is examined in some detail below. It is therefore clear that under the 1958 Constitution neither Parliament nor parliamentary statute is sovereign; the political ideology of the Revolution has thus been jettisoned in favour of political and legal pragmatism.

D. l'Etat de droit

1. The hierarchy of norms

The doctrine of *l'Etat de droit* (literally "State of law"; to be contrasted with a "police state") describes a system in which the governors (*les gouvernants*; including the administrative authorities) are not above the law, but subject to it, their powers over the governed (*les gouvernés*) being held by legal authority and exercised in accordance with the law. This submission of the state to the law confers ideological legitimacy on the state, even though in practice the state will never conform entirely to legal norms.

One aspect of the doctrine of *l'Etat de droit* is that public authorities must act in accordance with legal norms; this implies that there is a coherent hierarchical organisation of legal norms to be respected. In France, enacted laws are categorised according to a hierarchy of norms (*l'hiérarchie des norms*), with constitutional laws having greater value than parliamentary statute (*loi*) which in turn is in theory superior to government regulation (*règlement*). Each of the institutions which has power to enact law must therefore do so in accordance with this hierarchy; for example, parliamentary statute should not contradict constitutional norms. As has been seen, however, autonomous regulations (*règlements autonomes*) issued by the government do not fit neatly into this model.

Compliance with the hierarchy of norms is considered to be one of the fundamental principles of the French legal system. It means that a public authority which wishes to enact law (eg Parliament enacting a statute), or to reach a decision (eg a mayor granting a building permit), must do so in a way which does not contradict a norm of superior value in the hierarchy; thus the statute must not contradict a constitutional norm, nor the award of the building permit the provisions of a statute.

Increasingly since 1875 there has been a tendency to subject the law-making powers of the government, and more recently even of Parliament, to the doctrine of *l'Etat de droit*. At the same time, however, it has been recognised that the rights of the individual should additionally be protected by other means. This is shown by the creation of a version of the ombudsman, the *médiateur*, whose role is to mediate in disputes between public authorities and the individual (see below). The existence of watchdog bodies such as the *Commission d'accès aux documents administratifs (loi du 17.7.1978)* and the *Commission nationale informatique et liberté (loi du 6.1.1978)* should also be noted.

We will now examine each of the different norms in the hierarchy in turn, starting with the Constitution and parliamentary statute, then moving on to international and EC law, general principles of law, government regulations, ordinances, and presidential decisions.

2. The Constitution and parliamentary statute

(a) Introduction

The Constitutions of the French Republic have always been characterised by a certain degree of rigidity in that the provisions of the Constitution can be revised only in accordance with special procedures (eg *C.1958, Art. 89*). The Constitution is regarded as a text of supreme normative value with which lesser norms, especially parliamentary statute, must comply. However, because parliamentary statute was considered to be an expression of national sovereignty, there were no means of legally enforcing the superiority of the constitutional text. However, in the Fifth Republic the supreme value of the Constitution has effectively been realised by the submission of parliamentary statute to a control of constitutionality exercised by the *Conseil Constitutionnel*. The *Conseil* has grown in importance since its creation in 1958; not only has it sought to increase its influence, but also increasing recourse has been had to it, particularly by members of Parliament. There are now on average over ten references per year to the *Conseil* under *C.1958, Art.61* (see below). The increasing influence of the *Conseil* at the expense of the authority of Parliament has led some commentators to fear *gouvernement des juges*, fears which are strengthened by reason of the political nature of appointments to the *Conseil* (see below).

(b) Role of the Conseil Constitutionnel

(i) Introduction

The *Conseil Constitutionnel* has a variety of functions; these include ensuring that elections and referenda are properly carried out (*C.1958, Arts. 58, 59, 60*), and confirming the vacancy of the presidency or incapacity of the President (*C.1958, Art. 7*). However, its most important function is that of controlling the constitutionality of parliamentary statute. This is examined in more detail below.

(ii) Composition of the Conseil Constitutionnel

The President of the Republic and the presidents of the *Assemblée Nationale* and the *Sénat* each appoint (*C.1958, Art. 56*) three of the nine members of the *Conseil Constitutionnel* (known as *les neuf sages*). In addition, former Presidents are entitled to sit (as long as they are not members of the government or Parliament). The President of the Republic nominates the president of the *Conseil Constitutionnel*. The members, who in practice are eminent jurists or experienced politicians, are appointed in thirds for a non-renewable (and non-revocable) term of nine years. The political nature of appointments to the *Conseil* is at the heart of many of the criticisms levelled against the institution.

(iii) References to the Conseil Constitutionnel

The control of the constitutionality of parliamentary statutes operates by a reference being made to the *Conseil* before the bill has been promulgated. Such a reference may occur in a variety of ways. Firstly, *lois organiques* which are (*C.1958, Art. 46*) *lois* classified as organic by the Constitution (eg bills dealing with the status of *magistrats*; *C.1958, Art. 64*), must be referred to the *Conseil* before promulgation (*C.1958, Art. 61(1)*). Other government bills (*projets de loi ordinaires*) may be referred to the *Conseil Constitutionnel* at any time before

163

promulgation (*C.1958, Art. 61(2)*); originally this could be done only by the President of the Republic, the Prime Minister, or the presidents of either house. However, this was widened by the *loi du 29.10.1974* to enable a reference to be made by a group of 60 *députés* or 60 *sénateurs*.

This has led to an increase in references to the *Conseil Constitutionnel*; they are used by the opposition parties as a means of having a bill amended which they have failed to have rejected or amended during the parliamentary debates. In recent years, many major government reforms have been challenged in this way, such as the 1981 nation-alisations (*C.C., 16.1.1982, RDCC, 18*), the 1986 denationalisations (*C.C., 25−26.6.1986, RDCC, 61*) and the 1990 bill which sought to grant special status to Corsica and to recognise the existence of the Corsican people (*C.C., 9.5.1991*; see above and TEXTS, NO. 9).

The *Conseil Constitutionnel* has held (in a case on the referendum of 28 October 1962; *C.C., 6.11.1962; J.O., 1962, 10778;* TEXTS NO. 19) that its control of the constitutionality of statutes under *C.1958, Art. 61* does not extend to those adopted by referendum (*lois référendaires*) which are regarded as being a direct expression of national sovereignty; this confirms that the role of the *Conseil* is essentially one of controlling Parliament's exercise of its legislative power.

It has already been noted that if the government is of the opinion that the subject matter of a private member's bill (*proposition de loi*) that is going through Parliament should properly be regarded as being within the *domaine réglementaire* and not the *domaine de la loi* (or is contrary to a delegation made in favour of the government under *C.1958, Art. 38*), it may (*C.1958, Art. 41*) ask the president of the house to foreclose further debate on the bill, failing which the matter will be referred to the *Conseil Constitutionnel* for determination as to whether the subject matter of the bill is within the competence of Parliament or the government.

Sometimes a bill passes through both houses and is promulgated in the form of a *loi* even though its subject matter comes not within the *domaine de la loi* of *C.1958, Art. 34* but rather the *domaine réglementaire* of *C.1958, Art. 37*. It is therefore provided (*C.1958, Art. 37(2)*) that the Prime Minister may at any time after promulgation refer a statute (or a text having the force of a statute, such as an ordinance) to the *Conseil Constitutionnel* for determination as to whether it should be reclassified as a regulation; the process is known as *délégalisation*. It was used quite frequently in the early years of the Fifth Republic, but less so nowadays. Finally, the *Conseil Constitutionnel* can be seized before the ratification of a treaty, by the President of the Republic, the Prime Minister or the president of either the *Assemblée Nationale* or the *Sénat*, to determine whether or not the treaty is contrary to the Constitution, failing which the latter must be amended before ratification may take place (*C. 1958, Art. 54*). Such a reference by the Prime Minister in March 1992 in respect of the Maastricht agreement led to the decision of the *Conseil Constitutionnel* of 9 April 1992 which confirmed the necessity to amend the Constitution (see above; APPENDIX).

Over the years there have been various proposals to broaden the role of the *Conseil Constitutionnel*. A 1989 proposal of President Mitterand would have made it possible for an individual litigant in a case proceeding before the ordinary or administrative courts to claim that the provisions of a statute which was in issue in the case were unconstitutional as being against his "fundamental rights", and to instigate a reference to the *Conseil Constitutionnel* on the issue of constitutionality. The Senate rejected these proposals for direct reference in 1990, thereby frustrating the intended constitutional reform.

(iv) Effect of the decisions of the Conseil Constitutionnel

The decisions of the *Conseil Constitutionnel* are judicial in character, and are binding on all institutions (*C.1958, Art. 62*). A bill which is declared to be unconstitutional cannot be promulgated; if only some of the provisions of the bill are held to be unconstitutional, these can be severed from the rest. In the latter case the President of the Republic may promulgate the truncated text, or refer it to Parliament for further examination (under his *C.1958, Art. 10(2)* powers).

(c) Control of the constitutionality of parliamentary statutes

The *Conseil Constitutionnel* ensures the conformity of parliamentary statutes not only to the provisions of *C.1958, Art. 34* but also more widely to the text of the Constitution as a whole, and indeed to all norms to which the *Conseil* ascribes constitutional value, such as the principles set out in the 1789 Declaration and the preamble to the 1946 Constitution, and the "fundamental principles recognised by the laws of the Republic". This ensemble of constitutional norms is known collectively as *le bloc de constitutionnalité*. The broadening of the control of the *Conseil Constitutionnel* beyond a simple application of *C.1958, Art. 34* can be traced back to a 1971 case on a government bill which sought to introduce administrative control over the registration of associations (*C.C., 16.7.1971*, above; TEXTS, NO. 3). The *Conseil* declared the bill to be unconstitutional on the grounds of being contrary to the fundamental principles recognised by the law of the Republic. Since then the constitutionality of parliamentary bills has been adjudged by reference to a wide variety of norms, such as those based on the provisions of the 1789 Declaration (eg the right to freedom of *Art. 2 (C.C., 15.1.1975, D.1975, 529;* TEXTS, NO. 20); the right of equality before the law of *Art. 6 (C.C., 27.12.1973; J.O., 28.12.1974, 12949)*) and the 1946 preamble (eg the right of the child to the protection of health; *C.C., 15.1.1975*, above).

With this extension of the recognised norms of constitutionality, the *Conseil Constitutionnel* has given itself wide-ranging and flexible powers to control the constitutionality of parliamentary statutes. The *Conseil* is showing an increasing willingness to hold statutes unconstitutional; in particular it has shown itself to be the champion of the individual when confronted by what it considers to be the introduction by Parliament of unjustified restrictions on individual liberties. However, this increased intervention by the *Conseil Constitutionnel* has been the subject of some criticism; it has been argued that it has had the effect of dampening parliamentary creativity, and indeed that it is inappropriate for issues of a political nature to be submitted for scrutiny to a constitutional court.

3. International and EC law

(a) Constitutional provisions

The 1958 Constitution does not distinguish between international and EC law. Article 55 of the 1958 Constitution provides that treaties and agreements which are duly ratified or approved are accorded normative value superior to that of parliamentary statute. In practice, ratification is a matter for the President, approval for the Prime Minister. In order to protect parliamentary competence, *C.1958, Art. 53* provides that the ratification or approval of a wide range of important treaties and agreements must be authorised by Parliament. The intervention of the *Conseil Constitutionnel* is similarly required by *C.1958, Art. 54* where a treaty or agreement may violate the provisions of the Constitution; where any clause of a treaty is declared to be contrary to the Constitution, the treaty cannot be ratified or approved until the Constitution has been revised. In its decision of 9 April 1992 (see above; APPENDIX) the *Conseil Constitutionnel* decided that the 1992 Maastricht agreement on the European Union was contrary to the Constitution in respect of three matters: the right to vote and to stand as a candidate in municipal elections in the member state of residence (see above); the introduction of majority voting in the Council of Ministers in respect of visa requirements for non-EC nationals; and the creation of a single currency. These last two result, according to the *Conseil*, in the deprivation of a member state of competence in matters involving "the essential conditions of the exercise of national sovereignty". It was therefore necessary to amend the Constitution before approval to ratify the treaty could be given.

(b) Attitude of French courts

(i) Conseil Constitutionnel

In 1975 the *Conseil Constitutionnel* was asked to adjudge the constitutionality of an abortion bill by reference *inter alia* to an international treaty (the European Convention on Human Rights).

It refused to do so (*C.C., 15.1.1975*, above; TEXTS, NO. 20) on the grounds that it was not competent to examine the conformity of a parliamentary statute with the provisions of a treaty. Its role in such matters (eg the Maastricht agreement) is to determine whether or not a treaty conforms to the Constitution before it has been ratified or approved (*C.1958, Art. 54*). Once the treaty has been ratified or approved, its provisions become part of the French legal order and have superior authority to parliamentary statute by reason of *C.1958, Art. 55*; it is not the function of the *Conseil Constitutionnel* to implement that article. The *Conseil* confirmed this attitude in a decision of 3 September 1986, (*Rec., 135*), holding that, "In application of Article 55 it is for the various organs of state to apply international conventions within the framework of their respective competences".

(ii) Cour de Cassation

As a result of the 1975 decision of the *Conseil Constitutionnel*, it was left to the ordinary courts to apply *C.1958, Art. 55*. This they duly did soon afterwards in the *Société des Cafés Jacques Vabre* case (*Cass.Ch.Mixte, 24.5.1975, D.1975, 497*; TEXTS, NO. 21). The *Cour de Cassation* accepted the primacy of Art. 95 of the EEC Treaty over a subsequent parliamentary statute on import duties. Since then the *Cour de Cassation* has in its caselaw continued to give priority to international and EC law over incompatible parliamentary statutory provisions.

(iii) Conseil d'Etat

Compared with the other courts, it has taken the *Conseil d'Etat* longer to apply *C.1958, Art. 55*, particularly when faced with a subsequent incompatible parliamentary statute. Its role is, after all, to control the legality of government activity rather than hold Parliament to account for adopting statutes contrary to international obligations. However, in the case of *Nicolo (C.E., 20.10.1989, Rec., 190*; TEXTS, NO. 22) the *Conseil d'Etat* accepted that the provisions of the EEC Treaty (*Art. 227*) may take priority over a subsequent incompatible statute (*loi du 7.7.1977*) which delimited the constituencies for the elections to the European Parliament. Both the *Cour de Cassation* and the *Conseil d'Etat* have therefore accepted the full consequences of the primacy of both EC law and international law as set out in Article 55 of the 1958 Constitution.

4. General principles of law

As was seen in Chapter 2 (under the heading of "Modern techniques of interpretation of legislation"), the French courts, ordinary, administrative and constitutional, have all to varying degrees recognised and applied general principles of law as a source of law. These general principles have in effect been deduced by the courts from existing law, many from the principles set out in the 1789 Declaration or the preamble to the 1946 Constitution (and incorporated into the 1958 Constitution through the preamble), but sometimes also from the corpus of legislative texts (an example being the principle of freedom of association derived by the *Conseil Constitutionnel* from the *loi du 1.7.1901* on associations (*C.C., 16.7.1971*, above; TEXTS, NO. 3)). Due to their derivation from recognised legal norms, general principles are not regarded as having been created by the courts, which is of course not permitted in French legal theory; however by having recourse to general principles the court is, in reality, doing more than simply applying existing legal norms.

A major development of the notion of general principles was effected by the *Conseil d'Etat*, which particularly in the years following the Second World War increasingly adjudged administrative activity by reference to general principles that it had deduced from the law. There are a large number of general principles that have since been recognised, and the list is not yet closed. Some of them are grouped around basic notions such as the notion of equality (the principles of the equality of citizens before the law, and before fiscal and public obligations) and the notion of freedom (the principles of freedom of the individual, freedom of opinion and freedom of expression). In formulating these principles, the *Conseil d'Etat* has relied to a large extent on the 1789 Declaration (eg *C.E., 7.6.1957, Condamine, R.D.P., 1958, 98;* TEXTS, NO. 23) and the preamble to the 1946 Constitution (eg *C.E., 7.7.1950, Dehaene, Rec., 65;* TEXTS, NO. 24). Since 1958, the *Conseil d'Etat* has become bolder in its use of general principles, holding that not only autonomous regulations passed under *C.1958, Art. 37* (*C.E., 26.6.1959, Syndicat Général des Ingénieurs Conseils, Rec., 394,* below) but also ordinances passed under *C.1958, Art. 38* (*C.E., 24.11.1961, Fédération nationale des Syndicats de Police, D. 1962, 624,* above; TEXTS, NO. 25) are subject to them. The cases do not however give formal constitutional value to the general principles recognised by the *Conseil d'Etat*.

Let us take two examples of the recourse to a general principle by the *Conseil d'Etat*; that of the right of a person to have the opportunity to put a case in their defence (*le droit de la défence*). In the early case of *Trompier-Gravier* (*C.E., 5.5.1944, D, 1945, 110;* TEXTS, NO. 26) the decision of a prefect to close a newspaper kiosk in Paris was annulled on the grounds that the person affected was not given the opportunity of putting her case before the decision was taken. In the important case of *Canal, Robin et Godot* (*C.E., 19.10.1962, Rec., 552;* TEXTS, NO. 27) the *Conseil d'Etat* annulled a presidential ordinance of General de Gaulle which set up a military court of justice on the grounds of its being contrary to "essential defence rights and guarantees".

The *Conseil Constitutionnel* has subsequently used the same technique and, on the basis of the preambles to the 1958 and 1946 Constitutions, has adopted as norms in controlling the constitutionality of parliamentary statutes principles of both the 1789 Declaration and the preamble to the 1946 Constitution as well as "fundamental principles recognised by the laws of the Republic". These *principes fondamentaux*, being imposed on the legislature, in effect acquire constitutional value; they should therefore be contrasted with the *principes généraux* recognised by the *Conseil d'Etat*, which being imposed on government regulation (both derived and autonomous) have an authority which is superior to the latter, although inferior to that of parliamentary statute. Not all of the general principles of the *Conseil d'Etat* have been recognised by the *Conseil Constitutionnel* as fundamental principles. The recourse to general principles by the ordinary courts is examined in Chapter 2.

5. Government regulations; le pouvoir réglementaire

The phrase *le pouvoir réglementaire* describes the power held by the government and more widely by administrative authorities to enact regulations (*règlements*) of general normative value. Such regulations generally have a legal value which is inferior to parliamentary statute. The *pouvoir réglementaire* of the government is recognised in the Constitution (*C.1958, Art. 21*); however, the *Conseil d'Etat* long ago confirmed (*C.E., 8.8.1919, Labonne, Rec., 737*) that even without explicit constitutional authority, central government inherently has the power to make regulations. Article 21 of the 1958 Constitution provides that the Prime Minister "exercises the power to make regulations", but he is not alone in being able to do so; *C.1958, Art. 13* makes it clear that the President of the Republic also participates in the exercise of the *pouvoir réglementaire*. Individual ministers do not have inherent power to issue regulations, although they do have certain powers (see Chapter 2).

The government's power to make regulations is used in two ways. Firstly it permits the government to pass regulations in application of parliamentary statute (*règlements d'application*). Secondly, as we have seen, the power can be used in furtherance of *C.1958, Art. 37* to make autonomous regulations (*règlements autonomes*) in respect of matters which do not come within the parliamentary field of competence (set out in *C.1958, Art. 34*). The government exercises this autonomous power on its own initiative, independently of Parliament. The question of the legal value to be accorded to autonomous regulations is not expressly addressed in the Constitution, but has now been settled by the *Conseil d'Etat* (see above; also (below) the principle of legality).

As was seen in Chapter 2, various administrative authorities other than central government, particularly mayors and prefects, enjoy certain powers to issue regulations. The mayor, for example, has power to pass regulations (*arrêtés*) to ensure public order, security and public health within the municipality. The use of such powers is strictly controlled by the administrative courts by means of the principle of legality (see below).

6. Ordinances

The term *ordonnance* (ordinance), although used in the *Ancien Régime*, was unknown in preceding Republics until introduced in the 1958 Constitution. Generally, ordinances are administrative regulations passed by the *Conseil des Ministres* and signed by the President (*C.1958, Art. 13*) dealing with matters coming within parliamentary competence.

There are different types of ordinance. The Constitution provides for the use of ordinances in certain situations, for example where Parliament delays unduly in passing a finance bill (*C.1958, Art. 47*). Secondly, the use of ordinances may be authorised by referendum. For example, the *loi-référendaire* of 13.4.1962, which approved the *accords d'Evian* ending the war in Algeria, granted power to President de Gaulle to take all measures (whether legislative or regulatory in nature) by ordinance or decree to implement the agreement. As has already been mentioned, the resulting ordinances were subsequently held by the *Conseil d'Etat* to be subject to the control of the *Conseil* (*C.E., 19.10.1962, Canal, Robin et Godot*, above; TEXTS, NO. 27).

In practice, the most important type of ordinance are those passed under *C.1958, Art. 38*; the legislative competence of Parliament having been limited in 1958 to the matters set out in *C.1958, Art. 34*, and the government thus recognised as having autonomous power to enact law by regulation in other fields, it might have been thought appropriate that within the now restricted field of parliamentary competence, Parliament would not be permitted to delegate its legislative powers to the government. However, this is not the case, for by *C.1958, Art. 38* the government may, in order to carry out its programme, ask Parliament for authorisation (given by *loi d'habilitation*) to enact law (by means of ordinances) within the parliamentary field of competence for a particular time (in practice, usually between a month and a year). The enabling Act must specify the fields of law in which the government is empowered to enact ordinances. These fields may, however, be broad (eg see the *loi du 4.2.1960*; TEXTS, NO. 28). The advantage for the government is that once it has steered the enabling Act through Parliament, it can enact law rapidly by ordinance. Ordinances are passed by the government by simple decision of the *Conseil des Ministres* after vetting by the *Conseil d'Etat*, and become effective on publication. Once the enabling Act has been passed, Parliament loses its right to legislate in the fields delegated for the duration of the period of delegation; indeed, any attempt to do so may be blocked by the government under *C.1958, Art. 41*.

170

What is the legal value of ordinances by the government in pursuance of an authorised delegation? They have the value of parliamentary statutes in that they are capable of repealing or amending earlier statutes, but only once they have been ratified by Parliament within a fixed period. Until ratification, they only have the status of *actes réglementaires* and can therefore be controlled by the administrative courts and annulled if illegal (*C.E., Fédération nationale des Syndicats de Police,* above; TEXTS, NO. 25).

7. Presidential decisions

Measures taken by the President in application of his emergency powers under *C.1958, Art. 16* are known as *décisions*. As seen above, *décisions* taken in the *domaine de la loi* have legislative value; those in the *domaine réglementaire* have regulatory value, and are thus subject to the control of the *Conseil d'Etat (C.E., Rubin de Servens,* above; TEXTS, NO. 15).

8. The principle of legality

(a) Definition

By the principle of legality (*légalité*), administrative activities are required to comply with the law; it is the means by which the hierarchy of norms is applied to administrative activities. According to the principle, the *actes administratifs* (which include both regulations of general effect (*actes réglementaires*) and individual decisions (*actes individuels*)) of all administrative authorities must conform with the law; ie with constitutional norms, parliamentary statutes, general principles, and regulations. Moreover, they must be taken in the general interest. These norms to which the *actes administratifs* must conform are collectively known as *le bloc de légalité*. The principle of *légalité* may thus be seen as the application to the activities of the administration of the wider principle of *l'Etat de droit* (by which the powers of the organs of state over those it governs must be legally held and exercised in accordance with the law); furthermore, the control of the constitutionality of parliamentary statute which is exercised by the *Conseil Constitutionnel* is an extension of the principle to parliamentary activity.

The principle of legality not only protects the rights of individuals in their dealings with the administration, but it also encourages good administration and respect for the division of competence between the different administrative authorities. It may be enforced against the administration by the administrative courts in the context of proceedings commenced by individuals against allegedly illegal administrative activity (essentially by *recours pour excès de pouvoir*). The enforcement of the principle of *légalité* in this way should therefore be distinguished firstly from control exercised over the activities of an administrative body by a higher administrative authority; a person aggrieved by an administrative decision is always entitled to apply to a higher administrative authority (known as a hierarchical action; *recours hiérarchique*) for the decision to be reviewed. It should secondly be distinguished from the control which is exercised by the state through its representatives, such as the prefect, on the legality of activities of local authorities (municipal, departmental and regional).

(b) The content of the principle of legality

(i) Introduction

There has been a steady extension of the control exercised by the administrative courts on the *actes administratifs* of administrative authorities at all levels, from the mayor upwards.

(ii) The operation of the principle of legality

The way in which the principle of legality applies to any given administrative authority depends on the position that the authority has in the administrative hierarchy. Thus when an inferior administrative authority passes regulations (eg a mayor issuing by-laws (*arrêtés municipaux*)) these must conform to regulations on the matter which have been passed by superior authorities. Moreover, any decision of individual effect (eg the grant by the mayor of a building permit) must conform to the regulations that the authority has itself issued (in this example, *arrêtés municipaux*). Should it be desired to take an individual decision contrary to such regulations, the regulations will first have to be amended in accordance with the appropriate procedures.

The degree of control exercised by the administrative courts over *actes administratifs* depends on whether the administrative authority concerned had any discretion when exercising its power. Sometimes the administrative authority has no discretion in respect of the exercise of a particular power, in effect being under a mandatory duty (it is described as having a *compétence liée*). Where this is so, the court will simply examine whether or not the body has complied with its duty. Let us take as an example the registration of a society or association with the *préfecture* under the provisions of the *loi du 1.7.1901*. The 1901 statute states that upon presentation of the statutes and the appropriate forms, the *préfecture* will issue a formal receipt (*récépissé*) and the association will thereupon acquire legal capacity recognised by law; it gives no discretion to the prefect in the exercise of this function. In a 1971 case (*Trib. Adm. Paris, 25.1.1971, Dame de Beauvoir et sieur Leiris, A.J.D.A.1971, II, 229*) the prefect had refused to register an association (*l'Association des amis de la cause du peuple*) because of the political nature of its objects. It was held that as the 1901 statute gave the prefect no discretion in the exercise of his power, he had acted illegally, "whatever his reasons for his decision". His decision was accordingly annulled. This case led to the government of the day introducing a bill to amend the 1901 statute, and it was on the referral of this bill that the *Conseil Constitutionnel* took the seminal decision to adjudge the constitutionality of parliamentary statutes by reference to a wide body of constitutional norms including the principles of the 1789 Declaration (*C.C., 16.7.1971*, above; TEXTS, NO. 3).

Sometimes, however, the administrative authority may be granted a wide degree of discretion in the exercise of a power; this is known as a *pouvoir discrétionnaire* where the law leaves the administrative authority free to determine, according to the circumstances, whether to exercise its competence, and if so, how to do so. Between these poles there are instances where the authority is given a limited degree of discretion. Where statutory limits within which the discretion is to be exercised are set down, the administrative authority must exercise its discretion within those limits; otherwise its decision will be annulled on the grounds of being contrary to the principle of legality. However, if the limits are respected, the administrative court will not control the exercise of the discretion by the administrative authority; there is said to be no control of the opportuneness (*contrôle de l'opportunité*) of the decision.

The administrative courts have in practice intensified their control so as to limit increasingly the margin of discretion enjoyed by administrative authorities. They do so by the use of subtle distinctions which at times comes close to controlling the exercise of the discretion. We will now take as an example the way in which the courts have controlled administrative policing powers.

(iii) Control of policing powers (pouvoirs de police)

As is examined in more detail in Chapter 5, French law differentiates between two types of police functions, *la police administrative* and *la police judiciaire*. Judicial police functions are repressive: to seek out and bring to justice those who have committed criminal offences. Administrative police functions, on the other hand, are preventative: to prevent public disorder. We have already seen that the mayor is granted municipal administrative policing functions in order to ensure public order, security and public health within the municipality, and for this purpose the mayor may take all necessary measures (by way of *arrêtés*). These must, however, be taken in the general interest. If, therefore, an individual commences an action in the administrative courts in respect of *mesures de police* taken by the mayor, the court will ensure not only that the mayor had the legal authority to take the measures, but that in so doing he was acting in the public interest; moreover, in determining this, the court will assess whether the measures were necessary for the maintenance of public order. This is not regarded as a control of the opportuneness (*opportunité*) of the exercise of the policing powers of the mayor (*C.E., 19.2.1909, Abbé Olivier, S., 1909, III, 34;* TEXTS, NO. 29). One of the reasons is that in the exercise of policing powers, the issue of the proportionality of the measures taken to the seriousness of the prevailing circumstances is regarded as an element of the limits that define the legality of the exercise of the powers. This is understandable bearing in mind the rather delicate balance that must be drawn between upholding public order and safeguarding individual liberties. Let us take two examples. In the case of *Carlier (C.E., 18.11.49, Rec., 490;* TEXTS, NO. 30), the *Conseil d'Etat* held as unjustified a wholesale ban by *l'Administration des Beaux-Arts* on the plaintiff, a critic of theirs, which attempted to put a stop to his activities by prohibiting him from entering the cathedral at Chartres; the requirements of public order did not justify such a deprivation of individual liberties. However, in the case of *Ministre de l'Intérieur c.Epoux Leroy (C.E., 13.3.1968, Rec., 179;* TEXTS, NO. 31), the *Conseil d'Etat* held as justified a total ban by a prefect on the activities of unsolicited professional photographers during the summer season near Mont St. Michel on the basis that the dangers presented by these activities could not have been avoided by less wide-ranging measures.

(iv) Control of regulations passed under Art. 37

It has been seen that *C.1958, Art. 37* introduced a new category of regulations, *règlements autonomes*. These are autonomous in the sense that they are passed by the government without the need for parliamentary authorisation; they may be taken in fields other than those within the *domaine de la loi*. In view of the freedom that the government has in respect of *règlements autonomes*, the question arises as to whether or not such regulations are subject to the principle of legality. In the important case of *Syndicat Général des Ingénieurs Conseils (C.E., 26.6.1959, Rec., 394*; TEXTS, NO. 32), the *Conseil d'Etat* impliedly held that *règlements autonomes* are to be regarded as *actes administratifs* and thus subject to the principle of legality.

(c) Exceptions to the principle of legality

In certain circumstances the activities of the administration are not subject to a control of legality by the administrative courts. This occurs firstly in certain cases of crisis or emergency, where the principle of legality is effectively restricted; in some cases this happens on statutory authority (eg state of siege, state of emergency and the exercise of emergency powers by the President under *C.1958, Art. 16* (examined above)) – in other cases the exemption is a creation of the courts (eg the "theory of exceptional circumstances" (above)).

Also exempt from the control of the courts are administrative activities falling within the category of *actes de gouvernement*. This was confirmed by the *Conseil d'Etat* in the case of *Rubin de Servens (C.E., 2.3.1962,* above; TEXTS. NO. 15). This covers activities of the government connected with the functioning of the legislature or with international relations and the decision by the President to use his *C.1958, Art. 16* powers.

(d) Annulment proceedings; recours pour excès de pouvoir

A person who seeks to have an *acte administratif* annulled on the basis of its being contrary to the principle of legality will commence a *recours pour excès de pouvoir* in the administrative courts (see below). The *recours pour excès de pouvoir* was created by the *Conseil d'Etat*, and has been developed over many decades. A plaintiff will base his *recours* on one of the different grounds that have been recognised, the so-called *cas d'annulation*. These can be briefly outlined as follows: firstly, an *acte administratif* will be annulled for *incompétence* where the administrative authority which took it was not legally competent to do so. Secondly, annulment for *vice de forme* lies where the *acte administratif* was taken in breach of substantial requirements of formality (ie *formalités substantielles*). The third ground is *détournement de pouvoir*, where the *acte* was taken for improper reasons, one example being where a decision is made not in the general interest but for personal gain. The final catch-all *cas d'annulation* is *violation de la loi*, according to which an *acte administratif* will be annulled if taken in breach of any of the recognised legal norms (ie of the *bloc de légalité*). A *recours pour excès de pouvoir* should be distinguished from other categories of *recours*, particularly the *recours de pleine juridiction* in which the plaintiff seeks compensation for loss caused by administrative activity.

9. Le médiateur

(a) Function

The institution of the *médiateur de la République*, which was inspired by the Swedish model of the ombudsman, was created by the *loi du 3.1.1973* (since modified). It is a recognition of the fact that normal mechanisms, whether judicial or administrative, may at times be inappropriate or ineffective for resolving disputes between an individual and an administrative authority. The function of the *médiateur* is to make recommendations in an attempt to resolve such disputes. He has competence to deal with any complaints by an individual (whether French nationals or not) that an admininistrative body or authority (including private bodies carrying out public services) "has not functioned in accordance with its mission of public service".

(b) Status

The *médiateur* is appointed by *décret* for a non-renewable six-year term. His independence is guaranteed by the fact that he cannot be removed; is not answerable for the exercise of his functions; and cannot stand as a candidate for political office in either national or local elections. He is aided in the exercise of his functions by an administrative staff, and has correspondents in each *département*. Furthermore, each government ministry has a civil servant whose role is to collaborate with the *médiateur*. The functions of the *médiateur* are regarded as being administrative rather than judicial; therefore, it is possible for a reference to be made to him at the same time that proceedings are being pursued. His recommendations are not of such a nature as to be subject to review in the administrative courts.

(c) Reference

An individual is not able to refer a matter directly to the *médiateur*. A reference is made by the complainant's member of parliament (*député* or *sénateur*) once normal procedures for redress from the administrative authority concerned have been exhausted. This system of reference operates as a filter to weed out unjustified claims. However, in certain cases it is now possible (since a 1976 reform) for parliamentarians to make a reference to the *médiateur* on their own initiative.

(d) Powers

The *médiateur* makes recommendations to the administration as to how it should resolve the dispute, but he has no power to constrain the administration. He is, however, entitled to be informed of the measures that have been taken in furtherance of his recommendations. If the administration is refusing to comply with a judgment of the administrative courts, he can require it to do so within a certain period, failing which he will publicise the fact by issuing an official report in the *Journal officiel*. Furthermore he is empowered to issue proposals for improving management within, or reform of, an administrative authority. An annual report on his activities is published.

It can be seen that the effectiveness of the *médiateur* depends on the pressure that he can bring to bear on the errant administrative authority by reason of the authority of his office, and sometimes of his personal influence. In 1990, the *médiateur* examined some 23,000 references, a figure which represents an increase on 1989 of nearly 30 per cent.

Text and materials

1 Constitution du 4 octobre 1958

Le peuple français proclame solennellement son attachement aux Droits de l'homme et aux principes de la souveraineté nationale tels qu'ils ont été définis par la Déclaration de 1789, confirmée et complétée par le préambule de la constitution de 1946.

En vertu de ces principes et de celui de la libre détermination des peuples, la République offre aux territoires d'outre-mer qui manifestent la volonté d'y adhérer des institutions nouvelles fondées sur l'idéal commun de liberté, d'égalité et de fraternité et conçues en vue de leur évolution démocratique.

Art. 1er. La République et les peuples des territoires d'outre-mer qui, par un acte de libre détermination, adoptent la présente constitution instituent une Communauté.

La communauté est fondée sur l'égalité et la solidarité des peuples qui la composent.

TITRE 1er. – DE LA SOUVERAINETE

Art. 2. La France est une République indivisible, laïque, démocratique et sociale. Elle assure l'égalité devant la loi de tous les citoyens sans distinction d'origine, de race ou de religion. Elle respecte toutes les croyances.

L'emblème national est le drapeau tricolore, bleu, blanc, rouge.

L'hymne national est la Marseillaise.

La devise de la République est "Liberté, Égalité, Fraternité".

Son principe est: gouvernement du peuple, par le peuple et pour le peuple.

Art. 3. La souveraineté nationale appartient au peuple qui l'exerce par ses représentants et par la voie du référendum.

Aucune section du peuple ni aucun individu ne peut s'en attribuer l'exercice.

Le suffrage peut être direct ou indirect dans les conditions prévues par la constitution. Il est toujours universel, égal et secret.

Sont électeurs, dans les conditions déterminées par la loi, tous les nationaux français majeurs des deux sexes, jouissant de leurs droits civils et politiques.

Art. 4. Les partis et groupements politiques concourent à l'expression du suffrage. Ils se forment et exercent leur activité librement. Ils doivent respecter les principes de la souveraineté nationale et de la démocratie.

TITRE II. – LE PRESIDENT DE LA REPUBLIQUE

Art. 5. Le président de la République veille au respect de la constitution. Il assure, par son arbitrage, le fonctionnement régulier des pouvoirs publics ainsi que la continuité de l'Etat.

Il est le garant de l'indépendance nationale, de l'intégrité du territoire, du respect des accords de Communauté et des traités.

Art. 6. Le président de la République est élu pour sept ans au suffrage universel direct.

Les modalités d'application du présent article sont fixées par une loi organique.

Art. 7. Le président de la République est élu à la majorité absolue des suffrages exprimés. Si celle-ci n'est pas obtenue au premier tour, il est procédé, le deuxième dimanche suivant, à un second tour. Seuls peuvent s'y présenter les deux candidats qui, le cas échéant, après retrait des candidats plus favorisés, se trouvent avoir recueilli le plus grand nombre de suffrages au premier tour.

Le scrutin est ouvert sur convocation du Gouvernement.

L'élection du nouveau président a lieu vingt jours au moins et trente-cinq jours au plus avant l'expiration des pouvoirs du président en exercice.

En cas de vacance de la présidence de la République pour quelque cause que ce soit, ou d'empêchement constaté par le Conseil constitutionnel saisi par le Gouvernement et statuant à la majorité absolue de ses membres, les fonctions du président de la République, à l'exception de celles prévues aux articles 11 et 12 ci-dessous, sont provisoirement exercées par le président du Sénat et, si celui-ci est à son tour empêché d'exercer ses fonctions, par le Gouvernement.

En cas de vacance ou lorsque l'empêchement est déclaré définitif par le Conseil constitutionnel, le scrutin pour l'élection du nouveau président a lieu, sauf cas de force majeure constaté par le Conseil constitutionnel, vingt jours au moins et trente-cinq jours au plus après l'ouverture de la vacance ou la déclaration du caractère définitif de l'empêchement (. . .)

Art. 8. Le président de la République nomme le Premier ministre. Il met fin à ses fonctions sur la présentation par celui-ci de la démission du Gouvernement.

Sur la proposition du Premier ministre, il nomme les autres membres du Gouvernement et met fin à leurs fonctions.

Art. 9. Le président de la République préside le conseil des ministres.

Art. 10. Le président de la République promulgue les lois dans les quinze jours qui suivent la transmission au Gouvernement de la loi définitivement adoptée.

Il peut, avant l'expiration de ce délai, demander au Parlement une nouvelle délibération de la loi ou de certains de ses articles. Cette nouvelle délibération ne peut être refusée.

Art. 11. Le président de la République, sur proposition du Gouvernement pendant la durée des sessions ou sur proposition conjointe des deux assemblées, publiées au *Journal officiel*, peut soumettre au référendum tout projet de loi portant sur l'organisation des pouvoirs publics, comportant approbation d'un accord de Communauté ou tendant à autoriser la ratification d'un traité qui, sans être contraire à la constitution, aurait des incidences sur le fonctionnement des institutions.

Lorsque le référendum a conclu à l'adoption du projet, le président de la République, le promulgue dans le délai prévu à l'article précédent.

Art. 12. Le président de la République peut, après consultation du Premier ministre et des présidents des assemblées, prononcer la dissolution de l'Assemblée Nationale.

Les élections générales ont lieu vingt jours au moins et quarante jours au plus après la dissolution.

L'Assemblée Nationale se réunit de plein droit le deuxième jeudi qui suit son élection. Si cette réunion a lieu en dehors des périodes prévues pour les sessions ordinaires, une session est ouverte de droit pour une durée de quinze jours.

Il ne peut être procédé à une nouvelle dissolution dans l'année qui suit ces élections.

Art. 13. Le président de la République signe les ordonnances et les décrets délibérés en Conseil des ministres.

Il nomme aux emplois civils et militaires de l'Etat.

Les conseillers d'Etat, le grand chancelier de la Légion d'Honneur, les ambassadeurs et envoyés extraordinaires, les conseillers maîtres à la Cour des comptes, les préfets, les représentants du Gouvernement dans les territoires d'outre-mer, les officiers généraux, les recteurs des académies, les directeurs des administrations centrales sont nommés en conseil des ministres.

Une loi organique détermine les autres emplois auxquels il est pourvu en conseil des ministres ainsi que les conditions dans lesquelles le pouvoir de nomination du président de la République peut être par lui délégué pour être exercé en son nom.

Art. 14. Le président de la République accrédite les ambassadeurs et les envoyés extraordinaires auprès des puissances étrangères; les ambassadeurs et les envoyés extraordinaires étrangers sont accrédités auprès de lui.

Art. 15. Le président de la République est le chef des armées. Il préside les conseils et comités supérieurs de la défense nationale.

Art. 16. Lorsque les institutions de la République, l'indépendance de la nation, l'intégrité de son territoire ou l'exécution de ses engagements internationaux sont menacées d'une manière grave et immédiate et que le fonctionnement régulier des pouvoirs publics constitutionnels est interrompu, le président de la République prend les mesures exigées par ces circonstances, après consultation officielle du Premier ministre, des présidents des assemblées ainsi que du Conseil constitutionnel.

Il en informe la nation par un message.

Ces mesures doivent être inspirées par la volonté d'assurer aux pouvoirs publics constitutionnels, dans les moindres délais, les moyens d'accomplir leur mission. Le Conseil constitutionnel est consulté à leur sujet.

Le Parlement se réunit de plein droit.

L'Assemblée Nationale ne peut être dissoute pendant l'exercice des pouvoirs exceptionnels.

Art. 17. Le président de la République a le droit de faire grâce.

Art. 18. Le président de la République communique avec les deux assemblées du Parlement par des messages qu'il fait lire et qui ne donnent lieu à aucun débat.
Hors session, le Parlement est réuni spécialement à cet effet.

Art 19. Les actes du président de la République autres que ceux prévus aux articles 8 (1er alinéa), 11, 12, 16, 18, 54, 56 et 61 sont contresignés par le Premier ministre et, le cas échéant, par les ministres responsables.

TITRE III. – LE GOUVERNEMENT

Art. 20. Le Gouvernement détermine et conduit la politique de la nation.

Il dispose de l'administration et de la force armée.

Il est responsable devant le Parlement dans les conditions et suivant les procédures prévues aux articles 49 et 50.

Art. 21. Le Premier ministre dirige l'action du Gouvernement. Il est responsable de la défense nationale. Il assure l'exécution des lois. Sous réserve des dispositions de l'article 13, il exerce le pouvoir réglementaire et nomme aux emplois civils et militaires.

Il peut déléguer certains de ses pouvoirs aux ministres.

Il supplée, le cas échéant, le président de la République, dans la présidence des conseils et comités prévus à l'article 15.

Il peut, à titre exceptionnel, le suppléer pour la présidence d'un conseil des ministres en vertu d'une délégation expresse et pour un ordre du jour déterminé.

Art. 22. Les actes du Premier ministre sont contresignés, le cas échéant, par les ministres chargés de leur exécution.

Art. 23. Les fonctions de membre du Gouvernement sont incompatibles avec l'exercice de tout mandat parlementaire, de toute fonction de représentation professionnelle à caractère national et de tout emploi public ou de toute activité professionnelle.

Une loi organique fixe les conditions dans lesquelles il est pourvu au remplacement des titulaires de tels mandats, fonctions ou emplois.

Le remplacement des membres du Parlement a lieu conformément aux dispositions de l'article 25.

TITRE IV. – LE PARLEMENT

Art. 24. Le Parlement comprend l'Assemblée Nationale et le Sénat.

Les députés à l'Assemblée Nationale sont élus au suffrage direct.

Le Sénat est élu au suffrage indirect. Il assure la représentation des collectivités territoriales de la République. Les français établis hors de France sont représentés au Sénat.

Art. 25. Une loi organique fixe la durée des pouvoirs de chaque assemblée, le nombre de ses membres, leur indemnité, les conditions d'éligibilité, le régime des inéligibilités et des incompatibilités.

Elle fixe également les conditions dans lesquelles sont élues les personnes appelées à assurer, en cas de vacance du siège, le remplacement des députés ou des sénateurs jusqu'au renouvellement général ou partiel de l'assemblée à laquelle ils appartenaient.

Art. 26. Aucun membre du Parlement ne peut être poursuivi, recherché, arrêté, détenu ou jugé à l'occasion des opinions ou votes émis par lui dans l'exercice de ses fonctions.

Aucun membre du Parlement ne peut, pendant la durée des sessions, être poursuivi ou arrêté en matière criminelle ou correctionnelle qu'avec l'autorisation de l'Assemblée dont il fait partie, sauf le cas de flagrant délit.

Aucun membre du Parlement ne peut, hors session, être arrêté qu'avec l'autorisation du bureau de l'Assemblée dont il fait partie, sauf le cas de flagrant délit, de poursuites autorisées ou de condamnation définitive.

La détention ou la poursuite d'un membre du Parlement est suspendue si l'Assemblée dont il fait partie le requiert.

Art. 27. Tout mandat impératif est nul.

Le droit de vote des membres du Parlement est personnel.

La loi organique peut autoriser exceptionnellement la délégation de vote. Dans ce cas, nul ne peut recevoir délégation de plus d'un mandat.

Art. 28. Le Parlement se réunit de plein droit en deux sessions ordinaires par an.

La première session s'ouvre le 2 octobre, sa durée est de quatre-vingts jours.

La seconde session s'ouvre le 2 avril, sa durée ne peut excéder quatre-vingts jours.

Si le 2 octobre ou le 2 avril est un jour ferié, l'ouverture de la session a lieu le premier jour ouvrable qui suit.

Art. 29. Le Parlement est réuni en session extraordinaire à la demande du Premier ministre ou de la majorité des membres composant l'Assemblée Nationale, sur un ordre du jour déterminé.

Lorsque la session extraordinaire est tenue à la demande des membres de l'Assemblée Nationale, le décret de clôture intervient dès que le Parlement a épuisé l'ordre du jour pour lequel il a été convoqué et au plus tard douze jours à compter de sa réunion.

Le Premier ministre peut seul demander une nouvelle session avant l'expiration du mois qui suit le décret de clôture.

Art. 30. Hors les cas dans lesquels le Parlement se réunit de plein droit, les sessions extraordinaires sont ouvertes et closes par décret du président de la République.

Art. 31. Les membres du Gouvernement ont accès aux deux assemblées. Ils sont entendus quand ils le demandent.

Ils peuvent se faire assister par des commissaires du Gouvernement.

Art. 32. Le président de l'Assemblée Nationale est élu pour la durée de la législature. Le président du Sénat est élu après chaque renouvellement partiel.

Art. 33. Les séances des deux Assemblées sont publiques. Le compte rendu intégral des débats est publié au *Journal officiel*.

Chaque assemblée peut siéger en comité secret à la demande du Premier ministre ou d'un dixième de ses membres.

TITRE V. – DES RAPPORTS ENTRE LE PARLEMENT ET LE GOUVERNEMENT

Art. 34. La loi est votée par le Parlement.

La loi fixe les règles concernant:

– les droits civiques et les garanties fondamentales accordées aux citoyens pour l'exercice des libertés publiques; les sujétions imposées par la défense nationale aux citoyens en leur personne et en leurs biens;

– la nationalité, l'état et la capacité des personnes, les régimes matrimoniaux, les successions et libéralités;

– la détermination des crimes et délits ainsi que les peines qui leur sont applicables; la procédure pénale; l'amnistie, la création de nouveaux ordres de juridiction et le statut des magistrats;

– l'assiette, le taux et les modalités de recouvrement des impositions de toutes natures; le régime d'émission de la monnaie.

La loi fixe également les règles concernant:

– le régime électoral des assemblées parlementaires et des assemblées locales;

– la création de catégories d'établissements publics;

– les garanties fondamentales accordées aux fonctionnaires civils et militaires de l'Etat;

– les nationalisations d'entreprises et les transferts de propriété d'entreprises du secteur public au secteur privé.

La loi détermine les principes fondamentaux:

– de l'organisation générale de la défense nationale;

– de la libre administration des collectivités locales, de leurs compétences et de leurs ressources;

– de l'enseignement;

– du régime de la propriété, des droits réels et des obligations civiles et commerciales;

– du droit du travail, du droit syndical et de la sécurité sociale.

Les lois de finances déterminent les ressources et les charges de l'Etat dans les conditions et sous les réserves prévues par une loi organique.

Des lois de programme déterminent les objectifs de l'action économique et sociale de l'Etat.

Les dispositions du présent article pourront être précisées et complétées par une loi organique.

Art. 35. La déclaration de guerre est autorisée par le Parlement.

Art. 36. L'état de siège est décrété en conseil des ministres.

Sa prorogation au-delà de douze jours ne peut être autorisée que par le Parlement.

Art. 37. Les matières autres que celles qui sont du domaine de la loi ont un caractère réglementaire.

Les textes de forme législative intervenus en ces matières peuvent être modifiés par décrets pris après avis du Conseil d'Etat. Ceux de ces textes qui interviendraient après l'entrée en vigueur de la présente constitution ne pourront être modifiés par décret que si le Conseil constitutionnel a déclaré qu'ils ont un caractère réglementaire en vertu de l'alinéa précédent.

Art. 38. Le Gouvernement peut, pour l'exécution de son programme, demander au Parlement l'autorisation de prendre par ordonnances, pendant un délai limité, des mesures qui sont normalement du domaine de la loi.

Les ordonnances sont prises en conseil des ministres après avis du Conseil d'Etat. Elles entrent en vigueur dès leur publication mais deviennent caduques si le projet de loi de ratification n'est pas déposé devant le Parlement avant la date fixée par la loi d'habilitation.

A l'expiration du délai mentionné au premier alinéa du présent article, les ordonnances ne peuvent plus être modifiées que par la loi dans les matières qui sont du domaine législatif.

Art. 39. L'initiative des lois appartient concurremment au Premier ministre et aux membres du Parlement.

Les projets de loi sont délibérés en conseil des ministres après avis du Conseil d'Etat et déposés sur le bureau de l'une des deux assemblées. Les projets de loi de finances sont soumis en premier lieu à l'Assemblée nationale.

Art. 40. Les propositions et amendements formulés par les membres du Parlement ne sont pas recevables lorsque leur adoption aurait pour conséquence soit une diminution des ressources publiques, soit la création ou l'aggravation d'une charge publique.

Art. 41. S'il apparaît au cours de la procédure législative qu'une proposition ou un amendement n'est pas du domaine de la loi ou est contraire à une délégation accordée en vertu de l'article 38, le Gouvernement peut opposer l'irrecevabilité.

En cas de désaccord entre le Gouvernement et le président de l'assemblée intéressée, le Conseil constitutionnel, à la demande de l'un ou de l'autre, statue dans un délai de huit jours.

Art. 42. La discussion des projets de loi porte, devant la première assemblée saisie, sur le texte présenté par le Gouvernement.

Une assemblée saisie d'un texte voté par l'autre assemblée délibère sur le texte qui lui est transmis.

Art. 43. Les projets et propositions de loi sont, à la demande du Gouvernement ou de l'assemblée qui en est saisie, envoyés pour examen à des commissions spécialement désignées à cet effet.

Les projets et propositions pour lesquels une telle demande n'a pas été faite sont envoyés à l'une des commissions permanentes dont le nombre est limité à six dans chaque assemblée.

Art. 44. Les membres du Parlement et le Gouvernement ont le droit d'amendement.

Après l'ouverture du débat, le Gouvernement peut s'opposer, à l'examen de tout amendement qui n'a pas été antérieurement soumis à la commission.

Si le Gouvernement le demande, l'assemblée saisie se prononce par un seul vote sur tout ou partie du texte en discussion en ne retenant que les amendements proposés ou acceptés par le Gouvernement.

Art. 45. Tout projet ou proposition de loi est examiné successivement dans les deux assemblées du Parlement en vue de l'adoption d'un texte identique.

Lorsque, par suite d'un désaccord entre les deux assemblées, un projet ou une proposition de loi n'a pu être adopté après deux lectures par chaque assemblée ou, si le Gouvernement a déclaré l'urgence, après une seule lecture par chacune d'entre elles, le Premier ministre a la faculté de provoquer la réunion d'une commission mixte paritaire chargée de proposer un texte sur les dispositions restant en discussion.

Le texte élaboré par la commission mixte peut être soumis par le Gouvernement pour approbation aux deux assemblées. Aucun amendement n'est recevable sauf accord du Gouvernement.

Si la commission mixte ne parvient pas à l'adoption d'un texte commun ou si ce texte n'est pas adopté dans les conditions prévues à l'alinéa précédent, le Gouvernement peut, après une nouvelle lecture par l'Assemblée Nationale et par le Sénat, demander à l'Assemblée Nationale de statuer définitivement. En ce cas, l'Assemblée Nationale peut reprendre soit le texte élaboré par la commission mixte, soit le dernier texte voté par elle, modifié le cas échéant par un ou plusieurs des amendements adoptés par le Sénat.

Art. 46. Les lois auxquelles la constitution confère le caractère de lois organiques sont votées et modifiées dans les conditions suivantes.

Le projet ou la proposition n'est soumis à la délibération et au vote de la première assemblée saisie qu'à l'expiration d'un délai de quinze jours après son dépôt.

La procédure de l'article 45 est applicable. Toutefois, faute d'accord entre les deux assemblées, le texte ne peut être adopté par l'Assemblée Nationale en dernière lecture qu'à la majorité absolue de ses membres.

Les lois organiques relatives au Sénat doivent être votées dans les mêmes termes par les deux assemblées.

Les lois organiques ne peuvent être promulguées qu'après déclaration par le Conseil constitutionnel de leur conformité à la constitution.

Art. 47. Le Parlement vote les projets de loi de finances dans les conditions prévues par une loi organique.

Si l'Assemblée Nationale ne s'est pas prononcée en première lecture dans le délai de quarante jours après le dépôt d'un projet, le Gouvernement saisit le Sénat, qui doit statuer dans un délai de quinze jours. Il est ensuite procédé dans les conditions prévues à l'article 45.

Si le Parlement ne s'est pas prononcé dans un délai de soixante-dix jours, les dispositions du projet peuvent être mises en vigueur par ordonnance.

Si la loi de finances fixant les ressources et les charges d'un exercice n'a pas été déposée en temps utile pour être promulguée avant le début de cet exercice, le Gouvernement demande d'urgence au Parlement l'autorisation de percevoir les impôts et ouvre par décret les crédits se rapportant aux services votés.

Les délais prévus au présent article sont suspendus lorsque le Parlement n'est pas en session.

La Cour des comptes assiste le Parlement et le Gouvernement dans le contrôle de l'exécution des lois de finances.

Art. 48. L'ordre du jour des assemblées comporte, par priorité et dans l'ordre que le Gouvernement a fixé, la discussion des projets de loi déposés par le gouvernement et des propositions de loi acceptées par lui.

Une séance par semaine est réservée par priorité aux questions des membres du Parlement et aux réponses du Gouvernement.

Art. 49. Le Premier ministre, après délibération du conseil des ministres, engage devant l'Assemblée Nationale la responsabilité du Gouvernement sur son programme ou éventuellement sur une déclaration de politique générale.

L'Assemblée Nationale met en cause la responsabilité du Gouvernement par le vote d'une motion de censure. Une telle motion n'est recevable que si elle est signée par un dixième au moins des membres de l'Assemblée nationale. Le vote ne peut avoir lieu que quarante-huit heures après son dépôt. Seuls sont recensés les votes favorables à la motion de censure qui ne peut être adoptée qu'à la majorité des membres composant l'Assemblée. Si la motion de censure est rejetée, ses signataires ne peuvent en proposer une nouvelle au cours de la même session, sauf dans le cas prévu à l'alinéa ci-dessous.

Le Premier ministre peut, après délibération du conseil des ministres, engager la responsabilité du Gouvernement devant l'Assemblée Nationale sur le vote d'un texte. Dans ce cas, ce texte est considéré comme adopté, sauf si une motion de censure, déposée dans les vingt-quatre heures qui suivent, est votée dans les conditions prévues à l'alinéa précédent.

Le Premier ministre a la faculté de demander au Sénat l'approbation d'une déclaration de politique générale.

Art. 50. Lorsque l'Assemblée Nationale adopte une motion de censure ou lorsqu'elle désapprouve le programme ou une déclaration de politique générale du Gouvernement, le Premier ministre doit remettre au président de la République la démission du Gouvernement.

Art. 51. La clôture des sessions ordinaires ou extraordinaires est de droit retardée pour permettre, le cas échéant, l'application des dispositions de l'article 49.

TITRE VI. — DES TRAITES ET ACCORDS INTERNATIONAUX

Art. 52. Le président de la République négocie et ratifie les traités.

Il est informé de toute négociation tendant à la conclusion d'un accord international non soumis à ratification.

Art. 53. Les traités de paix, les traités de commerce, les traités ou accords relatifs à l'organisation internationale, ceux qui engagent les finances de l'Etat, ceux qui modifient les dispositions de nature législative, ceux qui sont relatifs à l'Etat des personnes, ceux qui comportent cession, échange ou adjonction de territoire, ne peuvent être ratifiés ou approuvés qu'en vertu d'une loi.

Ils ne prennent effet qu'après avoir été ratifiés ou approuvés.

Nulle cession, nul échange, nulle adjonction de territoire n'est valable sans le consentement des populations intéressées.

Art. 54. Si le Conseil constitutionnel, saisi par le président de la République, par le Premier ministre ou par le président de l'une ou l'autre assemblée, a déclaré qu'un engagement international comporte une clause contraire à la constitution, l'autorisation de le ratifier ou de l'approuver ne peut intervenir qu'après la révision de la constitution.

Art. 55. Les traités ou accords régulièrement ratifiés ou approuvés ont, dès leur publication, une autorité supérieure à celle des lois, sous réserve, pour chaque accord ou traité, de son application par l'autre partie.

TITRE VII. – LE CONSEIL CONSTITUTIONNEL

Art. 56. Le Conseil constitutionnel comprend neuf membres, dont le mandat dure neuf ans et n'est pas renouvelable. Le Conseil constitutionnel se renouvelle par tiers tous les trois ans. Trois des membres sont nommés par le président de la République, trois par le président de l'Assemblée Nationale, trois par le président du Sénat.

En sus des neuf membres prévus ci-dessus, font de droit partie à vie du Conseil constitutionnel les anciens présidents de la République.

Le président est nommé par le président de la République. Il a voix prépondérante en cas de partage.

Art. 57. Les fonctions de membres du Conseil constitutionnel sont incompatibles avec celles de ministre ou de membre du Parlement. Les autres incompatibilités sont fixées par une loi organique.

Art. 58. Le Conseil constitutionnel veille à la régularité de l'élection du président de la République.

Il examine les réclamations et proclame les résultats du scrutin.

Art. 59. Le Conseil constitutionnel statue, en cas de contestation, sur la régularité de l'élection des députés et des sénateurs.

Art. 60. Le Conseil constitutionnel veille à la régularité des opérations de référendum et en proclame les résultats.

Art. 61. Les lois organiques, avant leur promulgation, et les règlements des assemblées parlementaires, avant leur mise en application, doivent être soumis au Conseil constitutionnel, qui se prononce sur leur conformité à la constitution.

Aux mêmes fins, les lois peuvent être déférées au Conseil constitutionnel, avant leur promulgation, par le président de la République, le Premier ministre, le président de l'Assemblée Nationale, le président du Sénat ou soixante députés ou soixante sénateurs.

Dans les cas prévus aux deux alinéas précédents, le Conseil constitutionnel doit statuer dans un délai d'un mois. Toutefois, à la demande du Gouvernement, s'il y a urgence, ce délai est ramené à huit jours.

Dans ces mêmes cas, la saisine du Conseil constitutionnel suspend le délai de promulgation.

Art. 62. Une disposition déclarée inconstitutionnelle ne peut être promulguée ni mise en application.

Les décisions du Conseil constitutionnel ne sont susceptibles d'aucun recours. Elles s'imposent aux pouvoirs publics et à toutes les autorités administratives et juridictionnelles.

Art. 63. Une loi organique détermine les règles d'organisation et de fonctionnement du Conseil constitutionnel, la procédure qui est suivie devant lui, et notamment les délais ouverts pour le saisir de contestations.

TITRE VIII. – DE L'AUTORITE JUDICIAIRE

Art. 64. Le président de la République est garant de l'indépendance de l'autorité judiciaire.

Il est assisté par le Conseil Supérieur de la Magistrature.

Une loi organique porte statut des magistrats.

Les magistrats du siège sont inamovibles.

Art. 65. Le Conseil Supérieur de la Magistrature est présidé par le président de la République. Le ministre de la Justice en est le vice-président de droit. Il peut suppléer le président de la République.

Le Conseil Supérieur comprend en outre neuf membres désignés par le président de la République dans les conditions fixées par une loi organique.

Le Conseil Supérieur de la Magistrature fait des propositions pour les nominations de magistrats du siège à la Cour de cassation et pour celles de premier président de cours d'appel. Il donne son avis dans les conditions fixées par la loi organique sur les propositions du ministre de la Justice relatives aux nominations des autres magistrats du siège. Il est consulté sur les grâces dans les conditions fixées par une loi organique.

Le Conseil Supérieur de la Magistrature statue comme conseil de discipline des magistrats du siège. Il est alors présidé par le premier président de la Cour de cassation.

Art. 66. Nul ne peut être arbitrairement détenu.

L'autorité judiciaire, gardienne de la liberté individuelle, assure le respect de ce principe dans les conditions prévues par la loi.

TITRE IX. – LA HAUTE COUR DE JUSTICE

Art. 67. Il est institué une Haute Cour de Justice.

Elle est composée de membres élus, en leur sein et en nombre égal, par l'Assemblée Nationale et par le Sénat après chaque renouvellement général ou partiel de ces assemblées. Elle élit son président parmi ses membres.

Une loi organique fixe la composition de la Haute Cour, les règles de son fonctionnement ainsi que la procédure applicable devant elle.

Art. 68. Le président de la République n'est responsable des actes accomplis dans l'exercice de ses fonctions qu'en cas de haute trahison. Il ne peut être mis en accusation que par les deux assemblées statuant par un vote identique au scrutin public et à la majorité absolue des membres les composant; il est jugé par la Haute Cour de Justice.

Les membres du Gouvernement sont pénalement responsables des actes accomplis dans l'exercice de leurs fonctions et qualifié crimes ou délits au moment où ils ont été commis. La procédure définie ci-dessus leur est applicable ainsi qu'à leurs complices dans le cas de complot contre la sûreté de l'Etat. Dans les cas prévus au présent alinéa, la Haute Cour est liée par la définition des crimes et délits ainsi que par la détermination des peines telles qu'elles résultent des lois pénales en vigueur au moment où les faits ont été commis.

TITRE X. – LE CONSEIL ECONOMIQUE ET SOCIAL

Art. 69. Le Conseil économique et social, saisi par le Gouvernement, donne son avis sur les projets de loi, d'ordonnance ou de décret ainsi que sur les propositions de loi qui lui sont soumis.

Un membre du Conseil économique et social peut être désigné par celui-ci pour exposer devant les assemblées parlementaires l'avis du Conseil sur les projets ou propositions qui lui ont été soumis.

Art. 70. Le Conseil économique et social peut être également consulté par le Gouvernement sur tout problème de caractère économique ou social intéressant la République ou la Communauté. Tout plan ou tout projet de loi de programme à caractère économique ou social lui est soumis pour avis.

Art. 71. La composition du Conseil économique et social et ses règles de fonctionnement sont fixées par une loi organique.

TITRE XI. – DES COLLECTIVITES TERRITORIALES

Art. 72. Les collectivités territoriales de la République sont les communes, les départements, les territoires d'outre-mer. Toute autre collectivité territoriale est créée par la loi.

Ces collectivités s'administrent librement par des conseils élus et dans les conditions prévues par la loi.

Dans les départements et les territoires, le délégué du Gouvernement a la charge des intérêts nationaux, du contrôle administratif et du respect des lois.

(...)

TITRE XIV. – DE LA REVISION

Art. 89. L'initiative de la révision de la constitution appartient concurremment au président de la République sur proposition du Premier ministre et aux membres du Parlement.

Le projet ou la proposition de révision doit être voté par les deux assemblées en termes identiques. La révision est définitive après avoir été approuvée par référendum.

Toutefois, le projet de révision n'est pas présenté au référendum lorsque le président de la République décide de le soumettre au Parlement convoqué en congrès; dans ce cas, le projet de révision n'est approuvé que s'il réunit la majorité des trois cinquièmes des suffrages exprimés. Le bureau du Congrès est celui de l'Assemblée Nationale.

Aucune procédure de révision ne peut être engagée ou poursuivie lorsqu'il est porté atteinte à l'intégrité du territoire.

La forme républicaine du Gouvernement ne peut faire l'objet d'une révision.

(...)

La présente loi sera exécutée comme constitution de la République et de la Communauté.

Fait à Paris, le 4 octobre 1958.

2 Avis du Conseil d'Etat du 6.2.1953

Le Conseil d'Etat saisi par M. le Ministre d'Etat de la question de savoir «quelles sont la définition et la portée exacte de l'interdiction contenue dans l'article 13 de la Constitution, dans quelle mesure le gouvernement, à ce expressément autorisé par la loi, peut exercer son pouvoir réglementaire en des matières législatives et, en conséquence, abroger, modifier, ou remplacer des textes de loi par des dispositions réglementaires»;

Vu la Constitution du 27 octobre 1946;

Considérant qu'aux termes de l'article 13 de la Constitution du 27 octobre 1946 «l'Assemblée nationale vote seule la loi. Elle ne peut déléguer ce droit»;

Considérant qu'il ressort des débats ayant précédé l'adoption de cette disposition, dont le principe figurait dans l'article 55 du projet de Constitution élaboré par la première Assemblée nationale constituante, ainsi que de la procédure organisée aux articles 14 et suivants de la Constitution pour la discussion et le vote des lois, que les auteurs de ce texte ont entendu interdire le recours aux décrets pris en vertu des lois de pleins pouvoirs telles qu'elles furent votées sous la 3e République;

Considérant d'autre part que le législateur peut, en principe, déterminer souverainement la compétence du pouvoir réglementaire; qu'il peut, à cet fin, décider que certaines matières relevant de la compétence du pouvoir législatif entreront dans la compétence du pouvoir réglementaire, que les décrets pris en ces matières peuvent modifier, abroger ou remplacer les dispositions législatives; qu'ils pourront être eux-mêmes modifiés par d'autres décrets jusqu'à ce que le législateur évoque à nouveau les matières en question dans les conditions excluant dorénavant la compétence du pouvoir réglementaire;

Considérant toutefois que certaines matières sont réservées à la loi soit en vertu des dispositions de la Constitution, soit par la tradition constitutionnelle républicaine résultant notamment du préambule de la Constitution et de la Déclaration des Droits de l'Homme de 1789, dont les principes ont été réaffirmés par le préambule; que le législateur ne peut, dès lors, étendre à ces matières la compétence du pouvoir réglementaire;

Mais qu'il peut se borner à poser les règles essentielles en laissant au gouvernement le soin de les compléter;

Considérant enfin qu'en vertu de l'article 3 de la Constitution, la souveraineté nationale appartient au peuple français qui «l'exerce par ses députés à l'Assemblée nationale, en toutes autres matières que les matières constitutionnelles», que l'extension de la compétence du pouvoir réglementaire serait contraire à l'article 3 si, par sa généralité ou son imprécision, elle manifestait la volonté de l'Assemblée nationale d'abandonner au gouvernement l'exercice de la souveraineté nationale;

Est d'avis, qu'il y a lieu de répondre à la question posée dans le sens des observations qui précèdent.

3 Conseil Constitutionnel 16.7.1971, J.O., 18.7.1971, 7114

Le Conseil constitutionnel,

Saisi le 1er juillet 1971 par le président du Sénat, conformément aux dispositions de l'article 61 de la Constitution, du texte de la loi, délibérée par l'Assemblée nationale et le Sénat et adoptée par l'Assemblée nationale, complétant les dispositions des articles 5 et 7 de la loi du 1er juillet 1901 relative au contrat d'association;

Vu la Constitution, et notamment son préambule;

Vu l'ordonnance du 7 novembre 1958 portant loi organique sur le Conseil constitutionnel, notamment le chapitre II du titre II de ladite ordonnance;

Vu la loi du 1er juillet 1901 relative au contrat d'association modifiée;

Vu la loi du 10 janvier 1936 relative aux groupes de combat et milices privées;

Considérant que la loi déférée à l'examen du Conseil constitutionnel a été soumise au vote des deux Assemblées dans le respect d'une des procédures prévues par la Constitution, au cours de la session du Parlement ouverte le 2 avril 1971;

Considérant qu'au nombre des principes fondamentaux reconnus par les lois de la République et solennellement réaffirmés par le préambule de la Constitution il y a lieu de ranger le principe de la liberté d'association; que ce principe est à la base des dispositions générales de la loi du 1er juillet 1901 relative au contrat d'association; qu'en vertu de ce principe les associations se constituent librement et peuvent être rendues publiques sous la seule réserve du dépôt d'une déclaration préalable; qu'ainsi, à l'exception des mesures susceptibles d'être prises à l'égard de catégories particulières d'associations, la constitution d'associations, alors même qu'elles paraîtraient entachées de nullité ou auraient un objet illicite, ne peut être soumise pour sa validité à l'intervention préalable de l'autorité administrative ou même de l'autorité judiciaire;

Considérant que, si rien n'est changé en ce qui concerne la constitution même des associations non déclarées, les dispositions de l'article 3 de la loi dont le texte est, avant sa promulgation, soumis au Conseil constitutionnel pour examen de sa conformité à la Constitution ont pour objet d'instituer une procédure d'après laquelle l'acquisition de la capacité juridique des associations déclarées pourra être subordonnée à un contrôle préalable par l'autorité judiciaire de leur conformité à la loi;

Considérant, dès lors, qu'il y a lieu de déclarer non conformes à la Constitution les dispositions de l'article 3 de la loi soumise à l'examen du Conseil constitutionnel complétant l'article 7 de la loi du 1er juillet 1901, ainsi, par voie de conséquence, que la disposition de la dernière phrase de l'alinéa 2 de l'article 1er de la loi soumise au Conseil constitutionnel leur faisant référence;

Considérant qu'il ne résulte ni du texte dont il s'agit, tel qu'il a été rédigé et adopté, ni des débats auxquels la discussion du projet de loi a donné lieu devant le Parlement, que les dispositions précitées soient inséparables de l'ensemble du texte de la loi soumise au Conseil;

Considérant, enfin, que les autres dispositions de ce texte ne sont contraires à aucune disposition de la Constitution;

Décide:

ARTICLE PREMIER. Sont déclarées non conformes à la Constitution les dispositions de l'article 3 de la loi soumise à l'examen du Conseil constitutionnel complétant les dispositions de l'article 7 de la loi du 1er juillet 1901 ainsi que les dispositions de l'article 1er de la loi soumise au Conseil leur faisant référence.

ART. 2. Les autres dispositions dudit texte de loi sont déclarées conformes à la Constitution.

4 Loi du 25 février 1875 relative à l'organisation des pouvoirs publics

Art. 2. Le Président de la République est élu à la majorité absolue des suffrages par le Sénat et par la Chambre des Députés réunis en Assemblée Nationale. Il est nommé pour sept ans. Il est rééligible.

5 Loi du 14 août 1884

Art. 2. La forme républicaine du Gouvernement ne peut faire l'objet d'une proposition de révision – les membres des familles ayant régné sur la France sont inéligibles à la présidence de la République.

6 Ordonnance du 9 août 1944 du Général de Gaulle, Chef du Gouvernement provisoire de la République Française

Art. 1er: La forme du Gouvernement de la France est et demeure la République. En droit celle-ci n'a pas cessé d'exister.

2. Sont, en conséquence, nuls et de nul effet, tous les actes constitutionnels législatifs ou réglementaires, ainsi que les arrêtés pris pour leur exécution, sous quelque dénomination que ce soit, promulgués sur le territoire continental postérieurement au 16 juin 1940 et jusqu'au rétablissement du Gouvernement provisoire de la République française.

Cette nullité doit être expressément constatée.

3. Est expressément constatée la nullité des actes suivants:

L'acte dit «loi constitutionnelle du 10 juillet 1940»,

Tous les actes dits: «actes constitutionnels»,

(...)

7 Constitution du 27 octobre 1946

PREAMBULE

Au lendemain de la victoire remportée par les peuples libres sur les régimes qui ont été tenté d'asservir et de dégrader la personne humaine, le peuple français proclame à nouveau que tout être humain, sans distinction de race, de religion ni de croyance, possède des droits inaliénables et sacrés. Il réaffirme solennellement les droits et les libertés de l'homme et du citoyen consacrés par la déclaration des droits de 1789 et les principes fondamentaux reconnus par les lois de la République.

Il proclame, en outre, comme particulièrement nécessaires à notre temps, les principes politiques, économiques et sociaux ci-après:

La loi garantit à la femme, dans tous les domaines, des droits égaux à ceux de l'homme.

Tout homme persécuté en raison de son action en faveur de la liberté a droit d'asile sur les territoires de la République.

Chacun a le devoir de travailler et le droit d'obtenir un emploi. Nul ne peut être lésé, dans son travail ou son emploi, en raison de ses origines, de ses opinions ou de ses croyances.

Tout homme peut défendre ses droits et ses intérêts par l'action syndicale et adhérer au syndicat de son choix.

Le droit de grève s'exerce dans le cadre des lois qui le réglementent.

Tout travailleur participe, par l'intermédiaire de ses délégués, à la détermination collective des conditions de travail ainsi qu'à la gestion des entreprises.

Tout bien, toute entreprise, dont l'exploitation a ou acquiert les caractères d'un service public national ou d'un monopole de fait, doit devenir la propriété de la collectivité.

La nation assure à l'individu et à la famille les conditions nécessaires à leur développement.

Elle garantit à tous, notamment à l'enfant, à la mère et aux vieux travailleurs, la protection de la santé, la sécurité matérielle, le repos et les loisirs. Tout être humain qui, en raison de son âge, de son état physique ou mental, de la situation économique, se trouve dans l'incapacité de travailler a le droit d'obtenir de la collectivité des moyens convenables d'existence.

La nation proclame la solidarité et l'égalité de tous les Français devant les charges qui résultent des calamités nationales.

La nation garantit l'égal accès de l'enfant et de l'adulte à l'instruction, à la formation professionnelle et à la culture. L'organisation de l'enseignement public gratuit et laïque à tous les degrés est un devoir de l'Etat.

Le République française, fidèle à ses traditions, se conforme aux règles du droit public international. Elle n'entreprendra aucune guerre dans des vues de conquête et n'emploiera jamais ses forces contre la liberté d'aucun peuple.

Sous réserve de réciprocité, la France consent aux limitations de souveraineté nécessaires à l'organisation et à la défense de la paix.

La France forme avec les peuples d'outre-mer une union fondée sur l'égalité des droits et des devoirs, sans distinction de race ni de religion.

L'Union française est composée de nations et de peuples qui mettent en commun ou coordonnent leurs ressources et leurs efforts pour développer leurs civilisations respectives, accroître leur bien-être et assurer leur sécurité.

Fidèle à sa mission traditionnelle, la France entend conduire les peuples dont elle a pris la charge à la liberté de s'administrer eux-mêmes et de gérer démocratiquement leurs propres affaires; écartant tout système de colonisation fondé sur l'arbitraire, elle garantit à tous l'égal accès aux fonctions publiques et l'exercice individuel ou collectif des droits et libertés proclamés ou confirmés ci-dessus.

8 Conseil Constitutionnel 30 décembre 1975, Rec., 26

Le Conseil constitutionnel,
Saisi le 17 décembre 1975 par MM. Alain Vivien, Gaston Defferre (...)
députés à l'Assemblée nationale, dans les conditions prévues à l'article 61 de la

Constitution, du texte de la loi relative aux conséquences de l'autodétermination des îles des Comores, telle que cette loi a été adoptée par le Parlement;

Vu la Constitution;

Vu l'ordonnance du 7 novembre 1958 portant loi organique sur le Conseil constitutionnel, notamment le chapitre II du titre II de ladite ordonnance;

Ouï le rapporteur en son rapport;

Considérant que l'article 53, dernier alinéa, de la Constitution, dispose: «Nulle cession, nul échange, nulle adjonction de territoire n'est valable sans le consentement des populations intéressées»;

Considérant que les dispositions de cet article doivent être interprétées comme étant applicables, non seulement dans l'hypothèse où la France céderait à un État étranger ou bien acquerrait de celui-ci un territoire, mais aussi dans l'hypothèse où un territoire cesserait d'appartenir à la République pour constituer un État indépendant ou y être rattaché;

Considérant que l'île de Mayotte est un territoire au sens de l'article 53, dernier alinéa, de la Constitution, ce terme n'ayant pas dans cet article la même signification juridique que dans l'expression territoire d'outre-mer, telle qu'elle est employée dans la Constitution;

Considérant, en conséquence, que cette île ne saurait sortir de la République française sans le consentement de sa propre population; que, dès lors, les articles 1er et 2 de la loi déférée au Conseil constitutionnel font une exacte application de l'article 53, dernier alinéa, de la Constitution;

Considérant que cette loi n'a pour objet, dans aucune de ses dispositions, de définir ou de modifier l'organisation particulière d'un territoire d'outre-mer; qu'en conséquence l'article 74 ne saurait recevoir application dans le cas de l'espèce;

Considérant que l'île de Mayotte fait partie de la République française; que cette constatation ne peut être faite que dans le cadre de la Constitution, nonobstant toute intervention d'une instance internationale, et que les dispositions de la loi déférée au Conseil constitutionnel qui concernent cette île ne mettent en cause aucune règle du droit public international;

Considérant que le préambule de la constitution du 27 octobre 1946, confirmé par celui de la constitution du 4 octobre 1958, déclare que la République française n'emploiera jamais ses forces contre la liberté d'aucun peuple;

Considérant qu'aucune des dispositions de la loi déférée au Conseil constitutionnel ne tend à l'emploi des forces de la République contre la liberté de quelque peuple que ce soit; que, bien au contraire, son article 8 dispose «les îles de la Grande Comore, d'Anjouan et de Mohéli», dont les populations se sont prononcées, à la majorité des suffrages exprimés, pour l'indépendance, «cessent, à compter de la promulgation de la présente loi, de faire partie de la République française»;

Considérant que les autres dispositions de ce texte ne sont contraires à aucune disposition de la Constitution;

Considérant qu'il résulte de tout ce qui précède que la loi relative aux conséquences de l'autodétermination des îles des Comores ne contredit aucune disposition du préambule de la Constitution, aucun des textes auquel ce préambule fait référence, ni aucun article de la Constitution,

Décide:

Article premier – Les dispositions de la loi relative aux conséquences de l'autodétermination des îles des Comores déférée au Conseil constitutionnel ne sont pas contraires à la Constitution.

9 Conseil Constitutionnel 9 mai 1991, D.1991, 624

Le Conseil constitutionnel a été saisi, le 12 avril 1991, par MM. Pierre Mazeaud, Jacques Chirac, (...) députés, et le 15 avril 1991, d'une part, par M. Alain Poher, président du Sénat, et, d'autre part, par MM. François Giacobbi, Charles Ornano, (...) sénateurs, dans les conditions prévues à l'article 61, alinéa 2, de la Constitution, de la conformité à celle-ci de la loi portant statut de la collectivité territoriale de Corse;

Le Conseil constitutionnel,

Vu la Constitution du 4 octobre 1958;

Vu la Constitution du 27 octobre 1946 (...)

Considérant que l'article 1er de la loi est ainsi rédigé: «La République française garantit à la communauté historique et culturelle vivante que constitue le peuple corse, composante du peuple français, les droits à la préservation de son identité culturelle et à la défense de ses intérêts économiques et sociaux spécifiques. Ces droits liés à l'insularité s'exercent dans le respect de l'unité nationale, dans le cadre de la Constitution, des lois de la République et du présent statut.»;

Considérant que cet article est critiqué en ce qu'il consacre juridiquement l'existence au sein du peuple français d'une composante, «le peuple corse»; qu'il est soutenu par les auteurs de la première saisine que cette reconnaissance n'est conforme ni au préambule de la Constitution de 1958 qui postule l'unicité du «peuple français», ni à son article 2 qui consacre l'indivisibilité de la République, ni à son article 3 qui désigne le peuple comme seul détenteur de la souveraineté nationale; qu'au demeurant, l'article 53 de la Constitution se réfère aux «populations intéressées» d'un territoire et non pas au concept de peuple; que les sénateurs auteurs de la troisième saisine font valoir qu'il résulte des dispositions de la Déclaration des droits de 1789, de plusieurs alinéas du préambule de la Constitution de 1946, de la loi constitutionnelle du 3 juin 1958, du préambule de la Constitution de 1958 comme de ses articles 2, 3 et 91, que l'expression «le peuple», lorsqu'elle s'applique au peuple français, doit être considérée comme une catégorie unitaire insusceptible de toute subdivision en vertu de la loi;

Considérant qu'aux termes du premier alinéa du préambule de la Constitution de 1958 «le peuple français proclame solennellement son attachement aux droits de l'homme et aux principes de la souveraineté nationale tels qu'ils ont été définis par la Déclaration de 1789, confirmée et complétée par le préambule de la Constitution de 1946»; que la Déclaration des droits de l'homme et du citoyen à laquelle il est ainsi fait référence émanait des représentants «du peuple français»; que le préambule de la Constitution de 1946, réaffirmé par le préambule de la Constitution de 1958, énonce que «le peuple français proclame à nouveau que tout être humain, sans distinction de race, de religion ni de croyance, possède des droits inaliénables et sacrés»; que la Constitution de 1958 distingue le peuple français des peuples d'outre-mer auxquels est reconnu le droit à la libre détermination; que la référence faite au «peuple français» figure d'ailleurs depuis deux siècles dans de nombreux textes constitutionnels; qu'ainsi le concept juridique de «peuple français» a valeur constitutionnelle;

Considérant que la France est, ainsi que le proclame l'article 2 de la Constitution de 1958, une République indivisible, laïque, démocratique et sociale qui assure l'égalité devant la loi de tous les citoyens quelle que soit leur origine; que dès lors la mention faite par le législateur du «peuple corse, composante du peuple français» est contraire à la Constitution, laquelle ne connaît que le peuple français, composé de tous les citoyens français sans distinction d'origine, de race ou de religion;

Considérant en conséquence que l'article 1er de la loi n'est pas conforme à la Constitution; que toutefois il ne ressort pas du texte de cet article, tel qu'il a été rédigé et adopté, que ses dispositions soient inséparables de l'ensemble du texte de la loi soumise au Conseil constitutionnel;

Décide:

Article premier. – Ne sont pas conformes à la Constitution les dispositions suivantes de la loi portant statut de la collectivité territoriale de Corse;

– l'article 1er; (...)

10 Loi du 9 décembre 1905

Art. 1er. La République assure la liberté de conscience. Elle garantit le libre exercice des cultes sous les seules restrictions édictées ci-après dans l'intérêt de l'ordre public.

2. La République ne reconnaît, ne salarie ni ne subventionne aucun culte. En conséquence, à partir du 1er janvier qui suivra la promulgation de la présente loi, seront supprimées des budgets de l'Etat, des départements et des communes toutes dépenses relatives à l'exercice des cultes. Pourront toutefois être inscrites aux dits budgets les dépenses relatives à des services d'aumônerie et destinées à assurer le libre exercice des cultes dans les établissements publics, tels que lycées, collèges, écoles, hospices, asiles et prisons. – Les établissements publics du culte sont supprimés, sous réserve des dispositions énoncées à l'article 3.

11 Loi du 31 décembre 1959 ('loi Debré')

Art. 1er. – Suivant les principes définis dans la Constitution, l'Etat assure aux enfants et adolescents dans les établissements publics d'enseignement la possibilité de recevoir un enseignement conforme à leurs aptitudes dans un égal respect de toutes les croyances.

L'Etat proclame et respecte la liberté de l'enseignement et en garantit l'exercice aux établissements privés régulièrement ouverts.

Il prend toutes dispositions utiles pour assurer aux élèves de l'enseignement public la liberté des cultes et de l'instruction religieuse.

Dans les établissements privés qui ont passé un des contrats prévus ci-dessous, l'enseignement placé sous le régime du contrat est soumis au contrôle de l'Etat. L'établissement, tout en conservant son caractère propre, doit donner cet enseignement dans le respect total de la liberté de conscience. Tous les enfants sans distinction d'origine, d'opinions ou de croyances, y ont accès.

12 Avis du Conseil d'Etat du 27 novembre 1989

Le Conseil d'Etat saisi par le ministre d'Etat, ministre de l'Education nationale, de la Jeunesse et des Sports de la question de savoir:

1 – si, compte tenu des principes posés par la Constitution et les lois de la République et eu égard à l'ensemble des règles d'organisation et de fonctionnement de l'école publique, le port de signes d'appartenance à une communauté religieuse est ou non compatible avec le principe de laïcité;

2 – en cas de réponse affirmative, à quelles conditions des instructions du ministre, des dispositions du réglement intérieur des écoles, collèges et lycées, des décisions des directeurs d'école et chefs d'établissement pourraient l'admettre;

3 – si l'inobservation d'une interdiction du port de tels signes ou des conditions prescrites pour celui-ci justifieraient le refus d'accueil dans l'établissement d'un nouvel élève, le refus d'accès opposé à un élève régulièrement inscrit, l'exclusion définitive de l'établissement ou du service public de l'éducation, et quelles procédures et quelles garanties devraient alors être mises en oeuvre;

Vu (...)

Est d'avis de répondre aux questions posées dans le sens des observations ci-après:

1 – Le principe de laïcité trouve l'une de ses premières expressions dans la loi du 28 mars 1882, qui dispose que, dans l'enseignement primaire, l'instruction religieuse est donnée en dehors des édifices et des programmes scolaires et dans l'article 17 de la loi du 30 octobre 1886 sur l'organisation de l'enseignement primaire, aux termes duquel «dans les écoles publiques de tout ordre, l'enseignement est exclusivement confié à un personnel laïque».

Ce principe a été consacré par le préambule de la Constitution du 27 octobre 1946, qui fait de «l'organisation de l'enseignement public gratuit et laïque à tous les degrés un devoir de l'Etat» et par l'article 2 de la Constitution du 4 octobre 1958, qui proclame que «la France est une république ... laïque» et qu'«elle assure l'égalité devant la loi de tous les citoyens sans distinction d'origine, de race ou de religion».

Comme l'indique ce dernier texte, le principe de laïcité implique nécessairement le respect de toutes les croyances, déjà reconnu par l'article 10 de la Déclaration des droits de l'homme et du citoyen du 26 août 1789, aux termes duquel «Nul ne doit être inquiété pour ses opinions, même religieuses, pourvu que leur manifestation ne trouble pas l'ordre public établi par la loi».

La loi du 9 décembre 1905, tout en procédant à la séparation des Eglises et de l'Etat, a confirmé que «la République assure la liberté de conscience».

Cette liberté, qui doit être regardée comme l'un des principes fondamentaux reconnus par les lois de la République, s'exerce dans le domaine de l'éducation, dans le cadre des textes législatifs qui définissent la mission du service public et les droits et obligations des élèves et de leurs familles dans les termes suivants:

Article 1er de la loi du 31 décembre 1959 relative aux rapports entre l'Etat et les établissements de l'enseignement privé:

«Suivant les principes définis dans la Constitution, l'Etat assure aux enfants et adolescents dans les établissements publics d'enseignement la possibilité de recevoir un enseignement conforme à leurs aptitudes dans un égal respect de toutes les croyances.»

(...)

Article 1er de la loi d'orientation sur l'éducation du 10 juillet 1989:

(...)«Les écoles, les collèges, les lycées et les établissements d'enseignement supérieur ... contribuent à favoriser l'égalité entre les hommes et les femmes. Ils dispensent une formation adaptée dans ses contenus et ses méthodes aux évolutions technologiques, sociales et culturelles du pays et de son environnement européen et international».

Article 1er de la même loi: «Les obligations des élèves consistent dans l'accomplissement des tâches inhérentes à leurs études; elles incluent l'assiduité et le respect des règles de fonctionnement et de la vie collective des établissements.

Dans les collèges et les lycées, les élèves disposent, dans le respect du pluralisme et du principe de neutralité, de la liberté d'information et de la liberté d'expression. L'exercice de ces libertés ne peut porter atteinte aux activités d'enseignement ...»

Article 1er deuxième alinéa de la loi du 2 août 1989 relative aux conditions de séjour et d'entrée des étrangers en France: «Les agissements discriminatoires des détenteurs de l'autorité publique, des groupements ou des personnes privées, la provocation à la discrimination, à la haine ou à la violence, la diffamation et l'injure au motif de l'appartenance ou de la non-appartenance à une ethnie, une nation ou une religion sont interdits».

Article 2 de la même loi:

« ... L'école ... doit inculquer aux élèves le respect de l'individu, de ses origines et de ses différences».

(...) Il résulte des textes constitutionnels et législatifs et des engagements internationaux de la France sus-rappelés que le principe de la laïcité de l'enseignement public, qui est l'un des éléments de la laïcité de l'Etat et de la neutralité de l'ensemble des services publics, impose que l'enseignement soit dispensé dans le respect d'une part de cette neutralité par les programmes et par les enseignants et d'autre part de la liberté de conscience des élèves. Il interdit conformément aux principes rappelés par les mêmes textes et les engagements internationaux de la France toute discrimination dans l'accès à l'enseignement qui serait fondée sur les convictions ou croyances religieuses des élèves.

La liberté ainsi reconnue aux élèves comporte pour eux le droit d'exprimer et de manifester leurs croyances religieuses à l'intérieur des établissements scolaires, dans le respect du pluralisme et de la liberté d'autrui, et sans qu'il soit porté atteinte aux activités d'enseignement, au contenu des programmes et à l'obligation d'assiduité.

Son exercice peut être limité, dans la mesure où il ferait obstacle à l'accomplissement des missions dévolues par le législateur au service public de l'éducation, lequel doit notamment, outre permettre l'acquisition par l'enfant d'une culture et sa préparation à la vie professionnelle et à ses responsabilités d'homme et de citoyen, contribuer au développement de sa personnalité, lui inculquer le respect de l'individu, de ses origines et de ses différences, garantir et favoriser l'égalité entre les hommes et les femmes.

Il résulte de ce qui vient d'être dit que, dans les établissements scolaires, le port par les élèves de signes par lesquels ils entendent manifester leur appartenance à une religion n'est pas par lui-même incompatible avec le principe de laïcité, dans la mesure où il constitue l'exercice de la liberté d'expression et de manifestation de croyances religieuses, mais que cette liberté ne saurait permettre aux élèves d'arborer des signes d'appartenance religieuse qui, par leur nature, par les conditions dans lesquelles ils seraient portés individuellement ou collectivement, ou par leur caractère ostentatoire ou revendicatif, constitueraient un acte de pression, de provocation, de prosélytisme ou de propagande, porteraient atteinte à la dignité ou à la liberté de l'élève ou d'autres membres de la communauté éducative, compromettraient leur santé ou leur sécurité, perturberaient le déroulement des activités d'enseignement et le rôle éducatif des enseignants, enfin troubleraient l'ordre dans l'établissement ou le fonctionnement normal du service public.

2 – Le port de signes d'appartenance religieuse dans les établissements scolaires peut, en cas de besoin, faire l'objet d'une réglementation destinée à fixer les modalités d'application des principes qui viennent d'être définis, compte tenu de la situation propre aux établissements et dans les conditions énoncées ci-après:

La réglementation de la discipline dans les écoles et notamment des conditions dans lesquelles pourrait être restreint ou interdit, le port par les élèves de signes d'appartenance à une religion, relève, (...) de la compétence d'une part de l'inspecteur d'académie, qui arrête le règlement-type du département après consultation du Conseil de l'éducation nationale et d'autre part du conseil d'école, qui vote le règlement intérieur, compte tenu des dispositions du règlement-type du département (...)

Dans les lycées et collèges, cette réglementation est de la compétence du conseil d'administration de l'établissement qui, (...), adopte, sous réserve du contrôle de légalité, le règlement intérieur de l'établissement (...)

Le ministre auquel il appartient, au titre de ses pouvoirs hiérarchiques ou de tutelle, de prendre les mesures nécessaires au bon fonctionnement de l'administration placée sous son autorité, peut, par voie d'instructions, définir les orientations ou donner les indications susceptibles de guider les autorités compétentes dans l'élaboration de la réglementation intérieure des établissements scolaires et pour l'application de celle-ci.

3 – Il appartient aux autorités détentrices du pouvoir disciplinaire d'apprécier, sous le contrôle du juge administratif, si le port par un élève, à l'intérieur d'un établissement scolaire public ou dans tout autre lieu où s'exerce l'enseignement, d'un signe d'appartenance religieuse qui méconnaîtrait l'une des conditions énoncées au I du présent avis ou la réglementation intérieure de l'établissement, constitue une faute de nature à justifier la mise en oeuvre de la procédure disciplinaire et l'application, après respect des garanties instituées par cette procédure et des droits de la défense, de l'une des sanctions prévues par les textes applicables, au nombre desquelles peut figurer l'exclusion de l'établissement.

L'exclusion d'une école, d'un collège ou d'un lycée est possible, malgré le caractère obligatoire de l'instruction, dès lors que l'instruction de l'enfant peut être donnée, conformément à l'article 3 de l'ordonnance du 6 janvier 1959 portant prolongation de la scolarité obligatoire jusqu'à l'âge de seize ans «soit dans les établissements ou écoles publics ou libres, soit dans les familles par les parents, ou l'un d'entre eux, ou toute personne de leur choix», et que notamment l'élève peut être inscrit au centre public d'enseignement par correspondance (. . .)

Le directeur d'école, (. . .), et le chef d'établissement (. . .) sont responsables de l'ordre dans l'établissement et de son bon fonctionnement. Ils doivent notamment veiller à l'application du règlement intérieur. Ils peuvent dans la mesure et pour la durée nécessaires au rétablissement du déroulement normal des enseignements et de l'ordre dans l'établissement, refuser l'admission dans l'établissement ou à l'un des enseignements d'un élève régulièrement inscrit dont le comportement perturberait gravement le fonctionnement du service public, ou dont l'attitude a entraîné le déclenchement de poursuites disciplinaires, dans l'attente de la décision de l'autorité compétente. Un refus d'admission d'un élève mineur ne peut être exécuté sans que ses parents ou ses représentants légaux en aient été préalablement avertis.

Un refus d'admission dans une école d'un élève nouvellement inscrit ou un refus d'inscription dans un collège ou un lycée ne serait justifié que par le risque d'une menace pour l'ordre dans l'établissement ou pour le fonctionnement normal du service de l'enseignement.

13 Extrait de la conférence de presse du Général de Gaulle du 31 janvier 1964

(. . .) Mais, s'il doit être évidemment entendu que l'autorité indivisible de l'Etat est conférée tout entière au Président (. . .) qu'il n'en existe aucune autre, ni ministérielle, ni civile, ni militaire ni judiciaire, qui ne soit conférée et maintenue par lui, enfin qu'il lui appartient d'ajuster le domaine suprême qui lui est propre avec ceux dont il attribue la gestion à d'autres, tout commande, dans les temps ordinaires de maintenir la distinction entre la fonction et le champ d'action du Chef de l'Etat et ceux du Premier Ministre.

14 Conclusions (contraires) du Commissaire du Gouvernement Letourneur sur Conseil d'Etat 16 avril 1948, Laugier, S.1948, III, 36

Votre jurisprudence, soucieuse de ne pas entraver l'action de ceux qui, même dans les circonstances les plus difficiles, assument la charge et la responsabilité d'assurer, de façon permanente, la marche des services publics et de satisfaire les besoins essentiels de la Nation, a admis que des circonstances exceptionnelles de temps et de lieu peuvent rendre légitimes des décisions qui, en période normale, en vertu de la législation normale, ne le seraient pas. Mais vous connaissez aussi le danger de généraliser «les circonstances exceptionnelles», porte ouverte à la suppression de toute légalité, et vous exigez que soit devant vous démontré de la façon la plus nette, en premier lieu l'impossibilité où s'est trouvée l'autorité compétente d'agir légalement, suivant les voies habituelles du droit, en second lieu le caractère d'intérêt général de l'action effectuée qui n'est admissible que «pour pourvoir aux nécessités du moment».

15 Conseil d'Etat 2 mars 1962, Rubin de Servens, D.1962, 307

Cons. que les requêtes susvisées présentent à juger les mêmes questions; qu'il y a lieu de les joindre pour y être statué par une seule décision;

Cons. que, par décision en date du 23 avr. 1961, prise après consultation officielle du Premier ministre et des présidents des Assemblées et après avis du Conseil Constitutionnel, le Président de la République a mis en application l'art. 16 de la Constitution du 4 oct. 1958; que cette décision présente le caractère d'un acte de gouvernement dont il n'appartient au Conseil d'Etat ni d'apprécier la légalité ni de contrôler la durée d'application; que ladite décision a eu pour effet d'habiliter le Président de la République à prendre toutes les mesures exigées par les circonstances qui l'ont motivée et, notamment, à exercer dans les matières énumérées à l'art. 34 de la Constitution le pouvoir législatif et dans les matières prévues à l'art. 37 le pouvoir réglementaire;

Cons. qu'aux termes de l'art. 34 de la Constitution «la loi fixe les règles concernant ... la procédure pénale ... la création de nouveaux ordres de juridiction»; que la décision attaquée en date du 3 mai 1961, intervenue après consultation du Conseil Constitutionnel, tend d'une part à instituer un tribunal militaire à compétence spéciale et à créer ainsi un ordre de juridiction au sens de l'art. 34 précité, et, d'autre part, à fixer les règles de procédure pénale à suivre devant ce tribunal; qu'il s'ensuit que ladite décision, qui porte sur des matières législatives et qui a été prise par le Président de la République pendant la période d'application des pouvoirs exceptionnels, présente le caractère d'un acte législatif dont il n'appartient pas au juge administratif de connaître; ... (Rejet).

16 Loi du 14 juin 1791 ('loi le Chapelier')

Art. II. – Les citoyens d'un même état et profession, les entrepreneurs, ceux qui ont boutique ouverte, les ouvriers d'un art quelconque ne pourront, lorsqu'ils se trouveront ensemble se nommer ni président, ni secrétaire, ni syndics, tenir des registres, prendre des arrêtés, des délibérations, former des règlements, sur leurs prétendus intérêts communs.

Art. VIII. – Tous attroupements composés d'artisans, ouvriers, compagnons, journaliers ou excités par eux contre le libre exercice de l'industrie et du travail, appartenant à toute sorte de personnes et sous toute espèce de conditions convenues de gré à gré ou contre l'action de la police et l'exécution des jugements rendus en cette matière, ainsi que contre les enchères et adjudications publiques des diverses entreprises seront tenus pour attroupements séditieux et comme tels, seront dissipés par les dépositaires de la force publique sur les réquisitions légales qui leur seront faites, et punis selon toute la rigueur des lois, sur les auteurs, instigateurs et chefs des dits attroupements et sur tous ceux qui auront commis des voies de fait et des actes de violence.

17 Conseil Constitutionnel 30 décembre 1976, D.1977, 201

Le Conseil constitutionnel,

Sais le 3 décembre 1976, par le Président de la République, en application des dispositions de l'article 54 de la Constitution, de la question de savoir si la Décision du Conseil des Communautés européennes du 20 septembre 1976, relative à l'élection de l'Assemblée au suffrage universel direct, comporte une clause contraire à la Constitution;

Vu la Constitution;

Vu etc ...

Considérant que la Décision du Conseil des Communautés européennes du 20 septembre 1976 et l'acte qui y est annexé ont pour seul objet de stipuler que les représentants à l'Assemblée des peuples des Etats réunis dans la Communauté sont élus au suffrage universel direct et de fixer certaines conditions de cette élection;

Considérant que si le Préambule de la Constitution de 1946, confirmé par celui de la Constitution de 1958, dispose que, sous réserve de réciprocité, la France consent aux limitations de souveraineté nécessaires à l'organisation et à la défense de la paix, aucune disposition de nature constitutionnelle n'autorise des transferts de tout ou partie de la souveraineté nationale à quelque organisation internationale que ce soit;

Considérant que l'acte soumis à l'examen du Conseil constitutionnel ne contient aucune disposition ayant pour objet de modifier les compétences et pouvoirs limitativement attribués dans le texte des traités aux Communautés européennes et, en particulier, à leur Assemblée par les Etats membres ou de modifier la nature de cette Assemblée qui demeure composée de représentants de chacun des peuples de ces Etats;

Considérant que l'élection au suffrage universel direct des représentants des peuples des Etats membres à l'Assemblée des Communautés européennes n'a pour effet de créer ni une souveraineté ni des institutions dont la nature serait incompatible avec le respect de la souveraineté nationale, non plus que de porter atteinte aux pouvoirs et attributions des institutions de la République et, notamment, du Parlement; que toutes transformations ou dérogations ne pourraient résulter que d'une nouvelle modification des traités, susceptible de donner lieu à l'application tant des articles figurant au titre VI que de l'article 61 de la Constitution;

Considérant que l'engagement international (...) ne contient aucune stipulation fixant, pour l'élection des représentants français à l'Assemblée des Communautés européennes, des modalités de nature à mettre en cause l'indivisibilité de la République, dont le principe est réaffirmé à l'article 2 de la Constitution; que les termes de «procédure électorale uniforme» dont il est fait mention à l'article 7 de l'acte soumis au Conseil constitutionnel ne sauraient être interprétés comme pouvant permettre qu'il soit porté atteinte à ce principe; que, de façon générale, les textes d'application de cet acte devront respecter les principes énoncés ci-dessus ainsi que tous autres principes de valeur constitutionnelle;

Considérant que la souveraineté qui est définie à l'article 3 de la Constitution de la République française, tant dans son fondement que dans son exercice, ne peut être que nationale et que seuls peuvent être regardés comme participant à l'exercice de cette souveraineté les représentants du peuple français élus dans le cadre des institutions de la République;

Considérant qu'il résulte de tout ce qui précède que l'acte du 20 septembre 1976 est relatif à l'élection des membres d'une Assemblée qui n'appartient pas à l'ordre institutionnel de la République française et qui ne participe pas à l'exercice de la souveraineté nationale; que, par suite, la conformité à la Constitution de l'engagement international soumis au Conseil constitutionnel n'a pas à être appréciée au regard des articles 23 et 34 de la Constitution, qui sont relatifs à l'aménagement des compétences et des procédures concernant les institutions participant à l'exercice de la souveraineté française.

Déclare:

ARTICLE PREMIER – Sous le bénéfice des considérations qui précèdent, la Décision du Conseil des Communautés européennes en date du 20 septembre 1976 et l'acte qui y est annexé ne comportent pas de clause contraire à la Constitution.

18 Conseil Constitutionnel 18 novembre 1982, Rec., 66

Le Conseil Constitutionnel,

Considérant qu'en vertu de l'article 4 de la loi soumise à l'examen du Conseil les conseillers municipaux des villes de 3,500 habitants et plus sont élus au scrutin de liste; que les électeurs ne peuvent modifier ni le contenu ni l'ordre de présentation des listes et qu'en vertu de l'article L. 260 bis (du Code électoral): «Les listes de candidats ne peuvent comporter plus de 75% de personnes du même sexe»;

Considérant qu'aux termes de l'article 3 de la Constitution:

«La souveraineté nationale appartient au peuple qui l'exerce par ses représentants et par la voie du référendum.

«Aucune section du peuple ni aucun individu ne peut s'en attribuer l'exercice.

«Le suffrage peut être direct ou indirect dans les conditions prévues par la Constitution. Il est toujours universel, égal et secret.

«Sont électeurs, dans les conditions déterminées par la loi, tous les nationaux français majeurs des deux sexes, jouissant de leurs droits civils et politiques.»

Et qu'aux termes de l'article 6 de la Déclaration des Droits de l'homme et du citoyen: «Tous les citoyens étant égaux» aux yeux de la loi «sont également admissibles à toutes dignités, places et emplois publics, selon leur capacité et sans autre distinction que celles de leurs vertus et de leurs talents»;

Considérant que du rapprochement de ces textes il résulte que la qualité de citoyen ouvre le droit de vote et l'éligibilité dans des conditions identiques à tous ceux qui n'en sont pas exclus pour une raison d'âge, d'incapacité ou de nationalité, ou pour une raison tendant à préserver la liberté de l'électeur ou l'indépendance de l'élu; que ces principes de valeur constitutionnelle s'opposent à toute division par catégories des électeurs ou des éligibles; qu'il en est ainsi pour tout suffrage politique, notamment pour l'élection des conseillers municipaux;

Considérant qu'il résulte de ce qui précède que la règle qui, pour l'établissement des listes soumises aux électeurs, comporte une distinction entre candidats en raison de leur sexe, est contraire aux principes constitutionnels ci-dessus rappelés; qu'ainsi l'article L. 260 bis du Code électoral tel qu'il résulte de l'article 4 de la loi soumise à l'examen du Conseil Constitutionnel doit être déclaré contraire à la Constitution;

(...)

19 Conseil Constitutionnel 6 novembre 1962, J.O.1962, 10778

(. . .) Il résulte de l'esprit de la Constitution qui a fait du Conseil Constitutionnel un organe régulateur de l'activité des pouvoirs publics que les lois que la Constitution a entendu viser dans son Article 61 sont uniquement les lois votées par le Parlement et non point celles qui, adoptées par le peuple à la suite d'un référendum, constituent l'expression directe de la souveraineté nationale.

20 Conseil Constitutionnel 15 janvier 1975, D.1975, 529

Le Conseil constitutionnel,

Saisi le 20 décembre 1974 par MM. (. . .) (députés), dans les conditions prévues à l'article 61 de la Constitution, du texte de la loi relative à l'interruption volontaire de la grossesse, telle qu'elle a été adoptée par le Parlement;

Vu les observations produites à l'appui de cette saisine;

Vu la Constitution, et notamment son préambule;

Vu l'ordonnance du 7 novembre 1958 portant loi organique sur le Conseil constitutionnel, notamment le chapitre II du titre II de ladite ordonnance;

Ouï le rapporteur en son rapport;

Considérant que l'article 61 de la Constitution ne confère pas au Conseil constitutionnel un pouvoir général d'appréciation et de décision identique à celui du Parlement, mais lui donne seulement compétence pour se prononcer sur la conformité à la Constitution des lois déférées à son examen;

Considérant, en premier lieu, qu'aux termes de l'article 55 de la Constitution: «Les traités ou accords régulièrement ratifiés ou approuvés ont, dès leur publication, une autorité supérieure à celle des lois, sous réserve, pour chaque accord ou traité, de son application par l'autre partie»;

Considérant que, si ces dispositions confèrent aux traités, dans les conditions qu'elles définissent, une autorité supérieure à celle des lois, elles ne prescrivent ni n'impliquent que le respect de ce principe doive être assuré dans le cadre du contrôle de la conformité des lois à la Constitution prévu à l'article 61 de celle-ci;

Considérant, en effet, que les décisions prises en application de l'article 61 de la Constitution revêtent un caractère absolu et définitif, ainsi qu'il résulte de l'article 62 qui fait obstacle à la promulgation et à la mise en application de toute disposition déclarée inconstitutionnelle; qu'au contraire la supériorité des traités sur les lois, dont le principe est posé à l'article 55 précité, présente un caractère à la fois relatif et contingent, tenant, d'une part, à ce qu'elle est limitée au champ d'application du traité et, d'autre part, à ce qu'elle est subordonnée à une condition de réciprocité dont la réalisation peut varier selon le comportement du ou des Etats signataires du traité et le moment où doit s'apprécier le respect de cette condition;

Considérant qu'une loi contraire à un traité ne serait pas, pour autant, contraire à la Constitution;

Considérant qu'ainsi le contrôle du respect du principe énoncé à l'article 55 de la Constitution ne saurait s'exercer dans le cadre de l'examen prévu à l'article 61, en raison de la différence de nature de ces deux contrôles;

Considérant que, dans ces conditions, il n'appartient pas au Conseil constitutionnel, lorsqu'il est saisi en application de l'article 61 de la Constitution, d'examiner la conformité d'une loi aux stipulations d'un traité ou d'un accord international;

Considérant, en second lieu, que la loi relative à l'interruption volontaire de la grossesse respecte la liberté des personnes appelées à recourir ou à participer à une interruption de grossesse, qu'il s'agisse d'une situation de détresse ou d'un motif thérapeutique; que, dès lors, elle ne porte pas atteinte au principe de liberté posé à l'article 2 de la Déclaration des Droits de l'Homme et du Citoyen;

Considérant que la loi déférée au Conseil constitutionnel n'admet qu'il soit porté atteinte au principe du respect de tout être humain dès le commencement de la vie, rappelé dans son article 1ᵉʳ, qu'en cas de nécessité et selon les conditions et limitations qu'elle définit;

Considérant qu'aucune des dérogations prévues par cette loi n'est, en l'état, contraire à l'un des principes fondamentaux reconnus par les lois de la République ni ne méconnaît le principe énoncé dans le préambule de la Constitution du 27 octobre 1946, selon lequel la Nation garantit à l'enfant la protection de la santé, non plus qu'aucune des autres dispositions ayant valeur constitutionnelle édictées par le même texte;

Considérant, en conséquence, que la loi relative à l'interruption volontaire de la grossesse ne contredit pas les textes auxquels la Constitution du 4 octobre 1958 fait référence dans son préambule non plus qu'aucun des articles de la Constitution,

Décide:

ARTICLE PREMIER. Les dispositions de la loi relative à l'interruption volontaire de la grossesse, déférée au Conseil constitutionnel, ne sont pas contraires à la Constitution.

21 Cour de Cassation (Chambre Mixte) 24 mai 1975, Administration des douanes c/ Société 'Cafés Jacques Vabre', D.1975, 497

(...)

Sur le deuxième moyen:

Attendu qu'il est de plus fait grief à l'arrêt d'avoir déclaré illégale la taxe intérieure de consommation prévue par l'article 265 du Code des douanes par suite de son incompatibilité avec les dispositions de l'article 95 du traité du 25 mars 1957, au motif que celui-ci, en vertu de l'article 55 de la Constitution, a une autorité supérieure à celle de la loi interne, même postérieure, alors, selon le pourvoi, que s'il appartient au juge fiscal d'apprécier la légalité des textes réglementaires instituant un impôt litigieux, il ne saurait cependant, sans excéder ses pouvoirs, écarter l'application d'une loi interne sous prétexte qu'elle revêtirait un caractère inconstitutionnel; que l'ensemble des dispositions de l'article 265 du Code des douanes a été édicté par la loi du 14 décembre 1966 qui leur a conféré l'autorité absolue qui s'attache aux dispositions législatives et qui s'impose à toute juridiction française;

Mais attendu que le traité du 25 mars 1957, qui, en vertu de l'article susvisé de la Constitution, a une autorité supérieure à celle des lois, institue un ordre juridique propre intégré à celui des Etats membres; qu'en raison de cette spécificité, l'ordre juridique qu'il a créé est directement applicable aux ressortissants de ces Etats et s'impose à leurs juridictions; que dès lors, c'est à bon droit, et sans excéder ses pouvoirs, que la cour d'appel a décidé que l'article 95 du traité devait être appliqué en l'espèce, à l'exclusion de l'article 265 du Code des douanes, bien que ce dernier texte fût postérieur; d'où il suit que le moyen est mal fondé;

Sur le troisième moyen:

Attendu qu'il est au surplus reproché à l'arrêt d'avoir fait application de l'article 95 du traité du 25 mars 1957, alors, selon le pourvoi, que l'article 55 de la Constitution subordonne expressément l'autorité qu'il confère aux traités ratifiés par la France à la condition exigeant leur application par l'autre partie; que le juge du fond n'a pu, dès lors, valablement appliquer ce texte constitutionnel sans rechercher si l'Etat (Pays-Bas) d'où a été importé le produit litigieux a satisfait à la condition de réciprocité;

Mais attendu que, dans l'ordre juridique communautaire, les manquements d'un Etat membre de la Communauté économique européenne aux obligations qui lui incombent en vertu du traité du 25 mars 1957 étant soumis au recours prévu par l'article 170 dudit traité, l'exception tirée du défaut de réciprocité ne peut être invoquée devant les juridictions nationales; d'où il suit que le moyen ne peut être accueilli; (. . .) (Rejet.)

22 Conseil d'Etat 20 octobre 1989, Nicolo, Rec., 190

Vu la Constitution, notamment son article 55.

(. . .)

CONSIDÉRANT qu'aux termes de l'article 4 de la loi n° 77−729 du 7 juillet 1977 relative à l'élection des représentants à l'Assemblée des communautés européennes «le territoire de la République forme une circonscription unique» pour l'élection des représentants français au Parlement européen; qu'en vertu de cette disposition législative, combinée avec celles des articles 2 et 72 de la Constitution du 4 octobre 1958, desquelles il résulte que les départements et territoires d'Outre-mer font partie intégrante de la République française, lesdits départements et territoires sont nécessairement inclus dans la circonscription unique à l'intérieur de laquelle il est procédé à l'élection des représentants au Parlement européen;

Considérant qu'aux termes de l'article 227−1 du traité en date du 25 mars 1957 instituant la Communauté économique européenne; «Le présent traité s'applique . . . à la République française»; que les règles ci-dessus rappelées, définies par la loi du 7 juillet 1977, ne sont pas incompatibles avec les stipulations claires de l'article 227−1 précité du traité de Rome;

Considérant qu'il résulte de ce qui précède que les personnes ayant, en vertu des dispositions du chapitre 1er du titre 1er du livre 1er du code électoral, la qualité d'électeur dans les départements et territoires d'Outre-mer ont aussi cette qualité pour l'élection des représentants au Parlement européen; qu'elles sont également éligibles, en vertu des dispositions de l'article L.O. 127 du Code électoral rendu applicable à l'élection au Parlement européen par l'article 5 de la loi susvisée du 7 juillet 1977; que, par suite, M. Nicolo n'est fondé à soutenir ni que la participation des citoyens français des départements et territoires d'Outre-mer à l'élection des représentants au Parlement européen, ni que la présence de certains d'entre-eux sur des listes de candidats auraient vicié ladite élection; que, dès lors, sa requête doit être rejetée;

23 Conseil d'Etat 7 juin 1957, Condamine, R.D.P., 1958, 98

(. . .) Sur les conclusions dirigées contre l'arrêté, en date du 17 juillet 1948, par lequel le haut-commissaire de la République française au Cameroun a enjoint au sieur Condamine de quitter immédiatement le territoire du Cameroun:

Considérant, d'une part, que, si le requérant se prévaut, à l'appui de ses conclusions, de l'illégalité dont serait entaché le décret du 15 juin 1927, en application duquel a été pris l'arrêté contesté, il se borne à soutenir que ce décret méconnaîtrait les articles 8, 9 et 10 de la Déclaration des Droits de l'Homme, à laquelle se réfère le préambule de la Constitution, et la loi des 2 et 17 mars 1791; qu'il résulte de l'examen du décret précité du 15 juin 1927 que ses prescriptions ne sont contraires à aucune des dispositions ainsi invoquées par le sieur Condamine;

24 Conseil d'Etat 7 juillet 1950, Dehaene, Rec., 65

(. . .) En ce qui concerne le blâme:

Considérant que le sieur Dehaene soutient que cette sanction a été prise en méconnaissance du droit de grève reconnu par la Constitution;

Cons. qu'en indiquant dans le Préambule de la Constitution que «le droit de grève s'exerce dans le cadre des lois qui le réglementent», l'Assemblée constituante a entendu inviter le législateur à opérer la conciliation nécessaire entre la défense des intérêts professionnels dont la grève constitue une modalité et la sauvegarde de l'intérêt général auquel elle peut être de nature à porter atteinte;

Cons. que les lois des 27 décembre 1947 et 28 septembre 1948, qui se sont bornées à soumettre les personnels des compagnies républicaines de sécurité et de la police à un statut spécial et à les priver, en cas de cessation concertées du service, des garanties disciplinaires, ne sauraient être regardées, à elles seules, comme constituant, en ce qui concerne les services publics, la réglementation du droit de grève annoncée par la Constitution;

Cons. qu'en l'absence de cette réglementation la reconnaissance du droit de grève ne saurait avoir pour conséquence d'exclure les limitations qui doivent être apportées à ce droit comme à tout autre en vue d'en éviter un usage abusif ou contraire aux nécessités de l'ordre public; qu'en l'état actuel de la législation il appartient au gouvernement, responsable du bon fonctionnement des services publics, de fixer lui-même, sous le contrôle du juge, en ce qui concerne ces services, la nature et l'étendue desdites limitations;

Cons. qu'une grève qui, quel qu'en soit le motif, aurait pour effet de compromettre dans ses attributions essentielles l'exercice de la fonction préfectorale porterait une atteinte grave à l'ordre public, que, dès lors, le gouvernement a pu légalement faire interdire et réprimer la participation des chefs de bureau de préfecture à la grève de juillet 1948 (. . .)

25 Conseil d'Etat 24 novembre 1961, Fédération nationale des Syndicats de Police, D.1962, 624

(...)

Considérant qu'aux termes de l'article 34 de la Constitution du 4 octobre 1958 «la loi fixe ... les règles concernant ... les garanties fondamentales accordées aux fonctionnaires civils et militaires de l'Etat»; que si la loi du 4 février 1960 habilitait le gouvernement à prendre, pendant un délai limité, des «mesures comprises normalement dans le domaine de la loi et nécessaires pour assurer le maintien de l'ordre», et, par conséquent, à fixer par ordonnance prise en vertu de l'article 38 de la Constitution, les garanties fondamentales reconnues aux personnels de police de la Sûreté nationale, les dispositions attaquées de l'article 1er de l'ordonnance du 18 août 1960, loin de déterminer ces garanties, donnent au gouvernement tout pouvoir de régler par décrets en Conseil d'Etat le statut de ces personnels, les dispositions de l'ordonnance du 4 février 1959 portant statut général des fonctionnaires ne demeurant applicables à ceux-ci que dans la mesure où le gouvernement aura choisi de n'y pas déroger; qu'il s'ensuit que l'article 1er a pour effet de transférer au gouvernement d'une manière permanente le pouvoir de définir les garanties fondamentales accordées aux personnels de police de la Sûreté nationale; qu'en conséquence, la fédération requérante est fondée à soutenir que ledit article viole l'article 34 de la Constitution et à en demander pour ce motif l'annulation (...)

26 Conseil d'Etat 5 mai 1944, Trompier-Gravier, D.1945, 110

(...)

Cons. qu'il est constant que la décision attaquée, par laquelle le préfet de la Seine a retiré à la dame veuve Trompier-Gravier l'autorisation qui lui avait été accordée de vendre des journaux dans un kiosque sis boulevard Saint-Denis à Paris, a eu pour motif une faute dont la requérante se serait rendue coupable;

Cons. qu'eu égard au caractère que présentait, dans les circonstances susmentionnées, le retrait de l'autorisation et à la gravité de cette sanction, une telle mesure ne pouvait légalement intervenir sans que la dame veuve Trompier-Gravier eût été mise à même de discuter les griefs formulés contre elle; que la requérante, n'ayant pas été préalablement invitée à présenter ses moyens de défense, est fondée à soutenir que la décision attaquée a été prise dans des conditions irrégulières par le préfet de la Seine et est, dès lors, entachée d'excès de pouvoir; ... (Annulation).

27 Conseil d'Etat 19 octobre 1962, Canal, Robin et Godot, Rec., 552

(...)

Sur la fin de non-recevoir opposée par le ministre de la Justice et le ministre des Armées: – Considérant que l'article 2 de la loi du 13 avril 1962 adoptée par le peuple français par la voie du référendum, autorise le Président de la République «à arrêter, par voie d'ordonnance ou, selon le cas, de décrets en Conseil des ministres, toutes mesures législatives ou réglementaires relatives à l'application des déclarations gouvernementales du 19 mars 1962»; qu'il résulte de ses termes mêmes que ce texte a eu pour objet, non d'habiliter le Président de la République à exercer le pouvoir législatif lui-même, mais seulement de l'autoriser à user exceptionnellement, dans le cadre et les limites qui y sont précisés, de son pouvoir réglementaire, pour prendre, par ordonnances, des mesures qui normalement relèvent du domaine de la loi; qu'il suit de là que l'ordonnance attaquée du 1ᵉʳ juin 1962, qui a été prise en application de l'article 2 de la loi du 13 avril 1962, conserve le caractère d'un acte administratif et est susceptible, comme tel, d'être déférée au Conseil d'Etat par la voie du recours pour excès de pouvoir; ...

Sur les conclusions de la requête tendant à l'annulation de l'ordonnance du 1ᵉʳ juin 1962 instituant une Cour militaire de justice;

Sans qu'il soit besoin de statuer sur les autres moyens de la requête: – Considérant que, si l'article 2 de la loi du 13 avril 1962 précité a donné au Président de la République de très larges pouvoirs en vue de prendre toutes mesures législatives en rapport avec les déclarations gouvernementales du 19 mars 1962 relatives à l'Algérie et si de telles mesures pouvaient comporter, notamment, l'institution d'une juridiction spéciale chargée de juger les auteurs des délits et des infractions connexes commis en relation avec les événements d'Algérie, il ressort des termes mêmes aussi bien que de l'objet de la disposition législative précitée, que l'organisation et le fonctionnement d'une telle juridiction ne pouvaient légalement porter atteinte aux droits et garanties essentielles de la défense que dans la mesure où, compte tenu des circonstances de l'époque, il était indispensable de le faire pour assurer l'application des déclarations gouvernementales du 19 mars 1962;

Considérant qu'il ne résulte pas de l'instruction que, eu égard à l'importance et à la gravité des atteintes que l'ordonnance attaquée apporte aux principes généraux du droit pénal, en ce qui concerne, notamment, la procédure qui y est prévue et l'exclusion de toute voie de recours, la création d'une telle juridiction d'exception fût nécessitée par l'application des déclarations gouvernementales du 19 mars 1962; que les requérants sont, dès lors, fondés à soutenir que ladite ordonnance, qui excède les limites de la délégation consentie par l'article 2 de la loi du 13 avril 1962, est entachée d'illégalité; qu'il y a lieu, par suite, d'en prononcer l'annulation; (...)

28 Loi du 4 février 1960

L'Assemblée nationale et le Sénat ont adopté,

Le Président de la République promulgue la loi dont la teneur suit:

Art. 1ᵉʳ. – Sous la signature du général de Gaulle, Président de la République, conformément à l'article 13 de la Constitution, le Gouvernement actuellement en fonction est autorisé à prendre par ordonnances, dans les conditions prévues aux alinéas 2 et 3 de l'article 38 de la Constitution, les mesures comprises normalement dans le domaine de la loi et nécessaires pour assurer le maintien de l'ordre, la sauvegard de l'Etat et de la Constitution, la pacification et l'administration de l'Algérie.

Art. 2. – L'autorisation prévue à l'article précédent est valable pour une durée d'un an à dater du jour de la promulgation de la présente loi.

Art. 3. – Les projets de loi portant ratification des ordonnances prises en vertu de l'article 1ᵉʳ ci-dessus devront être déposés devant le Parlement au plus tard le 1ᵉʳ avril 1961.

Art. 4. – Les dispositions de la présente loi seront caduques en cas de dissolution de l'Assemblée nationale.

La présente loi sera exécutée comme loi de l'Etat.

Fait à Paris, le 4 février 1960.

29 Conseil d'Etat 19 février 1909, Abbé Olivier, S.1909, III, 34

(. . .) Considérant que, si le maire est chargé par l'article 97 de la loi du 5 avril 1884 du maintien de l'ordre dans la commune, il doit concilier l'accomplissement de sa mission avec le respect des libertés garanties par les lois; qu'il appartient au Conseil d'Etat, saisi d'un recours pour excès de pouvoir contre un arrêté rendu par application de l'article 97, précité, non seulement de rechercher si cet arrêté porte sur un objet compris dans les attributions de l'autorité municipale, mais encore d'apprécier, suivant les circonstances de la cause, si le maire n'a pas, dans l'espèce, fait de ses pouvoirs un usage non autorisé par la loi; (. . .)

30 Conseil d'Etat 18 novembre 1949, Carlier, Rec., 490

(. . .) Considérant que, si le directeur général des Beaux-Arts pouvait, en vue de faire respecter l'affectation des dépendances du domaine public dont il a la charge, prendre à l'égard des usagers les mesures nécessaires pour prévenir toute atteinte à la conservation de ces ouvrages, il lui incombait de concilier l'exercice de ce pouvoir avec le respect de la faculté qu'a tout usager d'utiliser les dépendances du domaine public conformément à leur affectation;

Considérant qu'il n'est pas établi que la protection de la cathédrale de Chartres contre les entreprises que l'attitude du sieur Carlier en septembre 1938 pouvait faire redouter de sa part n'aurait pu être efficacement assurée par des mesures autres que l'interdiction absolue d'accès qui a été prononcée contre le requérant; que, dès lors, celui-ci est fondé à soutenir que la décision du directeur général de Beaux-Arts lui interdisant l'accès des parties de la cathédrale de Chartres où n'est célébré aucun office du culte est illégale, et qu'elle a constitué une faute de nature à engager la responsabilité de l'Etat; (. . .)

31 Conseil d'Etat 13 mars 1968, Ministre de l'Intérieur c époux Leroy, Rec., 179

(. . .) Considérant que, par l'arrêté attaqué le préfet de la Manche a interdit l'activité des photographes-filmeurs pendant la saison touristique sur toute la portion de la route nationale conduisant au Mont-Saint-Michel, ainsi que sur les aires de stationnement aménagées de part et d'autre de cette route;

Considérant qu'il est constant que le Mont-Saint-Michel et ses abords immédiats connaissent, durant la saison estivale, une affluence exceptionnelle de touristes; qu'il résulte de l'instruction que l'activité des photographes-filmeurs sur cette voie publique particulièrement encombrée, où les véhicules automobiles sont normalement appelés à circuler, stationner et manoeuvrer au milieu des piétons, présentait à la date à laquelle l'arrêté précité a été pris, pour le maintien de l'ordre, des dangers auxquels il n'était pas possible de remédier par une mesure moins contraignante; que dans ces conditions le motif tiré par le tribunal administratif de ce que le préfet de la Manche ne pouvait, sans excéder les pouvoirs qu'il tient des articles 107 et 97 du Code de l'administration communale, apporter au principe de la liberté du commerce et de l'industrie les restrictions figurant dans son arrêté ne saurait justifier le dispositif du jugement susvisé par lequel ledit tribunal a annulé pour excès de pouvoir cet arrêté; (...)

32 Conseil d'Etat 26 juin 1959, Syndicat Général des Ingénieurs Conseils, Rec., 394

Sur la légalité du décret attaqué: (...) Cons. que le 25 juin 1947, alors que n'avait pas pris fin la période transitoire prévue par l'article 104 de la Constitution du 27 octobre 1946, le président du Conseil des ministres tenait de l'article 47 de ladite Constitution, le pouvoir de régler par décret, dans les territoires dépendant du ministère de la France d'outre-mer, en application de l'article 18 du sénatus-consulte du 3 mai 1854, les questions qui, dans la métropole, ressortissaient au domaine de la loi; que, dans l'exercice de ses attributions, il était cependant tenu de respecter, d'une part, les dispositions des lois applicables dans les territoires d'outre-mer, d'autre part, les principes généraux du droit qui, résultant notamment du préambule de la Constitution, s'imposent à toute autorité réglementaire même en l'absence de dispositions législatives;

Cons., en premier lieu, que la loi du 31 décembre 1940 n'était pas applicable dans les territoires visés par le décret attaqué; que les dispositions du Code civil, ayant été introduites dans ces territoires par décret, y avaient seulement valeur réglementaire; que, par suite, le syndicat requérant n'est pas fondé à soutenir que le décret attaqué serait entaché d'illégalité en tant qu'il méconnaîtrait les prescriptions de ces deux textes;

Cons., en second lieu, qu'en réservant aux architectes, dans les territoires qu'il concerne, le soin de «composer tous les édifices, d'en déterminer les proportions, la structure, la distribution, d'en dresser les plans, de rédiger les devis et de coordonner l'ensemble de leur exécution» et en interdisant ainsi aux membres d'autres professions de se livrer à ces activités, le décret attaqué, s'il est intervenu dans une matière réservée dans la métropole au législateur, n'a porté à aucun des principes susmentionnés une atteinte de nature à entacher d'illégalité les mesures qu'il édicte; (...)

Chapter 5

Criminal procedure

A. First principles

1. Characteristics

Criminal procedure in England and Wales is accusatorial in nature, both the prosecution and defence adducing evidence for their case, and the judge acting as independent arbiter. At the public trial, evidence is presented orally, witnesses being subject to cross-examination. In contrast, French criminal procedure is essentially inquisitorial; pre-trial procedure in particular is characterised by being written, secret and non-accusatorial. Since the implementation of the Napoleonic *Code d'Instruction Criminelle*, a clear distinction has been drawn between three different phases of criminal procedure, *l'enquête de police, l'instruction* and *le jugement*, each of which is under the control of different authorities. Following initial police inquiries (*l'enquête de police*), carried out under the control of the prosecutor, the file (in the case of more serious offences) is passed to the examining magistrate (*le juge d'instruction*), who is independent of the prosecutor, and whose role is to determine whether there is sufficient evidence for the suspect (or for that matter, another individual) to be formally charged and tried.

Instruction is essentially a secret procedure. However, the accused has a right to participate in the process by making oral or written representations; he is also entitled, but only after the initial police inquiries have taken place, to the advice and assistance of a lawyer, who will be kept informed of all the procedures being undertaken. The accused is entitled to remain silent, and his right to do so must be pointed out at the first questioning before the *juge d'instruction* (*Code de Procédure Pénale ("CPP"), Art. 114;* TEXTS, NO. 1). Having completed his investigation into the evidence, the examining magistrate is expected to reach an objective, disinterested decision as to whether a sufficient case exists for the accused to be sent to trial. If it is decided to proceed to trial, the dossier is sent to the trial court; however, in the case of serious crime a second level of *instruction* is first carried out by the *chambre d'accusation* of the *Cour d'Appel*.

At the trial court the hearing takes place in public. Although there is a degree of oral procedure at trial, it is not truly accusatorial, as the trial judge remains firmly in control of the process, and witnesses are not subject to cross-examination; nevertheless, questions can be put to the witnesses with the consent of the president of the court. Offences are classified according to their seriousness. Serious crimes (*crimes*) are those carrying a penalty of imprisonment of more than five years, and include murder, rape, and robbery. Intermediate offences (*délits*) are those carrying a penalty of imprisonment exceeding two months but not exceeding five years, or a fine exceeding 12,000 FF; this covers uch offences as causing death by dangerous driving, cases of assault which cause the victim to be off work for more than eight days, and most cases of theft. Minor offences (*contraventions*) are those carrying a penalty of imprisonment not exceeding two months, or a fine of 12,000 FF or less, and include minor assaults and many road traffic offences. In the case of *crimes*, trial in the *Cour d'Assises* is by jury and a panel of judges, who together determine both culpability and sentence. In respect of *délits* and *contraventions*, trial is before a court of professional judge(s) sitting without a jury (*Tribunal Correctionnel* and *Tribunal de Police* respectively). Note that a suspect is called an *inculpé* from the moment he is formally charged by the examining magistrate, and at trial he is called a *prévenu* in the lower courts or an *accusé* in the *Cour d'Assises*.

2. Historical development

The roots of French criminal procedure are to be found in the inquisitorial procedures of the ecclesiastical courts (see Chapter 1). Criminal procedure of the feudal courts of the time was accusatorial, but did not have recourse to modern means of proof. During the fourteenth century, with the creation of the office of public prosecutor (*procureur du roi*), and the growth of jurisdiction of the royal courts, the balance shifted in favour of procedures which were rational and under the control not of the parties themselves, but of professional lawyers. Thus legislative reforms introduced by a series of *ordonnances royales* from the fifteenth to the seventeenth centuries (especially those of 1498, 1539 and 1670) increasingly based criminal procedure on the inquisitorial model.

The absence of safeguards for the protection of the rights of the suspect during *instruction* was a cause of public dissatisfaction, particularly during the second half of the eighteenth century. *Instruction* was carried out entirely in secret, and without the presence of a lawyer; "confessions" were even obtained under torture. The arbitrary nature of the procedure was severely criticised by such writers as Voltaire and Montesquieu. Calls to reform criminal procedure featured prominently in the *cahiers de doléances*, the lists of collective grievances presented by delegates to the meeting of the Estates General in Versailles during May and June 1789, which was to lead to the creation of the revolutionary *Assemblée Nationale*.

In the law of the revolutionary period (*le droit intermédiaire*), the inquisitorial system was retained, though much reformed; *instruction* was made public, and the right to the assistance of a lawyer was introduced (*loi du 8.10.1789*). Jury trial (before a *jury de jugement* of twelve) was also introduced for serious offences (*loi du 16–29.9.1791*). An eight member *jury d'accusation* decided whether or not a suspect should be sent for trial until the creation in 1801 of the office of *juge d'instruction* (*loi du 7 pluviôse an IX*), marking a return to written procedure. The adoption in 1808 of the *Code d'Instruction Criminelle* marks the commencement of the modern system of criminal procedure, which is inquisitorial, at least until trial (see below). A reformed *Code de Procédure Pénale* was introduced in 1958.

3. Burden and means of proof

(a) Burden of proof

The 1789 *Déclaration des Droits de l'Homme et du Citoyen* states (*Art. 9*) that "a man is presumed innocent until he has been declared guilty", a presumption reaffirmed by Article 6 of the European Convention on Human Rights, which provides that "any person accused of an offence is presumed innocent until his guilt has been legally established". The provisions of the Convention, which France has ratified, take priority over statute by reason of the 1958 Constitution (*Art. 55*; see Chapter 4). In consequence of the presumption of innocence, the burden of proof (*la charge de la preuve*) is in principle on the prosecution. This, however, is not made clear in any provision of the *CPP*, which simply states (*Art. 427*; TEXTS, NO. 2) that judicial decisions must be founded on the basis of the evidence (*les preuves*) put before the courts at the public hearing. However, the *Cour de Cassation* has confirmed that "the accused being presumed innocent, the burden of proof of his guilt rests on the party commencing the action" (*Crim., 29.5.1980; Bull. crim., 164*). The onus of proof is recognised as being higher in criminal than civil cases, due to the presumption of innocence, and the accused must therefore be granted the benefit of any doubt (*in dubio pro reo*).

The application of the presumption of innocence to the phase of *instruction* is worth further examination. It does not prevent the lawful arrest or detention of the accused pending trial. Nor may the fact that the *juge d'instruction* commits the accused for trial be taken as evidence of guilt *per se*, the role of the *juge* being to determine whether or not there is sufficient evidence to send the accused for trial; it is the trial court that weighs this evidence and actually determines guilt. It should be noted that the accused is not asked to plead as to guilt or innocence at the start of the trial, as happens in the accusatorial system. The court therefore proceeds to examine the evidence against the accused, whether the latter has confessed or not.

It is incumbent on the prosecution to "prove all of the elements constituting the offence and the absence of any elements negating it" (*Crim., 24.3.1949; Bull. crim., 114*). In effect, three elements must be proved: the *élément matériel* (ie that the *actus reus* was committed by the accused), the *élément moral* (ie that the accused had the requisite *mens rea*), and the *élément légal* (for example, identify which provisions of the *Code Pénal* have been contravened, and show that the charges were brought within the limitation period (ten years for cases of *crimes*, three years for *délits*, one year for *contraventions*, time running from the date of commission of the offence; *CPP, Arts. 7–9*)).

However, the courts have taken the position that the burden of proof of certain defences falls on the accused. One example is provocation. Another is self-defence (*légitime défence*); *Code Pénal, Art. 328* provides for a presumption of self-defence in two particular cases – by adopting an interpretation *a contrario*, the courts have therefore determined that apart from those two cases, it is for the accused to prove self-defence. The accused also has the burden of proving defences which exonerate responsibility (*causes de non-imputabilité*) such as duress (*contrainte; Code Pénal, Art. 64*) and insanity (*démence; ibid*), although on the question of insanity the caselaw is less clear; but it is certainly for the accused at least to raise the issue of insanity.

The task of the prosecution in bearing the burden of proof is also aided by a variety of presumptions. There is a presumption which applies to *contraventions* (other than those requiring proof of "intentional or negligent fault" on the part of the accused) and a few *délits* (such as certain customs offences) to the effect that once the *actus reus* is proved, *mens rea* is in effect presumed (although the defendant may seek to absolve himself from responsibility by proof of *force majeure*). Also in respect of *contraventions* there is, unless otherwise provided by law, a rebuttable presumption of the truth of matters asserted in the formal reports of police inquiries (*procès-verbaux; CPP, Art. 537*); the rebuttal evidence must take the form of either written evidence or witness evidence. As regards other presumptions, the publication of material which is defamatory is presumed to have been carried out with the intention to defame, rebuttable only on proof of "good faith"; there is also a rebuttable presumption (*Code des Douanes, Art. 393*) that the captain of a ship or aircraft is liable for errors in the cargo manifest. The task of the prosecution is made easier in relation to serious offences by reason of the investigative role and wide-ranging powers of the *juge d'instruction*; for this reason the victim of a criminal offence will often seek redress as *partie civile* (below) before the criminal courts rather than commencing a separate civil action.

(b) Means of proof

In principle, the accused's guilt can be proved by any form of evidence, *CPP, Art. 427* (TEXTS, NO. 2) affirming that "apart from the cases where the law provides otherwise, offences may be proved by any means of proof". This is known as the principle of the freedom of means of proof (*principe de la liberté des preuves*). Moreover, the *Cour de Cassation* has accepted that where the law lays down a particular means of proof for a given offence, other means will be admissible as long as they are not expressly forbidden (*Crim., 24.1.1973, D.1973, 241*). Usual means of proof include confessions (*aveux*), witness statements (*témoignages*), material evidence (*les constatations matérielles*) such as fingerprints (*empreintes digitales*), photographic evidence, blood tests (*prélèvements sanguins*), and other forensic and expert evidence (*expertises*); also evidence obtained following searches and seizures (*perquisitions et saisies*) and body searches (*fouilles corporelles*). Also acceptable as means of proof are the results of breathalysers (*alcotest*), radar speed checks (*cinémomètres*), and tape recordings (although it should be noted that it is an offence (*Code Pénal, Art. 368*) to invade a person's privacy by tape recording conversations in a private place unless their consent is obtained). Evidence obtained by telephone tapping is admissible, despite *Code Pénal, Art. 368*, where the tap has been properly authorised by a *juge d'instruction* on suspicion of involvement in a specified offence (*CPP, Arts. 100 to 100–7*). The *Cour de Cassation* had shown (eg *Crim., 15.5.1990, Bacha*) that it was willing to take into account the criticisms levelled by the European Court of Human Rights (in the *Kruslin* case; *CEDH, 24.4.1990, Dr.Pén., 209*) concerning the absence of precision as to the circumstances in which tapping would be permitted. The *loi du 10.7.1991* has now specified that the authorisation of the *juge d'instruction* for a phone tap will last for a maximum period of four months. The authorisation must specify which calls may be tapped and the offences in respect of which the tap is authorised.

All the evidence obtained during the early phases of criminal procedure is only of probative value when actually produced at trial, *CPP, Art. 427(2)* providing that "the judge may base his decision only on evidence put before him and debated by the parties at the hearing". At the hearing, not only is the written dossier of evidence prepared by the *juge d'instruction* (where applicable) put before the court, but also the accused and witnesses (including expert witnesses) are examined and questioned. By way of exception, it is provided by *CPP, Art. 537*, as has been seen, that *contraventions* may be proved simply by means of *procès-verbaux*.

There are exceptions to the principle of freedom of means of proof, for although the objective of the preliminary phases of procedure is to unearth the truth, not every method of so doing can be permitted if the accused's individual liberties (such as those enshrined in the European Convention on Human Rights) are to be respected. The courts have shown their willingness to censor unfair practices such as the use of *agents provocateurs*, the administration of narcotics (ie truth drugs) to a suspect during questioning and the use of the polygraph.

There are few exclusionary rules of evidence; legal professional privilege is recognised by *CPP, Art. 432*, which excludes as written evidence "correspondence exchanged between the accused and his lawyer". There is, however, no hearsay rule as such; as we have seen, the basic principle is one of freedom of the means of proof, inquisitorial procedure being designed to enable the court to discover the truth. It should be borne in mind that the court will weigh the evidence produced to it and accord it such probative value as it thinks fit (see below).

The evidence that may be given by witnesses is wider than would be permitted in accusatorial procedure. A witness may give not only direct but also indirect evidence (*preuve indirecte*, which includes evidence of what he heard other people say). Furthermore, it is possible to call witnesses of character rather than fact, testifying as to the accused's character and background (see *CPP, Art. 331*). However, the witness is not entitled to give his opinion on the accused's guilt.

(c) The probative value of evidence

(i) The principle of "intime conviction"

What principles are there regarding the probative value to be accorded by the trial judge(s) (and jury, in the case of *crimes*) to the varying types of evidence unearthed during the preparatory phases of *enquête* and *instruction* and produced at trial? In the pre-revolutionary *Ancien Droit*, there existed a system of *preuve légale*, according to which different probative values were ascribed to different types of evidence; thus evidence of the accused's guilt consisting either of two corroborating witness statements, or a confession made in front of the instructing judicial authority, constituted *per se* sufficient proof for conviction. Such a system severely limited the discretion of the trial judge to weigh the probative value of the evidence, but has been recognised by doctrinal writers as having value in reducing the likelihood of arbitrary conviction by the judiciary at a time when inquisitorial criminal procedure was noted for its secrecy and non-accountability.

The 1808 *Code d'Instruction Criminelle* marked the introduction of a new principle in the weighing of evidence, the principle of *intime conviction*; henceforth the probative value of evidence was to be assessed by the trial judge (and/or jury) according to his/their own "inner conviction". The principle is enshrined in *CPP, Art. 427* (TEXTS, NO. 2), which provides that "apart from those cases where the law provides otherwise, offences may be proved by any means of proof, and the judge decides according to his inner conviction". In respect of jury trials in the *Cour d'Assises, CPP, Art. 353* (TEXTS, NO. 3) requires the following to be read out to the jury before they retire with the panel of three judges to consider their verdict: "the law does not make judges account for the means by which they reach their decisions, nor does it lay down rules with which they must comply as to the completeness or sufficiency of evidence; it requires them to ask themselves, silently and with composure, in all sincerity of conscience, what was the impression made on them by the evidence brought against the accused, and the evidence adduced in his defence. The law requires only that the following question, which encompasses their entire duty, be asked; 'do you have an inner conviction?'".

The court is therefore free to determine guilt or innocence without having to express what weight has been given to the various means of proof produced to it; this principle applies in theory to proceedings before all criminal courts, as well as to the process of *instruction*. However, judges of the *Tribunaux de Police* and *Tribunaux Correctionnels* must (*CPP, Arts. 543, 485;* TEXTS, NO. 4) state the grounds on which they reached their verdict, to enable the higher courts to exercise control over their decisions. Both the provisions of the *CPP* and the caselaw of the *Cour de Cassation* illustrate the large degree of discretion which is given to the trial judge by the principle of *intime conviction*. It is thus clear that he may decide to attach little or no weight to a confession (*CPP, Art. 428*) if he thinks, for example, that it is suspect. Conversely, he may choose to give it full weight, even though it was subsequently retracted (*Crim., 3.10.1967; Bull. crim., 238*); he may even "sever" that part of a confession which he thinks is unreliable (*Crim., 20.3.1974; Bull. crim., 123*). It is fair to say that the confession is no longer regarded as the "queen of proofs". Nor is the judge bound to accept expert evidence, which he should treat no differently from other types of evidence.

There are, however, exceptions to the principle of *intime conviction*, the most important of which concerns written evidence drawn up in a particular form, ie the *procès-verbal*. These may be drafted by the police (for example reports of interviews with the suspect and witnesses) and by certain other officials, such as a customs officer, or a clerk to a *juge d'instruction* (for example reports of interviews conducted by the *juge* with the accused and witnesses). Generally, as with any other evidence, the weight to be given to the facts referred to in a *procès-verbal* is to be determined by the trial judge (*CPP, Art. 430*). There are, however, two exceptions to this. Firstly, as has already been mentioned, certain types of *procès-verbaux* are taken to constitute proof of the facts they contain unless the contrary is proved. This is the case, for example, in respect of *procès-verbaux* produced as evidence of a *contravention* (*CPP, Art. 537*). The effect of this provision is to simplify the prosecution of the least serious category of criminal offence, for the simple production of the police *procès-verbaux* constitutes proof of its contents, and hence of the accused's guilt, unless rebuttal evidence is produced; in effect the burden of proof is reversed. It should however be noted that under this article the prosecution is not limited to the use of *procès-verbaux* for the proof of its case; the prosecution may choose to call witness evidence. The defence lawyer can also require witnesses and the *prévenu* to attend and give evidence, in which case the normal principle of *intime conviction* will apply. In practice, however, virtually all *contraventions* are proved by means of *procès-verbaux*. *Procès-verbaux* are also regarded as constituting *prima facie* evidence in this way in a variety of statutory provisions; examples include certain hunting offences (*loi du 10.7.1976*) and offences committed against railway property. The second exception is that a few types of *procès-verbaux* (such as those relating to customs offences (if signed by two customs officers), or forestry or certain fishing offences) are conclusive of the facts they refer to unless it can be proved that they were fraudulently drafted (*CPP, Art. 433*).

(ii) Exclusion of improperly obtained evidence

The first point to be made is that any physical mistreatment of suspects by police officers or other public agents is severely punished by the criminal law (eg *Code Pénal, Art. 186*). Furthermore, in an endeavour to prevent evidence being improperly obtained, the *CPP* lays down detailed rules for the carrying out of certain police procedures, such as searches and seizures, and the conduct of interviews of witnesses and the accused (although, as will be seen, the protection offered to the suspect by the *CPP* is generally effective only from the moment that the *juge d'instruction* becomes involved, being rather limited during the earlier *enquête*, during which time, of course, much of the evidence against him will have been obtained). The question that must be asked is the extent to which breaches of these statutory procedures are penalised by the exclusion of the evidence thereby obtained; the answer depends on whether it was obtained during the *enquête* or *instruction*.

Enquête de police: Procedural irregularities by the police during the initial *enquête de police* may lead to disciplinary action, or a civil claim for damages being taken against the police officer, but there is no general provision in the *CPP* which excludes the resulting evidence. There are limited statutory exclusions, however, an example being in respect of evidence obtained during irregular searches and seizures (*CPP, Art. 59*). In the absence of any general statutory provision, guidance must be sought from the caselaw of the *Cour de Cassation*. The *Cour de Cassation* has generally been reluctant to condemn irregular practices; it has thus held that such practices during police custody (*garde-à-vue*) do not lead to the exclusion of the evidence obtained as a result, particularly confessions, unless it can be shown that as a result of the irregularity "the search for the truth has been fundamentally vitiated" (*Crim., 17.3.1960, Kissari, JCP, 1960, II, 11641;* TEXTS, NO. 5). It is for the accused to prove such fundamental irregularity. Nor has the *Cour de Cassation* been willing to penalise illegal arrests by the police by excluding the resulting evidence (eg *Crim., 4.6.1964, Argoud, JCP, 1964, II, 13806*). Many commentators have been critical of the failure of the *Cour de Cassation* to give effective protection to suspects against improper police practices, especially during police custody.

Instruction: The proper exercise of the powers of the *juge d'instruction* is overseen by the *chambre d'accusation* of the *Cour d'Appel* (see below). Part of this function is to rule on the legality of the various measures (*actes d'instruction*) taken by the *juge d'instruction*, such as the formal questioning of witnesses (*auditions*) and suspects (*interrogatoires*), confrontation of the suspect with witnesses (*confrontations*) and the recourse to expert forensic evidence (*expertises*). An important limitation on the control exercised by the *chambre d'accusation* over the acts of the *juge d'instruction* is that claims for the annulment of allegedly illegal *actes d'instruction* can be referred to the *chambre d'accusation* only by the prosecutor or *juge d'instruction* himself (*CPP, Art. 171*) and not, as might be thought, by the accused, who may however petition either the prosecutor or *juge d'instruction* to do so. He may also in due course petition the trial court for such a reference. It should also be noted that procedural irregularities during *instruction* may constitute grounds for appeal on a point of law against conviction by way of *cassation* to the *Cour de Cassation* (see below).

The trial courts themselves have only limited powers to exclude evidence obtained irregularly. The *Tribunaux Correctionnels* and *Tribunaux de Police* have certain powers (*CPP, Art. 174*) of exclusion of *actes d'instruction* for procedural irregularity (particularly of evidence obtained in breach of *CPP, Arts. 114* (TEXTS, NO. 1), *118*). The *Cour d'Assises* has no such power.

Two categories of annulment of irregular *actes d'instruction* are recognised: *nullités textuelles,* and *nullités substantielles.* Let us examine each in turn.

Nullités textuelles: The *CPP* expressly provides for annulment for procedural irregularity, but only in respect of certain types of *actes d'instruction*, examples being the questioning of the accused under *CPP, Arts. 114, 118 (Art. 170)*, the effecting of property searches and seizures under *CPP, Art. 59(3)*, and the holding of identity checks (*CPP, Art. 78–3(11)*).

Nullités substantielles: In the absence of a general statutory power of annulment, the *Cour de Cassation* was quick to formulate the principle that failure to observe "substantial formalities" (eg questioning a suspect wrongfully under oath, as if he were a mere witness, contrary to *CPP, Art. 105*; TEXTS, NO. 6) might lead to an *acte d'instruction* being annulled. Article 172 of the *CPP* now provides that nullity may be pronounced for a breach of the "substantial" provisions of Book I Title III of the *CPP* (ie *Arts. 79–230*) particularly whenever the *acte d'instruction* had been carried out in a way which interferes with the accused's "rights of defence" (*droits de la défense*), for example (i) where correspondence between the accused and his *avocat* had been wrongfully seized (*Nanterre, 18.12.1980, GP, 1.2.1981*), and (ii) where the papers were sent to the accused's *avocat* in insufficient time to enable him to prepare (*Colmar, 3.6.1969, JCP, 1969, II, 16083*). However, violation of the accused's "rights of defence" are not the sole example of procedural irregularities which may lead to annulment; the courts have regarded "substantial" formalities as including additionally those formalities which are regarded as being *d'ordre public*, ie relating not primarily to the interests of the parties, but rather to the higher interests of the criminal justice system itself, such as the formalities of requiring various *actes d'instruction* to be signed or dated by the *juge d'instruction*.

Statutory limitation on annulment powers: An important limitation of the courts' powers of annulment for procedural irregularities was introduced by the *loi du 6.8.1975* (now *CPP, Art. 802;* TEXTS, NO. 7), annulment (in respect of both *nullités textuelles* and *nullités substantielles*) being limited to cases where "the irregularity has the effect of injuring the interests of the party concerned". Breaches of *CPP, Art. 105* (which grants a suspect certain rights during questioning) are expressly excluded from the ambit of this proviso.

Consequences of the annulment of an acte d'instruction: The consequences of an *acte d'instruction* being annulled are that the relevant material is removed from the file and may not be subsequently referred to in evidence (*CPP, Art. 173*). The annulment may extend to the procedure after the irregular *acte*, on the basis that the illegality has tainted the entire process. For example, such extension is expressly provided for by *CPP, Art. 170* in respect of a failure by the *juge d'instruction* to observe the procedures of *Arts. 114, 118* for the questioning of a suspect (such as the obligation to point out the right to have an *avocat* present). More generally, the *chambre d'accusation* is empowered to determine "whether the annulment should be limited to the irregular *acte* or extended to all or part of the subsequent procedure" (*CPP, Arts. 172(2), 206(2);* TEXTS, NO. 8). When an *acte* has been annulled, the *chambre d'accusation* may either send the file back to the original (or a different) *juge d'instruction* for the procedure to be carried out again, or it may do it itself (*CPP, Art. 206*).

A finding of irregularity may lead to disciplinary proceedings against the offending police officer. A civil action may also lie in serious cases. Furthermore, criminal charges may be brought against the *juge d'instruction* or prosecutor in the case of arbitrary detention (*CPP, Art. 126*).

B. Those involved in the criminal action

1. The police

(a) La police administrative and la police judiciaire

A distinction is drawn in France between administrative police functions (*la police administrative*) and judicial police functions (*la police judiciaire*). Administrative police functions include keeping the peace and preventing the commission of offences; such activities are under the control of the administrative authorities, and are subject to review by the administrative courts. Judicial police functions are defined in *CPP, Art. 14* (TEXTS, NO. 9) as "establishing the commission of offences, collecting evidence and seeking out offenders"; these activities are under the control of the prosecutor and are subject to review in the ordinary courts (*CPP, Art. 13*). However, this division of policing functions is a little obscured in practice because the functions are not exercised by two distinct bodies of police officers. Consequently, whether a police activity is subject to the control of the administrative or the ordinary courts may depend on the nature of the activity being undertaken.

(b) La gendarmerie nationale and la police nationale

Police officers are organised on a national basis into two separate bodies, the *gendarmerie nationale* and the *police nationale*. The *gendarmerie* has existed since the twelfth century (before 1791 it was known as *la maréchausée* (mounted constabulary)). It is organised along military lines, and is attached to the Ministry of Defence. There are currently some 85,000 *gendarmes*. There is a *gendarmerie départementale* for each *département*, whose members carry out both judicial and administrative functions. There is also a *gendarmerie mobile* which is kept in reserve for use in maintaining civil order.

The *police nationale*, on the other hand, is subject to the authority of the Minister of the Interior, and comprises some 113,000 police officers. It is organised into two forces, the *sûreté nationale* for the provinces, and the *préfecture de police* for the Paris area. The *sûreté nationale* is organised into different branches, some dealing with judicial police functions, and others with administrative functions; the *compagnies républicaines de sécurité* (*CRS*) are used among other things for controlling disturbances (*cf gendarmerie mobile*). The *préfecture de police* assures the full range of police services in the Paris area, different branches again dealing with judicial or administrative police functions. The police officers of the *préfecture de police* are in fact members of the *police nationale* who are regarded as having been put at the disposal of the *préfecture de police*.

Additionally, there are certain powers for a *commune* to have its own municipal police force; the functions of a municipal police force are largely administrative rather than judicial. Furthermore, both the prefect and the mayor have certain powers in respect of administrative policing functions (see Chapter 4).

(c) Officiers and agents de police judiciaire

Police personnel who have judicial police duties are classified into three categories (*CPP, Art. 15*): officers (*officiers de police judiciaire*), agents (*agents de police judiciaire*) and civil servants and agents regarded as having judicial police functions. The distinction is important, for the *CPP* provides that certain police functions (such as authorising police custody and the carrying out of investigations by delegation from the *juge d'instruction* (*commissions rogatoires*)) may be carried out only by an officer, not an agent. Furthermore, only the first two categories are entitled to carry out police inquiries on their own initiative (*CPP, Art. 75;* TEXTS, NO. 10).

Article 16 of the *CPP* defines *officiers de police judiciaire*; essentially they comprise senior and experienced members of the *gendarmerie* and *police nationale*, as well as mayors. Agents include (*CPP, Arts. 20, 21*) members of the *gendarmerie* and *police nationale* who do not have the status of officer. Examples of the third category, civil servants and agents who are attributed as having the functions of *police judiciaire*, are rural policemen (*gardes champêtres*), responsible for investigating offences relating to forestry and other rural property, and agents of public authorities accorded statutory judicial policing powers (eg tax, weights and measures, and railway inspectors).

2. The prosecution; le ministère public

(a) Composition and organisation

(i) Introduction

As was seen in Chapter 3, the members of the *ministère public* are *magistrats* (sometimes called *magistrats debouts* as they stand when they address the court, whereas the trial judges (*magistrats assis* or *du siège*) remain seated). Both types of *magistrats* are trained at the *Ecole nationale de la magistrature*, and it is even possible to move during a career from one branch to the other.

The members of the *ministère public* are attached to particular courts; each grouping is called a *parquet* (thought by some authors to originate from the fact that they did not sit with the judges, but made their submissions from the floor of the court). There are *parquets* attached to the *Cour de Cassation* (comprising a *procureur général de la Cour de Cassation*, a *premier avocat général* and *avocats généraux*), the *Cours d'Appel* (a *procureur général*, one or more *avocats généraux* and *substituts généraux; CPP, Art. 34*), and the *Tribunal de Grande Instance* (a *procureur de la République*, assisted by *procureur adjoints* (in major *Tribunaux* such as Paris, Lyon and Marseille) and *substituts; CPP, Arts. 39, 398−2*).

The *ministère public* of the *Cour d'Assises* is made up of members of the *parquet* of the *Cour d'Appel* where the *Cour d'Assises* sits at the seat of a *Cour d'Appel*, otherwise its membership is usually drawn from the *parquet* of the *TGI* (*CPP, Arts. 34, 39*). The *parquet* of the *TGI* provides prosecutors for the *Tribunal Correctionnel* and also in relation to matters of *instruction*. In the *Tribunal de Police*, the role is fulfilled either by prosecutors from the *TGI* or by a senior police officer (*commissaire;* or in exceptional circumstances by the mayor), depending on the seriousness of the *contravention* (*CPP, Arts. 45, 46*). As well as their role in criminal proceedings, members of the *ministère public* participate in civil proceedings; this is examined in Chapter 6.

(ii) Hierarchy

The structure of the *ministère public* is hierarchical, and those lower down the ranks must obey the orders of those above them all the way up to the Minister of Justice (although it should be noted that the *procureur général* of the *Cour de Cassation* has no authority over the members of other *parquets*). The minister may therefore require prosecution to be commenced in a given case (*CPP, Art. 36*), and more generally he may determine prosecution policies (particularly by issuing circulars). Failure to follow orders of superiors may lead to disciplinary sanctions.

There are, however, exceptions to the rule of hierarchical subordination. Firstly, the *procureur généraux* and *procureurs de la République* are recognised as having their own inherent authority; the effect of this is that should they contravene orders of superiors by, for example, refusing to commence a prosecution in a given case, although they may be liable to disciplinary sanctions, their decision itself remains valid. However, a *procureur de la République* may, where one of his *substituts* refuses to carry out his orders, remove the file from him, and either deal with it himself, or pass it on to another *substitut*. Another exception is that although a prosecutor must "follow the party line" in his written submissions to the court, he may orally give his own opinions ("*la plume est serve, mais la parole est libre*"; *CPP, Art. 33*).

(iii) Independence from juge d'instruction

It is important to note that the *ministère public*, which represents the executive, is independent from the other parties to the criminal action. The independence of the *ministère public* from the *juge d'instruction* is shown by the fact that only the former can decide to commence a prosecution and bring in the *juge d'instruction*; the latter is not competent to commence *instruction* on his own initiative (see below). Moreover, once a prosecution has been commenced, the *ministère public* cannot subsequently decide not to proceed; such a decision can be made only by the *juge d'instruction*. The trial court is also generally unable to instigate a prosecution itself (exceptions being the commission of offences (other than perjury) during a court hearing (*CPP, Art. 675*)).

(b) Liability

The *ministère public* is not generally liable in damages to a defendant, who is eventually acquitted, for having brought the prosecution, or for costs. Where, however, a prosecutor has been grossly personally negligent, a procedure known as *la prise à partie* (which applies also to other *magistrats*) may be commenced against him (*Code de l'Organisation Judiciaire, Art. L. 781; Ancien Code de Procédure Civile, Art. 505*).

(c) Role in prosecutions

The *ministère public* is a principal party to criminal proceedings; its role is to bring proceedings (*CPP, Arts. 1, 31;* TEXTS, NO. 11) and to pursue them as the representative of society before the courts. To enable him to fulfil this role, the *procureur de la République* may receive reports of the commission of offences directly from the public (*CPP, Art. 40;* TEXTS, NO. 12), as well as from the police who have to pass on to him "without delay" reports of the commission of offences that come to their attention (*CPP, Art. 19*). Indeed, the *procureur de la République* is given the duty of "carrying out all necessary steps to discover and prosecute offences" (*CPP, Art. 41;* TEXTS, NO. 13), and to this end has operational control of the inquiries carried out by the local *police judiciaire* (*CPP, Art. 12;* TEXTS, NO. 14).

The position of the *procureur de la République* as principal party to the proceedings, and as representative of the interests of society, gives him greater powers than the other parties, at both the *enquête* and *instruction* stages of procedure. In respect of the former, he is in charge of the preliminary police inquiries. As to the latter, during the course of *instruction* the *juge d'instruction* must consult the *procureur de la République* in respect of the exercise of certain of his powers (eg the issue of an arrest warrant (*mandat d'arrêt; CPP, Art. 131*), an order for detention pending trial (*détention provisoire; CPP, Art. 145*), and the lifting of conditions of judicial supervision (*contrôle judiciaire; CPP, Art. 140*)). The prosecutor is entitled to attend all sessions at which the accused is questioned (including *confrontations* with witnesses) by the *juge d'instruction*, and all hearings of the civil complainant (*partie civile* (see below); *CPP, Art. 119*). He may also call for the file from the *juge d'instruction* at any time, and even request the *juge d'instruction* to carry out certain inquiries which appear to the prosecutor to be appropriate for discovering the truth, and to take all necessary security measures (*CPP, Art. 82*). The *procureur de la République* may request the *chambre d'accusation* to annul any irregular *actes d'instruction* (*CPP, Art. 171*). Once the process of *instruction* has been completed, the *juge d'instruction* must give the *procureur de la République* three months (one month if the accused is in detention) to comment before a decision is made to drop the charges (*ordonnance de non-lieu*) or to pursue them (*ordonnance de renvoi*); *CPP, Art. 175*. The *procureur de la République* may appeal to the *chambre d'accusation* against any such order of the *juge d'instruction* (*CPP, Art. 185;* TEXTS, NO. 15), including an *ordonnance de non-lieu*.

The prosecution may (*CPP, Arts. 546, 497*) appeal against the decisions of the trial court in respect of culpability and sentence (although no appeal lies against a finding of "not guilty" by a jury at the *Cour d'Assises*; the equivalent of an Attorney General's reference is, however, permitted; *CPP, Art. 572*). Appeal also lies on a point of law to the *Cour de Cassation* (*CPP, Art. 621*). Following a finding of guilt, the *ministère public* must ensure the execution of criminal sentences (*CPP, Art. 32*), although in this context the role of the sentence execution judge (*le juge de l'application des peines*) must also be considered.

(d) The decision to prosecute

(i) Introduction

The *ministère public* has a discretion (known as *la règle de l'opportunité des poursuites*, recognised by *CPP, Art. 40*; TEXTS, NO. 12) as to whether or not to bring charges. An example of a reason for not doing so (*classement sans suite*) is an inability to identify the wrongdoer, or the insufficiency of the evidence against the accused. However, such a decision is administrative in nature, not judicial, and therefore the *ministère public* is not prevented from bringing charges at a later date (as long as the limitation period has not expired); nor does any appeal lie against a decision to prosecute or otherwise. Professor Pradel estimates (*Procédure Pénale, 6ème ed.*) that between 50 and 70 per cent of cases result in a *classement sans suite*. It should be noted that a decision not to prosecute may lead the victim to decide to sue the alleged offender as *partie civile*, the effect of which is to commence criminal proceedings (see below).

(ii) Direct reference to court

Introduction: If, as a result of the police inquiries (*enquête*), the prosecution decides to bring charges, there are two ways in which this can be done. In the case of serious offences (*crimes*) or complex cases, the prosecution can seize the *juge d'instruction* (by means of a *réquisitoire introductif*) who will thereupon commence the process of *instruction*. In the case of less complex *délits* and *contraventions*, where *instruction* is not appropriate, the prosecution will refer the matter directly to the trial court. There are three different methods of direct reference: the usual *citation directe* (direct summons), the more rapid *convocation par procès-verbal* (written summons) and *comparution immédiate* (immediate reference).

Citation directe: This is the normal way (*CPP, Arts. 388, 531*) of referring a *délit* (not being of such a nature as to warrant *instruction*) to the *Tribunal Correctionnel*; it is also used for referring to the *Tribunal de Police* those *contraventions* which are not dealt with under the simplified procedure of *CPP, Art. 524* (*l'ordonnance pénale*) which is available in respect of minor *contraventions*, and which is examined below in the context of trial procedure. It is also possible for the victim to use the procedure of *citation directe* as *partie civile*.

The *citation* must identify the accused; it is served on the defendant (or other persons at his residence, or at the *mairie*) by a *huissier* in the form of a procedural document known as an *exploit* (*CPP, Art. 551*). A simplified form of summons, the *convocation en justice*, is used when the *ministère public* is sure of being able to effect service in person (*CPP, Art. 390−1*). It may be served by a *huissier* or, where the accused is in detention, by the prison authorities. The *exploit de citation* or *convocation en justice* must state the facts and legal texts on which the charge against the accused is based. It must also give him at least ten days' notice of the date set for the hearing. At the hearing, the court proceeds to deal with the case there and then unless it decides that further inquiries need to be made, and gives a direction that an *information supplémentaire* be carried out by the prosecution.

A simplified alternative to a *citation* is available to the prosecution where the accused consents voluntarily to appear before the courts (*comparution volontaire*). In such a case, the simple notification (*avertissement*) of the charge against him and the date of a hearing is regarded as equivalent to a *citation* (*CPP, Arts. 388, 389, 531, 532*). Should the accused not appear, recourse will be had to a *citation*.

Convocation par procès-verbal and comparution immédiate: A *loi du 20.5.1863* introduced a special procedure permitting the immediate reference of a matter to court where the accused was caught in the act of committing a *délit* (*délit flagrant*; see below). This streamlined procedure was much modified during the 1970s and 1980s and is now found in the form of *la comparution immédiate*; it applies only to *délits*, but is no longer limited to *délits flagrants*. This has been complemented by a procedure of *convocation par procès-verbal*.

Convocation par procès-verbal is available (*CPP, Art. 394*) to the prosecution in respect of all *délits* other than those sufficiently complex to require *instruction*. The accused is summonsed in writing to appear before the court within between ten days and two months. Detention pending trial is not available, but if the prosecutor feels that judicial supervision pending trial (*contrôle judiciaire*; see below) is appropriate, he can apply to a judge of the *Tribunal Correctionnel* for *contrôle judiciaire*; the hearing takes place in chambers, and the accused is entitled to be represented.

A characteristic of comparution immédiate *CPP, Arts. 395-397−5*) is that the prosecution may apply for the accused to be detained pending trial if this is "justified by the facts of the case". The procedure is available with regard to *délits flagrants* which carry a maximum sentence of one to five years' imprisonment, and to "non-flagrant" *délits* which carry a maximum of two to five years where "it appears to the prosecutor that the charges are sufficient and the matter is in a state to be judged". If the *Tribunal Correctionnel* is sitting that day, the accused is brought before it at once. If it is not sitting that day, then unless the prosecutor is of the opinion that detention pending trial (*détention provisoire*) is not necessary (in which case he will revert to the procedure of *convocation*), he will apply for a detention order from a judge of the *Tribunal Correctionnel* at a hearing in chambers at which the accused and his *avocat* are entitled to be present. No appeal lies against the judge's decision. The accused must be brought before the court for trial within two days of the issue of the detention order, failing which the detention order comes to an end. When the accused appears before the trial court, he is informed that he can be judged on that day only if he so consents, in the presence of his *avocat*. The court may decide that the case is not yet in a triable state, and thus order detention pending the carrying out of further investigations (*un supplément d'information*) by the trial judges (who may delegate this to a *juge d'instruction*); or the court may decide that the case is sufficiently complex to warrant full *instruction*, and thus refer the matter via the prosecutor to a *juge d'instruction*. In any event, the trial must take place within two months of the first appearance of the accused before the trial court.

(iii) Reference to the juge d'instruction; réquisitoire introductif

Article 79 of the *CPP* provides that a reference to the *juge d'instruction* is obligatory in respect of *crimes* and certain *délits* (eg illicit speculation under *Code Pénal, Art. 419*). The *juge d'instruction* will also have to be brought in where an arrest warrant (*mandat d'arrêt*) is sought, where an investigation into the accused's background (*enquête de personnalité*) is necessary (eg juvenile offences) or where the identity of the offender is unknown. Unless the law provides otherwise, the *ministère public* has a discretion whether or not to have recourse to *instruction* in respect of *délits* and *contraventions*.

The *procureur de la République* refers a case to the *juge d'instruction* by means of a document called a *réquisitoire introductif* (*CPP, Art. 80;* TEXTS, NO. 16). The *réquisitoire* must be in writing, dated, state the facts in respect of which *instruction* is to be carried out, and specify the offence(s) to which the facts give rise. However, the alleged wrongdoer need not be identified, as it is possible to commence instruction against "persons unknown" (*réquisitoire contre personne non dénommée*). The *procureur* encloses the file of evidence collected during the police inquiries. We have already noted the general power of the *procureur de la République* to request the *juge d'instruction* to "carry out all acts which appear to him to be useful for the revelation of the truth, and all necessary security measures" (*CPP, Art. 82*). He may also request the use of certain powers by the *juge*, such as the issue of an arrest warrant (*mandat d'arrêt*).

Once a prosecution has been commenced by means of a *réquisitoire* it cannot be withdrawn by the *procureur de la République* even if he subsequently decides that the prosecution should not have been brought in the first place; *instruction* must be proceeded with. To allow otherwise would be to threaten the independence of the *juge d'instruction*. Nor is the prosecution entitled to reach a compromise (*une transaction*) with the accused (to the effect that the charges will be dropped in return for, say, the payment of compensation to the victim) except where legislation expressly permits such a practice; thus under *Art. L. 628 Code de la Santé Publique*, in cases of intoxication the prosecution may reach an agreement not to proceed with charges if the accused agrees to undergo detoxification treatment. Also, under *CPP, Art. 6*, where the prosecution is based on a complaint from the victim, the withdrawal of the complaint may lead to the dropping of the prosecution.

3. La partie civile; prosecution by the victim

(a) Introduction

The victim of a crime is of course entitled to sue the wrongdoer for compensation in the civil courts (*CPP, Art. 4*). If a criminal action has been commenced against the wrongdoer in respect of the same facts, then not only must the civil case be adjourned until after the criminal trial has been completed (*CPP, Art. 4*), but in addition the civil judge must not reach a decision which contradicts that of the criminal court (the principle of *la chose jugée au criminel a autorité sur le civil*). However, where a decision is reached first by the civil court, this does not bind the criminal court subsequently trying the case. Where the criminal action is barred, for example under the limitation rules, then the civil action must of course be commenced separately.

The victim has an alternative to commencing a separate civil action; he may (*CPP, Art. 3;* TEXTS, NO. 17) seek compensation from the accused by being joined as "civil party" (*partie civile*) to the criminal action. An advantage of pursuing the civil claim as *partie civile* is that the strongly inquisitorial nature of criminal procedure improves the victim's chances of obtaining damages. Where the victim is unaware of the identity of the offender, he has little choice but to adopt this course of action.

In order to be joined as *partie civile*, the victim will have to show that he personally suffered loss directly as a result of the offence (*CPP, Art. 2;* TEXTS, NO. 18). Extensive caselaw has developed on the interpretation of this article and of *CPP, Art. 3(2)*, which provides that the *partie civile* may recover for all types of loss. The courts have also had to grapple with the issue of precisely who is regarded as being a "victim" of a crime and thus able to be joined as *partie civile*. Particular problems have been caused in relation to the rights of the family of the victim and of third parties such as insurance companies who have paid the victim an indemnity for his loss.

(b) Procedure

There are two ways that a victim may become *partie civile*. The first is by requesting to be joined as party to criminal proceedings already instigated by the *ministère public*. Such a request can be made either during the course of *instruction* (*CPP, Art. 87*) or at the trial (*CPP, Arts. 419–421*), up to the point when the *procureur* makes his final address to the court.

If, on the other hand, no prosecution has been brought, the victim can hasten the intervention of the *ministère public* by commencing proceedings for compensation as *partie civile*. This automatically starts criminal proceedings, as no one may be *partie civile* in the absence of criminal proceedings (*CPP, Art. 3*). Where the alleged offence is a *délit* or *contravention*, the victim usually brings the matter directly before the trial court by means of a *citation directe* (*CPP, Art. 551*). The *ministère public* thereafter takes over the prosecution (although if he is not in agreement with the bringing of the prosecution, he can ask the court to find the accused not guilty).

However, where *instruction* is necessary (ie *crimes*) or desirable (eg serious or complex *délits*), proceedings are commenced by the making of a complaint by the victim to the *juge d'instruction* (in the form of a *plainte avec constitution de partie civile* (*CPP, Art. 85*; TEXTS, NO. 19)). This complaint, which must be in writing and must set out the facts alleged to constitute the offence and the fact that damages are being claimed, is transmitted to the *procureur de la République* by the *juge d'instruction* to enable the former to make his observations (*CPP, Art. 86*). Having received these, the *juge d'instruction* determines whether or not to allow the complainant to be constituted as *partie civile*; he does so if a *prima facie* case has been made out. If he does so, he will commence *instruction*. However, such *constitution de partie civile* may be contested by the *ministère public*, the accused, or another *partie civile* (*CPP, Arts. 87, 423*). Appeal also lies against a refusal to permit a *constitution de partie civile* (*CPP, Art. 186*). The *ministère public* takes over the prosecution of the case at the *Cour d'Assises* (or the *Tribunal Correctionnel* in the case of a *délit*).

Whether the *partie civile* commences an action by *citation directe* or *plainte*, he will, unless in receipt of legal aid, have to pay into court by way of deposit (*consignation; CPP, Arts. 88, R.236*) such sum as the court or *juge d'instruction* respectively thinks fit (taking into account both the likely costs and the resources of the *partie civile*) to cover the potential cost of the action.

If the accused is ordered to pay damages to the *partie civile*, he will (*CPP, Art. 374*) have to pay the latter's costs (ie *dépens*; see Chapter 3); he may also have to pay the cost of the fees of the *avocat* (*honoraires*) of the *partie civile* where it would be inequitable for him not to do so (*CPP, Arts. 375(2), 475–1, 543*). Conversely, a victim who commenced an action as *partie civile* (although not if he joined an action already started by the *ministère public*) runs the risk of being held liable for costs (ie *dépens* and *honoraires; loi du 10.7.1991, Art. 75*) if the accused is eventually found not guilty.

Starting a case as *partie civile* by *plainte* carries additional risks. Firstly, in an attempt to discourage unjustified proceedings, *CPP, Art. 91* provides that if the *juge d'instruction*, having completed *instruction*, decides not to send the matter to trial (*ordonnance de non-lieu*), the accused may obtain damages (in the *Tribunal Correctionnel* sitting in chambers) against the *partie civile* where he can show that the latter acted imprudently in commencing the action. Where the *partie civile* commences a prosecution by way of *citation directe* to the *Tribunal*

Correctionnel and the accused is found not guilty, he may seek damages from the trial court against the *partie civile* (*CPP, Art. 472*). Article 472 has been held not to apply to cases in the *Tribunal de Police* (*Crim., 2.2.1988, Bull. crim., 50*). An accused found not guilty by the *Cour d'Assises* may claim damages against the *partie civile* (*CPP, Art. 371*); such a claim is founded on the fault of the *partie civile* in wrongly commencing the action. Criminal proceedings may also be commenced against the *partie civile* for libellous denunciation (*dénonciation calomnieuse; Code Pénal, Art. 373*).

The *partie civile* is recognised as being a party to the criminal action, and as such has certain rights. For example, he is entitled to be represented by an *avocat*, and to have his *avocat* present when being questioned by the *juge d'instruction* (*CPP, Arts. 117, 118*); to be informed of important procedural steps and decisions of the *juge d'instruction*; to suggest *mesures d'instruction* to the *juge d'instruction*; to cite witnesses; and to make (through his *avocat*) submissions to the trial court. He also has certain rights of appeal against the decisions (of the *juge d'instruction, Tribunal Correctionnel* or *Tribunal de Police*) affecting his interest (*CPP, Arts. 186, 497(3), 546*), and a right of appeal by way of *cassation* (*CPP, Arts. 567, 573*).

(c) Determination of the civil claim

Where the defendant is acquitted, the criminal court generally cannot itself then find in favour of the civil claim of the *partie civile*. The *partie civile* may seek redress from the civil courts, but because the civil court cannot reach a decision which contradicts an earlier criminal decision, he will have to base the claim on grounds which were not rejected in the criminal court. However, by way of exception, *CPP, Art. 372* enables the *Cour d'Assises* to award damages despite an acquittal; this might occur where the bench (sitting without the jury for the purpose of determining the civil claim) decides that even though the accused has been found not guilty of a criminal offence, he is guilty of negligence sufficient to found the civil claim against him. It is also possible for the *Tribunal Correctionnel* and the *Tribunal de Police* to award damages to the victim of a road traffic accident even where a criminal prosecution is unsuccessful (*CPP, Arts. 470–1, 541*).

4. Prosecution by persons other than the ministère public and partie civile

The prosecution of certain categories of offence is granted by statute to those branches of the administration which have a particular interest in such prosecutions (cf *CPP, Art. 1*). Examples are the prosecution of customs offences by the *Administration des douanes* and of minor offences relating to indirect taxation by the *Administration des contributions indirectes*. These types of prosecution are in some ways different from those brought by the *ministère public*; for example, the prosecuting authority has much wider powers of reaching a compromise (*une transaction*) with the accused, being able to drop charges where, say, the accused pays an agreed sum in respect of unpaid duty. Furthermore, the prosecuting authority may be liable in costs to a defendant who is acquitted (which is not the case with the *ministère public*).

5. Juge d'instruction

(a) Role

The process of *instruction*, carried out by the examining magistrate (*juge d'instruction*), is obligatory in the case of *crimes* but discretionary in the case of *délits* and *contraventions*; it is used in serious or complex cases. There is a second level of *instruction* (by the *chambre d'accusation* of the *Cour d'Appel*) into *crimes*. The purposes of *instruction* are to carry out a judicial investigation into the facts referred to the *juge d'instruction* by the *ministère public* (or *partie civile*; see above), to identify the author of a crime, to assess evidence already obtained and to collect further evidence, and to determine whether the matter should be sent for trial.

For these purposes the *juge d'instruction* has wide powers to arrest and detain suspects, to order searches and seizures, to carry out investigations (using, where appropriate, members of the police force), to question suspects and witnesses, to order expert reports, and to carry out inquiries into the background of suspects. He must not act as judge in the trial of a case in respect of which he carried out *instruction* (*CPP, Art. 49*). *Juges d'instruction* are independent of the *ministère public*.

Juges d'instruction are judges from the *Tribunal de Grande Instance* appointed to the post for a three-year renewable term. In major conurbations, there are several *juges d'instruction*; in small provincial courts, there is only one, perhaps fulfilling this function part-time. Oversight of the activities of the *juge(s) d'instruction* is carried out by the president of the *chambre d'accusation* of the *Cour d'Appel* (*CPP, Art. 220*).

If there is more than one *juge d'instruction* attached to a court, the president of the court will assign a particular *juge d'instruction* to a given case. This may be done by means of a rota, which may take into account the specialisms of the *juges* (*CPP, Art. 83*). Article 84 of the *CPP* enables the *procureur de la République*, acting either on his own initiative, or at the request of the accused or the *partie civile*, to petition the president of the court to have a particular *juge d'instruction* replaced "in the interests of the good administration of justice", for example where there is evidence that there is a risk that he may not be impartial.

(b) Reference to the juge d'instruction

The *juge d'instruction* cannot commence *instruction* on his own initiative; he will be seized of a matter (*CPP, Art. 51*) by the *procureur de la République* (by means of a *réquisitoire introductif*) or by the victim of the crime (*plainte avec constitution de partie civile*). The *juge* is given wide investigative powers to carry out such steps as he thinks fit to arrive at the truth (*CPP, Art. 81*; TEXTS, NO. 20). On completing his investigations he may decide to drop the charges (*ordonnance de non-lieu*) or send the case for trial (*ordonnance de renvoi*); in the case of a *crime*, the matter is sent to the *chambre d'accusation* for further *instruction* before proceeding to trial. The *ministère public* has a wide power of appeal against the decisions of the *juge d'instruction*; the accused and the *partie civile* have reduced rights of appeal. The precise powers of the *juge d'instruction* are examined below in the context of *instruction*.

6. The chambre d'accusation of the Cour d'Appel

(a) Introduction

The main role of the *chambre d'accusation* is to act as a second tier of *instruction* in the case of *crimes* and to hear appeals from the decisions of the *juge d'instruction*. It is part of the local *Cour d'Appel*, and comprises a president and two *conseillers*, all three of whom are *Cour d'Appel* judges. Originally its procedure was of a particularly inquisitorial nature, being held in secret and entirely written. Although still not open to the public, proceedings do now take place in the presence of the parties and their *avocats*. Procedure is still largely written (*CPP, Art. 198*), although the *avocats* may make oral representations to the court (*CPP, Art. 199*). The court may – indeed must where dealing with the issue of pre-trial detention, and the accused so requests – require the parties to appear in person (*CPP, Art. 199*).

(b) Role

Apart from the major role that it plays in respect of *instruction* (see below), the *chambre d'accusation* deals with a variety of matters such as the exercise of disciplinary control over judicial police functions (*CPP, Art. 224*), extradition applications (*loi du 10.3.1927*) and rectification of criminal records (*casier judiciaire; CPP, Art. 778*).

7. The jury

(a) Introduction

The jury is found only in the *Cour d'Assises*, judging *crimes*. It is composed of nine jurors who sit with a panel of three judges to determine jointly both culpability and sentence.

(b) Composition

(i) Eligibility

French citizens over the age of 23 who can both read and write French, and have not lost their civic rights, are eligible for jury service (*CPP, Art. 255*). Those who are ineligible (*CPP, Art. 256*) include those condemned to a sentence in respect of a *crime* (*peine criminelle*) or who have spent at least one month in prison in respect of a *crime* or *délit*; there is a five-year ban for those who receive a lesser sentence for a *délit*. Also ineligible are undischarged bankrupts, civil servants who have been dismissed, disbarred professionals, those who have in the past failed to attend jury service, and those subject to guardianship (*tutelle*) or who are under a mental disability. Those who are exempt (*CPP, Art. 257*) include members of the government, Parliament, judges and prefects, senior civil servants and members of the armed forces, the prison service and the police. Those over 70 years of age and those with "strong reason" may apply to be excused jury service (*CPP, Art. 258*). It is an offence to fail without legitimate excuse to attend for service when called, or having attended, to fail to complete the service required (*CPP, Art. 288*). Jurors are entitled to claim for expenses and a daily allowance, which is based on the national minimum wage (*salaire minimum interprofessionnel de croissance*) (*CPP, Arts. R. 139–146*).

(ii) Selecting and empanelling the jury

The rules for selecting and empanelling the jury are set out in *CPP, Arts. 259–267, 282, 288–289, 293, 295–305*. With regard to selection, an annual list of jurors is drawn up for each *Cour d'Assises*. This is done by requiring the mayor of each *commune* (*arrondissement* in Paris) to hold a public random selection of names from the electoral register. These lists are put before a departmental commission of judges, lawyers and councillors, who weed out those who are ineligible and decide whether or not to excuse those who make such a request. The commission then randomly selects the requisite number of jurors for the annual list (1 per 1,300 inhabitants, with a minimum of 200; 1,800 for Paris). Then, one month before the opening of the assizes, the president of the *TGI* (or the first president of the *Cour d'Appel* where the *Cour d'Assises* sits at the seat of the *Cour d'Appel*) publicly and randomly selects the names of 35 jurors (plus 10 replacements) from the annual list, who will thus constitute the jury list for the session.

To enable the defence to exercise its right of challenge, the jury list, containing sufficient details to enable the jurors to be identified (date and place of birth, profession) is communicated to the accused at least two days before the hearing; the jurors' addresses, however, are made known only to counsel. The defendant is entitled to five peremptory challenges (a maximum which applies also to a case involving multiple defendants), and the prosecution to four. The jury is formed once the names of nine jurors have been drawn out of an urn (by the president of the court) without challenge. The jurors are then sworn in. One or more supplementary jurors are also randomly selected; they attend the hearings, and replace any juror who becomes indisposed.

Vetting of the jurors, at least to check that none who is ineligible has been selected, will have been carried out by the jury selection commission. Moreover, the trial of members of the armed forces for criminal offences where there is a risk of the divulgence of national defence secrets takes place before a specially constituted court; in respect of *crimes*, this is before a *Cour d'Assises* sitting without jury but with a panel of six assessors, who are professional judges (*CPP, Arts. 697, 697–1, 698–6,7*). A similarly constituted court also deals with terrorist cases (defined in *CPP, Art. 706–16* as certain offences, carried out either individually or as a collective enterprise, which are intended gravely to disturb public order by intimidation or terror) (*CPP, Art. 706–25*).

(c) Role

Since 1942, the nine jurors and three judges have together determined both guilt and sentence. Jurors are entitled to participate in the trial by asking questions of the accused and the witnesses with the consent of the president of the court (*CPP, Art. 311*). However, they are obliged to refrain, whilst so doing, from revealing their opinion on the culpability of the accused. In an attempt to prevent undue influence being exercised by the judges, it is provided that any decisions which are unfavourable to the accused (such as a finding of guilt, or rejection of attenuating circumstances) must be made by at least eight of the twelve members of the court (*CPP, Art. 359*); this may, however, be thought to leave room for "reasonable doubt" as to guilt. The court first deliberates on culpability; if a finding of guilt is forthcoming, the court goes on to determine sentence (determined by a simple majority, ie seven out of twelve: *CPP, Art. 362*). The panel of three judges sitting without the jury subsequently determines the civil claim of the *partie civile*.

No appeal lies to the *Cour d'Appel*, but appeal by way of *cassation* to the *Cour de Cassation* may lie (see below), including *recours en cassation* against the sentence if legal grounds for the *recours* can be found.

C. L'enquête de police

1. Purpose and characteristics

The *enquête*, or more precisely the *enquête de police*, is the police investigation into a criminal offence before a charge is brought. French criminal procedure has tended to concentrate more on *instruction*, the investigation carried out under the direction of the independent *juge d'instruction* following the referral of a matter to him by the *ministère public*. Instruction has been regarded as the appropriate stage for evidence to be collated and weighed with a view to determining whether or not to send the accused for trial; it is only therefore from the commencement of *instruction* that the suspect is recognised as being entitled to the protection of his "rights of defence". During the *enquête de police* phase, the suspect is thus not entitled to the protection of *CPP, Art. 114* (which enables him to have his *avocat* present during questioning by the *juge d'instruction*). When this lack of protection is coupled with the principle of liberty of means of proof (*CPP, Art. 427*; TEXTS, NO. 2), the reluctance of the courts to exclude evidence improperly obtained during police custody (*garde à vue; arrêt Kissari*, above; TEXTS, NO. 5) and the increased police powers granted by the *CPP* in the case of investigations into flagrant offences (see below), the dangers for the suspect are evident. It should, however, be noted that police custody is generally limited to a maximum of twenty-four hours

As has already been mentioned, the discretion to prosecute, and in the case of a serious offence the decision whether to send the matter for *instruction*, belongs to the *ministère public*. To enable him to exercise his discretion effectively, the police will obviously have had to have conducted an investigation into the case and drawn up a dossier of evidence. The pre-1958 *Code d'Instruction Criminelle* expressly regulated only *enquêtes* into flagrant offences (*enquêtes de flagrance*; see below). However, the practice of the police in holding *enquêtes préliminaires* into cases other than flagrant offences was given a legal foundation in the 1958 *CPP*, which affirms (*Art. 75*; TEXTS, NO. 10) that judicial police officers (and agents under the control of judicial police officers) may carry out *enquêtes préliminaires*. The judicial police are given the task (*CPP, Art. 14*; TEXTS, NO. 9) of establishing the commission of criminal offences, obtaining evidence in respect of the offence and seeking the offender.

The *enquête de police* is commenced either on the instructions of the *procureur de la République* on receipt of notification of the commission of an offence from the police or the public, or by the police acting on their own initiative (*CPP, Art. 75*), although in the latter case the *ministère public* will be informed when the file is passed to him. In both cases the *enquête de police* is carried out under the control of the *procureur de la République* (see *CPP, Arts. 41* (TEXTS, NO. 13), *12* (TEXTS, NO. 14)). It is he who decides whether or not to proceed with the matter. The *juge d'instruction* is usually not involved at this stage, although he can become involved in the case of an *enquête d'infraction flagrante* (see below).

The *enquête de police* displays the classic characteristics of inquisitorial criminal procedure. It is thus a secret procedure (*CPP, Art. 11*; TEXTS, NO. 21) which leads to the production of a written report (*procès-verbal*) by the police to the *procureur de la République* (*CPP, Art. 19*). The formal recognition in the 1958 *CPP* of the place of the *enquête préliminaire* in criminal procedure has perhaps reduced the importance of *instruction* and of the *juge d'instruction*, for by the time the latter is brought in, a large proportion of the investigative work will already have been carried out by the police under the supervision of the *procureur de la République*. It is also true that *instruction* occurs in only a small minority of cases.

2. L'enquête préliminaire and l'enquête de flagrance

A 1670 *ordonnance* first granted the police coercive powers (in respect of, for example, search, seizure, and detention for questioning) in cases where the suspect was caught in the act of committing a serious offence (*in flagrante delicto*) or within a short time afterwards. The increased powers of the *enquête de flagrance* were retained in the 1958 *CPP*. The extent of these powers is examined below.

What are the precise circumstances which are regarded as giving rise to an *enquête de flagrance* as opposed to an *enquête préliminaire*? The answer is provided by *CPP, Art. 53* (TEXTS, NO. 22). The first point to note is that an *enquête de flagrance* is applicable only to offences of a certain gravity, ie *crimes* and *délits* carrying the penalty of imprisonment. As to what is regarded as flagrance, *CPP, Art. 53* identifies four different cases. Firstly, an offence is flagrant if it is currently being committed. This obviously covers the case where a criminal is caught red-handed in the midst of, say, a burglary. In respect of a continuing offence, such as being in possession of an offensive weapon, there must be some exterior sign that an offence is being committed before the police officer can exercise any of his increased flagrance powers, such as that of search (eg *Crim., 21.7.1982, D.1982, 642*; TEXTS, NO. 23). Any other interpretation would broaden police powers unacceptably.

Secondly, offences which have just been committed are regarded as being flagrant. No period within which an offence remains flagrant is specified in the *CPP*. Caselaw on the equivalent pre-1958 provision accepted that the police could exercise their increased powers if they discovered an offence within 24 hours or so of its commission. The relevant provision of the *CPP, Art. 53* is clearly more restrictive, referring as it does to a "very short time" (*un temps très voisin de l'action*) after commission. This is taken to mean only a few hours within the commission of the offence.

Thirdly, an offence is flagrant where, within a short time of its commission, the suspect either (i) is pursued by public outcry (for example where the victim of a handbag snatch shouts "stop thief!"), or (ii) is found to be in possession of items or has upon his person traces or indications pointing to participation in the offence. In respect of (ii), it is again the case that there must be some exterior sign justifying the exercise of police search powers; were this not the case the police might be encouraged to "fish" for evidence.

The fourth case of flagrance is where the head of a household in which an offence has been committed invites a police officer or the *ministère public* to investigate the offence; for example, where a householder returns from a holiday to discover that his house has been burgled.

It should be noted that as long as the police commence their investigations during the time within which the offence remains flagrant, the increased powers of the *enquête de flagrance* remain available to them for as long as the investigation continues.

It is essentially for the police to determine whether or not an offence is flagrant. However, the issue of flagrance may be raised by the defendant's *avocat* at trial; he might argue, for example, that the results of a search carried out under the flagrance powers should not be admitted, the offence not having been flagrant.

3. Police powers and the rights of the suspect during the enquête de police

(a) Introduction

As has been seen, the police have coercive powers when carrying out an *enquête de flagrance*, the justification for which is stated to be the need to obtain evidence as quickly as possible in the case of a flagrant offence. They also have a duty (*CPP, Art. 54*) to report the offence to the *procureur de la République* at once. Police powers are greatly reduced in respect of inquiries into non-flagrant offences (*enquêtes préliminaires*), where generally they can be exercised only with the consent of those affected. Let us now examine the different police powers which may be exercised during the *enquête de police*, distinguishing where appropriate between the *enquête préliminaire* and the *enquête de flagrance*.

(b) Identity checks

It is only since 1981 that legislation has admitted a general power of the police to carry out identity checks (*contrôles d'identité*). Before then, such a power existed only in respect of *enquêtes de flagrance*. The relevant law can now be found in *CPP, Art. 78-2*. This article distinguishes two circumstances in which an identity check may be made. Firstly, a check may be made where there are indications that the person concerned has committed or attempted to commit an offence; or is about to commit a *crime* or *délit*; or may be able to provide information useful to police inquiries into a *crime* or *délit*; or is being sought by the police on judicial authority (for example, he is the subject of an arrest warrant). Secondly, a check may be made of the identity of any person on the grounds of preventing a breach of the peace, whether the threat is of injury to persons or damage to property.

If the person required to prove his identity refuses or fails satisfactorily to do so, a judicial police officer is entitled to detain him, either *in situ*, or by removal to the police station, for a maximum of four hours, for his identity to be established. It is possible for fingerprints and photographs to be taken on the authority of the *procureur de la République*; it is an offence to fail to comply.

(c) Expert reports

The *CPP* essentially provides for expert reports to be commissioned by *juges d'instruction* during the phase of *instruction*. However, in an attempt to prevent a *délit* being sent to a *juge d'instruction* solely for the purpose of obtaining expert reports, *CPP, Arts. 60, 77−1* authorise, during an *enquête de police* (whether flagrant or not), the recourse by a judicial police officer to technical or scientific examinations by duly qualified persons, where these need to be carried out without delay.

(d) Search and seizure

(i) Enquête préliminaire

In the absence of flagrance, police search powers are limited. Article 76 of the *CPP* provides that property searches (*perquisitions*), entry to an individual's home, and seizure of exhibits (*pièces à conviction*) may take place only with the express written consent of the person whose home it is. Even then, no search or visit may normally be undertaken between the hours of 9.00 pm and 6.00 am.

(ii) Enquête de flagrance

In an *enquête* into a flagrant offence, a judicial police officer has a duty (*CPP, Art. 54*) to report the offence to the *procureur de la République* immediately, to visit the scene of the crime and to carry out all useful inquiries. He must ensure the preservation of all traces and indications likely to reveal the truth. It should be noted that the *procureur de la République* (or the *juge d'instruction*) may attend the scene of the crime; where he does so, he takes over the conduct of the investigation.

By *CPP, Art. 56*, in cases of flagrance where, because of the nature of the crime, proof of culpability might be obtained by the seizure of papers, documents or objects in the possession of persons who appear to have participated in the crime or to be in possession of relevant articles or objects, a judicial police officer is empowered to carry out a search of the domicile (including any place of residence) of such persons (without the need to obtain a warrant or the consent of the homeowner) and to seize such items.

Searches must normally take place in the presence of the person whose home it is (or his nominee or, if neither of these is available, two witnesses) and commence between the hours of 6.00 am and 9.00 pm (*CPP, Arts. 57, 59*); it has been accepted by the courts that the power of search extends to a motor vehicle of a suspect (but because a motor vehicle is not a domicile, the formalities to be followed for *perquisitions* do not apply). The limitations on searches which have been outlined do not apply to some cases, such as searches for illegally held drugs.

In order to give some protection to documents subject to professional privilege (such as those of a lawyer or doctor), the searcher has a duty (*CPP, Art. 56*) to take all measures to ensure respect for professional secrets. It is also provided (*CPP, Art. 56−1*) that a search of the office or home of an *avocat* may be carried out only by a *magistrat* in the presence of the *bâtonnier* (see Chapter 3) or his agent. Furthermore, in no event may correspondence between an *avocat* and his client be seized. All *perquisitions* result in the drawing up of a written report. The police must be careful to comply with the formalities required by *CPP, Arts. 56, 57, 59*, as non-compliance may lead to the search being declared null, and the evidence obtained invalid (*CPP, Art. 59*).

Under the *CPP* the police do not have a power to carry out a body search (*fouille*) of a suspect; however the courts have recognised such a power, in respect of flagrant offences only, by analogy to *CPP, Art. 56*; indeed, the *fouille* is to be carried out in the same conditions as a *perquisition*. As *CPP, Art. 56* applies in respect of those "who appear to have participated in a crime", a body search will be permitted only where there are some indications that the suspect has so participated (eg a pistol is seen protruding from his pocket).

(e) Arrest and detention in police custody (garde à vue)

(i) Introduction

The police are given wide powers, particularly in respect of an *enquête de flagrance*, to detain for questioning, for a period of 24 hours (renewable once), anyone (including a suspect) who is likely to be able to provide information on the facts, or on evidence which has been seized. A dossier of the evidence thus obtained, including statements of the suspect and other witnesses, is drawn up. During this period of detention in police custody (*la garde à vue*), the so-called "rights of defence" are limited; as a result, the detainee is not entitled to obtain legal advice or benefit from the presence of his *avocat* during questioning. Such protection is accorded by the *CPP* only once the process of *instruction* (where appropriate) commences, or in respect of lesser offences (eg *délits*) when the suspect is brought before the *ministère public* at the end of police custody. This may be too late if the suspect has already made a damaging statement, although it is true that a confession may be retracted; it will then be for the trial court to determine what weight should be given to the retracted confession. As has been seen, the failure of the police to abide by the requirements of the *CPP* for the conduct of the *garde à vue* does not vitiate the *enquête de police* or lead to invalidation of the evidence so obtained.

(ii) Arrest

It is necessary to distinguish between a variety of powers of arrest and detention available at different stages of criminal procedure. The power to arrest for the purposes of an identity check under *CPP, Art. 78–3* has already been examined. Additionally, the judicial police, *procureur de la République* and *juge d'instruction* (*CPP, Art. 122*; below) have a variety of arrest powers. These police powers are greater in an *enquête de flagrance*.

Enquête préliminaire: The *CPP* gives the police no power to arrest persons for questioning or otherwise during the course of an *enquête préliminaire*, powers which they do have in the case of an *enquête de flagrance* (see below); a person can therefore only be requested (by *convocation*) to attend for questioning. However, paradoxically, the *CPP* does provide (*Art. 77*; TEXTS, NO. 24) for the detention in police custody (*garde à vue*) by a judicial police officer of any person who is at his disposition where this is required by "the needs of the investigation". This granting of a power of detention without a corresponding power of arrest to enforce it has been interpreted as having the effect of enabling the police to detain a person in custody under a *garde à vue* should he voluntarily respond to a request to come in for questioning.

Enquête de flagrance: In the case of an *enquête de flagrance*, *CPP, Art. 61* empowers a judicial police officer to prevent any person from leaving the scene of the crime whilst investigations there are continuing. Additionally, by *CPP, Art. 62* a judicial police officer can compel (by force if necessary, but only on the authority of the *procureur de la République*) anyone who is likely to be able to furnish information about the facts or about evidence which has been seized to attend at a police station and make a statement. This may lead to detention for questioning by way of *garde à vue* (see below). There is also (*CPP, Art. 63(2)*; TEXTS, NO. 25) a power of detention to enable a suspect against whom compelling evidence exists to be brought before the *procureur de la République* at the end of the period of police custody.

Furthermore, a wide power is accorded by *CPP, Art. 73* not only to the police but also to any citizen to arrest (known as *l'appréhension*)

someone who is committing or has committed (or is reasonably suspected of so doing) a flagrant *crime* or *délit* punishable with imprisonment. This power is designated to enable the arrest of offenders caught
in the act.

The *procureur de la République* himself may (at any time before
the *juge d'instruction* has been seized) issue an appearance warrant
(*mandat d'amener*; see below) in respect of a person suspected of
having participated in a *crime flagrant* (*CPP, Art. 70*).

(iii) Detention in police custody: garde à vue

Application and safeguards: Articles 63 and 77 of the *CPP* give a
judicial police officer powers of detention in custody for up to 24
hours where required by the "necessities of the *enquête*". In respect
of an *enquête de flagrance*, the power to detain applies to any person
who was at the scene of the crime, or who is likely to be able to furnish
information about the facts or about evidence which has been seized.
Surprisingly the power is wider in respect of *enquêtes préliminaires*,
applying to any person. The purpose of the *garde à vue* is to enable
the police to question witnesses and suspects effectively, and to prevent
the destruction of evidence or the warning of accomplices.

As has been seen, neither the *CPP* nor the caselaw of the *Cour de
Cassation* has provided much in the way of safeguards to the suspect
during police custody. Of particular concern is the silence of the *CPP*
on any right to have access to an *avocat*. It is only at the first appearance
before the *juge d'instruction* (where appropriate) that the accused will
be told that he is entitled to legal advice (*CPP, Art. 114*). A limited
exception applies in the case of an *enquête de flagrance* to a suspect who
is arrested following the issue of a *mandat d'amener* by the *procureur de
la République*; he will be brought before the *procureur de la République*
and questioned at once by him – although in such circumstances there
is again no right to legal advice, it is provided (*CPP, Art. 70*) that where
the suspect happens to arrive with a counsel, he may be questioned only
in the presence of his counsel. Note that in the case of a *délit* which
does not warrant *instruction*, the suspect will be told of his right to an
avocat and will be informed of the case against him when he is brought
before the *procureur* at the end of the *garde à vue* (*CPP, Art. 393*) for
a decision as to whether to send the matter to court for trial.

Duration and conditions: The *garde à vue* may last for up to 24 hours,
time running (*décret du 20.5.1903, Art. 124*) from the moment of arrest
or detention or instruction not to leave the scene of the crime (*CPP,
Art. 61*), or in the case of an *enquête préliminaire*, from the moment
of voluntary attendance at the police station in response to a request
to make a statement. The period may be extended by a further 24
hours by the *procureur de la République* (*CPP, Arts. 63, 77*). In
an investigation into a non-flagrant offence, normally an extension

can be granted only after the suspect has been brought before the *procureur* for examination; there are no specific grounds that have to be shown before an extension may be granted. In an investigation into a flagrant offence there is no need for the suspect to appear personally before the *procureur* for there to be an extension; however, there must be "serious and consistent evidence sufficient to justifying charges being brought". This is a rather surprising requirement; one might ask why, if there exists such evidence against the suspect, he is not simply charged at that point. The *garde à vue* may be extended up to a maximum of 96 hours in the case of drugs trafficking (*Code de la Santé Publique, Art. 627–1*) or terrorist offences (*CPP, Art. 706–23*). Where the *garde à vue* is extended beyond the initial 24 hours, the detainee has the right to require a medical examination (*CPP, Arts. 64, 77*); this is a safeguard against improper police treatment.

Questioning: The judicial police may, during the course of an *enquête de flagrance*, take the evidence of any person "likely to be able to furnish information on the facts or on evidence which has been seized" (*CPP, Art. 62*). Evidence is not given on oath. This provision is regarded as sufficient to justify the questioning (*interrogatoire*) of a suspect by the police. However, the suspect is not obliged to make a statement, and is entitled to remain silent.

It is accepted that the police are not permitted to use torture or coercive methods of interrogation (such as sleep deprivation, hypnosis or truth-drugs); although there are no provisions of the *CPP* directly on the point, inhuman and degrading treatment is forbidden by the European Convention on Human Rights. The issue of the admission of confessions obtained by the police by the use of ruses or tricks is left to the determination of the courts, which have shown themselves to be not very ready to penalise the use of such ruses during the *enquête* phase. It is rare for the evidence thus obtained to be excluded. However, disciplinary proceedings may be taken against the errant officer. There are no provisions in the *CPP* for the tape-recording of interviews of suspects. A confession made by a suspect may be withdrawn at any time (*Crim., 28.7.1981, D. 1982, 1, 185*); it is for the trial court to decide what weight to give to the withdrawn confession (*Crim., 18.12.1956; Bull crim., 846*). Finally, it should be noted that under *CPP, Arts. 70, 72*, both the *procureur de la République* and the *juge d'instruction* who attend the scene of a crime have certain powers of questioning.

Report: The written report (*procès-verbal*) of the *garde à vue* must (*CPP, Arts. 64, 78*) contain a custody record, giving details of the reasons for and duration of the detention; also of the duration of the periods of questioning and rest. There are no provisions setting down maximum questioning periods, or minimum rest periods.

4. Termination of l'enquête de police

Once the police have terminated their inquiries, the *procès-verbaux* and all evidence which has been obtained are transmitted to the *procureur de la République* for a determination as to whether or not to bring charges (see above). The suspect himself will be brought to the *procureur* at the end of a *garde à vue* if the police intend to proceed with the matter. If charges are brought and the accused is in custody under a *garde à vue*, detention may be extended either if the accused is brought to trial immediately by means of a *comparution immédiate* (see above), whereupon he will be informed of his right to legal advice, or in the case of serious crime the *procureur* will order *instruction* to be commenced (by *réquisitoire introductif*) and will send the suspect to the *juge d'instruction*. In the latter case, the suspect will be brought before the *juge d'instruction* by the police. The *juge* will proceed with the first hearing of the suspect (*interrogatoire de première comparution*) which represents the formal charging of the suspect (see below). At the end of the hearing, detention in custody may be ordered, but only in accordance with the procedure of *CPP, Art. 145* (see below).

D. Instruction

1. Purpose and nature of instruction

(a) Introduction

The purpose of *instruction* is to enable a judge (*le juge d'instruction*), who is independent of the prosecution, to examine all of the evidence which has thus far been unearthed, and to obtain such additional evidence as he thinks fit, with a view to determining whether or not the accused should be sent for trial.

His task is widely defined (*CPP, Art. 81*; TEXTS, NO. 20) as "carrying out all inquiries that he judges useful for the revelation of the truth". To enable him to do so, he is endowed by the *CPP* with wide powers to obtain evidence, effect searches and seizures, require witnesses to give statements, arrest (if not already in custody) and question the accused (for which purpose he has powers of judicial supervision and detention pending trial); he can even confront the accused face to face with the other witnesses in an endeavour to get at the heart of the matter. Most of these powers (save in particular the questioning of the suspect once he has been formally charged) may be, and often are, delegated, usually to police officers, by means of *commissions rogatoires.* As has already been mentioned, *instruction* is obligatory in the case of *crimes* and discretionary for *contraventions* and *délits* (*CPP, Art. 79*).

(b) Inquisitorial characteristics

(i) Non-accusatorial

Instruction has inquisitorial characteristics. The first of these is that it is non-accusatorial (*non-accusatoire*); it is the *juge d'instruction*, and not the *ministère public*, who conducts the inquiry, his purpose being to seek the truth. It should therefore be contrasted with committal proceedings in England and Wales, in which the prosecution seeks to prove a *prima facie* case against the accused. The *ministère public* does, however, have certain privileges during *instruction*. For example, he is entitled to be advised of and to be present at any questioning of the accused (*CPP, Art. 119*) and at procedural acts, such as searches, ordered by the *juge d'instruction* (*CPP, Art. 92*); to be consulted by the *juge d'instruction* in respect of decisions relating to judicial supervision (*contrôle judiciaire*) and detention pending trial (*détention provisoire*). He also has broad rights of appeal against the decisions of the *juge d'instruction*. Indeed, the privileged position of the *procureur de la République* is emphasised by the fact that he is entitled to request the *juge d'instruction* to carry out, *inter alia*, "such investigations as to him appear useful for the revelation of the truth", and the *juge d'instruction*, should he refuse to comply, must within five days give written reasons for his refusal (*CPP, Art. 82*).

The accused for his part is recognised as being entitled to certain "rights of defence" (*droits de la défense*), in particular the right to have his *avocat* present during questioning by the *juge d'instruction*. The accused also has a right to participate in *instruction*, by making observations to or asking questions of the *juge d'instruction*, orally or in writing, usually through his *avocat*, and by requesting the *juge* to carry out the investigations that he considers necessary. The *juge* is not, however, obliged to comply, although in the case of a request for an expert examination to be carried out, he has to give written reasons for a refusal (*CPP, Art. 156*). The accused has certain rights of appeal against the orders of the *juge d'instruction* under the terms of *CPP, Art. 186*.

(ii) Written

Instruction is also essentially written in nature; the evidence obtained during the procedure, including the statements made by witnesses and the accused, and formal reports (*procès-verbaux*) of all procedural steps undertaken by the *juge d'instruction* are incorporated into a written dossier of evidence (*dossier d'information*) by the *juge* (*CPP, Art. 81*). This dossier is passed to the trial court. By way of derogation from the principle of the written nature of *instruction*, there is a certain degree of oral procedure at the second tier of *instruction* into *crimes* by the *chambre d'accusation*, in that the *ministère public* and *avocats* of the parties are entitled to present summary oral observations in respect of their written reports (*CPP, Arts. 198, 199*).

(iii) Secret

A further inquisitorial characteristic of *instruction* is its secret nature (*CPP, Art. 11;* TEXTS, NO. 21). In the 1808 *Code d'Instruction Criminelle* the *juge d'instruction* was under no obligation to allow the accused access to the dossier that was being built up against him; nor was he under an obligation to specify the charge. Now *CPP, Art. 11* provides that the secrecy of *instruction* must not prejudice the accused's "rights of defence". He therefore is entitled to be informed of the nature of the charges against him and to have access to the file, although this latter right is exercisable only through his *avocat* (*CPP, Art. 118*). Similar access rights to the file are accorded to the *partie civile*.

Instruction is secret in the sense that it is a private procedure; for example, in respect of the second tier of *instruction* into *crimes*, the debates of the *chambre d'accusation* and the pronouncement of its decisions take place in chambers (*CPP, Art. 199*). Those participating in *instruction* (interpreted by the courts as referring to the judges, the prosecution and the police, but not the accused, the *partie civile* or witnesses) have an obligation (*CPP, Art. 11*) not to divulge evidence obtained during an *instruction* which is in progress. The publication, before a definitive decision has been reached by the trial court, of comments likely to influence the evidence to be given by witnesses or the decisions of either the *juge d'instruction* or trial court, is an offence (*Code Pénal, Art. 227*). By way of exception, however, the *juge d'instruction* and the *ministère public* may publish information relating to an investigation where this would be useful in the search for the truth.

2. Recourse to instruction

(a) Instruction in rem

The commencement of *instruction* by the *juge d'instruction* is known as the "opening of an inquiry" (*l'ouverture d'une information*). As has been seen above, the *juge d'instruction* cannot seize himself of a matter, but must be brought in either by the *ministère public* (by means of a *réquisitoire introductif*) or by the *partie civile* (by means of a *plainte avec constitution de partie civile*).

The *réquisitoire introductif* seizes the *juge d'instruction in rem*; in other words, he is given the task not of examining the case against a particular suspect, but rather of investigating the facts set out in the *réquisitoire*. He is not entitled to extend his investigation to other matters he unearths unless (*CPP, Art. 80(4)*), having informed the *ministère public* thereof, the latter so requires it by issuing a *réquisitoire supplétif*. The *réquisitoire introductif* may and usually will name a suspect. In such a case the *juge d'instruction* will formally charge (*inculpation*; see below) the suspect upon commencing *instruction*. The suspect is from that moment known as the accused (*l'inculpé*) and enjoys "rights of defence". The *juge d'instruction* is empowered to charge not only those suspects named by the *ministère public* in the *réquisitoire*, but anyone who appears to him to be implicated in the facts brought to his attention (*CPP, Art. 80(3)*), without the need to obtain a supplementary *réquisitoire* from the *ministère public*. Where the *réquisitoire* does not identify any suspect, *instruction* will be commenced against persons unknown (*contre "X"*).

(b) First acts of the juge d'instruction

Having determined that the case comes within his territorial jurisdiction (*CPP, Art. 52*), the *juge d'instruction* will decide whether he should proceed with *instruction* or not. He may refuse to do so (by issuing a reasoned *ordonnance de refus d'informer*, which can be appealed against by the *ministère public* or the *partie civile*) on the grounds that he is incompetent to deal with the matter; for example, where he is of the opinion that the facts set out in the *réquisitoire* do not constitute any criminal offence, or the limitation period (see above) has expired. Otherwise, he must proceed with *instruction*.

(c) Inculpation

Inculpation is the formal charging of a suspect by the *juge d'instruction* informing him that he is commencing an *instruction* into specified incriminating facts. There is a certain lack of clarity as to the precise relationship between the issuing of the *réquisitoire introductif* by the prosecutor, which is regarded as being the commencement of the public action (in the sense that time stops running against the state under the limitation period), and the *inculpation* of the suspect by the *juge d'instruction*, the importance of which is that upon acquiring the status of *inculpé* the accused enjoys the statutory "rights of defence", which are of particular importance during questioning by the *juge d'instruction* (see below).

It is for the *juge d'instruction*, and not the *ministère public*, to inculpate the accused (*CPP, Art. 80(3)*). However there is some authority (eg *Crim., 5.11.1985, D. 1986, IR, 303*) for the view that a suspect should be accorded the protection of *CPP, Art. 114* (giving him the right to an *avocat*; TEXTS, NO. 1) from the moment that the *réquisitoire introductif* is issued against him. Generally, there is no particular procedural formality required for the *inculpation* of a suspect by the *juge d'instruction*. The transition is usually marked either by the *juge d'instruction* starting his first session of questioning of the *inculpé* under *CPP, Art. 114* (*interrogatoire de première comparution*), at which the *juge d'instruction* must inform the suspect of his "rights of defence", or where he is not at the time in the custody of the *juge*, by the issue of one of the different warrants for enforced appearance under *CPP, Art. 122* (TEXTS, NO. 26). This is because the powers of both *CPP, Arts. 114 and 122* are stated to apply only to *inculpés*.

At what point should the *juge d'instruction* inculpate a suspect? A particular difficulty arises where, following the commencement of *instruction*, a witness who is being questioned by the *juge d'instruction* (or by a police officer following delegation by a *commission rogatoire*) makes a statement which is self-incriminating. In order to discourage the *juge d'instruction* from unduly delaying inculpating a suspect because he does not wish him thereby to have the right of access to a lawyer under *CPP, Art. 114*, it is provided by *CPP, Art. 105* (TEXTS, NO. 6) that as soon as there exist "serious and consistent indications of guilt" against a suspect, he may no longer be questioned as a mere witness (as opposed to an *inculpé*). In other words, he should be formally inculpated and thus be entitled to obtain legal advice before questioning continues. Also, following *inculpation*, the accused must be questioned personally by the *juge d'instruction*, delegation of this task to the police being thereafter forbidden (*CPP, Art. 152*). Article 80(3) of the *CPP* confirms that *inculpation* should occur when the *juge d'instruction* has evidence that the suspect has "taken part" in the offence. The *Cour de Cassation* has accepted (*Crim., 16.6.1981, Chatelain, D.1983, IR, 76*; TEXTS, NO. 27) that once a suspect who is being questioned as a witness has made a credible corroborated confession, the confession constitutes a "serious and consistent indication of guilt" with the effect that any further questioning without inculpation is unlawful, and the resulting statements will be struck from the dossier. However, *CPP, Art. 105*, on its own terms, applies only where the post-confession examination of the suspect as a witness is carried out "with the intention of frustrating the rights of defence". The courts have shown a reluctance to accept that the mere fact of a continuation of the questioning is evidence of the requisite intention, although they have done so in some cases, annulling the subsequently obtained evidence.

Where *instruction* has been commenced against the suspect following the bringing of an action by the *partie civile, CPP, Art. 104* provides that the suspect is entitled to access to a lawyer even though he is being questioned merely as a witness. The purpose of this article is to grant the suspect who has been denounced by the victim, rather than by the prosecution, rights of defence without the *juge d'instruction* having to move to an *inculpation* before he has made up his own mind on the evidence against the suspect.

3. Arrest, detention and questioning of the suspect

(a) Warrants (mandats) of the juge d'instruction

The *juge d'instruction* has in his armoury a range of warrants (*mandats*) that may be issued to bring the suspect before him for questioning (*CPP, Art. 122;* TEXTS, NO. 26). Where the suspect is thought to be likely to attend without any resort to force, the *juge d'instruction* will issue a *mandat de comparution* (judicial appearance summons) requiring him to attend for questioning at a given time and place; on appearing, he will be questioned at once (*CPP, Art. 125*). If he fails to do so, or where from the outset it is thought that recourse to force will be necessary, the *juge d'instruction* will issue a *mandat d'amener* (appearance warrant), which empowers the police to arrest the suspect whose whereabouts are known to them (the arrest of a suspect at his home may only be effected between 6.00 am and 9.00 pm; *CPP, Art. 134*) and bring him before the *juge d'instruction* for questioning. This will take place immediately after arrest, if possible; if not, he will be detained in a remand prison (*maison d'arrêt*; such prisons also house prisoners having less than a year of their term to run), but must be questioned by the *juge d'instruction* within 24 hours of arrest or he will be released (*CPP, Art. 125*; this period is extended if the accused is arrested more than 200 kilometres from the town where the *juge d'instruction* is based).

The two other warrants, the *mandat d'arrêt* (arrest warrant) and *mandat de dépôt* (custody warrant), that may be issued by the *juge d'instruction* are available only in respect of serious offences (at least a *délit* carrying a sentence of imprisonment; *CPP, Arts. 131, 135*) – and, in respect of a *mandat d'arrêt*, only after seeking the advice of the *procureur de la République* – as they lead to custody pending trial (*détention provisoire*). The *mandat d'arrêt* is an arrest warrant which is used when the accused is at large or resides overseas (*CPP, Art. 131*). On arrest, the suspect is taken to the *maison d'arrêt*, and will be questioned by the *juge d'instruction*, usually at the office of the *juge d'instruction*, within 24 hours (assuming he is arrested within 200 kilometres) and thereupon the *juge d'instruction* will deal with the issue of detention pending trial (in accordance with the procedure of *CPP, Art. 145*, below).

The *mandat de dépôt* (custody warrant) is used only where the suspect is already available to the *juge d'instruction*, usually following a *mandat de comparution* or a *mandat d'amener*, or where the accused has been brought before the *juge d'instruction* by the *ministère public* following detention under a *garde à vue* during the *enquête de police* phase. It presumes that the first hearing of the accused has taken place (*CPP, Art. 135*). The *mandat de dépôt* is an order to the prison governor to detain the accused pending trial, and the procedure of *CPP, Art. 145* (pre-trial detention hearing; see below) must therefore be followed (*CPP, Art. 135*).

(b) Questioning the accused (l'interrogatoire)

(i) Introduction

Central to *instruction* is the questioning of witnesses (*audition des témoins*) by the *juge d'instruction* or police acting on delegation, and the questioning of the accused (*interrogatoire de l'inculpé*) by the *juge d'instruction*. The accused is subject to a special regime of questioning, being entitled to be questioned by the *juge d'instruction* in the presence of his *avocat*. He is not obliged to make a statement, or to give his evidence on oath, as are witnesses; he may thus change his story during the course of *instruction* without committing the offence of giving false testimony. Indeed, in the search for the truth, the evidence of the accused is regarded by the courts as having particular importance, and caselaw confirms that the *juge d'instruction* is obliged to question the accused at least once during *instruction*. As is mentioned below, although the accused and witnesses subsequently give oral evidence at the trial court hearing (particularly at the *Cour d'Assises*), there is no testing of this evidence by cross-examination as such, questioning by the *avocats* for the parties being controlled by the trial judge. The accused's evidence is tested by his being questioned directly by the *juge d'instruction* and, where appropriate, by recourse by the *juge d'instruction* to the confrontation of the accused with the other witnesses; the resulting written reports form a part of the file of evidence which is put before the trial court. The evidence of the witnesses is given to the *juge d'instruction* on oath, the giving of false evidence constituting an offence.

(ii) L'interrogatoire de première comparution

At the first appearance of the accused before the *juge d'instruction* (*l'interrogatoire de première comparution*), *CPP, Art. 114* (TEXTS, NO. 1) imposes particular rules designed to safeguard the accused's "rights of defence". The *juge d'instruction* is required, having ascertained the identity of the accused, to inform him of the charges against him. He must then point out that he is not obliged to make a statement there and then; if, however, the accused expresses a desire to do so, the *juge* may receive the statement (but not question him on it at that stage; questioning should normally take place only in the presence of the accused's *avocat*). The *juge d'instruction* must also inform the accused that he is entitled to legal representation; if he does not already have an *avocat*, one will be appointed to represent him by the *bâtonnier*. If he states that he wants legal representation, the first appearance will come to an end at that point, with the *juge d'instruction* not proceeding to question the accused. The *avocat* is entitled to access to the file two clear days before subsequent appearances, which he may attend (*CPP, Art. 118*); where the accused is remanded in custody, he may freely consult his *avocat* (*CPP, Art. 116*).

If, however, the accused states that he does not wish to consult an *avocat* (although he can always change his mind later (*CPP, Art. 117*)) then the *juge d'instruction* may proceed with questioning (*CPP, Art. 118*); a disadvantage for the accused in such circumstances will be that he will not be permitted to see the file of evidence against him, as access is permitted only through an *avocat*. It is also possible for the accused to express his desire to obtain legal advice, but be willing to be questioned there and then.

If the *juge d'instruction* fails to comply with the requirements of *CPP, Arts. 114, 118*, the evidence obtained (then or subsequently) may be excluded by the *chambre d'accusation* (*CPP, Art. 170*). The *juge d'instruction* does not however have to comply with *CPP, Art. 114* where there is an urgency to proceed with investigations so as to prevent the disappearance of real evidence, or where there is a risk of the imminent decease of a witness, or where both the *juge d'instruction* and the *ministère public* are present at the scene of a flagrant offence and the *ministère public* requires the immediate commencement of *instruction* (*CPP, Art. 115*).

(iii) Subsequent questioning of the accused

If the accused exercises his right to legal advice at the first appearance before the *juge d'instruction*, it is during subsequent appearances that the substantive questioning of the accused will occur. The *juge d'instruction* may question the accused as many times during *instruction* as he thinks fit. Questioning may take a number of forms, including asking the accused to comment on the statements of the witnesses and other evidence (but only where communicated in advance to the accused's *avocat*), or the confrontation of the accused with witnesses, his co-accused or the *partie civile*. The *juge d'instruction* may also hold a reconstruction of the crime. Questioning takes place under the control of the *juge d'instruction*. The *procureur de la République* (who is entitled to be present at all *interrogatoires; CPP, Art. 119*) and the accused's *avocat* (also entitled to be present, and who will have prior access to the file) are permitted to ask questions only with the authorisation of the *juge d'instruction* (*CPP, Art. 120*). Because of the right of silence, the accused is not obliged to make a statement or respond to the questions put to him. Depositions (*procès-verbaux*) of the statements and responses to questions thus obtained will be signed by the accused, other individuals who have given evidence, and the *juge d'instruction* (*CPP, Arts. 106, 121*).

It should be noted that the *partie civile*, like the accused, does not give evidence under oath, and is similarly entitled to be questioned by the *juge d'instruction* (or confronted with the accused or witnesses) only in the presence of his *avocat*; this right may be renounced (*CPP, Art. 118*). The *avocat* of the *partie civile* will therefore participate in any confrontation between his client and the accused, and may ask questions with the consent of the *juge d'instruction*.

(c) Judicial supervision pending trial (contrôle judiciaire)

At the end of the first appearance of the accused before the *juge d'instruction*, the *juge d'instruction* will have to decide whether to allow the accused to remain at liberty during *instruction*, or to impose on him a judicial supervision order or an order for detention pending trial (see below). Article 137 of the *CPP* lays down the general principle that the accused should remain at liberty during *instruction*. The accused should not be subject to a judicial supervision order (*ordonnance de contrôle judiciaire*) unless this is required by the "necessities of instruction" or as a security measure (eg where he is likely to commit further offences) and the offence for which he is charged is at least a *délit* carrying a sentence of imprisonment (*CPP, Art. 138*).

If the *juge d'instruction*, either on his own initiative or following a request from the *ministère public*, issues an *ordonnance de contrôle judiciaire*, which he is empowered to do without the need either to hold a hearing or to specify the reasons for his decision, the accused will suffer one or more restrictions on his movements and social relationships (similar to bail conditions) for the duration of *instruction*. No appeal generally lies against the imposition or the terms of judicial control (although see below).

Usual conditions include (*CPP, Art. 138*) a curfew, the duty to remain within a particular locality, to report periodically to designated authorities (such as the police), to hand over a passport or driving licence, to refrain from consorting with certain named persons or carrying out certain named professional or social activities, and even to submit to medical examination and treatment (especially detoxification treatment). In addition, the accused may be required to pay bail money (*cautionnement; CPP, Art. 142*) firstly as a guarantee to ensure due compliance with the requirements of *instruction*, and secondly to cover any eventual liabilities (such as costs, fines and the award of damages to the *partie civile*). There is no system of sureties. Any of these terms may be varied, or indeed a judicial supervision order may be brought to an end at any time during *instruction* by the *juge d'instruction*, either on his own initiative, or on the request of the accused or the *procureur de la République* (*CPP, Arts. 139, 140*). The accused may appeal to the *chambre d'accusation* against a refusal to bring judicial supervision to an end (*CPP, Art. 186(1)*).

Where the accused fails to abide by the conditions of the supervision order, the *juge d'instruction* may remand him in custody (by issuing a *mandat d'arrêt* or a *mandat de dépôt*), whatever the maximum penalty the offence carries (*CPP, Art. 141–2*), although a hearing under *CPP, Art. 145* will have to be held (see below).

A judicial supervision order in respect of an accused charged with a *crime* continues until trial (*CPP, Art. 181*), but in respect of a *délit* will end with the closing of *instruction* unless (*CPP, Art. 179*) an order for its continuation is made by the *juge d'instruction*; this must be reasoned.

(d) Detention pending trial: détention provisoire

(i) Conditions

An order by the *juge d'instruction* for the accused to be detained pending trial (*ordonnance de détention provisoire*) is an exceptional measure which should be used only where justified by the necessities of *instruction* or as a security measure (*CPP, Art. 137*). In particular, it is available (*CPP, Art. 144*; TEXTS, NO. 28) only in respect of serious offences, ie *crimes*, or *délits* carrying a maximum penalty of at least two years' imprisonment (one year if a *délit flagrant*), where the imposition of a judicial supervision order would be insufficient and where one of the following conditions is met: (i) where pre-trial detention is the only means of retaining evidence or preventing interference with witnesses (or victims) or preventing "fraudulent manoeuvres" by the accused and accomplices; (ii) where pre-trial detention is necessary to preserve public order, to protect the accused, to prevent the recurrence of the offence, or to ensure the availability of the accused whilst proceedings are continuing; (iii) where the accused has failed to honour the conditions of a judicial supervision order, whatever the potential severity of the sentence (*CPP, Arts. 144, 141–2*).

(ii) Procedure

An order for detention pending trial can only be made (*CPP, Art. 145*) by the *juge d'instruction* after the holding of a hearing which is *contradictoire* in nature; ie both the *ministère public* and the accused are entitled to put their case to the *juge d'instruction*. The accused must be informed of his right to be present and to have access to an *avocat*. Indeed, he may insist on having the hearing deferred (for a maximum of five days) in order to consult his *avocat* and prepare his case; in such circumstances the accused will be detained in custody pending the hearing. At the hearing – which normally takes place in the chambers of the *juge d'instruction* – the *ministère public*, the accused and the latter's *avocat* may address the *juge d'instruction*.

Where a detention order is made, it must specify the matters of fact and law upon which is it based (with particular reference to the conditions set out in *CPP, Art. 144*; see *Crim., 24.6.1971, Bereni, D.1971, 546;* TEXTS, NO. 29). It is implemented by means of a *mandat de dépôt*. The accused (*CPP, Art. 186*) as well as the *ministère public* (*CPP, Art. 185*; TEXTS, NO. 15) may appeal against the decision of the *juge d'instruction* to the *chambre d'accusation*.

(iii) Duration

The maximum permitted duration of pre-trial detention is four months in the case of a *délit* and one year for a *crime* (*CPP, Arts. 145–1, 145–2*). These periods can be extended. For *crimes*, detention for further periods of one year, without upper limit, can be ordered, provided that for each period of one year a hearing is held by the *juge d'instruction*.

For *délits*, the position is that the initial four-month detention can be extended by one two-month period (ie a total of six months' detention) by the *juge* after receiving written evidence from the *ministère public* and the accused. However, where the accused has in the past been convicted of a serious offence (*CPP, Art. 145–1*) and the maximum penalty for the offence for which he is currently charged exceeds five years' imprisonment, detention can be ordered for successive periods of four months, on an examination of the parties' written evidence, up to a maximum of one year's detention, which may "exceptionally" be extended by four-month periods without limit on condition that a full hearing takes place in respect of each four-month extension beyond the initial year (*CPP, Art. 145–1*). Where the accused has been guilty of a serious offence, but does not risk imprisonment exceeding five years, the latter procedure applies but with a ceiling of two years' detention (*CPP, Art. 145–1*).

An accused on remand is detained (*CPP, Art. 714*) in a remand centre within the local prison (*maison d'arrêt*) and is entitled to certain privileges such as, where possible, the single occupancy of a cell and advantageous visiting and communication rights (*CPP, Art. 716*).

(iv) Release from detention (la mise en liberté)

There are a variety of ways in which the accused may regain his liberty before trial. It may firstly happen on the initiative of the *juge d'instruction* himself (having taken the advice of the *procureur de la République*), that of the *procureur de la République* (*CPP, Art. 147*) or even on the initiative of the *chambre d'accusation* (in respect of any case referred to it; *CPP, Art. 201(2)*). A judicial supervision order can be imposed in place of detention.

Secondly, under *CPP, Art. 148*, the accused (or his *avocat*) is entitled at any time to apply to the *juge d'instruction* for release from detention. The *juge d'instruction* will seek the written representations of the *ministère public* and the *partie civile*, and give a reasoned decision on the basis of these representations. This he must do within five days of transmitting the accused's request to the *ministère public*, failing which the accused may apply for release directly to the *chambre d'accusation*; the *chambre d'accusation* must give a reasoned decision within twenty days, otherwise the accused will automatically be released unconditionally. Appeal against the decision of the *juge d'instruction* by the accused or the *ministère public* (although in the latter case the accused will be granted his freedom pending appeal) lies to the *chambre d'accusation*. At the appeal the accused may insist on being heard by the court; the court has only fifteen days (twenty where the accused appears in person; *CPP, Art. 199(5)*) within which to make its decision *(CPP, Art. 194(2))*, otherwise automatic release follows.

Thirdly, a direct application may be made by the accused to the *chambre d'accusation* under *CPP, Art. 148–4* where more than four months have elapsed since an order for detention was made, and the *juge d'instruction* has not recalled the accused for a hearing to authorise continued detention.

The bringing to an end of the *instruction* phase by the *juge d'instruction* (by the issue of an *ordonnance de clôture*) also signals, in principle, the end of *détention provisoire* in respect of *délits* *(CPP, Art. 179)* although it is possible for an extension to be ordered by the *juge d'instruction* (by reasoned decision) until trial by the *Tribunal Correctionnel*, but only for a maximum period of two months *(CPP, Art. 179)*. In the case of a *crime*, detention continues into the second phase of *instruction* by the *chambre d'accusation* *(CPP, Art. 181)*.

After the end of *instruction* the accused may apply *(CPP, Arts. 148–1, 148–2)* for release at any time to the appropriate trial court (in the case of a *crime*, the *chambre d'accusation* rather than the *Cour d'Assises* until the latter is seized of the matter), which will make its decision (within ten days if a first instance court, twenty if an appeal court) after hearing both the accused and the *ministère public*. When the matter goes for trial, the trial court is empowered to order detention during the proceedings where justified as a security measure *(CPP, Arts. 215–1, 464–1, 465)*.

Time served during pre-trial detention (including detention under a *mandat d'arrêt* or a *mandat d'amener*) counts towards any eventual sentence *(Code Pénal, Art. 24)*. If the accused is detained pending trial and subsequently either the *juge d'instruction* determines that there is no case to answer *(ordonnance de non-lieu)* or the accused is found not guilty by the trial court (known as an *acquittement* in a jury trial in the *Cour d'Assises* and a *relaxe* in other trials), compensation is payable by the state *(CPP, Arts. 149, 150)* where the detention caused the detainee loss which is "manifestly abnormal and of particular gravity". Claims for such compensation must be addressed within six months of the acquittal to a special commission of three judges of the *Cour de Cassation* against whose decision no appeal is possible. The state may in its turn obtain an indemnity from an informant who acted in bad faith or a false witness where the actions of these provoked the remand in custody or increased its duration *(CPP, Art. 150)*. In 1990 compensation was granted in 34 cases, with an average award of 32,800 FF.

On 1 June 1992 there were 21,939 persons in *détention provisoire*.

4. Questioning of witnesses

The *juge d'instruction* is granted by *CPP, Art. 101* a wide power, including force if necessary, to require to appear before him to give evidence any person whose evidence appears to him to be useful. Certain professions, such as the medical and legal professions, cannot be compelled to give evidence in breach of professional confidence (*CPP, Art. 109; Code Pénal, Art. 378*). Failure to give evidence constitutes an offence (*CPP, Arts. 109, 111*). The evidence of witnesses is given either to the *juge d'instruction* or to a judicial police officer acting on *commission rogatoire*; normally, this is done neither in the presence of other witnesses nor the accused (*CPP, Art. 102*), although *confrontations* are possible.

The witness, before giving evidence, takes an oath (which may be religious in nature if he so wishes) to tell the whole truth and nothing but the truth (*CPP, Art. 103*). The resulting deposition is duly signed by the witness. It should be noted that because of the inquisitorial nature of French criminal procedure, witnesses are permitted to give evidence which to a British lawyer might be regarded as hearsay evidence, and also evidence as to the character of the accused or his past record. Witnesses should not, however, give evidence as to their opinions or deductions on the facts, especially in respect of the culpability of the accused.

5. Factual investigations

(a) Investigation by the juge d'instruction

As has been seen, much of the investigative work is carried out by the police during the *enquête de police*. However, the *juge d'instruction* is granted (*CPP, Art. 81*) wide powers to carry out all investigations which "he judges to be useful to the revelation of the truth", either personally or by delegation to judicial police officers. The type of factual investigation that the *juge* carries out personally includes visiting the scene of the crime (*transport sur les lieux; CPP, Art. 92*) in the presence of a clerk (*greffier*) and the *procureur de la République* (if the latter so desires), where he will interview witnesses and suspects, perhaps effect a search and even hold a reconstruction of the offence. A report (*procès-verbal*) of the visit is drafted.

(b) Delegation of powers; commissions rogatoires

The *juge d'instruction* is permitted, by means of a *commission rogatoire* (*CPP, Arts. 81* (TEXTS, NO. 20), *151* (TEXTS, NO. 30), *152*), to delegate his investigative powers to an agent, who may be a judge, another *juge d'instruction* or a judicial police officer, where it is not possible for the *juge d'instruction* to exercise his powers himself. A delegation may be in respect of a specific task, or general (although it should not be too wide). The power of the *juge d'instruction* to issue warrants (*mandats*), to make judicial orders (*ordonnances*) and to order expert reports cannot be delegated; nor can the power to question the accused or the confrontation of the accused with witnesses be delegated except to a *juge*.

Witnesses are required to give evidence to the agent, but can be forced to do so only by the delegating *juge d'instruction* (*CPP, Art. 153*). However, a police officer acting as agent is empowered to detain a person in custody (by way of *garde à vue*) for up to 24 hours by reason of "the necessities of the execution of the *commission rogatoire*" (*CPP, Art. 154*); detention for a further period of 24 hours may be permitted by the *juge d'instruction* after interviewing the person concerned. When the agent has completed his task (eg interviewing a witness), a written report will be submitted to the *juge d'instruction* (*CPP, Art. 154*), who will check that it has been properly carried out (*CPP, Art. 81(5)*); if he is not satisfied, he will require the task to be redone, or he will do it himself. The *chambre d'accusation* controls the use of *commissions rogatoires* by the *juge d'instruction* (*CPP, Art. 220*).

(c) Powers of search (perquisitions) and seizure (saisies)

The *juge d'instruction* may (*CPP, Arts. 94, 95*) effect a search (either personally or by delegation to his agent) of "any place where objects are to be found the discovery of which would be useful to the revelation of the truth". Such searches must take place between 6.00 am and 9.00 pm and, in the case of a search of residential premises, must be carried out in the presence of the occupier, two members of his family, or two witnesses (*CPP, Arts. 95, 96*). Breach of these rules will render the search illegal (*CPP, Arts. 95, 96, 57, 59*). When executing a search, the *juge d'instruction* (or his agent) must (*CPP, Art. 96(3)*) take all measures to ensure respect for professional secrets (ie those of lawyers and doctors) and the accused's rights of defence. The provisions of *CPP, Art. 56–1* (above), requiring a search of the premises of an *avocat* to be conducted by the *juge d'instruction* in the presence of the *bâtonnier*, are applicable. Professionally privileged documents (such as those passing between an accused and his *avocat*) cannot be seized.

When a search is for documents, the *juge d'instruction* (or his agent) is entitled to examine the documents that are found with a view to determining whether to effect a seizure (*CPP, Art. 97*); any unauthorised divulgence of their contents carries a criminal sanction (*CPP, Art. 98*). A power of seizure exists in respect of any articles or documents found during the search which appear to the *juge d'instruction* or his agent to be useful for revealing the truth (*CPP, Art. 97*), and includes articles over which third parties have rights. The power of seizure applies only to articles relevant to the offence in respect of which *instruction* has been commenced. A written report (*procès-verbal*) of the results of a search and seizure is drawn up. The accused and other interested parties may apply to the *juge d'instruction* at any time during *instruction* for the seized articles to be returned (*CPP, Art. 99*), or to the trial court thereafter.

6. Expert investigations

The *juge d'instruction* (also the *chambre d'accusation*, and the trial court) has power (*CPP, Art. 156*) to order a report from an expert witness on specified questions of a technical nature, either on his own initiative, or on the request of any of the parties. More than one expert will be instructed where this is "justified by the circumstances" (*CPP, Art. 159*); this may be requested by the parties. A refusal to appoint an expert, or more than one, may be appealed to the *chambre d'accusation*. Until a 1985 reform, two experts were automatically appointed where the matter to be investigated was fundamental to the case. The courts keep a list of recognised experts in different fields, although non-listed experts can be used if reasons are given (*CPP, Art. 157*).

The expert conducts his investigation under the control of and in liaison with the *juge d'instruction* (*CPP, Arts. 156, 161*). The expert investigation may include, where appropriate, the interviewing of witnesses and the accused, although the latter in such a case is entitled to the presence of his *avocat* and the *juge d'instruction* (*CPP, Art. 164*). In respect of *crimes* it is usual to appoint a medical practitioner to carry out a psychiatric examination of the accused; such examination takes place without the *juge d'instruction* or defence *avocat* being present. The parties may request the *juge d'instruction* to require the expert to examine certain facts or interview named individuals able to provide technical information (*CPP, Art. 165*).

The expert must report to the *juge d'instruction* within a period set down by the *juge d'instruction*, failing which he may be replaced (*CPP, Art. 161*). The report is transmitted to the parties by the *juge d'instruction* (*CPP, Art. 167*), who sets down a time limit within which they should make their observations and, if they wish, for lodging a request for a further expert opinion to be obtained. A decision by the *juge d'instruction* not to accede to this latter request must be reasoned, and can be appealed. The expert subsequently presents his findings in person to the trial court and may participate in the ensuing debate (*CPP, Art. 168*). It is for the court to determine the weight to be given to the expert evidence. The expert witness has the status of any other witness. In practice, however, the court is likely to accord a good deal of weight to the evidence. Psychiatric reports on the accused are often challenged at the *Cour d'Assises* by the accused's *avocat*.

7. Investigation of the background of the accused (l'enquête de personnalité)

As has been seen, the role of the *juge d'instruction* is to carry out any inquiries useful for revealing the truth (*CPP, Art. 81*). This article specifically provides for an inquiry (by the *juge* or more usually the police and the probation service as his agents) into the personality of the accused, and his material, family and social position. Such an inquiry (*l'enquête de personnalité*) is obligatory in the case of *crimes*, but discretionary for lesser offences. It should be noted that by *CPP, Art. 41(5)*, where the accused is under 21 years old, the *procureur de la République* will order an *enquête rapide* into the accused's material, family and social background; such an *enquête* is particularly useful in determining whether or not the accused should be detained pending trial.

The purpose of the *enquête de personnalité* is to enable the court to impose the appropriate sentence, should the accused in due course be found guilty. This is confirmed by *CPP, Art. D.16* (TEXTS, NO. 31) which provides that the purpose of the *dossier de personnalité* is to provide the judicial authorities with objective information on the accused's past and present mode of life; the article goes on to state categorically that it cannot be used as a means of proof of culpability. However, the information contained in the dossier, and in particular the accused's past criminal record, will be before the *juge d'instruction* when he makes his recommendations as to whether to send the accused to trial, and indeed before the trial court when determining guilt (see below). Moreover, the jurors in the *Cour d'Assises* are likely to be aware of the accused's previous convictions; although they do not have before them the written *dossier de personnalité*, the accused's background, including his previous convictions, will be discussed when the accused is being examined by the president of the court or by the *ministère public*. A medical or psychological examination may also be ordered by the *juge d'instruction*, on his own initiative, or at the request of the accused. A psychological examination is usually undertaken in the case of *crimes*.

8. Termination of instruction; ordonnances de clôture

Instruction is brought to an end when the *juge d'instruction* thinks fit. He will issue (*CPP, Art. 175*) an *ordonnance de soit-communiqué* sending the file to the *procureur de la République* for the latter to make his *réquisitions* within one month (or three months if the accused is not in custody). The *juge d'instruction* will then make his final decision on whether or not to send the matter for trial. He will issue one of the *ordonnances de règlement* (or *de clôture*) which will set out the facts, and the reasons for his decision. If he is of the opinion that the facts do not constitute an offence, or that the author of the offence is unknown, or that there is insufficient evidence against the accused, the charges will be dropped by an *ordonnance de non-lieu* (*CPP, Art. 177*). Where dropped on the grounds of law (eg the limitation period has expired, or the accused is found to be legally not responsible for his actions (eg insanity)), the matter cannot be raised again. However, where the case is dropped on the facts, new charges may be brought by the *ministère public* (by a *réquisitoire à fin de reprise; CPP, Art. 190*) against the accused where fresh evidence comes to light which strengthens the case against the accused or throws new light on the facts originally investigated (*CPP, Art. 189*). Fresh charges can however be brought only within the limitation period.

Where, on the other hand, the *juge d'instruction* decides that the facts investigated constitute an offence, he will issue an *ordonnance de renvoi*, sending the case to the appropriate trial court and passing the file to the *procureur de la République* (*CPP, Arts. 178, 179, 180*), or in respect of a *crime* an *ordonnance de transmission des pièces* which results in the sending of the file to the *procureur de la République* and then on to the *chambre d'accusation* for a second level of *instruction* to be held (*CPP, Art. 181*). The *procureur de la République* has the right to appeal against any *ordonnance* of the *juge d'instruction*, including an *ordonnance de non-lieu* (*CPP, Art. 185*; TEXTS, NO. 15). Appeal is to the *chambre d'accusation*. The accused, on the other hand, has no right of appeal against any of the *ordonnances de clôture*; the *partie civile* may for his part appeal against an *ordonnance de non-lieu* (*CPP, Art. 186*).

9. The chambre d'accusation of the Cour d'Appel

(a) Control of the activities of the juge d'instruction by the chambre d'accusation

(i) Introduction

The *chambre d'accusation* of the *Cour d'Appel*, in addition to undertaking a second level of *instruction* into *crimes* (see below), is given the task of controlling the exercise of powers by the *juge d'instruction*. Control is necessary because of the wide-ranging powers enjoyed by *juges d'instruction*. It takes several forms.

(ii) Appeal against ordonnances

We have noted above the wide-ranging rights of appeal that the *ministère public* has against the *ordonnances* of the *juge d'instruction* and the more restricted rights of appeal of the *partie civile*. As for the accused, he has no right to appeal against the *ordonnances de clôture* of the *juge* which terminate *instruction*. He can however appeal against the so-called *ordonnances juridictionnelles*, such as those relating to the *constitution de partie civile*. He may also apply for the ending of judicial supervision or detention pending trial. Appeals by the *procureur de la République* must be lodged within five days of notification of the *ordonnance*, and by the other parties within ten days. In principle, on an appeal of this type, the *chambre d'accusation* will rule solely on the matter of the *ordonnance*, and will not exercise its wider powers of *révision* of *instruction* (see below).

(iii) Control of legality (régularité)

As has been seen in some detail earlier in this chapter, the *chambre d'accusation* is empowered (*CPP, Art. 206*; TEXTS, NO. 8) to rule on the "regularity" of the various *actes d'instruction* carried out by the *juge d'instruction*. These, it will be recalled, may be annulled where statute expressly provides (*nullité textuelle*), or where there is a breach of "substantial formality" (*nullité substantielle*). Annulment is limited to cases where "the irregularity has the effect of injuring the interests of the party concerned" (*CPP, Art. 802*; TEXTS, NO. 7); see above.

The issue of the legality of an *acte d'instruction* may be brought up by the *chambre d'accusation* itself when a case comes before it (*CPP, Art. 206*), or by the *juge d'instruction* on his own initiative, or by the *procureur de la République* (*CPP, Art. 171*). There is, however, no statutory right for the accused or the *partie civile* to seize the *chambre d'accusation* for annulment; all they may do is petition the *juge d'instruction* or the *procureur de la République* to do so, or in due course ask the trial court to refer the matter. A further watering-down of the rights of the accused is to be found in *CPP, Arts. 170(2), 172*: the former provides that the accused who formally renounces his right to legal representation during questioning will not subsequently be able to argue that any confession he makes is void through want of formality; the latter provides that the parties may expressly renounce their right to press for the annulment of any irregular procedures where annulment would be in their sole interest (although renunciation is not possible in respect of the breach of a rule *d'ordre public* (see above)). It must be asked whether these statutory provisions risk encouraging pressure to be put on the accused not to take full advantage of the annulment procedures designed to protect his interests. It could however be argued that in the light of the many grounds for the annulment of *actes d'instruction* recognised by the *CPP*, criminal procedure would be unduly slowed down unless limits are put on the right of review.

(iv) Power of revision

In addition to the powers we have just examined, the *chambre d'accusation* has an inherent right of control of *instruction* once a case has been referred to it. In effect, it can check that the *juge d'instruction* has carried out his task properly. It may thus (*CPP, Arts. 201, 205*) require the holding of additional inquiries (*un supplément d'information*) such as re-interviewing certain witnesses, or obtaining an expert report on a particular question of fact. It may also require the bringing of further charges against the accused, or fresh charges against those who have not yet been charged (*CPP, Arts. 202, 204*).

(b) Second level instruction in respect of crimes

By *CPP, Art. 181*, where the *juge d'instruction* decides to send the accused for trial in respect of a *crime*, the matter must be sent to the *chambre d'accusation* for the carrying out of a second level of *instruction*. The *chambre* may order any additional measures of *instruction* that it considers appropriate. It may decide that the charges should be dropped (*arrêt de non-lieu; CPP, Art. 212*), or that the facts justify charging the accused only with a *contravention* or *délit* (*CPP, Art. 213*). If it decides that the matter should be sent for trial to the *Cour d'Assises*, it will issue a reasoned *arrêt de mise en accusation* (*CPP, Art. 215*). Appeal lies on a point of law only (ie *pourvoi en cassation*), against the *arrêts* of the *chambre d'accusation* (including an *arrêt de non-lieu*), to the *Cour de Cassation* (*CPP, Art. 567*). All parties enjoy this right of appeal *en cassation*, although the accused cannot usually appeal in this way against a decision of the *chambre d'accusation* to send him for trial for a *contravention* (to the *Tribunal de Police*) or for a *délit* (to the *Tribunal Correctionnel; CPP, Art. 574*).

E. Trial

1. Characteristics

It is at the trial stage that French criminal procedure displays the fewest inquisitorial traits, being public rather than secret, oral rather than written, and accusatorial (*contradictoire*) in the sense that the parties will usually be present in person, and each witness may be questioned by all parties, although this takes place under the control of the president of the court, and there is no cross-examination as such. The hearing must be public (*CPP, Arts. 306, 400, 535*), except where secrecy is justified by public order or morality, and in the case of juvenile and certain sexual offences. It is generally permissible to publish reports of trial proceedings as long as these are accurate and published in good faith; however there are exceptions, such as juvenile cases, and matters involving state security.

Witnesses give their evidence under oath and orally, although the president may permit them to refer to written documents (*CPP, Arts.*

331, 452); however, it is possible for the written evidence of a witness to be received where the witness fails to attend in person. The jury in a trial at the *Cour d'Assises* is not normally given copies of the depositions of witnesses obtained during *instruction*; nor is the jury given expert reports.

Generally the accused must appear personally (*CPP, Arts. 320, 410, 544*) at his trial, to ensure that the proceedings are *contradictoire*. However, if charged with a *délit* punishable with no more than two years' imprisonment or a *contravention* carrying only a fine, he may request to be tried in his absence, although his *avocat* must be present; however, the court may insist on his presence in respect of a *délit* (*CPP, Arts. 411, 544*).

If the accused fails to attend the hearing or to instruct an *avocat* to represent him, he can be judged in his absence (*CPP, Arts. 410, 544, 627–641*; this is known as *jugement par défaut* or, in the *Cour d'Assises, jugement par contumace*). It is possible for the matter to be subsequently reopened; in respect of *crimes* this is by a procedure known as *purge de contumace*; in respect of *délits* and *contraventions* it is by the appeal procedure of *opposition* (see below).

2. Trial procedure

The president of the court is in control of procedure, and thus has a discretion as to the order in which evidence is heard. Usually, the trial will start with the president confirming the identity of the accused (*CPP, Arts. 294, 406*) and proceeding to receive his evidence and to examine him (*CPP, Arts. 328, 442*). The accused does not take the oath; nor does he plead to the charge. In questioning the accused, the president may refer to admissions or statements made by the accused during the *enquête de police* or *instruction*. Indeed, questions may be put which will reveal the accused's background and past criminal record (in practice this often emerges when the accused is being questioned by the *ministère public*). The president must not, however, reveal during the questioning his opinion on guilt (which he will, of course, have had the opportunity of formulating from reading the file before the trial commences).

The accused is entitled to remain silent and to refuse to make a declaration or answer questions, but the court can draw its own conclusions from this silence, because of the principle of liberty of means of proof. Questions can be put to the accused by the *ministère public, avocats* for the accused and the *partie civile* and, in a jury trial, by jurors (as long as the jurors do not thereby reveal their views on culpability; *CPP, Art. 311*). However, all such questioning is done by permission of the president who is in control of the procedure, rather than it being truly accusatorial (*CPP, Arts. 309, 311, 312* (TEXTS, NO. 32), *401*). He may permit the questioner to ask questions directly, or do so himself; it is normal for the *ministère public* and the *avocats* to be permitted to question the accused (and witnesses) directly. The president will disallow any questions which "compromise the dignity of the proceedings or prolong them without there being reason to believe that they will lead to greater certainty in the result" (*CPP, Art. 309*).

After the accused has been heard, the witnesses (who can be compelled to give evidence; *CPP, Arts. 326, 439*) will be called (they remain outside the courtroom until they give their evidence). They give their evidence on oath (*CPP, Arts. 331, 446*). This evidence, which is delivered orally (although reference to documents may be permitted; eg *CPP, Art. 452*), may relate "only to the facts in respect of which the accused is charged, or to his personality or morality" (*CPP, Art. 331*). The witness will then be questioned by the president (including questions on earlier depositions) and then by the *ministère public*, the parties' *avocats* and jurors (in a jury trial), again under the control of the president (*CPP, Arts. 311, 312, 332, 454*). The accused and witnesses can be confronted with real evidence and their observations noted (*CPP, Arts. 341, 455*); indeed, witnesses may be confronted with each other, or with the accused (*CPP, Arts. 338, 454*).

Expert witnesses are then examined on oath in a similar fashion; they may refer to their reports (*CPP, Art. 168*). The court will also examine the real evidence and the depositions. A jury trial, however, is essentially oral, and therefore the jury is not entitled to see the depositions of witnesses and experts who give evidence at trial (or of confrontations between the accused and witnesses) at least until after they have given evidence in court; this, however, is rarely done, the jurors usually relying on the evidence given orally. Other written evidence, such as depositions of witnesses who are not going to be produced in court, may be disclosed to the jury. If the court is of the opinion that certain matters require further clarification, the court may require further investigations to be carried out (*un supplément d'information; CPP, Arts. 283, 463*) before reaching a verdict.

The lawyers then make their oral representations (*plaidoiries* of the *avocats* or *réquisitoire* of the *ministère public*). They may also submit written representations (*conclusions* of the *avocats*, or *réquisitoire* of the *ministère public*); this is often done in the *Tribunal Correctionnel* (*CPP, Arts. 346, 458, 459, 460*). The representations are made in the following order: first, the *avocat* for the *partie civile*, then the *ministère public*, and finally the *avocat* for the accused. The *avocat* for the *partie civile* and the *ministère public* are then entitled to respond to the arguments of the defence, but the defence always has the last word.

The court will reach its verdict (either *ex tempore* or after retiring for consideration) and determine sentence. Decisions of the *Tribunal Correctionnel*, if not unanimous, can be by a majority of two of the three judges; the judgment must be reasoned (*CPP, Art. 485;* TEXTS, NO.

4). The verdict is read out in open court (*CPP, Arts. 366, 400*). Where the accused is found guilty, he will be liable for costs (see Chapter 3) (*CPP, Arts. 366, 473, 543*).

3. Modified trial procedure in the Cour d'Assises

At the *Cour d'Assises* there is a pre-trial hearing (*CPP, Arts. 272–277*) at least five days before the trial, at which the president of the court interviews the accused, confirms his identity, ensures that he understands the nature of the charges against him and the procedure, and that he is represented by an *avocat* (which is obligatory in the *Cour d'Assises; CPP, Art. 317*); if he has no *avocat*, one will be assigned to his case (*CPP, Art. 274*). The accused is given a copy of the dossier of witness and expert evidence against him (*CPP, Art. 279*). The *partie civile* and the *ministère public* must give at least 24 hours' notice before proceedings commence of the witnesses (and experts, in the case of the *ministère public*) whom they intend to call, failing which the accused may object to their being called. At this stage the president can, if he thinks it necessary, order further *instruction* to be carried out (*CPP, Art. 283*).

The procedure for the selection and empanelling of the jury of nine has been examined above.

At the commencement of the trial, the clerk (*greffier*) reads out the charges (*arrêt de renvoi; CPP, Art. 327*). During a trial in the *Cour d'Assises*, the president has a wide discretionary power to "take all measures which he believes to be useful for the discovery of the truth" (*CPP, Art. 310*). To this end he may call any person to give evidence, even where this may not be given under oath (including evidence given by close relatives of the accused who under *CPP, Art. 335* may not give evidence on oath against the accused). He may also order the production of any piece of evidence (such as the taking of fingerprints) even if such evidence has not been disclosed to the accused before trial. This power is very wide, the judge being entitled to take, without having to give reasons, any measures which are not contrary to the provisions of the law. It is regarded as justified on the grounds that once the hearing of the *Cour d'Assises* has commenced, it may not be discontinued until a verdict is reached (*CPP, Art. 307*), and it is thus impracticable thereafter for additional investigations (*suppléments d'instruction*) to be carried out (these usually being ordered, where appropriate, by the president before the hearing commences); hence the need for a wide discretion to be recognised in favour of the president if the "search for the truth" is not to be compromised.

The president does not sum up to the jury as such (*CPP, Art. 347*); there is no need, as he will be retiring with the jury. He does, however, set out the questions of fact which the court should answer to determine culpability. He also reads out to the jury the wording of *CPP, Art. 353*

(TEXTS, NO. 3) describing the degree of proof required for conviction (the principle of *intime conviction*; see above). The jury of nine then retires with the three judges to deliberate. A written, secret vote (*CPP, Arts. 356–358*) is taken on the issue of culpability (and, where appropriate, aggravating circumstances). At least eight of the twelve members of the court must agree for a conviction to be returned; if the voting is seven for and five against conviction, the accused will be found not guilty. Once culpability has been determined, the court and the jury immediately turn their attention to the issue of sentence, their decisions being made on the basis of a simple majority vote (ie seven from twelve; *CPP, Art. 362*). The court then deals with the civil claim of the *partie civile*; the decision is taken by the three judges alone sitting without the jury. The court may receive the parties' observations before reaching its decision on the civil claim (*CPP, Art. 371*).

4. Simplified trial procedure in the Tribunal de Police

By *CPP, Art. 524*, the *ministère public* may decide to deal with a *contravention* by means of a simplified procedure, that of *l'ordonnance pénale*. The case will be referred to the judge of the *Tribunal de Police*; he may decide that the matter should be tried in the normal way, or that the offence warrants a penalty greater than a fine, but if not, he will there and then determine culpability on an examination of the papers, without the accused appearing or being represented. The maximum penalty that may be imposed is a fine. The decision (*une ordonnance pénale*) does not have to be reasoned. The convicted party may within thirty days apply for the case to be tried according to normal trial procedure (*CPP, Art. 527*).

There is also a scheme of "on the spot" payment of set fines (*amendes forfaitaires*) for certain traffic offences under *CPP, Art. 529*; these are payable either there and then or within thirty days. The accused may, alternatively, decide to contest the matter, again within thirty days, in which case proceedings will be commenced against him. Offenders are encouraged to pay their fines "on the spot" by the fact that if they do so, they are given a 30 per cent "discount".

F. Voies de recours; appeals

1. Introduction

We have already examined appeals against the various *actes d'instruction*. In this section we concentrate on the different types of substantive appeal, of which there are several. Firstly there is *appel*, which in effect is appeal on a point of law or fact, in respect of conviction and sentence from decisions of the *Tribunal de Police* and *Tribunal Correctionnel*, to the regional *Cour d'Appel* which will retry the case. It should be noted that no such appeal lies from a decision of the *Cour d'Assises* – the only recourse is appeal on a point of law (*pourvoi en cassation*) to the *Cour de Cassation*. Secondly there is the procedure of *opposition*, which is available in certain cases where judgment was reached in default; the case will be re-examined by the trial court. Thirdly there is an appeal on a point of law (*pourvoi en cassation*) to the *Cour de Cassation*, requesting the quashing (*cassation*) of a decision. Finally, it is possible for a case to be reopened when, for example, fresh evidence is unearthed; such appeals, known as *pourvois en révision*, are heard by the *Cour de Cassation*.

2. Appel

Appel lies to the *Cour d'Appel* against a judgment of the *Tribunal de Police* (*CPP, Art. 546*) in respect of offences for which the maximum sentence exceeds five days' imprisonment or a fine of 1300 FF, or where the sentence imposed was one of imprisonment, or where damages were awarded to the *partie civile*. *Appel* also lies to the *Cour d'Appel* from decisions of the *Tribunal Correctionnel* (*CPP, Arts. 496, 497*). Appeal may be on the facts or on a point of law (*CPP, Arts. 516, 520*). The offender and the *partie civile* have ten days within which to appeal, the *ministère public* two months (*CPP, Art. 498*). Appeal is possible by the prosecution against a finding of not guilty or against sentence (the *Cour d'Appel* in such a case being able on appeal to find the acquitted accused guilty or, where he has been convicted, to increase sentence; *CPP, Art. 515*). Appeal by the *partie civile* lies against a refusal to award him damages or against the amount of damages (which cannot be reduced on appeal). The person who has been convicted may appeal in respect of either culpability or sentence, and also against the award of damages to the *partie civile*; the danger for him in appealing is that if he does so, the *ministère public* is likely to enter a counter-appeal, in which case the *Cour d'Appel* may increase the sentence on appeal.

The *CPP* recognises no separate right of appeal against sentence, an appeal generally being against the entirety of the judgment. If, however, the appellant expressly limits his appeal to certain aspects of the decision of the lower court, the *Cour d'Appel* may limit its re-examination to these aspects. When the offender appeals, his sentence may not be increased on appeal (nor may the award in favour of the *partie civile* be increased); sentence may, however, be increased if the counter-appeal is made by the *ministère public*.

On appeal the *Cour d'Appel* (more precisely the *chambre des appels correctionnels* of the *Cour d'Appel*, comprising three judges) retries the case following a modified form of the procedure of the *Tribunal Correctionnel*. An oral report will be made by a reporting judge, and the defendant will be examined. The court has a discretion as to which witnesses to examine; it may choose simply to rely on the evidence given by a witness at the first instance trial (*CPP, Arts. 512, 513, 547*). The court has a discretion to hear evidence from witnesses who did not appear at the first instance trial where this may provide further information for the court. It may even order further investigations (*un supplément d'information*) to be carried out by one of its number, which may lead to fresh evidence being obtained. The parties may also introduce new arguments (*moyens*) in favour of their case (*Crim., 20.10.1986; Bull. crim., 291*). Where the appeal is rejected, the appellant (other than the *ministère public*) will be liable for the costs (*dépens*; see Chapter 3) of the appeal (*CPP, Art. 514*).

3. Opposition

This is a procedure available (*CPP, Arts. 489, 545*) to the accused in the *Tribunal Correctionnel* or *Tribunal de Police* who has been judged in his absence, where he did not receive notification of the trial or had a valid excuse for non-appearance. It is not available where he failed to appear without good reason. The *opposition* procedure, which must be commenced within ten days of notification of the judgment (*CPP, Art. 491*), renders the judgment void (*CPP, Art. 489*) and the trial court is seized to retry the case in accordance with normal procedure. An analogous procedure (*purge de contumace*) is available in the *Cour d'Assises*.

4. Pourvoi en cassation

Appeal on a point of law by *pourvoi en cassation* to the *chambre criminelle* of the *Cour de Cassation* is available to the *ministère public*, the accused and the *partie civile*, within five days of judgment, in respect of final judgments of the *Cour d'Appel*, decisions of the *Tribunal de Police* in respect of which no appeal lies, of the *chambre d'accusation* and of the *Cour d'Assises* on the grounds of illegality (*violation de la loi; CPP, Arts. 567, 591*). It should however be noted that an acquittal by the *Cour d'Assises* can neither be appealed against by the prosecution to the *Cour d'Appel* (as has been seen) nor be the subject of appeal *en cassation* (apart from a *pourvoi en cassation* in the interests of the law by the *ministère public* or by order of the Minister of Justice where there has been an error of law; it is similar to an Attorney-General's reference in that the acquittal will stand (*CPP, Art. 572*)).

The appellant must allege one of the following grounds (*moyens de cassation*): that the court against whose decision *cassation* is being sought was not properly constituted or the proceedings did not take place in public (*constitution irrégulière de la juridiction; CPP, Art. 592*); that the court was not competent to reach the decision it did (*incompétence;* see *CPP, Art. 599*); that the court took decisions which were *ultra vires* (*excès de pouvoir*); that there were procedural irregularities (either statutory formalities or those regarded by caselaw as being "substantial") (*violation des règles de forme;* but see the limitations imposed by *CPP, Arts. 594, 599, 802* (TEXTS, NO. 7), (see above)); that the court's reasoning was unsatisfactory (*défaut, insuffisance ou contradiction des motifs; CPP, Art. 593;* the *Cour de Cassation* may, however, in the case of *contradiction des motifs* substitute its own reasoning and uphold the decision); or that the decision taken was illegal (*violation de la loi; CPP, Art. 591*), the appellant citing the provisions of a statute which he alleges the court did not correctly interpret or apply.

The *Cour de Cassation* will not retry the case, but will simply hear legal arguments. The parties may not introduce legal arguments (*moyens*) not put before the court against whose decision *cassation* is being sought (apart from *moyens d'ordre public* (see above), such as that of the lack of competence of the court).

The court receives a report on the case from one of its members, then examines the written evidence and hears the oral observations of the parties' *avocats* (although the appellant may simply submit written arguments himself) and the *ministère public* before reaching its decision. This may be to reject the appeal (*rejet,* in which case the unsuccessful appellant will be liable for costs; *CPP, Arts. 607, 608*) or it may be to quash (*cassation; CPP, Art. 609*) the decision. In the latter case, the matter will usually be sent back (*cassation avec renvoi*) to a different court of the same type and same hierarchical level for the case to be retried because the *Cour de Cassation,* being able to judge matters of law alone, cannot substitute its own decision for the one it has quashed. A *renvoi* will not be ordered where it would serve no purpose (eg due to the limitation period having expired). On retrial, the trial court is free to determine the case as it thinks fit; if, however, it fails to abide by the decision of the *Cour de Cassation* its judgment is liable to be subject to a second *pourvoi en cassation* – the resulting decision of the *Cour de Cassation,* sitting formally *en assemblée plénière* (see Chapter 3) will then be sent to another court of the appropriate level for implementation (*CPP, Art. 619*).

5. Pourvoi en révision

This is an application to the *Cour de Cassation* for the reopening of an allegedly wrongful conviction (which perhaps is less likely to occur because appeals to the *Cour d'Appel* take the form of a retrial). It was introduced in 1895 as a result of the infamous Dreyfus case. It is available only where all other rights of appeal have been exhausted.

Any person found guilty of a *crime* or *délit* (or, if that person has died, their next of kin) and the Minister of Justice may at any time apply (*CPP, Arts. 622, 623*) for *révision* to a special commission of five judges of the *Cour de Cassation* in the following cases: where, after a conviction for homicide, evidence is produced that the alleged victim is still alive (!); where, in a separate criminal prosecution, another individual has been convicted for the offence for which the appellant was convicted, thus proving the latter's innocence; where one of the witnesses has since been convicted of giving false evidence against the appellant; where, after the conviction, "new facts or elements have been revealed which were not produced to the trial court and which give rise to a doubt as to the culpability of the offender". Such "new facts" have been held by the courts to include revised forensic evidence which undermines the prosecution case (*Crim., 28.12.1923; Bull. crim., 449*); the retraction by a witness of evidence which was central to the prosecution case (*Crim., 18.12.1930; Bull. crim., 307*); and where an incriminating letter alleged to have been written by the appellant is scientifically proved to have not been written by him (*Crim., 9.11.1955; Bull. crim., 474*).

The *Cour de Cassation* is entitled, in its sole discretion, to determine the importance and effect of the evidence brought before it in support of a *pourvoi en révision* (*Crim., 28.10.1980; Bull. crim., 280*). The commission of five judges will proceed, itself or through *commissions rogatoires*, to carry out a full investigation of the case (*CPP, Art. 623*), including examining and confronting the convicted person and witnesses, and it will determine whether or not to refer the case to the *chambre criminelle* of the *Cour de Cassation* for review. No appeal lies against this decision.

If a review is held, the *chambre criminelle* may proceed to carry out before the hearing such further investigations as it thinks appropriate. The parties are entitled to appear at the hearing and make written and oral representations (*CPP, Art. 625*). The court will then give a reasoned decision, again from which no appeal lies, either rejecting the application and confirming the conviction, or quashing the conviction.

Where the conviction is quashed, and it is impossible or useless to refer the matter back to a trial court − for example where there is no possibility, for technical reasons, of the appellant being subsequently convicted, or where he is clearly innocent − the *Cour de Cassation* will itself proceed to annul definitively the conviction. However, where there exists a possibility that the appellant may still be subsequently convicted, the matter will be referred back to an appropriate trial court for retrial. A person whose conviction is annulled is entitled to compensation (*CPP, Art. 626*).

G. Proposals for reform

In 1990 the *Commission Delmas-Marty*, which had been set up by the Ministry of Justice to report on the reform of the criminal justice system, submitted its report. Among the commission's suggestions for reform are that a suspect should be entitled to access to an *avocat* during the *enquête de police*, and that the accused should be allowed to plead guilty, in which case a simplified procedure would apply. The commission also calls into question the role of the *juge d'instruction*, recommending the separation of his investigative and judicial functions. The investigative functions should, it recommends, be carried out by the *ministère public*, and the judicial functions (eg issuing an order for detention pending trial) should be carried out by a judge or a bench of judges. The reform proposals had not, at the time of writing, been implemented. However, in February 1992 the government proposed more limited reforms, which would increase the rights of suspects. Essentially, the *inculpation* (formal charge) of a suspect, which in practice is too often confused with culpability, would be replaced by his being *mise en cause* (ie by stating that he is implicated in the matter without being formally charged). He would be entitled to have the assistance of an *avocat* as from the moment of *mise en cause*. Moreover, a decision to make an order of *détention provisoire* (pre-trial detention) would have to be made by a panel of judges.

Texts and materials

1 Code de Procédure Pénale, Art. 114

Lors de la première comparution, le juge d'instruction constate l'identité de l'inculpé, lui fait connaître expressément chacun des faits qui lui sont imputés et l'avertit qu'il est libre de ne faire aucune déclaration. Mention de cet avertissement est faite au procès-verbal.

Si l'inculpé désire faire des déclarations, celles-ci sont immédiatement reçues par le juge d'instruction.

Le magistrat donne avis à l'inculpé de son droit de choisir un conseil parmi les avocats inscrits au tableau ou admis au stage, ou parmi les avoués, et à défaut de choix, il lui en fait désigner un d'office, si l'inculpé le demande. La désignation est faite par le bâtonnier de l'Ordre des avocats s'il existe un conseil de l'Ordre et, dans le cas contraire, par le président du tribunal.

Mention de cette formalité est faite au procès-verbal.

La partie civile a également le droit de se faire assister d'un conseil dès sa première audition (. . .)

2 Code de Procédure Pénale, Art. 427

(Tribunal Correctionnel)

Hors les cas où la loi en dispose autrement, les infractions peuvent être établies par tout mode de preuve et le juge décide d'après son intime conviction.

Le juge ne peut fonder sa décision que sur des preuves qui lui sont apportées au cours des débats et contradictoirement discutées devant lui.

3 Code de Procédure Pénale, Art. 353

(Cour d'Assises)

Avant que la cour d'assises se retire, le président donne lecture de l'instruction suivante, qui est, en outre, affichée en gros caractères dans le lieu le plus apparent de la chambre des délibérations:

«La loi ne demande pas compte aux juges des moyens par lesquels ils se sont convaincus, elle ne leur prescrit pas de règles desquelles ils doivent faire particulièrement dépendre la plénitude et la suffisance d'une preuve; elle leur prescrit de s'interroger eux-mêmes, dans le silence et le recueillement, et de chercher, dans la sincérité de leur conscience, quelle impression ont faite, sur leur raison, les preuves rapportées contre l'accusé, et les moyens de sa défense. La loi ne leur fait que cette seule question, qui renferme toute la mesure de leurs devoirs: «Avez-vous une intime conviction?»»

4 Code de Procédure Pénale, Art. 485

(Tribunal Correctionnel)

Tout jugement doit contenir des motifs et un dispositif.

Les motifs constituent la base de la décision.

Le dispositif énonce les infractions dont les personnes citées sont déclarées coupables ou responsables ainsi que la peine, les textes de loi appliqués, et les condamnations civiles.

Il est donné lecture du jugement par le président ou par l'un des juges; cette lecture peut être limitée au dispositif. Dans le cas prévu par l'alinéa premier de l'article 398, elle peut être faite même en l'absence des autres magistrats du siège.

5 Cass. crim., 17 mars 1960, Kissari et autres, Bull.Crim., no. 156, J.C.P. 1960, II, 11641

LA COUR: – Statuant sur les pourvois de: 1° Abassi Abdesselem; 2° Kissari Djillali contre un jugement du Tribunal permanent des Forces armées du Département de la Saoura, en date du 9 février 1960, les condamnant à la peine de mort pour tentative d'assassinat et complicité; – Sur le second moyen de cassation, pris de la violation des articles 63, 64 et 172 du Code de Procédure pénale, de l'article 7 de la loi du 20 avril 1810, défaut de motifs et manque de base légale, en ce que le Tribunal, saisi par la défense de conclusions contestant la régularité des mesures de garde à vue prises notamment contre Kissari, les a rejetées au motif que si l'accusé a été arbitrairement détenu, il lui appartient de saisir les autorités compétentes, et que ce fait ne peut entacher la valeur du procès-verbal, alors que les dispositions relatives à la garde à vue sont substantielles et essentielles à la protection des droits de la défense, qu'elles entrent dans les prévisions de l'article 172, alinéa 1er, du Code de Procédure pénale, et que, dès lors, leur violation doit entraîner soit l'annulation de l'acte vicié, soit l'annulation de tout ou partie de la procédure ultérieure; – Attendu qu'il résulte des constatations du jugement et des pièces auxquelles il se réfère que les procès-verbaux d'enquête argués de nullité par les accusés, comme ne satisfaisant pas aux formalités exigées par la loi en matière de garde à vue, ne comportent aucune des irrégularités dont il leur était fait grief; – Que dès lors, c'est à bon droit que le Tribunal a rejeté les conclusions prises par les demandeurs sur ce point; – Attendu d'ailleurs que les règles énoncées aux articles 63 et 64 du Code de Procédure pénale ne sont pas prescrites à peine de nullité; que leur inobservation, si elle engage, même au regard de la loi pénale, la responsabilité personnelle des officiers de police judiciaire qui les auraient méconnues, ne saurait par elle-même entraîner la nullité des actes de la procédure, lorsqu'il n'est pas démontré que la recherche et l'établissement de la vérité s'en sont trouvés viciés fondamentalement; – D'où il suit que le moyen n'est pas fondé; ...

Par ces motifs, rejette les pourvois.

6 Code de Procédure Pénale, Art. 105

Le juge d'instruction chargé d'une information, ainsi que les magistrats et officiers de police judiciaire agissant sur commission rogatoire, ne peuvent, dans le dessein de faire échec aux droits de la défense, entendre comme témoins des personnes contre lesquelles il existe des indices graves et concordants de culpabilité.

7 Code de Procédure Pénale, Art. 802

En cas de violation des formes prescrites par la loi à peine de nullité ou d'inobservation des formalités substantielles, à l'exception toutefois de celles prévues à l'article 105, toute juridiction, y compris la Cour de cassation, qui est saisie d'une demande d'annulation ou qui relève d'office une telle irrégularité ne peut prononcer la nullité que lorsque celle-ci a eu pour effet de porter atteinte aux intérêts de la partie qu'elle concerne.

8 Code de Procédure Pénale, Art. 206

La chambre d'accusation examine la régularité des procédures qui lui sont soumises.

Si elle découvre une cause de nullité, elle prononce la nullité de l'acte qui en est entaché et, s'il y échet, celle de tout ou partie de la procédure ultérieure.

Après annulation, elle peut soit évoquer et procéder dans les conditions prévues aux articles 201, 202 et 204, soit renvoyer le dossier de la procédure au même juge d'instruction ou à tel autre, afin de poursuivre l'information.

9 Code de Procédure Pénale, Art. 14

Elle (la police judiciaire) est chargée, suivant les distinctions établies au présent titre, de constater les infractions à la loi pénale, d'en rassembler les preuves et d'en rechercher les auteurs tant qu'une information n'est pas ouverte.

Lorsqu'une information est ouverte, elle exécute les délégations des juridictions d'instruction et défère à leurs réquisitions.

10 Code de Procédure Pénale, Art. 75

(Des Enquêtes)

Les officiers de police judiciaire et, sous le contrôle de ceux-ci, les agents de police judiciaire désignés à l'article 20 procèdent à des enquêtes préliminaires soit sur les instructions du procureur de la République, soit d'office.

Ces opérations relèvent de la surveillance du procureur général.

11 Code de Procédure Pénale, Art. 31

Le ministère public exerce l'action publique et requiert l'application de la loi.

12 Code de Procédure Pénale, Art. 40

Le procureur de la République reçoit les plaintes et les dénonciations et apprécie la suite à leur donner. Il avise le plaignant du classement de l'affaire ainsi que la victime lorsque celle-ci est identifiée.

Toute autorité constituée, tout officier public ou fonctionnaire qui, dans l'exercice de ses fonctions, acquiert la connaissance d'un crime ou d'un délit est tenu d'en donner avis sans délai au procureur de la République et de transmettre à ce magistrat tous les renseignements, procès-verbaux et actes qui y sont relatifs.

13 Code de Procédure Pénale, Art. 41

Le procureur de la République procède ou fait procéder à tous les actes nécessaires à la recherche et à la poursuite des infractions à la loi pénale.

A cette fin, il dirige l'activité des officiers et agents de la police judiciaire dans le ressort de son tribunal (. . .)

14 Code de Procédure Pénale, Art. 12

La police judiciaire est exercée, sous la direction du procureur de la République, par les officiers fonctionnaires et agents désignés au présent titre.

15 Code de Procédure Pénale, Art. 185

Le procureur de la République a le droit d'interjeter appel devant la chambre d'accusation de toute ordonnance du juge d'instruction.

Cet appel formé par déclaration au greffe du tribunal, doit être interjeté dans les cinq jours qui suivent la notification de la décision (. . .)

16 Code de Procédure Pénale, Art. 80

Le juge d'instruction ne peut informer qu'en vertu d'un réquisitoire du procureur de la République, même s'il a procédé en cas de crime ou de délit flagrant.

Le réquisitoire peut être pris contre personne dénommée ou non dénommée.

Le juge d'instruction a le pouvoir d'inculper toute personne ayant pris part, comme auteur ou complice, aux faits qui lui sont déférés.

Lorsque des faits, non visés au réquisitoire, sont portés à la connaissance du juge d'instruction, celui-ci doit immédiatement communiquer au procureur de la République les plaintes ou les procès-verbaux qui les constatent.

En cas de plainte avec constitution de partie civile, il est procédé comme il est dit à l'article 86.

17 Code de Procédure Pénale, Art. 3

L'action civile peut être exercée en même temps que l'action publique et devant la même juridiction.

Elle sera recevable pour tous chefs de dommages, aussi bien matériels que corporels ou moraux, qui découleront des faits objets de la poursuite.

18 Code de Procédure Pénale, Art. 2

L'action civile en réparation du dommage causé par un crime, un délit ou une contravention, appartient à tous ceux qui ont personnellement souffert du dommage directement causé par l'infraction.

La renonciation à l'action civile ne peut arrêter, ni suspendre l'exercice de l'action publique, sous réserve des cas visés à l'alinéa 3 de l'article 6.

19 Code de Procédure Pénale, Art. 85

Toute personne qui se prétend lésée par un crime ou un délit peut en portant plainte se constituer partie civile devant le juge d'instruction compétent.

20 Code de Procédure Pénale, Art. 81

Le juge d'instruction procède, conformément à la loi, à tous les actes d'information qu'il juge utiles à la manifestation de la vérité.

Il est établi une copie de ces actes ainsi que de toutes les pièces de la procédure; chaque copie est certifiée conforme par le greffier ou l'officier de police judiciaire commis mentionné à l'alinéa 4. Toutes les pièces du dossier sont cotées par le greffier au fur et à mesure de leur rédaction ou de leur réception par le juge d'instruction (...)

Si le juge d'instruction est dans l'impossibilité de procéder lui-même à tous les actes d'instruction, il peut donner commission rogatoire aux officiers de police judiciaire afin de leur faire exécuter tous les actes d'information nécessaires dans les conditions et sous les réserves prévues aux articles 151 et 152.

Le juge d'instruction doit vérifier les éléments d'information ainsi recueillis.

Le juge d'instruction procède ou fait procéder soit par des officiers de police judiciaire, conformément à l'alinéa 4, soit par toute personne habilitée dans les conditions déterminées par décret en Conseil d'Etat, à une enquête sur la personnalité des inculpés, ainsi que sur leur situation matérielle, familiale ou sociale. Toutefois, en matière de délit, cette enquête est facultative.

Le juge d'instruction peut prescrire un examen médical, confier à un médecin le soin de procéder à un examen médico-psychologique ou ordonner toutes autres mesures utiles. Si ces examens sont demandés par l'inculpé ou son conseil, il ne peut les refuser que par ordonnance motivée.

Le juge d'instruction peut également commettre, suivant les cas, le comité de probation et d'assistance aux libérés, le service compétent de l'éducation surveillée ou toute personne habilitée en application de l'alinéa qui précède à l'effet de vérifier la situation matérielle, familiale et sociale d'un inculpé et de l'informer sur les mesures propres à favoriser l'insertion sociale de l'intéressé. A moins qu'elles n'aient été déjà prescrites par le ministère public, ces diligences doivent être prescrites par le juge d'instruction chaque fois qu'il envisage de placer en détention provisoire un majeur âgé de moins de vingt et un ans au moment de la commission de l'infraction lorsque la peine encourue n'excède pas cinq ans d'emprisonnement.

21 Code de Procédure Pénale, Art. 11

Sauf dans le cas où la loi en dispose autrement et sans prejudice des droits de la défense, la procédure au cours de l'enquête et de l'instruction est secrète.

Toute personne qui concourt à cette procédure est tenue au secret professionnel dans les conditions et sous les peines de l'article 378 du Code pénal.

22 Code de Procédure Pénale, Art. 53

Est qualifié crime ou délit flagrant, le crime ou le délit qui se commet actuellement, ou qui vient de se commettre. Il y a aussi crime ou délit flagrant lorsque, dans un temps très voisin de l'action, la personne soupçonnée est poursuivie par la clameur publique, ou est trouvée en possession d'objets, ou présente des traces ou indices, laissant penser qu'elle a participé au crime ou au délit.

Est assimilé au crime ou délit flagrant tout crime ou délit qui même non commis dans les circonstances prévues à l'alinéa précédent a été commis dans une maison dont le chef requiert le procureur de la République ou un officier de police judiciaire de le constater.

23 Cass.Crim., 21 juillet 1982, Bull. Crim., no. 196, D.1982, 642

LA COUR: − Statuant sur le pourvoi formé par l'Administration des Douanes, partie civile, contre un arrêt de la chambre d'accusation de la cour d'appel de Pau, en date du 17 févr. 1982, qui a annulé les pièces de la procédure suivie contre X ..., Y ... et Z ... des chefs de trafic de stupéfiants et d'importation en contrebande de marchandises prohibées.

Sur les deux moyens réunis: − Attendu qu'il appert de l'arrêt attaqué que le 22 sept. 1981 deux fonctionnaires de la police, informés anonymement que des stupéfiants étaient transportés par des personnes dont la description leur avait été communiquée, les ont interpellées et palpées sommairement; qu'ils ont trouvé sur X ... une boîte contenant une certaine quantité «d'un dérivé de la morphine»; qu'ils ont procédé à l'arrestation du susnommé et de Y ... qui l'accompagnait; que, par les éléments de l'enquête, il a été établi ensuite que de la drogue avait été importée en contrebande par ces deux individus, qui en avaient vendu une partie à Z ..., lequel en a revendu à d'autres; que l'administration des douanes a dressé procès-verbal de ces faits, le 23 sept. 1981, en se fondant sur les constatations des procès-verbaux de police; que, sur plainte de ladite administration, les trois susnommés ont été poursuivis et inculpés par le juge d'instruction d'infractions à la législation sur les stupéfiants et à la législation douanière; – Attendu que, pour annuler le procès-verbal d'interpellation et de saisie, ainsi que toutes les pièces de la procédure subséquente, et notamment le procès-verbal des douanes ci-dessus mentionné, l'arrêt énonce que «les enquêteurs ne peuvent avoir agi en flagrant délit», la flagrance n'ayant commencé qu'avec la découverte de la drogue, alors que l'enquête de flagrance devait suivre et non précéder le délit flagrant; que, d'autre part, ces fonctionnaires «agissaient en enquête préliminaire et auraient dû, aux termes de l'art. 76 c. pr. pén., obtenir l'assentiment exprès de la personne intéressée, ce qu'ils n'ont pas fait»; qu'enfin, «la fouille à corps est assimilée à une perquisition»; – Attendu qu'en l'état de ces constatations et énonciations; la cour d'appel, loin de violer les textes visés aux moyens, en a fait, au contraire, l'exacte application;

Qu'en effet, d'une part, la «fouille à corps», assimilable à une perquisition, est nulle, ainsi que les actes qui ont suivi, si elle a été pratiquée par un officier de police judiciaire, alors qu'aucune information n'était ouverte et que l'existence d'un délit imputable à la personne fouillée n'était révélée par aucun indice apparent; que d'autre part, sont nulles les perquisitions et saisies pratiquées par un agent de police judiciaire sans l'assentiment exprès de la personne chez qui l'opération a eu lieu, alors qu'aucune information n'était ouverte et qu'aucun indice apparent d'un comportement délictueux ne pouvait révéler l'existence d'une infraction répondant à la définition donnée des crimes et délits flagrants par l'art. 53 c. pr. pén; que, par voie de conséquence, est également nul le procès-verbal de douane établi sur la base de l'acte annulé; d'où il suit que les moyens ne sauraient être accueillis;

Par ces motifs, rejette.

24 Code de Procédure Pénale, Art. 77

Lorsque pour les nécessités de l'enquête préliminaire, l'officier de police judiciaire est amené à retenir une personne à sa disposition plus de vingt-quatre heures, celle-ci doit être obligatoirement conduite avant l'expiration de ce délai devant le procureur de la République.

Après audition de la personne qui lui est amenée, le procureur de la République peut accorder l'autorisation écrite de prolonger la garde à vue d'un nouveau délai de vingt-quatre heures (...)

A titre exceptionnel, cette autorisation peut être accordée, par décision motivée, sans que la personne soit conduite au Parquet.

25 Code de Procédure Pénale, Art. 63

Si, pour les nécessités de l'enquête, l'officier de police judiciaire est amené à garder à sa disposition une ou plusieurs des personnes visées aux articles 61 et 62, il ne peut les retenir plus de vingt-quatre heures.

S'il existe contre une personne des indices graves et concordants de nature à motiver son inculpation, l'officier de police judiciaire doit la conduire devant le procureur de la République sans pouvoir la garder à sa disposition plus de vingt-quatre heures.

Le délai prévu à l'alinéa précédent, peut être prolongé d'un nouveau délai de vingt-quatre heures par autorisation écrite du procureur de la République ou du juge d'instruction (...)

26 Code de Procédure Pénale, Art. 122

Le juge d'instruction peut, selon les cas, décerner mandat de comparution, d'amener, de dépôt ou d'arrêt.

Le mandat de comparution a pour objet de mettre l'inculpé en demeure de se présenter devant le juge à la date et à l'heure indiquées par ce mandat.

Le mandat d'amener est l'ordre donné par le juge à la force publique de conduire immédiatement l'inculpé devant lui.

Le mandat de dépôt est l'ordre donné par le juge au chef de l'établissement pénitentiaire de recevoir et de détenir l'inculpé. Ce mandat permet également de rechercher ou de transférer l'inculpé lorsqu'il lui a été précédemment notifié.

Le mandat d'arrêt est l'ordre donné à la force publique de rechercher l'inculpé et de le conduire à la maison d'arrêt indiquée sur le mandat, où il sera reçu et détenu.

27 Cass.crim., 16 juin 1981, Chatelain, Bull. Crim., no. 207, J.C.P 1982, II, 19,838

LA COUR: − Attendu qu'il appert des pièces de la procédure qu'une information ayant été ouverte contre X ..., à la suite d'une tentative de vol avec prise d'otages au cours de laquelle Neiburt Régine, épouse Forest allait trouver la mort et son mari être blessé, le juge d'instruction a donné commission rogatoire à la section des recherches de la gendarmerie de Chambéry aux fins d'identifier le ou les auteurs de ces crimes; que l'enquête aboutit aux interpellations successives de Chatelain Jean-François, Cacciani Stéphane et Fauvette Marie-Joëlle; que tous trois ont reconnu leur participation aux faits, objet de la poursuite;

Que, plus particulièrement, Chatelain était entendu, en qualité de témoin, les 12 et 13 février 1981; que lors de sa dernière audition, il avouait être l'un des auteurs de l'agression dont les époux Forest avaient été les victimes, exposait en détail la préparation et l'exécution des faits, reconnaissait que c'était lui qui avait, par deux fois, fait feu sur les époux Forest et dénonçait Fauvette Marie-Joëlle, sa maîtresse, et Cacciani Stéphane comme étant ses complices; qu'il s'offrait, enfin «pour prouver la véracité de ses dires» à conduire les enquêteurs dans une sapinière où il avait caché deux sacs contenant les armes utilisées; que ces sacs furent effectivement découverts à l'endroit indiqué; que le lendemain, 14 février, Chatelain, était une nouvelle fois entendu, à sa demande, et identifiait chacun des objets saisis et notamment le fusil avec lequel il avait tiré; qu'à cet instant, les officiers de police judiciaire «devant les indices graves et concordants réunis contre lui» interrompaient son audition et lui notifiaient que «conformément à l'article 105 du Code de procédure pénale», il allait être conduit devant le juge d'instruction;

Que, par requête fondée sur l'article 171 du Code de procédure pénale, le procureur de la République a saisi la Chambre d'accusation aux fins d'annulation de la dernière audition de Chatelain en qualité de témoin qui «lui semblait avoir été faite au mépris des dispositions de l'article 105 du Code de procédure pénale»;

Que, par l'arrêt attaqué, la Cour faisait droit à une requête, sans constater cependant que les officiers de police judiciaire avaient agi dans le dessein de faire échec aux droits de Chatelain;

Que, contrairement à ce qui est allégué au moyen, c'est à bon droit que la Chambre d'accusation s'est bornée à l'annulation de cette dernière audition, ayant jugé qu'il avait été régulièrement procédé aux auditions antérieures;

Qu'en effet, alors que Chatelain sur qui ne pesaient que de simples soupçons et qui persistait à nier toute participation aux faits, objets de l'enquête, sans que puissent lui être opposés des arguments déterminants, sa décision soudaine «d'avouer clairement les faits tels qu'ils s'étaient passés» commandait aux officiers de police judiciaire de le laisser s'expliquer et de vérifier ensuite si ses aveux étaient corroborés par des éléments objectifs permettant de conclure à l'existence de charges de nature à engager sa responsabilité pénale;

Qu'enfin, la Cour ayant refusé, à bon droit, d'annuler dans sa totalité le procès-verbal d'audition de Chatelain, en qualité de témoin, il ne peut lui être fait grief de n'avoir pas annulé le déposition de la partie civile devant le juge d'instruction, au motif qu'elle se référait aux déclarations de Chatelain rapportées dans le procès-verbal critiqué;

D'où il suit que le moyen ne saurait être accueilli;

Rejette le pourvoi.

28 Code de Procédure Pénale, Art. 144

En matière criminelle et en matière correctionnelle si la peine encourue est égale ou supérieure soit à un an d'emprisonnement en cas de délit flagrant, soit à deux ans d'emprisonnement dans les autres cas et si les obligations du contrôle judiciaire sont insuffisantes au regard des fonctions définies à l'article 137, la détention provisoire peut être ordonnée ou maintenue:

1° Lorsque la détention provisoire de l'inculpé est l'unique moyen de conserver les preuves ou les indices matériels ou d'empêcher soit une pression sur les témoins ou les victimes, soit une concertation frauduleuse entre inculpés et complices;

2° Lorsque cette détention est nécessaire pour préserver l'ordre public du trouble causé par l'infraction ou pour protéger l'inculpé, pour mettre fin à l'infraction ou prévenir son renouvellement ou pour garantir le maintien de l'inculpé à la disposition de la justice.

La détention provisoire peut également être ordonnée, dans les conditions prévues par l'article 141−2, lorsque l'inculpé se soustrait volontairement aux obligations du contrôle judiciaire.

29 Cass. crim., 24 juin 1971, Bereni, Bull. Crim., no. 358, D.1971, 546

LA COUR: − Statuant sur le pourvoi formé par Bereni Antoine, contre un arrêt de la chambre d'accusation de la cour d'appel de Paris en date du 2 mars 1971, qui, dans une information suivie des chefs de fabrication de faux documents administratifs, usage et complicité, escroquerie et complicité, infraction à la législation sur les chèques, a confirmé une ordonnance du juge d'instruction rejetant une demande de mise en liberté du demandeur;

Sur le moyen unique de cassation, pris de la violation des art. 138, 144, 145, 148, 198, 216, 591 et 593 c. pr. pén. et de l'art. 7 de la loi du 20 avr. 1810, défaut de motifs, manque de base légale;

Attendu qu'il résulte de la combinaison des art. 144, 145 al. 1er, et 148 al. 3, c. pr. pén., qu'en matière correctionnelle, la décision d'une juridiction d'instruction rejetant une demande de mise en liberté doit, comme celle prescrivant la détention provisoire, être spécialement motivée d'après les éléments de l'espèce par référence aux dispositions de l'art. 144 du même code; que ces dispositions sont substantielles; − Attendu que, pour confirmer l'ordonnance du juge d'instruction qui avait rejeté la demande de mise en liberté du demandeur, la chambre d'accusation énonce «que la détention provisoire de l'inculpé est l'unique moyen de conserver les preuves et les indices matériels et d'empêcher soit une pression sur les témoins soit une concertation frauduleuse entre les inculpés»;

Mais attendu qu'en se bornant à reproduire les termes généraux de l'art. 144 c. pr. pén., sans se référer aux éléments de l'espèce, la cour d'appel a violé le principe ci-dessus rappelé; que, dès lors, la cassation est encourue sans qu'il y ait lieu d'examiner les autres griefs formulés au moyen;

Par ces motifs, casse ..., renvoie devant la chambre d'accusation de la cour d'appel d'Amiens.

30 Code de Procédure Pénale, Art. 151

Le juge d'instruction peut requérir par commission rogatoire tout juge de son tribunal, tout juge d'instruction ou tout officier de police judiciaire, qui en avise dans ce cas le procureur de la République, de procéder aux actes d'information qu'il estime nécessaires dans les lieux où chacun d'eux est territorialement compétent.

La commission rogatoire indique la nature de l'infraction, objet des poursuites. Elle est datée et signée par le magistrat qui la délivre et revênue de son sceau.

Elle ne peut prescrire que des actes d'instruction se rattachant directement à la répression de l'infraction visée aux poursuites.

31 Code de Procédure Pénale, Art. D.16

L'enquête sur la personnalité des inculpés ainsi que sur leur situation matérielle, familiale ou sociale prévue à l'article 81, alinéa 6, du Code de procédure pénale et les examens, notamment médical et médico-psychologique, mentionnés à l'alinéa 7 dudit article, constituent le dossier de personnalité de l'inculpé.

Ce dossier a pour objet de fournir à l'autorité judiciaire, sous une forme objective et sans en tirer de conclusion touchant à l'affaire en cours, des éléments d'appréciation sur le mode de vie passé et présent de l'inculpé.

Il ne saurait avoir pour but la recherche des preuves de la culpabilité.

32 Code de Procédure Pénale, Art. 312

(Cour d'Assises)

Sous réserve des dispositions de l'article 309, le ministère public, l'accusé, la partie civile, les conseils de l'accusé et de la partie civile peuvent poser des questions, par l'intermédiaire du président, aux accusés, aux témoins et à toutes personnes appelées à la barre.

Chapter 6

Civil and administrative procedure

A. Introductory matters

1. Growth of litigation

Recent years have seen a rapid growth in litigation in both civil and administrative courts. The number of cases heard by the *Tribunaux de Grande Instance* has grown from some 250,500 in 1977 to approximately 460,000 in 1989. In the *Conseils de Prud'hommes* the figures have increased in the same period from some 80,000 to almost 150,000. This great pressure of business on the courts has led to reforms to streamline civil procedure. A similarly substantial increase has occurred in the administrative courts which, as has been mentioned (Chapter 2), led to the creation in 1989 of the *Cours Administratives d'Appel* so as to reduce the load on the *Conseil d'Etat*.

2. Roles of the judge and the parties

As a matter of terminology, the plaintiff is known as the *demandeur* and the defendant the *défendeur*. The word *plaideur* is a general term referring to any party to an action, any litigant.

The respective roles of the judge and the parties in civil and administrative procedure will be examined at three stages of the proceedings: the commencement of an action, the *instruction* phase, and trial. As will be seen, administrative procedure is essentially inquisitorial in nature, whereas civil procedure is not, although the civil judge does have powers to force the pace of pre-trial procedure.

(a) Commencement of an action

The commencement of a civil action almost always depends entirely on the initiative of the parties; a principle which is affirmed in the very first article of the *Nouveau Code de Procédure Civile* ("*NCPC*"; this came into effect on 1 January 1976, replacing the 1806 *Code de*

Procédure Civile). *Art. 1* provides that "only the parties may commence an action (*introduire une instance*) apart from the cases where the law states otherwise ...". It is rare that the judge may seize himself of a matter (*se saisir d'office*); an example is to be found in *Code Civil, Art. 375* where the judge may of his own initiative take protective measures where there is a threat to the "health, safety or morality" of a juvenile. It is also for the parties to determine the ambit of the case (in the pleadings: *NCPC, Art. 4*), the civil judge not being permitted to adjudge matters other than those submitted to him by the parties (*NCPC, Art. 5*).

(b) Instruction

The second phase is that of *instruction*; as with criminal procedure, this is the phase preceding the hearing, during which time much of the evidence which will be relied on at the trial is produced. That civil procedure is not essentially inquisitorial is shown by the fact that it is for the parties and not the judge to direct this phase of pre-trial procedure; this is clear from *NCPC, Arts. 2, 4*, which provide that it is for the parties to conduct the action. The role of the judge is to oversee procedure, ensuring that it is properly conducted, and to order the carrying out of the appropriate measures of *instruction*; in particular he must (*NCPC, Art. 16*) ensure compliance with the principle of *contradiction*, both sides having to disclose to the other side the grounds of fact and law on which their claim is based (*NCPC, Art. 15*). Nevertheless, legislation has, in recent years, increased the power of the judge to intervene during the *instruction* phase so as to maintain the progress of the proceedings, and indeed to promote the "search for the truth". In the *Tribunal de Grande Instance*, a judge (known as *le juge de la mise en état*) is appointed to oversee the *instruction* phase. Although some commentators have found in these developments certain traces of inquisitorial procedure, the accusatorial nature of civil procedure has not been fundamentally undermined; the burden of proof remains on the plaintiff, and the parties are always at liberty to drop their claim or reach a settlement (*une transaction*).

In administrative procedure, the *instruction* phase is and always has been inquisitorial, directed not by the parties but by the judge. This distinction is usually explained by the fact that administrative proceedings usually involve an individual who is in dispute with an administrative body; the resulting lack of parity between the parties thus needs to be redressed by according the judge wide inquisitorial powers such as, for example, the power to require the administrative body concerned to disclose the precise reasons why a particular decision was taken. It is obviously difficult for the aggrieved individual to obtain such information on his own. The onus of proof on the plaintiff is naturally affected (in favour of the plaintiff) by these inquisitorial powers of the administrative judge.

(c) Trial and judgment

In civil as in administrative procedure, the final phase of the proceedings is that of trial and judgment, comprising a hearing (*le débat*) in which the *avocats* make their oral addresses (*plaidoiries*) to the court, the *délibéré*, when the judge(s) retires to examine the dossier and the evidence, and the pronouncement of the judgment (*le prononcé du jugement*). There has been a tendency in recent years in civil procedure (and even more so in administrative procedure) for the *plaidoiries* of the *avocats* to be shorter than has traditionally been the case.

3. Procedure: secret or public?

Whereas the *instruction* phase of both civil and administrative procedure is carried out in private, the court hearing and pronouncement of judgment in principle take place in public (*NCPC, Art. 433*). A hearing is held in camera (*en chambre du conseil*) where the law so provides, for example in respect of divorce proceedings (*Code Civil, Art. 248*), affiliation proceedings (*NCPC, Art. 1149*), and consent orders (*matières gracieuses*; found, for example, in cases of adoption and divorce by mutual consent). Sometimes the law gives the judge a certain discretion; thus under *NCPC, Art. 435* the hearing may be held in private in response to a request by both of the parties, or where a public hearing might compromise the intimacy of people's private lives. Judgment must be pronounced in open court, in both civil (*NCPC, Art. 451*) and administrative cases. There are statutory exceptions in respect, for example, of consent orders. In divorce cases the full judgment of the court is not read out, only confirmation of the fact and effective date of divorce (*NCPC, Art. 1081*).

4. Procedure: written or oral?

In the civil courts, a distinction must be drawn between the *Tribunaux de Grande Instance* and *Cours d'Appel* on the one hand, and the specialised courts on the other. In the former, procedure is very largely written, the writ (*assignation*) and pleadings (*conclusions*) being written, and a degree of oral procedure is found only at the hearing. However, in proceedings in specialised courts (*Tribunaux d'Instance, Tribunaux de Commerce, Conseils de Prud'hommes*) procedure is essentially oral (*NCPC, Arts. 843, 871; Code du Travail, Art. R. 516–6*); indeed an action can be commenced by the oral declaration of the plaintiff. Nor are written *conclusions* obligatory, although usually they are found in practice.

In administrative cases, procedure is essentially written, both the writ (*requête*), which starts an action, and the pleadings (*mémoires*) submitted by the parties being written. Moreover, at the public hearing, the representations of the *avocats* to the court are essentially written, although supplementary oral representations may be made.

5. Burden and means of proof

(a) In the civil courts

By *NCPC, Arts. 6, 9*, it is for the parties to prove, in a way which is in conformity with the law, the facts on which their case rests. Thus they must find and produce the documentary, witness and other evidence sufficient to convince the court. However, a party may well be helped by one of the various statutory legal presumptions (*présomptions légales*); for example, the presumption of legitimacy (*Code Civil, Art. 312*). Common to both civil and administrative procedure is the principle that the judges of the trial court are entitled to accord such weight as they think fit to the different evidence which is adduced. There is no test equivalent to that of proof on the balance of probabilities. However, it should be noted in respect of contracts that, although there are important exceptions, proof must in principle be in writing (see below).

The judge, however, is not a passive referee. As will be seen, he is accorded powers, especially during the phase of *instruction*, of overseeing the obtaining of evidence and furthermore of ensuring that the evidence that is produced is relevant and sufficient to enable the trial court to reach a decision; indeed, if not, he may of his own initiative order further inquiries to be carried out.

As to the means of proof which may be used, *Ancien Droit* was traditionally based on a system of "legal proof" (*preuve légale*) according to which types of evidence were classified into different categories and were accorded different probative values. Of particular value were admissions (*aveux*) and oaths of admission (*serments*).

In modern French law, of determinative probative value are an *aveu judiciaire* (*Code Civil, Art. 1356*), which is a formal admission to the judge, either in the pleadings (*conclusions*) or orally, and a *serment décisoire*, where one party is required by the other party formally to swear an oath before the judge as to the truth of the facts founding his claim, or have his claim struck out (*Code Civil, Arts. 1357 et seq.*). As a general rule, however, parties may now prove their claims by any means. Important exceptions must be noted; the first is in respect of proof of civil status (eg birth, death) which is normally proved by means of an official certificate (*acte d'état civil*). More importantly, in the matter of means of proof, a distinction is drawn between proof of facts and proof of an *acte juridique* (being defined in civil law as a manifestation of intention intended to have legal consequences; eg a contract). Facts may in principle be proved by any means. On the other hand, *actes juridiques* (and contracts in particular) may be proved (*Code Civil, Art.*

1341) only by written document. This document may take one of two forms. Firstly, it may take the form of a deed of a public officer (*acte authentique*; eg of a *notaire*); the facts that it certifies are presumed to be true unless the *acte* can be shown to be a forgery. Secondly, it may take the form of an *acte sous seing privé* (private signed document), which is a document simply signed by the parties to the *acte juridique* (eg a contract signed by the contracting parties). An *acte sous seing privé* is proof of its contents, but this may be rebutted by evidence to the contrary (such evidence must itself be in writing).

There are several exceptions to the general principle that an *acte juridique* may be proved only by written document; where an exception applies, proof may be by any means. They are as follows: firstly, where the plaintiff has *prima facie* evidence of the existence of the contract in some written form (such as a letter, or a draft contract) emanating from the defendant or his agent (*commencement de preuve par écrit; Code Civil, Art. 1347*). Article 198 of the *NCPC* gives this exception greater importance by providing that where during *instruction* one or all of the parties are required to attend before the judge to give oral evidence (*comparution personnelle;* see below) the judge is entitled to treat the evidence thus given, or even a failure to give evidence, as constituting *prima facie* written evidence, thus obviating the need to prove the contract by written document. A second exception is any *acte juridique* the subject matter of which does not exceed a certain value (currently 5,000 FF); eg contracts for goods or services not exceeding 5,000 FF in value. Thirdly are exempted (*Code Civil, Art. 1341; Code de Commerce, Art. 109*) contracts between traders (*commerçants;* see below), whatever their value; where the contract is only "commercial" for one of the parties (eg where a consumer purchases goods from a *commerçant*) then only the other party (ie the consumer) benefits from the exemption, and the *commerçant* must normally, in accordance with the principle of *Code Civil, Art. 1341*, prove the contract by written document (assuming, for example, that the goods exceed 5,000 FF in value). The final exemption is in respect of contracts which cannot realistically be expected to be proved by written document, for example contracts made in emergency conditions, such as salvage contracts.

As has been seen, apart from *actes juridiques*, as a general rule proof may be by any means; the means of proof to which the parties will have recourse are varied. One type of evidence to which recourse is often had is documentary evidence; however, this can be relied on only where the document is disclosed to the other party and exchanged during the *instruction* phase of civil procedure, failing which the judge may decide to exclude it (*NCPC, Art. 135*). The court is entitled to draw its own inferences from the facts proved.

During *instruction*, recourse may be had to a variety of measures (*mesures d'instruction*) which may be ordered by the judge with a view to "uncovering the truth". Such measures may be requested by the parties, but it is for the judge to determine whether or not to order them. Indeed, the court may do so on its own initiative where it is of the opinion that further evidence is necessary for the matter to be tried (*NCPC, Art. 144*).

Mesures d'instruction are wide ranging in their scope. Firstly, the judge may decide to carry out investigations himself (*les vérifications*), for example by visiting the scene of a road accident; a written report (*procès-verbal*) will be produced. Secondly, the *mesures d'instruction* may relate to the production of witness evidence (*témoignages*), either in the form of written statements (*attestations*) or evidence given orally to the judge in chambers (by the procedure of *enquête*). An *attestation*, which must be signed and dated by the witness, may relate only information that the person deposing personally ascertained. By means of the procedure of *enquête* it is possible to obtain oral witness evidence by requiring any person (other than non-compellable witnesses, such as parents and spouses, and those subject to professional privilege) to attend at the chambers of the judge (during *instruction*) and give their oral evidence in the presence of the parties; this will be written up in the form of a deposition.

The judge may decide (although he rarely does in practice) to require the parties to the action to give oral evidence to him in chambers (*comparution personnelle*); this will in principle take place in the presence of the other parties, who may themselves put questions through the judge. A *procès-verbal* of the statements made to the judge will be drawn up and form part of the evidence; the court may draw such inferences as it thinks fit from the evidence given, silence in response to a question, or failure to attend a *comparution personnelle*.

Enquêtes, comparutions personnelles and other *mesures d'instruction*, such as *expertises*, are used to obtain further evidence to confirm or disprove facts alleged by a party. However, the onus of proof of any particular fact lies on the party alleging that fact, not on the judge. The parties will produce their evidence to the trial court, which will accord it such probative value as it determines.

L'attestation, les comparutions personnelles and *l'enquête* are examined in more detail below in the context of *instruction*.

(b) In the administrative courts

In administrative procedure, the general principle is that the burden of proof is on the plaintiff, and that all means of proof, written and oral, may be used. However, as has already been mentioned, administrative procedure is very largely written, even at the hearing. In addition, the largely inquisitorial nature of administrative procedure and in particular the wide investigative powers of the judges tend to assist the plaintiff in bearing the burden of proof when suing the administration. The judges of the administrative court will give such weight to the evidence produced as they think fit.

6. Role of the ministère public and commissaire du gouvernement

We have already seen that the members of the *ministère public* are technically *magistrats*, whose function is not to judge but to oversee the proper application of the law, in their role of representing the interests of society. We have already examined their function in criminal cases of bringing prosecutions. However, they also have a role in civil cases.

They may firstly be joined as *partie jointe* to a civil action, either of their own initiative, or on the request of the judge, their role being to give an opinion representing the general interest. The advice of the *ministère public* must be sought in certain cases such as affiliation, guardianship (*tutelle*) (*NCPC, Art. 425*) and consent orders (*matière gracieuse; NCPC, Art. 798*). In other cases the court has a discretion as to whether or not to bring in the *ministère public* (*NCPC, Art. 427*). The advice of the *ministère public* was obtained, for example, in a case in 1984 in which a young widow sought to obtain possession from a sperm bank of the frozen sperm that had been deposited by her husband who had since deceased.

Secondly, the *ministère public* may (*NCPC, Arts. 422, 423*) commence a civil action himself (as *partie principale*) in the public interest, in respect either of cases where he is given specific statutory authority to do so (eg to contest the French nationality of an individual (*NCPC, Art. 1040*), or cases involving a protection order in respect of an adult (*Protection des majeurs; Code Civil, Arts. 488 et seq.*)), or more generally in respect of cases involving considerations of public order.

In the administrative courts, an advisory role (similar in some ways to that of the *ministère public* when intervening as *partie jointe*) is played by the *commissaire du gouvernement*, who is a member of the administrative court appointed to the role for a limited period. He cannot himself commence an action as *partie principale*. His intervention is limited to indicating to the court the solution to the case which appears most in conformity with the law. The *commissaire du gouvernement* does not, as his name appears to suggest, represent the interests of the government, but is independent and may express his own impartial views. This can be seen from a case which took place in the 1970s in the *Tribunal Administratif* of Nantes following a mid-air collision. The accident occurred whilst the civil air-traffic controllers were on strike, and therefore air-traffic control was being carried out, on the direction of the government, by the military. The *commissaire du gouvernement* argued in favour of liability being laid entirely at the door of the administration. The opinions of *commissaires du gouvernement* are held in high respect, and are usually followed by the administrative courts.

As has been seen, civil procedure and administrative procedure are not of the same nature; the latter is essentially inquisitorial, the former not. We will therefore examine the rules of civil and administrative procedure separately.

B. Civil procedure in cases before the Tribunal de Grande Instance

We will examine the rules of civil procedure by following through a matter coming within the competence of the *Tribunal de Grande Instance* which, as has been seen, is the court of general competence (*de droit commun*) for civil matters. We will then examine the principal characteristics of interlocutory procedures and the simplified rules of procedure which apply to cases brought before the courts of special jurisdiction.

1. Commencement of an action

(a) Writ (assignation)

In the *Tribunal de Grande Instance* an action is in principle commenced either by a writ (*assignation*) or a petition (*requête conjointe*) (*NCPC, Art. 750*). An *assignation* is (*NCPC, Art. 55*) an official document (*acte d'huissier*) served on the defendant (by a *huissier* acting for the plaintiff) in which the plaintiff summons the defendant to appear at court to answer the case against him. The *assignation*, which is drafted by an *avocat*, is not issued by the court before service; indeed, the court will be seized of the matter by the parties after service.

All *assignations* must include (*NCPC, Arts. 56, 752*): details of the court in which the case is being brought; the nature and extent of the plaintiff's claim (*objet de la demande*) and the grounds (*moyens*) and documents (if any) on which it is based; also the fact that unless the defendant enters an appearance (*comparaître*), judgment may be entered against him.

Furthermore, because in the *TGI* it is obligatory for the pre-trial procedure (*la représentation*) to be carried out by an *avocat*, an *assignation* by the *TGI* must also indicate the identity of the plaintiff's *avocat* and the time limit (fifteen days in the *TGI*) within which the defendant must himself notify his choice of *avocat*.

In principle, service (*la signification*) is personal (*NCPC, Art. 654*); in the case of a corporate defendant, the *assignation* is served on the corporation's representative. Where personal service on the defendant is not possible, service may be effected on (*NCPC, Arts. 655, 656*) any person present at the defendant's home (including a caretaker) or even on a neighbour, but only where the recipient agrees to accept the writ and gives his name and address. Otherwise a copy of the writ will be lodged at the local town hall (*mairie*). Where service is not effected personally, it is necessary for the *huissier* to leave a memorandum of service at the defendant's residence. If the defendant has no known place of residence or employment, a copy of the writ will be sent to the last known address by registered letter.

After service, the court is seized of the matter by one or other of the parties (usually the plaintiff) submitting a copy of the writ to the secretariat of the court. This must be done within four months from the date on which the writ was served on the defendant, failing which the writ will expire (*NCPC, Art. 757*).

(b) Requête conjointe

In the vast majority of *TGI* cases, an action is commenced by *assignation*. Alternatively, however, an action may be commenced by petition (*requête conjointe*). This is a formal document addressed directly to the court jointly by the two parties, setting out their respective claims and arguments, and the points on which they disagree (*NCPC, Art. 57*); such procedure is rarely used. *Requêtes* of a different type (*requêtes gracieuses*) are also used in respect of consent orders (*matière gracieuse; NCPC, Art. 60*).

2. The instruction phase

(a) Introduction

During *instruction*, which as we have seen takes place between the commencement of an action and trial, the parties exchange pleadings and documentary evidence, and other measures are carried out in an endeavour to procure evidence to substantiate their respective cases. The introduction in 1971 of the *juge de la mise en état*, who is given important powers of direction of a civil case during *instruction*, is indicative of the fact that although it remains essentially for the plaintiff to prosecute the case, the judge has been granted important powers to ensure that pre-trial procedure is carried out effectively.

(b) Pre-trial review

Once the court has been seized of a matter, the president of the court will call the parties' *avocats* to a pre-trial review (*audience de l'appel des causes*) before the president of the division (*chambre*) to which the matter has been assigned. This hearing, which usually takes place within two months, enables the divisional president to assess the state of readiness of the case (*NCPC, Arts. 758, 759*). If the case is ready to proceed to trial, the president will declare that *instruction* is closed and will set the matter down for trial, which may even take place the same day (*NCPC, Art. 760*). In practice this simplified procedure is used only where the case is simple or, more unusually, where the parties have already exchanged pleadings (*conclusions*) and the documents on which they will be relying. If the parties have started such exchanges but have not yet completed them, the divisional president may decide to give them a time limit for the exchanges to be completed and for a further pre-trial review; if by that date the case is ready to proceed to trial, it will be set down (*NCPC, Art. 761*). All cases which in the opinion of the divisional president are not at the time of the *audience de l'appel des causes* ready to be tried, will proceed (*NCPC, Arts. 762, 763*) to *instruction* under the control of a judge acting as *juge de la mise en état*.

(c) Instruction

(i) Role of the juge de la mise en état

The *juge de la mise en état* has the role of ensuring that pre-trial procedure is properly carried out, and that prompt exchange of the pleadings and documents occurs. His powers are wide ranging: thus he may, for example, call the parties to appear before him (*NCPC, Art. 767*), normally in the presence of each other; he may use the opportunity to try to effect a conciliation under the general power of *NCPC, Art. 21* (cf *NCPC, Art. 768*).

The judge may suggest and, indeed, if necessary require the parties' *avocats* to carry out the various procedural steps within such time limits as he shall, after consultation with the *avocats*, determine having regard to the nature, urgency and complexity of the case (*NCPC, Art. 764*). The *juge de la mise en état* has a good deal of discretion, and the way in which he exercises these wide powers varies greatly with the individual. It is in fact usual for the judge to meet with the *avocats* and come to an agreement as to the time limits within which the various procedural steps will be taken. Should the *avocats* fail to carry out the procedural steps within the time limit set, the *juge de la mise en état* may (on his own initiative or on the request of one of the parties) close *instruction* at that point, the parties thereafter being unable to submit further *conclusions* or evidence in support, and set the matter down for trial; no appeal lies against such decisions (*NCPC, Arts. 780, 782*).

(ii) Pleadings (conclusions) and exchange of documentary evidence (pièces)

Instruction of a civil *TGI* case entails the carrying out of two sets of procedural steps. The first is the exchange by the parties of pleadings (*conclusions*) and documentary evidence. The second is the ordering by the judge of *mesures d'instruction*, such as the obtaining of the oral testimony of the parties or witnesses and the appointment of expert witnesses. We will examine each in turn.

Conclusions: *Conclusions* (pleadings) may be defined as the written documents drafted and signed by the parties' *avocats*, in which the parties set out the extent and nature of their claims (*le dispositif*) and their arguments in support (*les motifs*). The importance of the *conclusions* is evident from the fact that the court is seized to determine only those issues which are raised by the parties in the pleadings (*NCPC, Art. 4*). Furthermore, by *NCPC, Art. 7*, the court may base its decision on only those facts which have been put in issue (*qui sont dans le débat*), although this includes facts which are in issue even though not specifically relied on by the parties.

Compared with English law, there are few rules relating to the exchange of pleadings. Pleadings are exchanged between the parties' *avocats*, and copies are submitted to the court (*NCPC, Arts. 815, 816*). Usually the plaintiff starts the process by serving on the defendant the *assignation* (writ). Although the *assignation* is regarded (*NCPC, Art. 56*) as being the equivalent of *conclusions*, it is normal for the plaintiff thereafter to submit *conclusions en demande*, in which he develops the points raised in the *assignation*. The defendant then replies by his *conclusions en défense*; there is no formal requirement to rebut all of the allegations of the plaintiff, but the defendant will of course usually do so, also disputing, where appropriate, the plaintiff's assertions of points of law.

Beyond these *demandes initiales* the parties may submit *demandes incidentes*. The most usual of these is where the defendant in his *conclusions en défense* makes a counterclaim (*demande reconventionnelle; NCPC, Art. 64*). The plaintiff may reply to the *conclusions en défense* by submitting further *conclusions*; however, he will in practice do so only either where the defendant raises issues of fact or law not dealt with in the *assignation*, or where the defendant submits a counterclaim. Other *demandes incidentes* are the *demande additionnelle* (*NCPC, Art. 65*) where a party wishes to modify earlier claims, and the *intervention* which is used where it is sought to join a third party to an existing action; an *intervention* may be submitted by the third party himself (*NCPC, Art. 66*).

Such *conclusions* as are submitted must be transmitted to the other party in time (*en temps utile*) to enable that party to examine them and reply, if he so wishes, by submitting further *conclusions*. This is in accordance with the general principle that each party must be given the opportunity to respond to the other parties' claims; each party must disclose to the other parties the facts on which his allegations are based, the means by which he intends to prove those allegations, and the principles of law on which the claim is founded (*le principe de la contradiction; NCPC, Arts. 15, 16*).

Discovery of pièces: The parties must of their own initiative exchange not only their *conclusions* but also all documents (*pièces*), such as letters, plans, receipts, photographs and other documents (eg the witness statements (*attestations*) that they have obtained) on which they intend to rely (*NCPC, Art. 132*). Exchange must be effected in time to enable the adversary to reply; failure to do so may lead to the documents being excluded by the court (*NCPC, Art. 135*), although this rarely occurs in practice. Documents do not have to be produced where there is a legitimate excuse for non-production (*empêchement légitime; NCPC, Art. 11*). A legitimate excuse includes the fact that the documents are confidential (eg correspondence between a lawyer and his client, and other documents covered by professional privilege (*le secret professionnel*: above)). The *juge de la mise en état* may (*NCPC, Arts. 11, 133, 134, 138, 142*), on the application of one of the parties (but not on his own initiative), require any of the parties (or even a third party) to produce a document that he has in his possession (*la production forcée*). Failure to comply may lead to the imposition of a daily penalty (*astreinte*) which will vary depending on the degree of resistance shown by the defaulter. It may thus, for example, accumulate for each day of non-compliance.

(iii) Les mesures d'instruction

Role of judge: As has been seen, as a general principle it is for each party to prove the facts supporting his claims (*NCPC, Art. 9*). Often the facts on which the decision of the court is based are established by measures carried out during the *instruction* phase (known as *mesures d'instruction*). In principle these measures are ordered (*NCPC, Art. 143*) by the *juge de la mise en état* (in the *TGI*) either on his own initiative or on the request of the parties, but the judge always has a discretion as to whether to order them or not. The judge, if of the opinion that there is insufficient evidence for the case to be tried, may order (*NCPC, Art. 144*) further *mesures d'instruction* to be carried out.

Only limited rights of appeal lie against the judge's decisions in respect of *mesures d'instruction* (*NCPC, Arts. 150, 272*). In effect, no appeal (*appel* or *cassation*) lies independently of an appeal against the eventual substantive decision, with the exception of matters relating to the appointment of expert witnesses. It is evident that *mesures d'instruction* can be ordered to establish only matters of fact, not matters of law which are for the judge to determine (*NCPC, Art. 12*). The *NCPC*, effective from 1976, has sought to simplify the use of *mesures d'instruction* and to reinforce the powers of the judge, in order to accelerate procedure and to permit more readily the "discovery of the truth".

Vérifications: Amongst the *mesures d'instruction* that the judge can order may be cited, firstly, *les vérifications* (*NCPC, Arts. 179–183*) personally carried out by the judge at the scene of the litigation (eg where the case involves defective building construction). Such visits, at which the parties are invited to be present, are rare.

Comparutions personnelles: Under *NCPC, Arts. 184–198*, the judge has a discretion to require, on the request of one of the parties or on his own initiative, any or all of the parties (or in the case of a corporation, its representative) to appear personally before him in chambers (*la comparution personnelle*) usually in the presence of the other parties and their *avocats*. *Comparutions personnelles* may also be ordered by the trial court. The judge may confront the parties with each other or with other persons, such as witnesses. The party who is called to appear may have questions put to him by the other parties through the judge. The statements that are obtained will be written down, signed, and put with the file. The procedure of *comparution personnelle* enables the judge to obtain his own impression of the parties. It might for example be used in paternity cases, or in cases involving an appreciation of the *bona fides* of a contracting party. The judge is entitled to draw such inferences as he sees fit from the declarations made by parties, from their refusal to comment on a point, or even from their absence.

Attestations: A third *mesure d'instruction* is the obtaining of witness evidence, whether written (*attestations*) or oral (*enquêtes*) (*NCPC, Art. 199*). It is worth at this point recalling that, as discussed above, proof by testimony is not always admissible; in particular the existence and contents of *actes juridiques* such as contracts (apart from those of 5,000 FF or less in value and contracts between *commerçants*) may usually be proved only by a written document emanating from the parties (*Code Civil, Art. 1341*).

In practice, the parties of their own initiative frequently obtain written witness statements (*attestations; NCPC, Arts. 200, 202*). Although the judge can order their production (*NCPC, Art. 200*), he very rarely does so. Despite the precautions taken to ensure the credibility of *attestations* (thus they must cite details of the witness, be signed by the witness and contain an indication that any false testimony may give rise to prosecution for the offence of false testimony (*NCPC, Art. 202*)), their probative effect is very variable. This is essentially because most *attestations* are obtained from the witnesses not by the judge, but by the party who wishes to produce them in evidence. The probative value of an *attestation*, as with other evidence, will be determined in due course by the trial court.

Enquêtes: The procedure of *enquête*, by which oral testimony is given by witnesses to the judge (regulated by *NCPC, Arts. 199, 204–231*), usually occurs during *instruction*, the examination taking place in chambers. However, witnesses may also be required to give evidence at the trial itself. Failure to give evidence without legitimate excuse may lead to the imposition of a fine. An *enquête*, as with other *mesures d'instruction*, may be ordered on the judge's own initiative, or on the application of one of the parties. Where one of the parties requests an *enquête*, he must specify the facts that he wishes to be examined and must draw up a list of the names of the persons whom he wishes to give evidence (*NCPC, Arts. 222–224*). In accordance with the principle of *contradiction*, once the holding of an *enquête* has been ordered, any other party or parties is entitled to have the witnesses of his choice examined by the judge on the same facts at the *enquête* (*NCPC, Art. 204*). When it has been decided to hold an *enquête*, the judge may, on his own initiative or that of a party, order any person whose examination appears to be useful for the revelation of the truth to attend to give evidence (*NCPC, Art. 218*).

The parties and their *avocats* are of course entitled to attend the examination of the witnesses. The witnesses normally give their evidence separately under oath (unless, for example, they are under a legal disability). After the witness has given his evidence to the judge, the parties may be permitted to put questions to the witness through the judge. The judge may indeed decide to confront one witness with another, with the parties or with a technical expert. The procedure of *enquête* may be used to obtain oral evidence from a witness who has submitted a written *attestation*. Written depositions of the evidence obtained during the *enquête* will be drawn up. In practice, the procedure of *enquête* is rarely used, due partly to the time it takes. The judge has a more general power to take evidence on the spot from any person where this seems to him to be useful for the revelation of the truth (*NCPC, Art. 231*).

Expert evidence; introduction: The last group of *mesures d'instruction* are those carried out by technical experts (*techniciens*). *NCPC, Art. 232* provides that the judge may appoint "any person of his choice" to examine a question of fact which requires clarification by a technical expert. The court, however, is not bound to accept the findings of fact of the technical expert, who should carry out his task conscientiously with impartiality and objectivity (*NCPC, Art. 237*). In the *NCPC* it is sought to limit recourse to a full expert inquiry (*une expertise*) by an *expert* because of the implications of cost and delay. Therefore (*NCPC, Arts. 249–262*), rather than an *expertise*, the judge may require the carrying out of simplified inquiries such as *constatations* by a *constatant* (simple investigations of fact) or a *consultation* by a *consultant* on a purely technical point. *Constatations* and *consultations* may be ordered not only during *instruction*, but also during the course of the trial. The *technicien* will give his evidence to the court either orally or in writing (*NCPC, Art. 245*). In practice, judges continue to have wide recourse to *expertises* even though they should do so only in respect of complex investigations for which a *constatation* or *consultation* is insufficient (*NCPC, Art. 263*).

Expertises: The provisions of the *NCPC* have considerably increased the role of the judge in determining whether or not to hold an *expertise* (*NCPC, Arts. 263 to 284–1*), the way in which the procedure is to be carried out, and what weight is to be given to the expert's report. However, the principle of *contradiction* continues to apply; in this context this means that the parties and their *avocats* are entitled to be informed of the investigations and to be present when they are carried out (where appropriate); they may also comment on the investigations that are being effected and on the final report of the *expert*.

The judge may on his own initiative order the holding of an *expertise*, but it is more usual for him to do so following a request by one of the parties. The judge must, on appointing the *expert*, not only identify the reasons which make the *expertise* necessary, but also specify the limits of the investigation and the time within which it must be carried out (*NCPC, Art. 265*). The parties may appeal against decisions relating to the ordering of an *expertise* independently of the substantive issue (*NCPC, Art. 272*).

It is for the judge to choose the expert (or experts, if more than one appears to him to be necessary). The expert is entitled, once appointed, to seek the opinion of other experts on matters outside his technical expertise (*NCPC, Art. 278*; this is to be contrasted with *constatants* and *consultants*, who must carry out their investigations alone). The NCPC seeks to bring about collaboration between the *expert* and the judge in the way that the *expertise* is carried out; the *expert* must thus inform the judge of the progress of his investigations and of any difficulties that he comes up against which might require an extension of the time limit (*NCPC, Arts. 273, 279*). For his part the judge is entitled to be present at the investigations, although in practice he rarely is present. He may also restrict or extend the limits of the *expertise*.

The report of the expert will be presented orally or in writing to the trial court (*NCPC, Art. 282*). In practice, the expert usually reports in writing, and the court normally accepts his conclusions. Where more than one expert has been appointed, although only one report is drafted, each expert may express his own opinion. Types of expert report that are often found in practice include engineers' reports on the faulty construction of buildings, medical reports on the cause and extent of bodily injury, and accountants' reports in company law cases. The court is not bound to accept the expert's conclusions (*NCPC, Art. 246*). The costs of the *expertise* are usually paid initially by the party who requested it, or jointly by the parties in such proportions as the judge determines (*NCPC, Art. 269*); these costs will eventually be borne by the party paying the costs of the action; this is usually the loser (see Chapter 3).

(iv) Bringing instruction to an end

When the *juge de la mise en état* (in the *TGI*) considers that the case is ready to be tried, he will issue an *ordonnance de clôture de l'instruction* (*NCPC, Art. 779*); thereafter the parties may generally not submit new *conclusions* or adduce fresh evidence (*NCPC, Art. 783*). The case is then set down for trial.

The role of the *juge de la mise en état* is different from that of the *juge d'instruction* in criminal cases. In civil procedure it is essentially for the parties and not the *juge de la mise en état* to carry out the process of *instruction*; the judge is there to oversee and control the process (*NCPC, Arts. 763, 777*). Therefore, unlike his colleague in the criminal process, who at the end of *instruction* gives a reasoned decision, he does not generally have to produce a written report of the case at the end of *instruction*, although the divisional president does have a discretion to order him to do so if of the opinion that the case requires it (*NCPC, Art. 785*). This also contrasts with administrative procedure (see below) where the judge who has been overseeing *instruction* not only drafts a report but also acts as *rapporteur* to the trial court, giving a summary of the case at the start of the hearing. Where the civil *juge de la mise en état* is required to draft a *rapport* under *NCPC, Art. 785*, he will act as *rapporteur* to the *TGI* in this way (*NCPC, Art. 440*).

3. Hearing and judgment

(a) Introduction

At the public hearing the *avocats* for each party present their *dossiers* and make their oral submissions to the court. The court hearing (*audience publique*) is not as central to French civil procedure as it is in English procedure which relies heavily on the presentation of evidence, particularly the oral examination and cross-examination of the parties and witnesses, before the trial court. In France, the success of a claim depends more on the quality of the *dossier* drawn up by the parties' *avocats* during the pre-trial phase and the *conclusions* and documents in support which it contains. The court hearing consists essentially of the presentation to the court of these *dossiers* and arguments based on them by the *avocats* of the parties. As we have seen, the parties must have an *avocat* to represent them during pre-trial procedure; however, although they usually have an *avocat* to present their case at the hearing, they are not obliged to, as they are entitled to make their own oral representations to the court (*NCPC, Art. 441*).

This phase of procedure is traditionally divided into three parts, the *débats*, when the *avocats* present their case, the *délibéré*, when the judges deliberate, and the *jugement*. Let us examine each in turn.

(b) Les débats

The president of the court is in charge of proceedings at the hearing (*NCPC, Arts. 438, 440*). Except in the rare case that the *juge de la mise en état* has been required to make a written report which he will present to the court at the outset (see above), the president gives the first word to the plaintiff's *avocat*. In his *plaidoirie*, the plaintiff's *avocat* sets out his client's claim and the grounds upon which he is relying. He will also refute those arguments of his adversary which he knows about as a result of the defendant's *conclusions*. It is then the turn of the defence *avocat* to do likewise. In practice, this usually brings the *plaidoiries* to an end. The court may (*NCPC, Art. 442*) seek further elucidation from the *avocats* (or the parties) on matters of fact or law which the court considers to be in need of clarification or where this appears necessary. The president is entitled to bring the addresses of the *avocats* to an end when the court has been sufficiently enlightened (*NCPC, Art. 441*), but generally he does not intervene. The last word is given to the *ministère public*, in cases where he is intervening as *partie jointe* (*NCPC, Art. 443*).

There is no examination and cross-examination of the parties and witnesses as such; it should be recalled that where oral witness evidence is permitted (eg not, in principle, to prove a contract; see above), this will very largely have been obtained by the *juge de la mise en état* during the pre-trial procedure (*l'enquête*; see above) and thus form part of the dossier, although, as has been seen, it is possible for *enquêtes* to be ordered by the trial court. The court does not rely just on the oral *plaidoiries* of the *avocats*, as the dossier of the respective pleadings, documents in support and evidence obtained by way of *mesures d'instruction* will have been deposited with the secretariat of the court (*NCPC, Art. 727*), and therefore is available to the judges during the hearing; moreover, the *avocats*, on finishing their interventions, will hand over their own dossiers to the court.

At the end of the *plaidoiries* the president closes the hearing (*clôture des débats*), after which the parties cannot produce any further written memoranda (*notes en délibéré*) in support of their case (apart from where the president so requires, for example to clarify certain points or in response to the arguments of the *ministère public* (*NCPC, Art. 445*)), because in accordance with the *principe de la contradiction* each side must be given the opportunity of responding to the other side's arguments. However, the president does have a certain discretion (*NCPC, Art. 444*) to reopen the *débats*, for example to enable the debate of issues which were brought to his attention only after the end of the proceedings.

(c) Le délibéré

The judges of the trial court all participate in the deliberation (*le délibéré*), retiring to discuss the case and determine by majority decision the judgment of the court (*NCPC, Arts. 447–449*). In civil procedure it is rare for the judges to reach an immediate decision; the pronouncement of the decision (*le prononcé du jugement*) is usually deferred (*mis en délibéré*) to a future date (often two months).

(d) Le jugement

There are numerous detailed rules which govern the drafting of the text of the judgment (both in the *TGI* and in other civil courts). For example, *NCPC, Art. 454* requires the written judgment to indicate a certain number of matters, such as the names of the parties, the *avocats*, and the judges giving the judgment. *NCPC, Art. 451* sets out the general rule that the judgment of the court must be pronounced in public. A further set of detailed rules specifies the method by which the judgment is to be notified to the parties (*NCPC, Arts. 675–682*). A breach of these rules relating to judgments may in certain cases lead to the annulment of the judgment.

Another issue is that of the effect of a judgment, which is generally regarded not as creating new rights but as simply declaring the pre-existing rights of the parties. From a procedural point of view the judgment is regarded as having two effects. Firstly, the judgment has binding authority on the parties (*le jugement a l'autorité de la chose jugée*). The parties are therefore barred from starting further proceedings in respect of the same matter (ie involving the same parties, having the same objective and based on the same legal foundations as the earlier case).

Secondly, a judgment cannot be executed until it has acquired *la force de la chose jugée*; in effect, a judgment cannot as a general rule be executed whilst (*NCPC, Art. 500*) it remains subject to *appel* or *opposition*. However, in two cases a judgment may be immediately enforced despite being subject to such appeals. Firstly, the law provides that certain types of judgment are immediately enforceable (*jugements exécutoires à titre provisoire*), for example (*NCPC, Art. 514*) summary decisions (*ordonnances de référé*; see below). Secondly, the court may decide (on its own initiative or on application by one of the parties) that in the light of the nature of the case, judgment should be treated as immediately enforceable (*NCPC, Art. 515*). Where it is the judge who orders *exécution provisoire*, appeal lies to the first president of the *Cour d'Appel*, who may stay execution if immediate execution is likely to have manifestly excessive consequences (*NCPC, Art. 524*).

4. Voies de recours (appeals)

(a) Introduction

Voies de recours are the means by which judicial decisions are contested; the phrase covers the differing types of appeal and motions for rehearing. That which is most frequently exercised is appeal (*appel*) to the *Cour d'Appel* which, as has been mentioned above, takes the form of a rehearing of the case. We will concentrate on *appel*, dealing in a more summary fashion with the other *voies de recours*.

(b) Appel

(i) Introduction

L'appel, according to *NCPC, Art. 542*, is the means by which a judgment of first instance may be reversed or annulled by the *Cour d'Appel*. As a general principle, appeal lies against any first instance decision, even in respect of consent orders (*matières gracieuses*), unless otherwise provided by law (*NCPC, Art. 543*).

(ii) Conditions

The right of appeal is subject to certain conditions. These are not unduly restrictive, on account of the general principle of the *double degré de juridiction* whereby the parties to an action are in effect given two bites at the litigious cherry. For *appel* to lie, three main groups of conditions must be satisfied. Firstly, the judgment must be one which is capable of being the subject of an appeal. Although, as has been seen, this is generally true of all first instance judgments, legislation precludes the right to appeal against judgments of "first and last resort", ie involving less than 13,000 FF (18,200 FF against judgments of the *Conseil de Prud'hommes* (1992 figure)). The value of the litigation is not the only reason for the exclusion of appeal; *appel* is not available, for example, against certain judgments relating to the judicial liquidation of a company.

The second condition is that only a party who has an interest in the case may appeal (*NCPC, Art. 546*); essentially, this is any party to the first instance case who did not obtain entire satisfaction. The party who takes the initiative of appealing is said to lodge an *appel principal*, and his adversary, if he has not obtained total satisfaction at first instance, may himself launch an *appel incident*.

The third condition is that the *appel* must be made within a certain time limit. In principle this is one month from the date of the notification of the judgment (*NCPC, Art. 538*). However, this time limit may in certain cases be shorter; eg 15 days in respect of a consent order (*en matière gracieuse*) or for a summary *ordonnance de référé* (*NCPC, Art. 490*).

(iii) Effect of appel

Traditionally, *appel* has been regarded as having both a suspensive and a devolutive effect. There is a suspensive effect in that *appel* to the *Cour d'Appel* suspends the execution of the first instance judgment. It is important to note that this suspensive effect operates not only from the date when an *appel* is actually lodged, but also during the period in which appeal is available against a first instance judgment, which as we have seen means that during this period the judgment cannot normally be executed.

The second effect of *appel* is its *effet dévolutif*. This means that an *appel* refers a case which has been judged at first instance to the appeal court for review of matters both of fact and law (*NCPC, Art. 561*). The *Cour d'Appel* may examine only the aspects of the first instance judgment (*chefs du jugement*) against which *appel* has been made.

The *Cour d'Appel*, although in theory seized to rehear the case in respect of matters of both fact and law, will not usually do so unless the appellant is arguing for the first instance decision to be annulled *in toto*; in most cases the appeal is limited by the parties to particular issues of fact or law, and the court will examine and rule on those aspects only (*NCPC, Art. 562*).

The devolutive effect of *appel* also means that the *Cour d'Appel* may only take cognisance of that which has been judged at first instance. *NCPC, Art. 564* sets out in this respect the principle that the parties cannot on appeal submit new claims (*prétentions*) to the court. Nevertheless there are a number of exceptions to this principle. Firstly it is considered that a party does not submit a new claim where he simply produces new *moyens*, ie new evidence or new arguments supporting his claim. Accordingly it is thus possible for a party on appeal to produce new legal arguments and new evidence (including documentary evidence) to support the claim he made at first instance (*NCPC, Art. 563*). It is also possible for a party to modify on appeal the legal basis of his claim, as long as he is seeking the same ends as he was at first instance (*NCPC, Art. 565*); for example, where a claim for damages at first instance was based on contract, on appeal arguments based on tortious liability may be raised. Furthermore, a counterclaim (*demande reconventionnelle*) may be raised by the defendant, and third parties may intervene in a case for the first time on appeal (*NCPC, Arts. 554, 555, 567*). Finally, *NCPC, Art. 568* provides that where *appel* is launched in respect of a *mesure d'instruction* (or certain other procedural issues) the *Cour d'Appel* may in certain circumstances proceed to judge the substantive case (*juger au fond*) without sending the matter back to the first instance court; this procedure is known as *l'évocation*.

(iv) Procedure in the Cour d'Appel

Ordinary procedure in the *Cour d'Appel* starts with the lodging of an appeal (*la déclaration d'appel*) by the appellant (*l'appelant*) to the secretariat of the *Cour d'Appel* which will at once inform the respondent (known as the *intimé*) of the appeal. The *déclaration d'appel* must identify (*NCPC, Art. 901*), *inter alia*, the parts of the judgment (*chefs du jugement*) against which the appeal is limited (if indeed it is limited in this way) and the name of the appellant's *avoué* (the *représentation* of the parties in pre-trial procedure by an *avoué* is obligatory in most cases (*NCPC, Art. 899*), although there are exceptions, for example in respect of appeals from decisions of the *Conseils de Prud'hommes, Tribunaux des Affaires de Sécurité Sociale* and *Tribunaux Paritaires des Baux Ruraux*). The parties will usually be represented at the hearing by an *avocat*.

One of the parties (usually the appellant) must within two months of the lodging of the *déclaration d'appel* request that the matter be set down for trial, failing which the appeal will lapse. The first president of the *Cour d'Appel* will remit the case to a particular division; one of the judges of that division, acting as *conseiller de la mise en état*, will proceed to *instruction* in a way which is similar to that which occurs in the *Tribunal de Grande Instance* (*NCPC, Art. 910*). However, if the case is urgent or appears to be in a state to be judged forthwith, the divisional president may set it down for hearing directly. The procedure of the *Cour d'Appel* is essentially the same as that of the *Tribunal de Grande Instance*, the drafting of *conclusions* and the exchanges of *pièces* being carried out not by *avocats* but *avoués* representing the parties.

(c) Other voies de recours

(i) Opposition

L'opposition is a procedure by which a person against whom judgment by default was given may, within one month of notification of the decision, seize the court which gave the judgment with a view to having the judgment retracted and the case reheard (*NCPC, Arts. 571–578*). In the past, this procedure was often used simply as a way of delaying matters; to prevent this, *NCPC, Art. 473* gives a restrictive definition of "judgment by default" (*jugement par défaut*) against which *opposition* lies.

(ii) Tierce opposition

La tierce opposition is a *voie de recours* enabling a third party to have reversed or varied, in respect of matters of fact or law, a judgment to which he was not a party (and at which he was not represented) but which affects his interests (*NCPC, Arts. 582–592*). It is available in respect of any judgment unless expressly excluded by law. It might be used where, for example, an adoption order has been made without the participation of one of the natural parents; *tierce opposition* will lie if the adopting parents are shown to be guilty of fraud or fraudulent misrepresentation (*Code Civil, Art. 353–1*). A claim of *tierce opposition* must be brought before the court which reached the original decision within 30 years of the date of the judgment complained of (or where the third party received official notification of the judgment, within two months thereof). Such proceedings do not have suspensive effect.

(iii) Recours en révision

This is a *voie de recours* used by a party against a judgment which has acquired *la force de la chose jugée* (ie against which *appel* no longer lies); it seeks the revocation of the judgment on the grounds that an error of fact has been made (*NCPC, Arts. 593–603*). *Recours en révision*, which is made to the court which gave the judgment complained of, must be used within two months of the facts which form the basis of the *recours* coming to the attention of the appellant. The grounds on which *recours en révision* lies are as follows: that the judgment was obtained by fraud, or was based on documents or witness evidence which have since been shown to have been falsified; or that since the judgment was given, documentary evidence has come to light which had been retained by another party. The court which is seized by way of *recours en révision* makes a preliminary determination as to whether or not the *recours* is admissible. If the *recours* is admissible, the court proceeds to review both matters of fact and law.

(iv) Pourvoi en cassation

Grounds for lodging a pourvoi: A *pourvoi en cassation*, which is regulated by *NCPC, Arts. 604–639*, is made to the *Cour de Cassation* by a party against a judgment of last resort of an inferior court, with a view to having that judgment quashed on the grounds that it is not in conformity with the law. We have already seen in Chapter 3 that the *Cour de Cassation* does not retry a case, but simply examines the issues of law raised in the *pourvoi*; if the decision of the lower court is quashed, it will be sent back for retrial. In this chapter we will concentrate on the procedural aspects of the *pourvoi en cassation*.

It is important to note that the issuing of a *pourvoi en cassation* does not generally have the effect of suspending the judgment complained of; the judgment can therefore be executed by the successful party. Indeed, it is even provided (*NCPC, Art. 1009–1*) that the first president of the *Cour de Cassation* may decide not to examine the *pourvoi* until the appellant has complied with the judgment of the inferior court (unless to do so is likely to give rise to "manifestly excessive consequences"). However, the lodging of a *pourvoi en cassation* may exceptionally have the effect of suspending execution; this is the case in such matters as divorce and judicial separation. Despite the general non-suspensive effect, it is obviously risky for a party who was successful in the inferior court to execute the judgment in his favour whilst a *recours en cassation* is pending, as the judgment may be quashed by the *Cour de Cassation*; should he proceed with execution in the interim, he does so at his own risk.

Procedure in the Cour de Cassation: Procedure is regulated by *NCPC, Arts. 973–1031*. Both parties must normally be represented by an *avocat au Conseil d'Etat et à la Cour de Cassation* (*NCPC, Art. 973*) although there are exceptions, such as in respect of *recours* against decisions of the *Conseils de Prud'hommes* (*Code du Travail, Art. R. 517–10*). The *pourvoi* is lodged by the appellant (*demandeur en pourvoi*) by means of a *déclaration* (to which is attached a copy of the judgment complained of) which is submitted to the secretariat (*le greffe*) who will inform the respondent (*défendeur au pourvoi*). The case proceeds with an exchange of *mémoires* drafted by the *avocats* containing their respective legal arguments; the appellant's *mémoire ampliatif* must be submitted within five months of the *déclaration*, and the respondent's *mémoire en défence* must follow within two months of the *mémoire ampliatif*. The division of the *Cour de Cassation* which is competent appoints a judge to act as *rapporteur*; his role is to draw up a report on the case which he presents to the court at the beginning of the *audience publique*. Thereafter the *avocats* are entitled to make oral representations supplementary to their written *mémoires* "if they ask to do so", but in practice this is rare. The parties may also be heard in person with the authorisation of the president. The *ministère public* is then asked to give his opinion. The court subsequently retires and gives its verdict in due course. We have examined in Chapter 3 the effect of a decision of rejection or quashing of the *pourvoi en cassation*.

5. Voies d'exécution: enforcement of judgments

Once judgment has been pronounced, the question of its enforcement arises. In the absence of voluntary execution, the judgment debtor can be required to comply with the judgment by means of *voies d'exécution*. Recourse to these supposes that the judgment creditor has had his right to execute judgment recognised in an official document capable of execution (*titre exécutoire*) of which the best example is a court judgment from which appeal no longer lies or which benefits from being immediately enforceable (*jugement exécutoire*; see above).

In practice, most types of *voies d'exécution* that are used to obtain the payment of monetary sums take the form of *saisies*. A *saisie* entails the sequestration and sale (*vente forcée*) of goods belonging to the judgment debtor in order to pay the judgment debt. *Saisies* may in principle be effected over all assets of the judgment debtor, whether movable property (*biens meubles*) or immovable (*biens immeubles*) (*Code Civil, Art. 2092*). However, certain assets are exempt from seizure, in particular those which constitute the minimum necessary for daily life, such as a table and chairs, a bed, clothes, work tools, and a certain fraction of the judgment debtor's income.

It is essentially for the judgment creditor to have the judgment executed; this will be done through a *huissier* (see Chapter 3). For the simpler types of *voies d'exécution*, such as *saisies* of movable property, the intervention of a *huissier* may be sufficient. For the more complex, especially *saisies* of immovable property, the *Tribunal de Grande*

Instance oversees the procedure, and the public auction (*vente aux enchères*) takes place during a hearing held by the court. The procedure followed is basically the same for all *saisies*; the property which is seized is rendered inalienable during the time necessary for organising a public auction. The proceeds of sale are then used to pay the judgment creditor. However, the *saisie-arrêt* (known as the *saisie-attribution* since the *loi du 10.7.1991* which modernised *saisies* over movable property) is of a different nature. It enables the judgment debt to be paid out of sums owed by a third party to the judgment debtor; such *saisies* are often made against sums held by the judgment debtor's banker, employer or notary.

In cases where the judgment does not require the payment of a sum of money but rather requires the judgment debtor to do or refrain from doing something, the use of *saisies* is evidently inappropriate. The execution of such judgments may be facilitated by the judge attaching to the judgment an *astreinte*. This is a pecuniary penalty which is payable to the judgment creditor; it may be fixed at a certain sum per day, week or month of default. Where, however, the *astreinte* fails to persuade the judgment debtor to comply with the judgment, the judgment creditor may apply to court to have the *astreinte* liquidated. The court will fix a sum of money which is based, where the judge specifies the *astreinte* to be an *astreinte définitive*, on the total amount of the *astreinte* that has not been paid; if, however, the judge specifies the *astreinte* to be an *astreinte provisoire*, there is a discretion in the fixing of the amount of the liquidated sum. This sum is thereafter regarded as a judgment debt, and the judgment creditor may enforce the payment in the usual way.

Generally, the non-payment of civil debts does not lead to the imposition of criminal sanctions, although there are some exceptions, such as the non-payment of a *pension alimentaire* (periodic payments ordered to be paid to a spouse or child).

C. Particular procedures

1. Introduction

Having examined the principal procedural steps for an action taking place before the *Tribunal de Grande Instance*, we will now look briefly at certain preliminary procedures, the simplified procedure followed before other first instance civil courts, and non-judicial methods of dispute resolution.

2. Procedures for simple and urgent matters (les procédures d'urgence)

Two sets of procedure are applicable in this context. The first set are summary procedures (*la procédure des référés* and *l'ordonnance sur requête*) used in respect of urgent matters and certain preliminary matters; summary procedures have been a part of French civil procedure since before the Revolution. The second set (*l'injonction de payer* and *l'injonction de faire*) are simplified procedures for obtaining satisfaction.

(a) Ordonnances de référé and l'ordonnance sur requête

According to *NCPC, Art. 484*, an *ordonnance de référé* is a provisional decision given at the request of one party against the other party, present or called, in cases where the law gives a judge, who is not called to rule on the substantive claim, the power to order immediately any measures which are necessary.

A characteristic of *le référé* is the speed of the procedure. This explains, firstly, the fact that the power to issue *ordonnances de référé* is given not to the full court but rather to the president of the principal civil jurisdictions sitting alone; ie *Tribunal de Grande Instance, Tribunal d'Instance, Tribunal de Commerce, Tribunal Paritaire de Baux Ruraux, Conseil de Prud'hommes* (president and vice-president sitting together) and *Cour d'Appel* (first president).

It also explains the conditions in which the procedure of *référé* is available. Traditionally, this was limited to cases where the need for the intervention of the courts was urgent, and where the measure which was being sought was not likely to be seriously contested. Although this remains true (*NCPC, Art. 808*), nowadays it is often possible to obtain an *ordonnance de référé* upon proof that the rights invoked by the plaintiff cannot seriously be contested by the defendant, even if there is no urgency. This is particularly true (*NCPC, Arts. 808, 809(2), 849(2), 873(2)*) where a creditor demands the award of an interim payment (*une provision*) in respect of an obligation which is not in serious dispute (known in practice as a *référé provision*); eg a demand for a provisional award of damages in respect of a personal injury claim. Caselaw has accepted that in such cases the plaintiff need not show that it was "urgent" for him to obtain this interim payment.

The *juge des référés* is not infrequently asked, before the substantive matter is dealt with (and before the appointment of a *juge de la mise en état* in the *TGI*), to appoint an expert to verify the existence, extent and cause of the loss which has occurred; this is known as a *référé expertise* (*NCPC, Art. 145*). This article may be used to seek *mesures d'instruction* for the conservation or establishment of evidence; however the fact that the *référé* procedure is *contradictoire*, giving the other party the right to participate, may in this context act to the disadvantage of the party seeking to use the procedure; the latter might therefore prefer to have recourse to the ex-parte procedure of *l'ordonnance sur requête* (see below).

The *juge des référés* may (*NCPC, Art. 809(1)*), even in cases which are contested, take protective measures (*mesures conservatoires*) either to bring to an end a disturbance which is manifestly illegal (such as an illegal occupation of premises by striking workers) or to prevent imminent loss (eg to prevent the publication of material which is in breach of the right of privacy (see *Code Civil, Art. 9*), or to prevent the unauthorised use of a trade-name or trade-mark (*la concurrence déloyale*)). The procedure of *le référé* may also be used by a judgment creditor to resolve difficulties in the execution of a judgment (*NCPC, Art. 811*).

It can be seen that there are many ways in which the *juge des référés* may intervene; however, his decisions are not definitive. *NCPC, Art. 488* reiterates the traditional rule that an *ordonnance de référé* is not accorded *l'autorité de la chose jugée*; as a result, the court which subsequently deals with the substantive case does not have to keep to the ruling of the *juge des référés*. However, in practice *ordonnances de référé* are unlikely to be overturned. There are two reasons for this. The first is because such orders have the status of being immediately enforceable (*exécutoire de droit*); indeed, enforcement may be made subject to an *astreinte* (*NCPC, Art. 491*). The second reason is because in many cases, as has just been seen, the *juge des référés* will issue the *ordonnance de référé* on the basis that the plaintiff's claim is not seriously contestable, making it unlikely that the trial court will take a different view. In practice, *ordonnances de référé* are in fact provisional only where the measures taken do not prejudice the substantive decision, such as a decision to appoint an expert.

In some cases, the plaintiff may obtain sufficient satisfaction from the *ordonnance de référé* not to proceed with the substantive case; this is particularly true where the *juge des référés* exercises his power under *NCPC, Art. 809(2)*, available in cases where the existence of an obligation is not seriously contestable, to make not just a provisional award in favour of the creditor, but to order the performance of the obligation *in toto*.

An application for an *ordonnance de référé* is made by writ (*assignation*) to the court from which the order is sought on one of the days (which is often each week) when the court deals with matters of *référé*. As *référé* proceedings are *inter partes*, the judge must make sure that the other party has had time to prepare his defence (*NCPC, Art. 486*). Appeal (*appel*) may be lodged against an *ordonnance de référé* within 15 days of its being issued, unless it emanates from the first president of the *Cour d'Appel* or where appeal is generally excluded because of the amount involved.

An *ordonnance sur requête* is a provisional order available on an ex-parte application, usually to a judge (of a first instance civil court or the *Cour d'Appel*) sitting alone. Apart from instances where its use is specifically authorised by statute (eg in respect of certain *saisies*,

308

vesting orders in favour of universal legatees (*Code Civil, Art. 1008*) and certain matrimonial orders (*Code Civil, Art. 220−1; NCPC, Art. 1290*)), an *ordonnnance sur requête* may be obtained from a judge where in the circumstances an ex-parte application is shown to be justified, particularly in cases of urgency (*NCPC, Arts. 493, 812*). The procedure is often used in practice to prevent the removal of assets that might be used to pay a judgment debt. Appeal lies to the *Cour d'Appel*, unless the order was made by the first president of the *Cour d'Appel* (*NCPC, Art. 496*).

(b) Injonction de payer and injonction de faire

The procedure of *injonction de payer* is regulated by *NCPC, Arts. 1405−1425*. It applies mainly to liquidated debts in respect of a contract, enabling the creditor to obtain a rapid judgment in accordance with a simplified procedure. Application is made for an *ordonnance portant injonction de payer* to the *Tribunal d'Instance* or *Tribunal de Commerce*; all supporting documentation is submitted with the application. If the judge refuses the application (against which decision no appeal is possible), the plaintiff will have to follow normal procedures to recover his debt. However, the judge will issue the *ordonnance* if he is of the opinion that "in the light of the documents produced, the plaint appears founded, at least in part" (*NCPC, Art. 1409*). A copy of the order will be served on the debtor, who may within one month appeal to the court that issued it by way of *opposition* − this will usually result (*NCPC, Art. 1408*) in the case being automatically transferred for hearing in the normal way. If the defendant does not appeal in this way, the plaintiff may request to be given leave to execute the order forcibly.

This procedure of *injonction de payer* is often used by business creditors (eg high street shops and credit companies) against small debtors or against those who are not contesting the contractual obligation. There is no pecuniary ceiling limiting the availability of the procedure to the creditor.

A related procedure, which in practice benefits consumers, is that of *l'injonction de faire*, introduced in 1988 (now *NCPC, Art. 1425−1 to 1425−9*). Its purpose essentially is to enable consumers to obtain judgment rapidly against those who have contracted to provide goods or services but have failed to do so. It is available in respect of contractual obligations (of a value not exceeding the jurisdiction of the *Tribunal d'Instance*) where at least one party did not contract as a trader (*commerçant*). The plaintiff applies to the *Tribunal d'Instance* for an *injonction de faire*, enclosing supporting documentary evidence. If the court thinks that the claim is not founded, the plaintiff will have to follow normal procedures. If, however, the court accepts the plaintiff's case, it will issue an *injonction*, against which no appeal lies, for the obligation to be executed by a certain date (a hearing date being provisionally fixed for the court to deal with any non-compliance).

3. Procedure in respect of consent orders (matière gracieuse)

The intervention of the French judge is sometimes required in matters which are not contentious. It is thus necessary for a judge to approve certain agreements reached between the parties, such as an agreement by a couple to divorce by mutual consent (*NCPC, Art. 1008*) or to change the name of a natural child (*NCPC, Art. 1153*). He must also authorise certain operations (such as the rectification of a certificate of civil status (*acte d'état civil*)).

The usual rules of procedure which apply to contested cases are considered inappropriate for such consent orders. Instead, an action (*NCPC, Arts. 25–29*) is started by a petition (*requête gracieuse*) addressed by one or more parties to the appropriate court. The judge may of his own initiative proceed to order such *mesures d'instruction* as he considers useful. He may without formality hear not only those whose interests might be affected, but also any person whose evidence he considers may be of value. In the *TGI*, a judge is appointed to act as *rapporteur*, and the *ministère public* is required to give his opinion (*NCPC, Arts. 797–800*). The court may reach a decision without holding a full hearing; where a full hearing does take place, it is held in chambers. The judgment, which may be based not only on facts alleged by the parties, but also on any facts which relate to the case, is not pronounced publicly (*NCPC, Art. 451*). The applicants may appeal against the judgment if they have not obtained satisfaction (*NCPC, Art. 543*). Third parties whose interests are adversely affected by the judgment may appeal (by means of *appel*) only if the judgment has been officially notified to them (as it will be if the court has had notice of their interest); if not, their only recourse is appeal by way of *tierce opposition* (*NCPC, Art. 583(2)*).

4. Simplified procedure before courts of special jurisdiction

(a) Introduction

In order to render justice before courts of special jurisdiction such as the *Tribunaux d'Instance, Tribunaux de Commerce* and *Conseils de Prud'hommes* more rapid, less expensive and more accessible to litigants, simplified rules of procedure apply. Particularly significant is the fact that in these courts the parties may carry out the procedural steps themselves, and even represent themselves in court. Indeed they may choose to have both of these functions carried out by someone other than an *avocat*. However, their choice of representatives is limited. In the *Tribunal d'Instance* this choice is essentially limited to members of their family (and, in the case of an employer, someone from his business), although in the *Conseil de Prud'hommes* it includes representatives of unions or employers' organisations, and in the *Tribunal de Commerce* it extends to *conseils juridiques* and *huissiers de justice* (*NCPC, Arts. 827, 828, 853, 879 (Code du Travail, Art. R. 516−4, 5)*). Another characteristic of all three courts is that procedure is essentially oral, and the parties are not required to submit written *conclusions*, although in practice they will often do so.

(b) Tribunal d'Instance

The procedural rules applying to actions heard by the *Tribunal d'Instance* (*NCPC, Arts. 827 to 852−1*) are particular in that the *juge d'instance* is given the role of attempting to effect a conciliation between the parties before proceeding to try the case.

The plaintiff may decide simply to seize the court (by a *citation à seule fin de conciliation*) for the purpose of attempting conciliation. If this occurs, the parties will be called to a meeting at which the judge will try to resolve the matter by conciliation. If this fails, the plaintiff will have to commence an action by writ in the normal way unless the parties agree to the judge proceeding to try the case on the spot.

Usually, however, an action is commenced by an *assignation à toutes fins*; even under this procedure, the judge is obliged at least to attempt conciliation before proceeding to trial. If the judge decides that the matter is not ready, he will order the appropriate *mesures d'instruction* to be carried out, and defer the trial to a future date.

In principle, procedure at trial is oral, although the parties may, and in practice often do, submit written *conclusions* as well as appearing in person. The judge ensures that both parties put their case on the issues raised by their respective claims, and may require either party to provide such explanations or documentary evidence as he considers necessary for the proper resolution of the case.

In TEXTS, NOS. 1−5 can be found the procedural documents (and judgment) in respect of a typical *TI* case.

(c) Tribunal de Commerce

In the *Tribunal de Commerce*, procedure (*NCPC, Arts. 853−878*) is not dissimilar to that of the *Tribunal de Grande Instance*. An action is usually commenced by means of an *assignation*. If the matter is not ready to be tried, a member of the court may be appointed to act as *juge rapporteur*, enjoying some of the powers of the *juge de la mise en état* (of the *TGI*) to oversee the *instruction* phase of procedure. He may call the parties to appear before him, and invite them to produce such evidence as he considers necessary for the matter to be tried, or he may bring *instruction* to a close and set the matter down for trial. He may endeavour to effect a conciliation between the parties. No *appel* lies against the *mesures d'instruction* that he orders independently of *appel* against the substantive judgment. The powers of the *juge rapporteur* during *instruction* are not as extensive as those of a *juge de la mise en état* in the *TGI*. His powers are limited because the legislature felt unable to endow a non-professional judge with the considerable powers of his professional counterpart. Where a matter does not require *instruction* before it can be ready for trial, it will be tried at the first hearing for which it was set down. At the hearing the procedure is essentially oral, although the parties are entitled to submit written *conclusions* if they wish.

(d) Conseils de Prud'hommes

An action is commenced in the *Conseil de Prud'hommes* either by letter or by the application to the court secretariat. Procedure (*NCPC, Art. 879; Code du Travail, R. 516–0 to R.518–2*) is divided into two stages. The first stage is when the parties appear in person before the *bureau de conciliation* whose mission, evident from its name, is to seek to conciliate the parties in a private hearing. A written report of these proceedings is drawn up.

If conciliation proves not to be possible, the case is referred to the full *bureau de jugement* for hearing. However, even where the case is referred in this way, the *bureau de conciliation* retains competence (*NCPC, Art. 879; Code du Travail, R. 516–18*) to take certain interlocutory measures, such as a decision to award the employee sums in respect of unpaid salary, or to require the delivery to him of certain documents such as a certificate of work and notification of salary; such decisions are immediately enforceable, and may have *astreintes* attached to them. The *bureau de conciliation* may also itself order the carrying out of *mesures d'instruction*, or appoint one or two of its number, acting as *conseiller rapporteur*, to oversee *instruction*; the latter can of his own initiative order the production of documents held by the parties (*Code du Travail, R. 516–23(2)*). No appeal (*appel*) lies against these *mesures d'instruction* independently of an *appel* against the substantive decision.

The hearing before the *bureau de jugement* may be held immediately after a failed attempt at conciliation, although this is rare; the case is normally adjourned to a future date. It might be decided that further *instruction* is necessary. Procedure at the hearing is again essentially oral. Unless there is good reason (such as illness), the parties must attend in person.

5. Arbitration

It is possible for the parties to have recourse to arbitration in two ways (*NCPC, Arts. 1442 et seq.*). Firstly the parties may have included in their contract a *clause compromissoire*, an agreement by which parties to a contract agree to submit any litigation arising out of the contract to arbitration (*NCPC, Art. 1442*); such a clause is valid in international contracts and commercial contracts, but not in civil contracts (*Code*

Civil, Art. 2061). The second method is by entering into an arbitration agreement known as a *compromis d'arbitrage* after the conflict has arisen; this is possible even if an action has already been commenced (*NCPC, Arts. 1447, 1450*).

In both cases the dispute is brought before a *juridiction arbitrale* made up of one or a greater odd number of arbitrators (*NCPC, Art. 1453*). The arbitrator is not generally required to abide by the rules of court procedure, unless the parties have provided otherwise in the arbitration agreement. Nevertheless, he must respect certain fundamental principles of civil procedure, such as the burden of proof and the requirement that the proceedings be *contradictoire* (see above) (*NCPC, Art. 1460*). The parties may be represented by an *avocat* or by another person of their choice (*NCPC, Art. 1472*).

The arbitrator must in principle arbitrate the matter in accordance with the relevant principles of law.

However, the parties may agree to permit him to arbitrate as *amiable compositeur*; in such a case he is entitled to arbitrate not strictly in accordance with the rules of law, but rather in accordance with equity and justice (*en équité*) (*NCPC, Art. 1474*).

The decision of the arbitrator (*une sentence arbitrale*), which must be reasoned, and reached by majority if there is more than one arbitrator, does not have the same force as the judgment of a court. It thus cannot be executed forcibly unless and until the successful party obtains from the local *Tribunal de Grande Instance* authority to do so (*une décision d'exequatur (NCPC, Art. 1477)*). The *sentence arbitrale* is normally subject to *appel* to the *Cour d'Appel*, except where the parties have renounced this right in the arbitration agreement; even then, *recours en annulation* may lie to the *Cour d'Appel* (where, for example, the arbitration proceedings failed to respect the principle that proceedings must be *contradictoire (NCPC, Arts. 1484, 1486)*). Where the arbitrator has been given the task of arbitrating as *amiable compositeur*, appeal is not available unless the parties have expressly reserved the right (*NCPC, Art. 1482*). Appeal by way of *opposition* or *cassation* does not lie from a decision of the arbitrator, although *tierce opposition* (*NCPC, Art. 1481*) and *recours en révision* (*NCPC, Art. 1491*) are available.

6. Non-judicial dispute resolution

In the light of the increasing number of actions which are being commenced in the courts, the government has sought to reduce the work-load of the courts by introducing new methods of dispute resolution. In a broad way, *NCPC, Art. 21* provides that it is within the power of any judge to seek to effect a conciliation between the parties; how this might occur is set out in *NCPC, Arts. 127–131*. The courts have thus been given the opportunity of bringing litigation to an early resolution by encouraging conciliation. These general provisions supplement specific provisions permitting particular instances of conciliation (eg in cases taking place before the *Tribunal d'Instance* and the *Conseil de Prud'hommes*; see above).

Furthermore, in recent years the government has sought to direct certain categories of litigation away from the courts towards non-judicial institutions with a view to their contractual resolution. A *décret du 20.3.1978* created the (unpaid) office of conciliator (*concilateur*). They are appointed by the first president of the *Cour d'Appel* on the advice of the *procureur général*. Their role is to facilitate, without recourse to judicial procedures, the contractual resolution (*le règlement amiable*) of conflicts. As the dispute is resolved by agreement, and not by judicial decision, no *appel* lies.

This initiative has received some hostility from certain members of the judiciary and the legal professions, who do not approve of conferring the role of conciliation on persons not necessarily having any legal training, and who therefore may effect a conciliation without reference to the rules of law appropriate to the case. In an attempt to meet the criticisms levelled at the institution, the Minister of Justice has proposed radical reforms whereby the *juge* would have a discretion, to be exercised with the agreement of the parties, to send certain types of litigation to a mediator (*médiateur*), who would try to resolve the dispute, but would throughout remain in contact with the *juge*.

D. Administrative court procedure

1. Introduction

Administrative contentious procedure displays the characteristics of inquisitorial court procedure. Not only is the *instruction* phase inquisitorial, being under the control of the court rather than the parties, but procedure is largely written, even during the trial stage. Most contentious administrative proceedings involve a claim by an individual against an administrative body; the considerable powers which are accorded to the administrative judge (for example to require the parties – particularly the administration – to produce their files and explain the reasons why a decision was taken) are sometimes justified on the basis that they are required to enable the court to correct the in-built imbalance between the parties. The fact that the judges of the administrative courts are themselves trained as civil servants, mostly graduates of the *Ecole nationale d'administration*, also helps to explain the degree of reliance on written procedure.

2. Different types of administrative proceedings (recours)

(a) Introduction

Proceedings in the administrative courts are known as *recours* rather than *actions en justice*. The word *recours* should not be confused with the term *voies de recours* which, as has been seen, refers to the different types of appeal (*appel, cassation, opposition, révision,* etc) available against a judgment. The use of the word *recours* may be explained by the fact that in most cases proceedings started in the administrative courts are in effect a *recours* against an earlier decision of an administrative body.

There are several types of proceedings available to the litigant; the one which will be chosen depends on the remedy sought from the courts. The plaintiff may simply be requesting that administrative regulations (or an administrative decision) be annulled as being illegal; he may however be seeking damages for loss that he has suffered. The different *recours* are often classified by modern writers (such as Professor René Chapus) into those which are objective and those which are subjective. According to this classification, the *recours* is objective where its purpose is to determine the conformity of administrative regulations or an administrative decision to the general provisions of the law (eg where it is claimed that government regulations which have been passed are contrary to recognised norms of legality), and is subjective where at issue is the violation of a subjective right of the plaintiff (eg where the plaintiff claims damages for loss suffered as a result of administrative activity).

(b) Recours pour excès de pouvoir

The most important type of objective proceedings is the *recours pour excès de pouvoir*, in which is sought the annulment of an illegal administrative *acte* (ie a decision of individual effect − such as the grant or refusal of a building permit − or a regulation of general effect, for example a municipal by-law (*arrêté*) regulating parking). When seized on this basis, the function of the court is limited to adjudging the legality of the administrative *acte*, which will be annulled if illegal. If a regulation of general effect is annulled, such annulment will itself be of general effect.

Because of the public interest of such proceedings, *recours pour excès de pouvoir* are more widely available than *recours de pleine juridiction* (see below). In particular, a plaintiff does not have to show a subjective interest to have *locus standi*, as is the case for a *recours de pleine juridiction*, although he must show some interest (see below). A further procedural advantage of the *recours pour excès de pouvoir* is that it is not necessary to be represented by an *avocat* (see below).

315

A second type of objective action, the *recours en appréciation de légalité*, arises as a matter of preliminary reference (*question préjudicielle*). As we have seen (Chapter 3), where in proceedings taking place before the civil courts the matter of the legality of an *acte administratif* is in issue, the civil courts cannot rule on the matter (although criminal courts can do so by way of *exception d'illégalité*). In such a case, the matter must be adjourned and referred to the administrative court on a preliminary reference by *recours en appréciation de légalité* for the administrative court to issue a declaration on the legality of the *acte*; the declaration will then be transmitted to the civil court, which will proceed with the case in the light of the ruling of the administrative court. The requirement for the plaintiff to be represented by an *avocat* does not apply to such proceedings.

A third type of objective action is the *recours en déclaration d'inexistence*, by which the plaintiff seeks from the court a declaration that the *acte administratif* is so gravely illegal that it should be regarded as never having existed. It is rarely found in practice.

(c) Contentieux de pleine juridiction

Recours de pleine juridiction (full jurisdiction proceedings; classified as *recours subjectifs*) are so called because of the fullness of the powers of the court to right a wrong caused to the plaintiff by the administration, whether tortious (eg the commission of a wrongdoing in the operation of a public service) or contractual; it extends however to other wrongs, such as the wrongful assessment of the plaintiff to tax. The administrative court has, in such cases, "full" powers in that in addition to declaring void the administrative action, it can award damages for the loss caused. Such proceedings are usually subjective because the judge is pronouncing on the existence and extent of subjective rights claimed by the plaintiff. Moreover, the decision of the court will affect only the parties to the action. However, *recours de pleine juridiction* may sometimes be objective, in the sense of dealing with the objective legality of certain categories of administrative activity. This is particularly so, for example, in respect of proceedings connected with the holding of elections, or with the assessment of an individual to tax. In both cases the proceedings are "full" proceedings because of the extensive powers of the court (eg to amend the tax assessment).

(d) Criminal and disciplinary jurisdiction

There is a category of administrative proceedings which does not fit easily into the objective/subjective analysis; this is the limited criminal jurisdiction exercised by the administrative courts. This includes the power to impose sanctions (usually only a fine) for a limited category of "highway" offences (*contraventions de grande voirie*) in respect of certain categories of public property (*le domaine public*) such as canals, electricity pylons, and railway level crossings, and also proceedings before certain administrative disciplinary jurisdictions (such as the *Conseil de discipline des universités*).

3. Non-suspensive effect of administrative proceedings

A particular characteristic of administrative procedure is that, as a general principle, commencement of a *recours* does not have the effect of suspending the coming into operation of the administrative decision or regulations complained of. This principle accords with the notion of the inherent power of the administration (*la puissance publique*); without it, the commencement of an action against the administration would paralyse that part of its operations.

However, to prevent the rule having the consequence of frustrating an eventual finding in favour of the plaintiff, it is possible for the plaintiff to obtain a suspension of the operation (*sursis à exécution*) of the *acte administratif* if he can show that its coming into effect might cause irreparable consequences; he must also, of course, show that he has a *prima facie* case for the decision or regulations to be annulled.

4. Conditions for proceedings to lie (conditions de recevabilité des recours)

(a) Locus standi

To be able to commence proceedings, the plaintiff must show that he has *locus standi* (*intérêt pour agir*). In the case of subjective proceedings (*recours de pleine juridiction*) he must show a personal interest. However in respect of objective proceedings, in particular the *recours pour excès de pouvoir*, it will suffice if the plaintiff can show that he belongs to a group or category of people who are affected by the administrative *acte*; thus a local taxpayer has *locus standi* to challenge a decision of the municipal council to provide free medical services (*C.E., 29.3.1901, Casanova, Rec., 333*); moreover an *intérêt moral* may suffice, such as the interest of religious believers in the holding of religious ceremonies according to the rites of their faith (*C.E., 8.2.1908, Abbé Deliard, Rec., 127*).

(b) La règle de la décision préalable

By the preliminary decision rule (*la règle de la décision préalable*), a plaintiff is entitled to commence an action in the administrative courts only after the administration has actually reached a decision in respect of the subject matter of the proceedings.

In the case of a *recours pour excès de pouvoir*, in which the plaintiff is seeking the annulment of a decision which has been taken or regulations which have been issued, the administration has by definition already reached a decision on the matter; accordingly, all the plaintiff need do is append to the petition (*requête*) a copy of the offending decision or regulations. However, the rule assumes greater significance for the plaintiff in the case of a *recours de pleine juridiction*, where he is seeking compensation for loss. Here the court action may be commenced only after a claim for compensation has been made to the administration, and rejected. Such rejection may be express, but will in any event be implied after four months' silence following the submission of the claim. The preliminary decision rule does not apply to cases in which a person is claiming that he has suffered loss as a result of the carrying out of public works (*travaux publics*). The rule can perhaps be best understood as a hangover of the early doctrine of the "minister-judge" (*ministre-juge*), abolished by the *Conseil d'Etat* in the case of *Cadot* (*C.E., 13.12.1889, Rec., 1148*), according to which complaints against the administration had to be brought initially before the appropriate minister, who in effect acted as a first instance jurisdiction, the administrative courts (at the time the *Conseil d'Etat*) in effect hearing appeals from the minister's decision. The rule does have the advantage of giving the administration the opportunity of settling a dispute before the matter is taken to court.

(c) Limitation period (le délai de recours)

As a general principle, the plaintiff must lodge his *recours* within two months (of the publication of regulations of general effect; or of the notification of a decision of individual effect; or of the rejection of a claim for damages against the administration). As has been seen, four months' silence by the administration to a claim is regarded as constituting an implied rejection of the claim.

There are, however, exceptions to the general principle. Firstly, where the plaintiff seeks damages by way of a *recours de pleine juridiction*, in order to protect his interests, time does not run against him until an express rejection is forthcoming from the administration. Secondly, by a *décret du 28.11.1983*, special rules apply where an administrative decision is taken by a state administrative service or state public corporation (*établissement public de l'Etat*) following a request from a member of the public. The administrative body must issue a formal receipt (*un accusé de réception*) in response to such a request, and time cannot run until a valid receipt has been issued. Thirdly, there is an exception in the matter of preliminary references (*questions préjudicielles*) from the ordinary courts to the administrative courts for a ruling on the legality of administrative regulations, for which there is no limitation period. Nor does the limitation period apply to claims for loss arising from the carrying out of public works (*travaux publics*). Another relevant rule which should be borne in mind is that a debt owed by the administration must generally be paid within four years or it becomes time-barred (known as *la règle de la prescription quadriennale*).

The expiry of the limitation period has the effect of barring the commencing of proceedings in respect of the allegedly illegal *acte*. However, the issue of the illegality of administrative regulations of general effect may still be raised after the expiry of the limitation period in criminal proceedings; ie where the defendant argues in his defence that relevant administrative regulations (eg the *règlements* which regulate the *contravention* of which he is charged) are illegal (*l'exception d'illégalité*).

(d) Recours administratifs préalables

In an endeavour to bring about a conciliated settlement, legislation provides in an increasing number of cases that before an administrative action may be commenced, the plaintiff must first seek redress either from the administrative body with whom he is in dispute (*recours gracieux*) or from that body's hierarchical superior (*recours hiérarchique*). Even where it is not required by statute, the *recours gracieux* may be used. Indeed, a plaintiff may always use a *recours gracieux* in respect of *recours pour excès de pouvoir*. Where a *recours gracieux* is started, time (for limitation purposes) does not start to run against the litigant until a response to the claim has been received (four months' silence generally constituting an implied rejection).

5. Procedure in the administrative courts

(a) Commencing proceedings

The plaintiff commences an action by means of a petition (*requête*), addressed directly to the competent jurisdiction. The petition does not have to be in any particular form, but must identify the plaintiff (known as the *requérant*), set out the facts and grounds (*moyens*) upon which the claim is based, and be accompanied, where appropriate, by a copy of the decision or regulations which are the subject of the claim. It should be noted that the interlocutory procedure of *référé* is available in the administrative courts (by application to the president of the court) to order the carrying out of preliminary or urgent measures.

As has been seen, in the case of the *recours pour excès de pouvoir* and the *recours en appréciation de légalité*, it is not necessary for an *avocat* to carry out the pre-trial procedure (*la représentation*), although for the other types of *recours* this is necessary. Generally, it is not necessary for the parties to be represented by an *avocat* at the trial (*l'audience publique*) itself, although this frequently occurs in practice.

(b) Instruction

A member of the court is appointed to act as *rapporteur* to direct the process of *instruction* (in the *Conseil d'Etat* the *sous-section* to which the case is assigned will appoint one of its members as *rapporteur*). *Instruction* is essentially a written, inquisitorial procedure, the initiative for the carrying out of procedural steps coming from the judge and not from the parties. It thus differs somewhat from *instruction* in civil proceedings. The administrative body which is the subject of the claim is required to present its defence (in a *mémoire en défense*) to the plaintiff's *requête*. Thereafter the parties may address to the court, within time limits determined by the judge, written *mémoires* setting out their respective counter-arguments. *Instruction* is *contradictoire* in that both sides must be given proper opportunity to put their own case and to raise arguments against the allegations of the other party. The *rapporteur* may order all measures of *instruction* which to him appear to be necessary (such as the hearing of witnesses (*l'enquête*) and, in appropriate cases, the ordering of *expertises*; *expertises* are more frequent in cases taking place before the *Tribunal Administratif*). He may also constrain the parties (and in particular the administration) to produce documents and evidence and to give reasons for the administrative decisions that have been taken; refusal to do so may lead to adverse inferences being drawn.

The *instruction* phase, which may last several months or even longer, is brought to a close when the *rapporteur* decides that sufficient information has been disclosed for the case to proceed to trial. At the end of *instruction*, the *rapporteur* has the duty of drawing up a report synthesising all the issues in the case; he then presents the report to the court (in the *Conseil d'Etat*, to the *sous-section* to which the case has been assigned).

(c) Commissaire du gouvernement

In addition to the involvement of the *rapporteur*, the case is referred to a member of the court acting as *commissaire du gouvernement*, who in his report on the case (*conclusions*) proposes to the court the appropriate solution to the matter. It is worth reiterating that, contrary to the implication of his title, the *commissaire du gouvernement* does not represent the interests of the government, but is independent in respect of the opinion that he gives. The *conclusions* of *commissaires du gouvernement* often look at the development of relevant caselaw over the years and sometimes even suggest the appropriate direction for its future evolution.

(d) Trial

The proceedings at the trial (*audience publique*) are to a large extent written. They commence with the *rapporteur* reading his report, outlining to the court the issues in the case. The parties' *avocats* (or, with the exception of proceedings before the *Conseil d'Etat*, the parties themselves, with the permission of the court) may then address the court, but only to make oral observations to supplement their written *mémoires*. However, such oral addresses are rare in the *Conseil d'Etat*; indeed, the parties themselves are unlikely to be present. The *commissaire du gouvernement* is then called upon to present his *conclusions* to the court. The judges subsequently retire to deliberate, and adjourn to a later date the public pronouncement of the court's reasoned judgment (known as a *jugement* in the *Tribunaux Administratifs* and an *arrêt* in the *Cours Administratives d'Appel* and the *Conseil d'Etat*).

(e) Voies de recours

The different types of appeal and review (*voies de recours*) that we have already discussed in respect of proceedings before the ordinary courts are also found in administrative proceedings; ie *appel* from a judgment of the *Tribunal Administratif* either to the *Cour Administrative d'Appel* or to the *Conseil d'Etat* (depending on the type of proceedings); *opposition, tierce opposition* and *recours en révision* (in certain circumstances) to the court whose decision is being contested; *recours en cassation* to the *Conseil d'Etat* in respect of judgments of last resort. See below, and Chapter 3.

(f) Enforcement

The enforcement of the judgments of administrative courts presents certain difficulties, because of the separation of administrative and judicial functions imposed by the *loi des 16–24 août 1970* (see Chapter 3). As a result, it has traditionally not been possible for an injunction to be issued against an administrative authority. Nor has recourse been permitted to methods of enforced execution of a judgment against the administration; therefore, in principle, none of the private law *voies d'exécution* can be used against the administration or an administrative body which fails to comply with an administrative court judgment. This immunity has been justified theoretically on the basis that the property of the administration cannot be seized to satisfy a judgment in favour of an individual, as it is held by the administration for the purposes of the provision of public services. The judgment however remains obligatory and must be complied with by the administration.

In fact, the administration, when liable, usually does comply voluntarily with the judgment, even if on occasion it takes some time to do so. The *Conseil d'Etat (section du rapport et des études)* plays a role in seeking to encourage compliance, by explaining to the administration the way in which the judgment might be complied with and by discussing with it any difficulties of compliance. The judgment creditor may also (via his M.P.) bring in the *médiateur* (see Chapter 4) to help resolve the issue.

Neither of these methods of enforcement is coercive. In recent years, however, coercive measures (although without recourse to seizures (*saisies*)) have been introduced in order to constrain the administration to carry out administrative court judgments. The *loi du 16.7.1980* has given the *Conseil d'Etat* the power to enforce a judgment, which has not been complied with within six months, by means of *astreintes* (a sum which is payable for each day, week or month of default). The *astreinte* is in principle payable by the defaulting administrative body to the judgment creditor, although it may be decided by the *Conseil* that a certain proportion be paid instead to an equipment fund for local authorities. This power may be exercised by the *Conseil* on its own initiative, or on that of the unsatisfied judgment creditor. The *astreinte* may be liquidated (see above). Where an *astreinte* has been levied against the administration, the civil servant responsible for the non-execution of the judgment may be held by the *Cour de Discipline Budgétaire et Financière* to be personally liable to a fine.

Furthermore, under the 1980 law, in the case of the administration failing to execute within four months a judgment which requires it to pay a sum of money, the unsatisfied judgment creditor may apply for an order of enforced payment. In the case of a judgment obtained against an organ of the state, the application is made to the public accounts auditors (*comptables publics*) of the organ concerned, who will enforce payment. If judgment was obtained against a public collectivity (eg *département, commune*), the application is made to the authority with supervisory power (*l'autorité de tutelle*; eg the prefect) over the recalcitrant collectivity, and this authority will ensure compliance.

Texts and materials

Exemple schématique d'un procès civil fictif devant le Tribunal d'Instance:-
1. *Formule traditionnelle de citation devant le Tribunal d'Instance;*
2. *Conclusions résumées du demandeur à propos d'une affaire fictive;*
3. *Conclusions résumées de la défenderesse à propos de cette affaire;*
4. *Liste des pièces qui auraient pu être échangées entre les parties à cette affaire;*
5. *Jugement.*

1. Formule traditionnelle de citation en justice devant le Tribunal d'Instance

ASSIGNATION A TOUTES FINS

date

Cachet de   (prénoms et nom de
l'huissier   l'huissier de justice)
de justice
                  Huissier de Justice

                  (adresse et numéro de téléphone)

                  à

                  M. (Mme ou Mlle) ... (prénoms,
                  nom et domicile du défendeur
                  destinataire ou, s'il s'agit d'une personne morale: sa
                  dénomination et son siège social).

Je vous fais connaître que M. (Mme ou Mlle) ... (prénoms, nom, profession, qualité, date et lieu de naissance, nationalité, domicile du demandeur, avec élection de domicile en France s'il est étranger; si le demandeur est une personne morale, sa dénomination, sa forme, son siège social, l'organe qui la représente légalement) qui a pour avocat M ..., vous invite à comparaître devant le Tribunal d'Instance de ..., siégeant à ... le ... (jour et heure) à ... aux fins d'un préliminaire de conciliation au sujet du différend ci-après détaillé qui vous divise et, à défaut d'accord, aux fins de faire trancher toute contestation entre vous par ledit Tribunal.

En effet ... (exposé sommaire par le demandeur de l'objet du litige et du schéma de ses conclusions (qu'il déposera plus tard)).

Très important

Cette affaire est inscrite à l'audience qui se tiendra le ... (date et heure) au Tribunal d'Instance de ... (adresse du Tribunal) pour qu'il soit procédé à une

323

tentative de conciliation et, faute d'y parvenir, il sera plaidé sans désemparer au fond.

Vous êtes tenu:

– soit de vous présenter personnellement à cette audience seul ou assisté d'un membre de votre famille (conjoint, parent ou allié en ligne directe, parent ou allié en ligne collatérale jusqu'au troisième degré inclus) ou d'une personne exclusivement attachée à votre service personnel ou à votre entreprise:

– soit de vous y faire représenter par un avocat ou par l'une des autres personnes ci-dessus énumérées à condition qu'elle soit munie d'un pouvoir écrit que vous aurez spécialement établi pour ce procès.

Si vous ne le faites pas, vous vous exposez à ce qu'un jugement soit rendu contre vous sur les seuls éléments fournis par votre adversaire.

Les personnes dont les ressources sont insuffisantes pour faire valoir leurs droits en justice peuvent, si elles remplissent les conditions prévues par la loi, bénéficier d'une aide judiciaire. Elles doivent, pour demander cette aide, s'adresser au bureau d'aide judiciaire compétent pour connaître de la demande.

(Mentions de la remise de l'acte par l'huissier de justice et coût de l'acte, sont précisés dans l'assignation.)

2. Conclusions résumées du demandeur à propos d'une affaire fictive

RESUME DES CONCLUSIONS DU DEMANDEUR

TRIBUNAL D'INSTANCE
DE MARSEILLE

CONCLUSIONS

POUR: Monsieur, Yann BERNARD pâtissier, demeurant à CARRY
            LE ROUET (Bouches du Rhône)

            Demandeur

            Maître Jaulin, avocat

Contre: Madame Claudette GILBERT, serveuse, demeurant à
            MARSEILLE (Bouches du Rhône)

            Défenderesse

            Maître Trudel, avocat

                                                PLAISE au Tribunal

Faits:
Le 6 juillet 1990 Madame GILBERT a vendu à M. BERNARD un véhicule VOLVO 240 Break immatriculé 7783.OM.13 pour un prix total de 23,000 Francs. Le compteur indiquait que le véhicule avait roulé 130,000 kms. Le

prix a été payé en deux fois: 15,000 Francs par un chèque remis immédiatement au vendeur et 8,000 Francs remis en numéraire huit jours plus tard.

Aussitôt après cet achat M. BERNARD a constaté un mauvais fonctionnement du véhicule. Un garagiste lui a indiqué que la présence d'huile dans le circuit de refroidissement laissait supposer que le joint de culasse était détérioré.

M. BERNARD a donc écrit à la venderesse par lettre recommandée pour lui demander de procéder à la remise en état du moteur. Aucune réponse ne lui a été adressée. Il a ensuite invité sans plus de succès Mme. GILBERT à participer à une expertise amiable réalisée par M. CHANTELOUP. Enfin il a fait convoquer Mme. GILBERT devant le Tribunal d'Instance à une audience de conciliation, et son adversaire ne s'y est pas présenté.

Les demandes que M. BERNARD est donc obligé de présenter en justice portent sur trois points:

1. Annulation du contrat

A) L'expertise amiable réalisée par M. CHANTELOUP montre que le véhicule était atteint d'un vice caché; l'altération du joint de culasse et les dégats qui en résultent pour le moteur rendent le véhicule inutilisable. L'action en garantie des vices cachés peut donc être exercée par M. BERNARD et permet l'annulation du contrat.

B) Pour s'y opposer Mme. GILBERT invoque un document signé par M. BERNARD indiquant: «le véhicule est pris par moi dans l'état où il se trouve sans qu'aucun recours ne puisse être exercé contre Mme. GILBERT. Je donne décharge entière et définitive».

Cette clause de non-responsabilité est obscure et imprécise: surtout, il est clair que Mme. GILBERT ne pouvait ignorer que le véhicule avait été sommairement réparé juste avant la vente dans le seul objectif de le vendre. Elle a reconnu que c'était son oncle, garagiste retraité, qui avait fait cette réparation sommaire.

Dans ce genre d'hypothèse, la jurisprudence considère que le vendeur est de mauvaise foi et n'accorde aucune valeur à la clause de non-responsabilité.

C) En conséquence de l'annulation, Mme. GILBERT devra donc restituer le prix versé par M. BERNARD soit 23,000 Francs. Plusieurs témoins affirment qu'il s'agit du prix convenu alors que le prix porté sur l'acte signé par M. BERNARD est de 19,000 Francs: M. BERNARD peut d'ailleurs prouver qu'il a retiré 8,000 Francs de son livret de caisse d'épargne le 8 juillet 1990 et cette somme a permis de payer le solde du prix.

2. Indemnité pour résistance abusive

M. BERNARD est en droit de réclamer à Mme. GILBERT des indemnités pour le préjudice qui lui a été causé du fait de ses manoeuvres dilatoires et de sa mauvaise foi après la naissance du litige, alors que la responsabilité de la venderesse était évidente.

Le préjudice constitué par les tracas d'une procédure rendue nécessaire par la résistance injustifiée de Mme. GILBERT peut être évalué à 3,000 Francs.

3. Indemnisation au titre de l'Article 700 Nouveau Code de Procédure Civile

Tout ce qui précède montre qu'il serait inéquitable de laisser à la charge de M. BERNARD tous les frais non compris dans les dépens et il est donc légitime de lui attribuer à ce titre la somme de 2,000 Francs.

PAR CES MOTIFS:

– annuler la vente intervenue entre les parties le 6 juillet 1990;

– condamner Mme. GILBERT à payer 23,000 Francs à M. BERNARD en restitution du prix de vente;

– condamner Mme. GILBERT à payer 3,000 Francs au titre de dommages-intérêts pour resistance abusive;

– condamner Mme. GILBERT à payer une somme de 2,000 Francs au titre de l'article 700 du NCPC;

– condamner Mme. GILBERT aux entiers dépens.

3. Conclusions résumées de la défenderesse à propos de cette affaire

RESUME DES CONCLUSIONS DE LA DEFENDERESSE

TRIBUNAL D'INSTANCE
DE MARSEILLE

CONCLUSIONS

POUR: Madame Claudette GILBERT, serveuse, demeurant à MARSEILLE (Bouches du Rhône)

   Défenderesse

   Maître Trudel, avocat

Contre: Monsieur Yann BERNARD, pâtissier, demeurant à CARRY LE ROUET (Bouches du Rhône)

   Demandeur

   Maître Jaulin, avocat

PLAISE au Tribunal

1. Sur le prix

Il est incontestable que le bon de commande porte clairement la somme de 19,000 Francs et qu'il est signé de l'acheteur. Les témoignages ou attestations invoqués par l'acheteur ne peuvent prouver contre le contenu de cet acte.

2. Sur la clause de non-responsabilité

La clause signée par l'acheteur est parfaitement claire et précise. Elle indique clairement que le véhicule est pris dans son état actuel sans aucune possibilité de recours.

3. Sur le vice caché allégué par l'acheteur

La réparation réalisée sur le véhicule vendu a été faite par l'oncle de Mme. GILBERT. Celui-ci est en retraite après avoir été garagiste professionnel pendant 30 ans (en tant que salarié puis propriétaire de son entreprise). Il n'est pas concevable qu'il ait bricolé hâtivement la réparation d'un véhicule que Mme. GILBERT, sa nièce, a conduit plusieurs semaines avant de le vendre.

Il est donc exclu que le vice allégúe ait été connu de Mme. GILBERT au moment où la vente a eu lieu. Sa bonne foi ne peut être mise en doute.

Il est plus probable que le véhicule a été utilisé dans des conditions défectueuses par M. BERNARD ce qui a créé ou en tout cas aggravé la panne. En tout cas ces circonstances interdisent d'exclure le jeu de la clause de non-responsabilité.

Il convient donc de débouter M. BERNARD de toutes ses demandes.

PAR CES MOTIFS:

- débouter M. BERNARD de toutes ses demandes;

- le condamner à payer 3,000 Francs au titre de l'article 700 NCPC;

- le condamner aux dépens.

4. Liste des pièces qui auraient pu être échangées entre les parties à cette affaire

LISTE DES PIECES ECHANGEES PAR LES PARTIES

1. Pièces communiquées par Maître JAULIN, avocat de M. BERNARD:

- lettre recommandée adressée par M. BERNARD à Mme. GILBERT le 25 juillet 1990 (retournée à l'expéditeur);

- diverses factures des garagistes pour interventions sur le véhicule litigieux après le 6 juillet 1990;

- bulletin de non-conciliation remis au demandeur attestant que Mme. GILBERT ne s'est pas présentée à la tentative de conciliation devant le tribunal;

- photocopie d'un document bancaire attestant du retrait de 8,000 Francs le 8 juillet 1990, par M. BERNARD;

- attestations écrites signées par des tiers et conformes à l'article 202 NCPC déclarant que le prix convenu entre les parties était de 23,000 Francs.

2. Pièces communiqués par Maître TRUDEL, avocat de Mme. GILBERT:

– bon de commande signé par M. BERNARD et comportant la clause de non-responsabilité;

– facture des fournitures acquises par M. ROGET, oncle de Mme. GILBERT, pour procéder au changement du joint de culasse;

– pièces attestant de l'exercise pendant 30 ans par M. ROGET de la profession de garagiste;

– attestation d'une voisine de Mme. GILBERT affirmant que le véhicule vendu était entretenu régulièrement par M. ROGET et que ce véhicule était en parfait état.

5. Jugement

SECRETARIAT GREFFE
DU
TRIBUNAL D'INSTANCE
DE MARSEILLE
(Bouches du Rhône)

COPIE
DU JUGEMENT

Aff: Monsieur BERNARD

C/

Madame GILBERT

EXTRAIT
DES MINUTES DU SECRETARIAT GREFFE

DU TRIBUNAL D'INSTANCE

DE MARSEILLE

Département des Bouches du Rhône

REPUBLIQUE FRANCAISE

AU NOM DU PEUPLE FRANCAIS

L'an mil neuf cent quatre vingt onze
et le quatre mars

Le Tribunal d'Instance de MARSEILLE
Départment des Bouches du Rhône

sis à Marseille, place Jules Verne

a rendu en audience publique le Jugement
dont la teneur suit:

Rôle No 87/0058

le 4 mars 1991
Jugement
Contradictoire

M. BERNARD
C/
Mme. GILBERT

TRIBUNAL D'INSTANCE
DE MARSEILLE

AUDIENCE PUBLIQUE DU
TRIBUNAL D'INSTANCE DE MARSEILLE

tenue le QUATRE MARS MIL NEUF CENT
QUATRE VINGT ONZE,

au siège du Tribunal, place Jules Verne

Par Gérard MARTIN, Juge du Tribunal d'Instance,

Assisté de Josette MATOU, Greffier.

ENTRE:

Monsieur Yann BERNARD, né le 31 avril 1953 à TOULON, pâtissier, demeurant 3 place de l'Eglise à CARRY LE ROUET

DEMANDEUR

Représenté par Maître JAULIN – Avocat au Barreau de Marseille

ET:

Madame Claudette GILBERT, serveuse, demeurant 26 impasse Erdre à MARSEILLE

DEFENDERESSE

Représentée par Maître TRUDEL – Avocat au Barreau de Marseille

*
* *

LE TRIBUNAL

Après avoir tenté de concilier les parties, a entendu leurs conseils en leurs plaidoiries à l'audience publique du 20 janvier 1991, puis a mis l'affaire en délibéré à ce jour où le jugement suivant a été rendu.

-:- JUGEMENT -:-

Par acte d'huissier en date du 16 octobre 1990, Monsieur Yann BERNARD a fait citer Madame Claudette GILBERT devant le Tribunal d'Instance de Marseille pour voir annuler la vente d'un véhicule, intervenue le 6 juillet 1990 en raison de l'existence de vices cachés, et entendre Madame GILBERT condamnée à lui payer le prix de vente de ce véhicule, soit 23,000 Francs, la somme de 3,000 Francs à titre de dommages-intérêts pour résistance abusive et celle de 2,000 Francs sur le fondement de l'article 700 du Nouveau Code de Procédure Civile.

Monsieur BERNARD forme sa demande en annulation de la vente du véhicule pour vice caché; il se fonde sur un rapport d'expertise amiable établi à sa demande, selon lequel le véhicule est entaché d'un défaut grave le rendant impropre à sa destination dont l'origine est à rechercher dans des réparations effectuées au coût le moins élevé en vue de la revente, en dehors de toutes règles élémentaires; il soutient que la clause de non-responsabilité, trop générale, doit être écartée dans la mesure où Madame GILBERT ne pouvait ignorer l'existence des vices cachés; enfin, il maintient que le prix de vente s'est élevé à 23,000 Francs et non à 19,000 Francs comme le prétend la venderesse, le bon de commande produit par celle-ci ayant été complété par elle par la mention du prix après la vente.

Madame GILBERT conclut au débouté et demande reconventionellement une somme de 3,000 Francs en vertu des dispositions de l'article 700 du Nouveau Code de Procédure Civile.

Elle reconnaît que les réparations ont été effectuées par son oncle, ancien garagiste aujourd'hui retraité, mais fait valoir que la compétence de celui-ci ne saurait être mis en doute et que les conditions dans lesquelles le véhicule a été entretenu et utilisé pendant les premières semaines qui ont suivi la vente ont été de nature à provoquer les dégradations constatées par le technicien consulté par Monsieur BERNARD; enfin, elle rappelle que l'acheteur a signé une clause de décharge de responsabilité sans restriction ni réserve dont le libellé ne laisse place à aucune ambiguïté.

DISCUSSION

Attendu qu'aucune des parties ne remet en cause les constatations techniques effectuées par Monsieur CHANTELOUP expert judiciaire, intervenu à la demande de Monsieur BERNARD; que Madame GILBERT conteste seulement ses conclusions selon lesquelles les avaries constatées proviendraient de réparations effectuées hâtivement, sans respecter les règles de l'art les plus élémentaires.

Attendu qu'il résulte des pièces versées aux débats et de l'audition des parties que dès l'origine des désordres, soit une huitaine de jours après l'achat, le garagiste de Monsieur BERNARD puis le concessionnaire VOLVO ont diagnostiqué une anomalie due à une altération du joint de culasse, anomalie provoquée par le fait que cette pièce aurait été trop serré ou au contraire pas assez serré, mais en tout hypothèse mal posée.

Attendu que Monsieur CHANTELOUP a confirmé l'altération du joint de culasse et découvert un mauvais état de la segmentation du moteur; qu'il en attribue la cause essentielle à des réparations effectuées au moindre coût, sans respecter les plus élémentaires règles de l'art, s'agissant d'un organe vital du véhicule, et selon lui en vue de la vente, par un mécanicien réalisant un travail 'au noir'.

Attendu qu'il a été établi que les réparations dont la qualité est remise en cause ont été effectuées par l'oncle de Madame GILBERT; que celui-ci, qui est retraité depuis 1982, travaille sans disposer des installations nécessaires et semble-t-il, selon les dires mêmes de Madame GILBERT, dans des conditions particulières, les réparations ayant été effectués en deux temps.

Que, sans vouloir remettre en cause les compétences de cet ancien garagiste, il convient de constater que de l'avis unanime de trois professionnels en exercice ces réparations n'ont pas été effectuées correctement et qu'elles ne pouvaient avoir pour résultat que d'entraîner des avaries graves dans un proche avenir; que cette manière de procéder ne peut s'expliquer que par le fait que Madame GILBERT envisageait de vendre son véhicule et a fait procéder au moindre coût à des réparations sommaires lui permettant de le proposer sur le marché.

Qu'il ne peut en effet être envisagé qu'un ancien garagiste professionnel ait pu réaliser un travail d'aussi mauvaise qualité si le véhicule devait demeurer entre les mains de sa nièce.

Attendu que celle-ci ne pouvait de toute évidence ignorer les conditions de cette réparation faite avec son accord; que dès lors, la clause restrictive ne peut être considérée comme valable, dans la mesure où elle connaissait l'existence des vices cachés pour lesquels elle a stipulé la non responsabilité.

Que l'action en annulation formée par Monsieur BERNARD est dès lors recevable.

Attendu que celui-ci prétend se voir restituer la somme de 23,000 Francs; qu'il soutient en effet avoir réglé, d'une part, une somme de 15,000 Francs par chèque à la commande et d'autre part, une somme de 8,000 Francs en espèce à la livraison; que Madame GILBERT affirme pour sa part n'avoir reçu que la somme de 19,000 Francs.

Attendu que le prix de 19,000 Francs est mentionné à deux reprises sur le bon de commande signé le 6 juillet 1990 par les parties; qu'il est indiqué d'une part, que la vente est faite pour le prix net de 19,000 Francs, frais de carte grise et de vignette en sus, et que les parties convenaient du versement d'un acompte de 15,000 Francs à la commande et du solde de 4,000 Francs à la livraison; qu'aucun élément sérieux ne permet d'établir que ce bon de commande aurait été complété par Madame GILBERT après sa signature par Monsieur BERNARD, lequel aurait alors fait preuve d'une grave négligence; que le fait que Monsieur BERNARD ait, à cette époque, prélevé une somme de 8,000 Francs sur son livret de Caisse d'Epargne ne peut en aucune façon être retenue comme la preuve du prix; qu'il est de même de l'attestation d'un témoin qui aurait entendu parler de 23,000 Francs.

Attendu dès lors, qu'il y a lieu de condamner Madame GILBERT à restituer le prix de 19,000 Francs.

Attendu que l'attitude de celle-ci s'est avéré particulièrement dilatoire; qu'elle n'a pas répondu aux lettres de Monsieur BERNARD, qu'elle a refusé l'expertise amiable du véhicule, qu'elle ne s'est pas présentée à la tentative de conciliation; qu'elle a, de ce fait, causé un préjudice complémentaire à Monsieur BERNARD, le contraignant à engager une action en justice et retardant la solution du litige, alors que Monsieur BERNARD est privé de l'usage du véhicule; qu'il y a lieu, dans ces conditions, de faire droit à la demande de dommages-intérêts et de la condamner à payer la somme de 3,000 Francs à titre de dommages-intérêts.

Attendu qu'il serait inéquitable de laisser à la charge du demandeur les frais non compris dans les dépens; qu'il y a lieu de lui allouer une somme de 1,800 Francs sur le fondement de l'article 700 du Nouveau Code de Procédure Civile.

-:- PAR CES MOTIFS -:-

Statuant publiquement, contradictoirement, et en premier ressort,

Le Tribunal,

PRONONCE l'annulation de la vente du véhicule VOLVO intervenue le 6 juillet 1990 entre Madame Claudette GILBERT et Monsieur Yann BERNARD

CONDAMNE Madame GILBERT à restituer à Monsieur BERNARD la somme de DIX NEUF MILLE Francs (19,000F),

CONDAMNE Madame GILBERT à payer à Monsieur BERNARD:

– la somme de TROIS MILLE Francs (3,000F) à titre de dommages-intérêts,

– la somme de MILLE HUIT CENTS Francs (1,800F) sur le fondement de l'article 700 du Nouveau Code de Procédure Civile,

REJETTE toutes autres demandes des parties,

CONDAMNE Madame GILBERT aux entiers dépens.

*
* *

AINSI JUGE ET PRONONCE en audience publique, le quatre mars mil neuf cent quatre vingt onze, et nous avons signé avec le Greffier.

Le Greffier   Le Juge d'Instance
    Josette MATOU   Gérard MARTIN

EN CONSEQUENCE

La République Française mande et ordonne,

A tous Huissiers de Justice, sur ce requis, de mettre ledit jugement à exécution.

Aux Procureurs Généraux et aux Procureurs de la République près les Tribunaux de Grande Instance, d'y tenir la main.

A tous Commandants et Officiers de la Force Publique de prêter main forte lorsqu'ils seront légalement requis.

En foi de quoi, le présent jugement a été signé par le Président et le Greffier.

POUR COPIE CERTIFIEE CONFORME,

P/Le Greffier en Chef,
P. Lambert.

Appendix

Constitutional implications of the Maastricht treaty

The ratification of the Maastricht treaty has necessitated constitutional reforms in France. In April 1992 the *Conseil Constitutionnel* held that the treaty was contrary to the 1958 Constitution, thereby requiring the amendment of the latter before ratification could be proceeded with. A bill reforming the Constitution was duly passed by both houses sitting *en congrès* in June 1992. The issue of the ratification of the treaty is to be put to a referendum during September 1992. The decision of the *Conseil Constitutionnel* of 9 April 1992 and the reform bill passed on 23 June 1992 (to become the *loi constitutionnelle du 25 juin 1992)* are set out in this Appendix.

1. Conseil Constitutionnel 9 avril 1992, J.C.P.II, 21853

«Le Conseil constitutionnel a été saisi, le 11 mars 1992, par le président de la République, conformément à l'article 54 de la Constitution, de la question de savoir si, compte tenu des engagements souscrits par la France et des modalités de leur entrée en vigueur, l'autorisation de ratifier le traité sur l'Union européenne signé à Maastricht le 7 février 1992 doit être précédée d'une révision de la Constitution; (...)

»Considérant que le quatorzième alinéa du preámbule de la Constitution de 1946, auquel se réfère le préambule de la Constitution de 1958, proclame que la République française «se conforme aux règles du droit public international»; qu'au nombre de celles-ci figure la règle *pacta sunt servanda* qui implique que tout traité en vigueur lie les parties et doit être exécuté par elles de bonne foi; que l'article 55 de la Constitution de 1958 dispose, en outre, que «les traités ou accords régulièrement ratifiés ou approuvés ont, dès leur publication, une autorité supérieure à celle des lois, sous réserve, pour chaque accord ou traité, de son application par l'autre partie»;

»Considérant qu'il appartient au Conseil constitutionnel saisi (...)

d'un traité qui modifie ou complète un ou plusieurs engagements internationaux déjà introduits dans l'ordre juridique interne de déterminer la portée du traité soumis à son examen en fonction des engagements internationaux que ce traité a pour objet de modifier ou compléter;

»Considérant que le peuple français a, par le préambule de la Constitution de 1958, proclamé solennellement «son attachement aux droits de l'homme et aux principes de la souveraineté nationale tels qu'ils ont été définis par la Déclaration de 1789, confirmée et complétée par le préambule de la Constitution de 1946»;

»Considérant que dans son article 3, la Déclaration des droits de l'homme et du citoyen énonce que «le principe de toute souveraineté réside essentiellement dans la nation»; que l'article 3 de la Constitution de 1958 dispose, dans son premier alinéa, que «la souveraineté nationale appartient au peuple qui l'exerce par ses représentants et par la voie du référendum»;

»Considérant que le préambule de la Constitution de 1946 proclame, dans son quatorzième alinéa, que la République française se «conforme aux règles du droit public international» et, dans son quinzième alinéa, que «sous réserve de réciprocité, la France consent aux limitations de souveraineté nécessaires à l'organisation et à la défense de la paix»;

»Considérant que, dans son article 53, la Constitution de 1958 consacre, comme le faisait l'article 27 de la Constitution de 1946, l'existence de «traités ou accords relatifs à l'organisation internationale»; que ces traités ou accords ne peuvent être ratifiés ou approuvés par le président de la République qu'en vertu d'une loi;

»Considérant qu'il résulte de ces textes de valeur constitutionnelle que le respect de la souveraineté nationale ne fait pas obstacle à ce que, sur le fondement des dispositions précitées du préambule de la Constitution de 1946, la France puisse conclure, sous réserve de réciprocité, des engagements internationaux en vue de participer à la création ou au développement d'une organisation internationale permanente, dotée de la personnalité juridique et investie de pouvoirs de décision par l'effet de transferts de compétences consentis par les Etats membres;

»Considérant toutefois qu'au cas où des engagements internationaux souscrits à cette fin contiennent une clause contraire à la Constitution ou portent atteinte aux conditions essentielles d'exercice de la souveraineté nationale, l'autorisation de les ratifier appelle une révision constitutionnelle;

»Considérant que c'est au regard de ces principes qu'il revient au Conseil constitutionnel de procéder à l'examen du traité sur l'Union européenne; (...)

»Considérant qu'aux termes du paragraphe 2 de l'article F du traité sur l'Union européenne: «l'Union respecte les droits fondamentaux, tels qu'ils sont garantis par la Convention européenne des droits de l'homme et des libertés fondamentales, signée à Rome le 4 novembre 1950, et tels qu'ils résultent des traditions constitutionnelles communes aux Etats membres, en tant que principes généraux du droit communautaire»; que leur respect est assuré par la Cour de justice des Communautés européennes notamment à la suite d'actions engagées à l'initiative des particuliers;

»Considérant que les stipulations du paragraphe 2 de l'article F, conjuguées avec l'intervention des juridictions nationales statuant dans le cadre de leurs compétences respectives, sont à même de garantir les droits et libertés des citoyens; qu'à cet égard, l'engagement international soumis au Conseil constitutionnel ne porte pas atteinte aux règles et principes de valeur constitutionnelle;

»Considérant qu'il ressort de l'article B du traité sur l'Union européenne que l'Union se donne notamment pour objectif de «renforcer la protection des droits et des intérêts des ressortissants de ses Etats membres par l'instauration d'une citoyenneté de l'Union»; que l'article G du traité précité, modifie le traité de Rome du 25 mars 1957 instituant la Communauté économique européenne afin d'instituer la Communauté européenne; que, dans sa nouvelle rédaction, l'article 8 de ce dernier traité stipule qu'il est «institué une citoyenneté de l'Union» et précise qu' «est citoyen de l'Union toute personne' ayant la nationalité d'un Etat membre»; (...)

»Considérant qu'aux termes du paragraphe 1 de l'article 8 B ajouté au traité instituant la Communauté européenne, «tout citoyen de l'Union résidant dans un Etat membre dont il n'est pas ressortissant a le droit de vote et d'éligibilité aux élections municipales dans l'Etat membre où il réside, dans les mêmes conditions que les ressortissants de cet Etat»; qu'il est prévu que ce droit sera exercé sous réserve des modalités à arrêter par le Conseil formé par un représentant de chaque Etat membre au niveau ministériel, statuant à l'unanimité, sur proposition de la Commission et après consultation du Parlement européen; que l'article 8 B, paragraphe 1, stipule in fine que «ces modalités peuvent prévoir des dispositions dérogatoires lorsque des problèmes spécifiques à un Etat membre le justifient»;

»Considérant que les «modalités à arrêter» auront pour objet de fixer les règles applicables à l'exercice du droit de vote et d'éligibilité; qu'au nombre de celles-ci, figurent notamment la preuve de la jouissance des droits civiques dans l'Etat d'origine, la durée de résidence dans l'Etat dont l'intéressé n'est pas le ressortissant ainsi que la prohibition de doubles inscriptions; (...)

»Considérant que l'article 3 de la Constitution dispose dans son premier alinéa que «la souveraineté nationale appartient au peuple qui l'exerce par ses représentants et par la voie du référendum»; que le même article dispose, dans son troisième alinéa, que «le suffrage peut être direct ou indirect dans les conditions prévues par la Constitution. Il est toujours universel, égal et secret»; qu'il est spécifié au quatrième alinéa de l'article 3 que «sont électeurs, dans les conditions déterminées par la loi, tous les nationaux français majeurs des deux sexes, jouissant de leurs droits civils et politiques»;

»Considérant qu'en vertu de l'article 24 de la Constitution, le Sénat, qui est élu au suffrage indirect, «assure la représentation des collectivités territoriales de la République»; qu'aux termes du premier alinéa de l'article 72 de la Constitution «les collectivités territoriales de la République sont les communes, les départements, les territoires d'outre-mer. Toute autre collectivité territoriale est créée par la loi»; que selon le deuxième alinéa du même article «ces collectivités s'administrent librement par des conseils élus et dans les conditions prévues par la loi»;

»Considérant qu'il résulte de ces dispositions que l'organe délibérant d'une collectivité territoriale de la République ne peut procéder que d'une élection effectuée au suffrage universel; que le Sénat doit, dans la mesure où il assure la représentation de collectivités territoriales de la République, être élu par un corps électoral qui est lui-même l'émanation de ces collectivités; qu'il s'ensuit que la désignation des conseillers municipaux a une incidence sur l'election des sénateurs; qu'en sa qualité d'Assemblée parlementaire le Sénat participe à l'exercice de la souveraineté nationale; que, dès lors, le quatrième alinéa de l'article 3 de la Constitution implique que seuls les «nationaux français» ont le droit de vote et d'éligibilité aux élections effectuées pour la désignation de l'organe délibérant d'une collectivité territoriale de la République, et notamment pour celle des conseillers municipaux ou des membres du Conseil de Paris;

»Considérant, qu'en l'état, l'article 8 B, paragraphe 1, ajouté au traité instituant la Communauté européenne par l'article G de l'engagement international soumis au Conseil constitutionnel, est contraire à la Constitution;

»Considérant que le paragraphe 2 de l'article 8 B rapproché de l'article 138, paragraphe 3, maintient la possibilité d'instituer une procédure uniforme pour l'élection du Parlement européen sous réserve de son adoption par les Etats membres, conformément à leurs règles constitutionnelles respectives;

»Considérant que, sans préjudice de ces stipulations, l'article 8 B, paragraphe 2, dispose que: «Tout citoyen de l'Union résidant dans un Etat membre dont il n'est pas ressortissant a le droit de vote et d'éligibilité aux élections au Parlement européen dans l'Etat membre où il réside dans les mêmes conditions que les ressortissants de cet Etat. Ce droit sera exercé sous réserve des modalités à arrêter, avant le 31 décembre 1993, par le Conseil, statuant à l'unanimité sur proposition de la Commission et après consultation du Parlement européen; ces modalités peuvent prévoir des dispositions dérogatoires lorsque des problèmes spécifiques à un Etat membre le justifient»; (...)

»Considérant qu'il ressort des dispositions combinées du quatrième alinéa de l'article 3 de la Constitution et des autres alinéas du même article que la règle constitutionnelle qui limite le droit de vote aux «nationaux français» ne s'impose que pour l'exercice du droit de suffrage «dans les conditions prévues par la Constitution»;

»Considérant que le Parlement européen a pour fondement juridique, non les termes de la Constitution de 1958, mais des engagements internationaux souscrits, sur une base de réciprocité, dans le cadre des dispositions de valeur constitutionnelle mentionnées précédemment; qu'au demeurant, selon l'article E du traité sur l'Union européenne, le Parlement européen exerce ses attributions dans les conditions et aux fins prévues, d'une part, par les dispositions des traités instituant les Communautés européennes et des traités et actes subséquents qui les ont modifiés et complétés, et, d'autre part, par les autres stipulations du traité sur l'Union européenne; (. . .) qu'il est stipulé que le Parlement européen, à l'instar des autres institutions communautaires, agit «dans les limites des attributions qui lui sont conférées» par chacun des traités précités;

»Considérant qu'il suit de là que la reconnaissance au profit de tout citoyen de l'Union européenne, sur une base de réciprocité, du droit de vote et d'eligibilité aux élections au Parlement européen dans un Etat membre de la Communauté européenne où il réside, sans en être ressortissant, ne contrevient pas à l'article 3 de la Constitution;

»Considérant au surplus que le traité sur l'Union européenne, n'a pas pour conséquence de modifier la nature juridique du Parlement européen; que ce dernier ne constitue pas une assemblée souveraine dotée d'une compétence générale et qui aurait vocation à concourir à l'exercice de la souveraineté nationale; que le Parlement européen appartient à un ordre juridique propre, qui, bien que se trouvant intégré au système juridique des différents Etat membres des Communautés, n'appartient pas à l'ordre institutionnel de la République française;

»Considérant, dans ces conditions, que le paragraphe 2 de l'article 8 B ajouté au traité instituant la Communauté européenne par l'article G du traité sur l'Union européenne n'est contraire à aucune règle non plus qu'à aucun principe de valeur constitutionnelle;

»Considérant que l'article B du traité sur l'Union européenne fait figurer au nombre des objectifs que se donne l'Union la promotion d'un progrès économique et social équilibré et durable par l'établissement en particulier d'une Union économique et monétaire comportant à terme «une monnaie unique»; que l'article G du traité qui, ainsi qu'il a été dit ci-dessus, modifie le traité de Rome instituant la Communauté économique européenne, comprend plusieurs stipulations tendant à la réalisation de l'objectif précité;

»Considérant que la nouvelle rédaction de l'article 2 du traité de Rome intègre parmi les missions de la Communauté la réalisation d'une «union économique et monétaire»; que l'article 3 A stipule, en son paragraphe

2, que l'action des Etats membres et de la Communauté comporte, dans les conditions et selon les rythmes et les procédures prévus par le traité, «la fixation irrévocable des taux de change conduisant à l'instauration d'une monnaie unique, l'écu, ainsi que la définition et la conduite d'une politique monétaire et d'une politique de change uniques»; que l'article 4 A institue, selon les procédures prévues par le traité, un système européen de banques centrales et une Banque centrale européenne (...);

»Considérant que l'entrée en vigueur de la troisième phase de l'Union économique et monétaire interviendra au plus tard le 1er janvier 1999; (...) que, pour les Etats membres remplissant les conditions objectives requises, et qui ne peuvent, par suite, prétendre au bénéfice d'une dérogation, l'entrée dans la troisième phase entraîne en particulier la mise en oeuvre aussi bien d'un politique monétaire unique que d'une politique de change unique;

»Considérant que, s'agissant de la politique monétaire, il convient de relever qu'est posé par l'article 107 le principe de l'indépendance tant de la Banque centrale européenne que des banques centrales nationales, lesquelles constituent le système européen de banques centrales; qu'il revient à ce dernier, conformément aux dispositions combinées de l'article 105, paragraphe 2, et de l'article 3 du protocole numéro 3 de «définir et mettre en oeuvre la politique monétaire de la Communauté»; que la Banque Centrale Européenne (BCE) est, en vertu du paragraphe 1 de l'article 105 A, «seule habilitée à autoriser l'émission de billets de banque dans la Communauté»; que le paragraphe 2 du même article ne permet aux Etats membres d'émettre des pièces que «sous réserve de l'approbation, par la BCE, du volume de l'émission»; qu'en outre, suivant le deuxième alinéa de l'article 109 G, «dès le début de la troisième phase, la valeur de l'écu est irrévocablement fixée, conformément à l'article 109 L, paragraphe 4»; que, selon ce texte, le jour de l'entrée en vigueur de la troisième phase, le Conseil des ministres des Communautés, statuant à l'unanimité des Etats membres non dérogataires, «arrête les taux de conversion auxquels leurs monnaies sont irrévocablement fixées et le taux irrévocablement fixé auquel l'écu remplace»; les monnaies des Etats concernés; que l'Ecu deviendra ainsi «une monnaie à part entière»; que, suivant la même procédure, le Conseil «prend également les autres mesures nécessaires à l'introduction rapide de l'écu en tant que monnaie unique» des Etats membres non dérogataires;

»Considérant que, s'agissant de la politique de change, le paragraphe 1 de l'article 109 investit le Conseil des ministres des Communautés, statuant à l'unanimité des Etats membres non dérogataires, du pouvoir de conclure des «accords formels portant sur un système de taux de change pour l'écu, vis-à-vis des monnaies non communautaires»; qu'il lui revient aussi, en se prononçant à la majorité qualifiée des Etats membres non dérogataires, d'«adopter, modifier ou abandonner les cours centraux de l'écu dans le système des taux de change»; que cette procédure de décision est également applicable, en vertu du paragraphe 2 de l'article 109, à l'effet de permettre au conseil de formuler les orientations générales de politique de change vis-à-vis d'une ou de plusieurs monnaies non communautaires, en l'absence de système de taux de change;

»Considérant qu'il résulte des dispositions applicables à compter du début de la troisième phase de l'Union économique et monétaire que la réalisation d'un semblable objectif se traduira par la mise en oeuvre d'une politique monétaire et d'une politique de change uniques suivant des modalités telles qu'un Etat membre se trouvera privé de compétences propres dans un domaine où sont en cause les conditions essentielles d'exercice de la souveraineté nationale;

»Considérant que, dans leur état, les dispositions de la Constitution font obstacle à ce que la France s'intègre à l'Union économique et monétaire instituée par le traité;

»Considérant que, pour ces motifs, sont contraires à la Constitution:

– l'article B du traité sur l'Union européenne en tant qu'il prévoit l'établissement d'une union économique et monétaire comportant à terme une monnaie unique;

– l'article G du traité précité, en tant qu'il a pour objet d'insérer dans le traité instituant la Communauté européenne, l'article 3 A, paragraphe 2, l'article 105, paragraphe 2, l'article 105 A, l'article 107, l'article 109, l'article 109 G, alinéa 2, l'article 109 L, paragraphe 4;

– les autres dispositions des chapitres II, III et IV du titre VI ajouté au traité instituant la Communauté européenne ainsi que celles des protocoles nos 3 et 10, dans la mesure où elles sont indissociables des articles précités;

»Considérant que, dans sa rédaction issue de l'article G du traité sur l'Union européenne, l'article 3 du traité instituant la Communauté comporte dans les conditions et selon les rythmes prévus par ce traité: «d) des mesures relatives à l'entrée et à la circulation des personnes dans le marché intérieur conformément à l'article 100 C»;

»Considérant qu'aux termes du paragraphe 1 de l'article 100 C, le Conseil des ministres des Communautés européennes, «statuant à l'unanimité sur proposition de la Commission et après consultation du Parlement européen, détermine les pays tiers dont les ressortissants doivent être munis d'un visa lors du franchissement des frontières extérieures des Etats membres»; qu'il est stipulé au paragraphe 2 du même article que «dans le cas où survient dans un pays tiers une situation d'urgence confrontant la Communauté à la menace d'un afflux soudain de ressortissants de ce pays, le Conseil peut, statuant à la majorité qualifiée sur recommandation de la Commission, rendre obligatoire, pour une période ne pouvant excéder six mois, l'obtention d'un visa par les ressortissants du pays en question»; qu'il est précisé que cette obligation peut être prorogée selon la procédure définie au paragraphe 1;

»Considérant que le paragraphe 3 de l'article 100 C énonce qu'à compter du 1ᵉʳ janvier 1996, le Conseil adoptera «à la majorité qualifiée les décisions visées au paragraphe 1» dudit article et qu'avant cette date le Conseil, statuant à la majorité qualifiée sur proposition de la Commission et après consultation du Parlement européen, arrête les mesures relatives à l'institution d'un modèle type de visa; que le paragraphe 4 C de l'article 100 C prescrit que, dans les domaines «visés» audit article, «la Commission est tenue d'instruire toute demande formulée par un Etat membre et tendant à ce qu'elle fasse une proposition au Conseil»; que, selon le paragraphe 5, «le présent article ne porte pas atteinte à l'exercice des responsabilités qui incombent aux Etats membres pour le maintien de l'ordre public et la sauvegarde de la sécurité intérieure»;

»Considérant que les engagements internationaux souscrits par les autorités de la République française ne sauraient affecter l'exercice par l'Etat de compétences qui relèvent des conditions essentielles de sa souveraineté; que ne sont pas contraires à cette exigence les dispositions de l'article 100 C qui sont relatives à la détermination des pays tiers dont les ressortissants doivent être munis d'un visa lors du franchissement des frontières extérieures des Etats membres, dès lors qu'elles concernent la période antérieure au 1ᵉʳ janvier 1996; qu'en effet la politique commune des visas à l'égard des pays tiers est décidée par le Conseil des ministres des Communautés à l'unanimité, sous la seule réserve de mesures de sauvegarde motivées par l'urgence et temporaires dans leurs effets; qu'en revanche, l'abandon de la règle de l'unanimité à compter du 1ᵉʳ janvier 1996, comme le prévoit le paragraphe 3 de l'article 100 C, pourrait conduire, en dépit des dispositions des paragraphes 4 et 5 du même article, à ce que se trouvent affectées des conditions essentielles d'exercice de la souveraineté nationale;

»Considérant qu'il suit de là qu'en l'état le paragraphe 3 de l'article 100 C, ajouté au traité instituant la Communauté européenne par l'article G du traité sur l'Union européenne est contraire à la Constitution;

»Considérant qu'aucune des autres dispositions de l'engagement international soumis au Conseil constitutionnel au titre de l'article 54 de la Constitution n'est contraire à celle-ci;

»Considérant que, pour les motifs ci-dessus énoncés, l'autorisation de ratifier en vertu d'une loi le traité sur l'Union européenne exige une révision constitutionnelle;

(Le Conseil constitutionnel décide:)

»**Article premier** – L'autorisation de ratifier en vertu d'une loi le traité sur l'Union européenne ne peut intervenir qu'après révision de la Constitution.

»**Article 2** – La présente décision sera notifiée au président de la République et publiée au *Journal officiel* de la République française.

2. Décret du 19 juin 1992 tendant à soumettre un projet de loi constitutionnelle au Parlement convoqué en Congrès

Le Président de la République,

Sur le rapport du Premier ministre,

Vu l'article 89 de la Constitution,

Décrète:

Art. 1er − Le projet de loi constitutionnelle ajoutant à la Constitution un titre: «Des Communautés européennes et de l'Union européenne», voté en termes identiques par le Sénat le 16 juin 1992 et par l'Assemblée nationale le 18 juin 1992, et dont le texte est annexé au présent décret, est soumis au Parlement convoqué en Congrès le 23 juin 1992.

Art. 2. − L'ordre du jour du Congrès est fixé ainsi qu'il suit:

Vote sur le projet de loi constitutionnelle ajoutant à la Constitution un titre: «Des Communautés européennes et de l'Union européenne».

Art. 3 − Le présent décret sera publié au *Journal officiel* de la République française.

Fait à Paris, le 19 juin 1992.

FRANÇOIS MITTERRAND

Par le Président de la République:

Le Premier ministre,
PIERRE BÉRÉGOVOY

ANNEXE
PROJET DE LOI CONSTITUTIONNELLE
AJOUTANT À LA CONSTITUTION UN TITRE:
«DES COMMUNAUTÉS EUROPÉENNES
ET DE L'UNION EUROPÉENNE»

Article 1er

Après le premier alinéa de l'article 2 de la Constitution du 4 octobre 1958, il est inséré un alinéa ainsi rédigé:

«La langue de la République est le Français.»

Article 2

L'article 54 de la Constitution est ainsi rédigé:

«Art. 54 − Si le Conseil constitutionnel, saisi par le Président de la République, par le Premier ministre, par le président de l'une ou l'autre assemblée ou par soixante députés ou soixante sénateurs, a déclaré qu'un engagement international comporte une clause contraire à la Constitution, l'autorisation de ratifier ou d'approuver l'engagement international en cause ne peut intervenir qu'après la révision de la Constitution.»

Article 3

La dernière phrase de l'article 74 de la Constitution est remplacée par deux alinéas ainsi rédigés:

«Les statuts des territoires d'outre-mer sont fixés par des lois organiques qui définissent, notamment, les compétences de leurs institutions propres, et modifiés, dans la même forme, après consultation de l'assemblée territoriale intéressée.

«Les autres modalités de leur organisation particulière sont définies et modifiées par la loi après consultation de l'assemblée territoriale intéressée.»

Article 4

Le titre XIV et le titre XV de la Constitution deviennent respectivement le titre XV et le titre XVI.

Article 5

Il est inséré, dans la Constitution, un nouveau titre XIV ainsi rédigé:

«TITRE XIV

«DES COMMUNAUTÉS EUROPÉENNES
ET DE L'UNION EUROPÉENNE

«Art. 88−1. − La République participe aux Communautés européennes et à l'Union européenne, constituées d'Etats qui ont choisi librement, en vertu des traités qui les ont instituées, d'exercer en commun certaines de leurs compétences.

«Art. 88−2. − Sous réserve de réciprocité, et selon les modalités prévues par le Traité sur l'Union européenne signé le 7 février 1992, la France consent aux transferts de compétences nécessaires à l'établissement de l'union économique et monétaire européenne ainsi qu'à la détermination des règles relatives au franchissement des frontières extérieures des Etats membres de la Communauté européenne.

«Art. 88−3. − Sous réserve de réciprocité et selon les modalités prévues par le Traité sur l'Union européenne signé le 7 février 1992, le droit de vote et d'éligibilité aux élections municipales peut être accordé aux seuls citoyens de l'Union résidant en France. Ces citoyens ne peuvent exercer les fonctions de maire ou d'adjoint ni participer à la désignation des électeurs sénatoriaux et à l'élection des sénateurs. Une loi organique votée dans les mêmes termes par les deux assemblées détermine les conditions d'application du présent article.

«Art. 88−4. − Le Gouvernement soumet à l'Assemblée nationale et au Sénat, dès leur transmission au Conseil des Communautés, les propositions d'actes communautaires comportant des dispositions de nature législative.

«Pendant les sessions ou en dehors d'elles, des résolutions peuvent être votées dans le cadre du présent article, selon des modalités déterminées par le règlement de chaque assemblée.»

Selected bibliography

1 The French Legal System and its Historical Development

Amos and Walton, *An introduction to French Law*. 3rd edn by Lawson, Anton, and Brown. 1967. Oxford University Press.

Aubert, *Introduction au Droit*. 3rd edn. 1988. Armand Colin.

Carbonnier, *Droit Civil. Introduction*. 18th edn. 1990. Presses Universitaires de France.

David, *French Law. Its Structure, Sources and Methodology*. Translated by Kindred. 1972. Louisiana State University Press.

David, *English Law and French Law*. 1980. Stevens and Eastern Law House.

David and Brierly, *Modern Legal Systems of the World Today*. 3rd edn. 1985. Stevens.

David and de Vries, *The French Legal System*. 1958. Oceana.

De Vries, *Civil Law and the Anglo-American Lawyer*. 1976. Oceana.

Guidicelli-Delage, *Institutions Judiciaires et Juridictionnelles*. 1987. Presses Universitaires de France.

Harouel, Barbey, Bournazel et Thibaut-Payen, *Histoire des Institutions de l'Epoque Franque à la Révolution*. 3rd edn. 1990. Presses Universitaires de France.

Kahn-Freund, Levy and B. Rudden, *A Source-book on French Law*. 3rd edn by B. Rudden. 1991. Clarendon Press.

Lemarignier, *La France Médiévale. Institutions et Société*. 1970. Armand Colin.

Merryman, *The Civil Law Tradition: an Introduction to the Legal Systems of Western Europe and Latin America*. 2nd edn. 1985. Stanford University Press.

Perrot, *Institutions Judiciaires*. 4th edn. 1992. Montchrestien.

Robinson, Fergus and Gordon, *An Introduction to European Legal History*. 1985. Professional Books.

Sautel, *Histoire des Institutions Publiques depuis la Révolution Française*. 7th edn. 1990. Dalloz.

Stein, *Legal Institutions. The Development of Dispute Settlement*. 1984. Butterworths.

Supiot, *Les Juridictions du Travail*. 1987. Sirey.

Tanguy, *La Recherche Documentaire en Droit*. 1991. Presses Universitaires de France.

Vincent, Guinchard, Montagnier et Varinard, *La Justice et ses Institutions*. 3rd edn. 1991. Dalloz.

Weill et Terré, *Droit Civil. Introduction Générale*. 4th edn. 1979. Dalloz.

Weston, *An English Reader's Guide to the French Legal System*. 1991. Berg.

2 Public law

Ardant, *Institutions Politiques et Droit Constitutionnel.* 1989. Librairie Générale de Droit et Jurisprudence.

Brown and Garner, *French Administrative Law.* 3rd edn. 1983. Butterworths.

Chantebout, *Droit Constitutionnel.* 1986. Nathan.

Chapsal, *La Vie Politique sous la Ve République.* 1984. Presses Universitaires de France.

Chapus, *Droit du Contentieux Administratif.* 2nd edn. 1990. Montchrestien.

Debbasch et Ricci, *Contentieux Administratif.* 5th edn. 1990. Dalloz.

Duverger, *Eléments de Droit Public.* 12th edn. 1988. Presses Universitaires de France.

Gicquel, *Droit Constitutionnel et Institutions Politiques.* 10th edn. 1989. Montchrestien.

Gounelle, *Introduction au Droit Public (Institutions, Fondements, Sources).* 2nd edn. 1989. Montchrestien.

Lavroff, *Le Système Politique Français, la Ve République.* 4th edn. Dalloz. 1986.

Mény, *Le Système Politique Français.* 1991. Montchrestien.

Pactet, *Institutions Politiques. Droit Constitutionnel.* 9th edn. 1988. Masson.

Rivero, *Droit Administratif.* 13th edn. 1990. Dalloz.

3 Procedure

Code de Procédure Pénale, (Editions Dalloz or Litec, updated annually).

Couchez, *Procédure Civile.* 7th edn. 1992. Sirey.

Croze et Morel, *Procédure Civile.* 1988. Presses Universitaires de France.

Gabolde, *Traité Pratique de la Procédure des Tribunaux Administratifs.* 10th edn. 1988. Thémis.

Héron, *Droit Judiciaire Privé.* 1991. Montchrestien.

Nouveau Code de Procédure Civile, (Editions Dalloz or Litec, updated annually).

Pradel, *Procédure Pénale.* 6th edn. 1992. Cujas.

Rassat, *Procédure Pénale.* 1990. Presses Universitaires de France.

Solus et Perrot, *Droit Judiciaire Privé, T.1* (1961), *T.2* (1973), *T.3* (1991). Sirey.

Stefani, Levasseur et Bouloc, *Procédure Pénale.* 14th edn. 1990. Dalloz.

Vincent et Guinchard, *Procédure Civile.* 22nd edn. 1991. Dalloz.

Vogler, *A Guide to the French Criminal Justice System,* 1989. Prisoners Abroad.

Index

351